Comfortable Words

Comfortable Words

Essays in Honor of Paul F. M. Zahl

EDITED BY
TODD BREWER
AND JOHN D. KOCH JR.

PICKWICK *Publications* · Eugene, Oregon

COMFORTABLE WORDS
Essays in Honor of Paul F. M. Zahl

Pickwick Publications
An Imprint of Wipf and Stock Publishers
199 W. 8th Ave., Suite 3
Eugene, OR 97401

www.wipfandstock.com

ISBN 13: 978-1-61097-787-6

Cataloguing-in-Publication data:

Comfortable words : essays in honor of Paul F. M. Zahl / edited by Todd Brewer and John D. Koch Jr. ; Foreword by Tullian Tchividjian.

xviii + 278 p. ; 23 cm. Includes bibliographical references.

ISBN 13: 978-1-61097-787-6

1. Zahl, Paul F. M. 2. Bible. New Testament—Theology. 3. Theology. I. Brewer, Todd. II. Koch, John D. Jr. III. Tchividjian, Tullian. IV. Title.

BS2397 C50 2013

Manufactured in the U.S.A.

Dedicated to Paul F. M. Zahl
on the occasion of his 60th birthday

Hear what comfortable words our Saviour Christ saith unto all who truly turn to him.

COME unto me, all ye that travail and are heavy laden, and I will refresh you. *St. Matt.* xi. 28.

So God loved the world, that he gave his only-begotten Son, to the end that all that believe in him should not perish, but have everlasting life. *St. John* iii. 16.

Hear also what Saint Paul saith.

This is a true saying, and worthy of all men to be received, That Christ Jesus came into the world to save sinners. *1 Tim.* i. 15.

Hear also what Saint John saith.

If any man sin, we have an Advocate with the Father, Jesus Christ the righteous; and he is the Propitiation for our sins. *1 St. John* ii. 1, 2.

THE BOOK OF COMMON PRAYER, 1928[1]

. . . whoever knows well how to distinguish the Gospel from the Law should give thanks to God and know that he is a real theologian.

MARTIN LUTHER'S LECTURES ON GALATIANS, 1535[2]

Now this mountain I must climb
Feels like a world upon my shoulders
And through the clouds I see love shine
It keeps me warm as life grows colder

"I WANT TO KNOW WHAT LOVE IS" —FOREIGNER

1. Episcopal, *The Book of Common Prayer, and Administration of the Sacraments and Other Rites and Ceremonies of the Church, According to the Use of the Protestant Episcopal Church in the United States of America; Together with the Psalter or Psalms of David.*

2. Luther's Works 26:115

Contents

Contributors

C. FitzSimons Allison is the twelfth bishop of the Diocese of South Carolina, retired.

Todd Brewer is a doctoral candidate (New Testament) at Durham University, Durham, England.

George Carey, Lord Carey of Clifton, was Archbishop of Canterbury (1991–2002).

James D. G. Dunn, is Emeritus Lightfoot Professor of Divinity, Durham University, Durham, England.

Susan G. Eastman is Associate Professor of the Practice of Bible and Christian Formation and Director of the Doctor of Theology Program at Duke Divinity School, Durham, North Carolina.

Mark Mattes is Professor of Philosophy and Religion at Grand View University in Des Moines, Iowa.

Geiko Müller-Fahrenholz is a retired Lutheran pastor and lives in Bremen, Germany.

Justin S. Holcomb is adjunct professor of theology and philosophy at Reformed Theological Seminary; and co-author of *Rid of my Disgrace* and *Save Me from Violence*.

John D. Koch Jr. is a doctoral candidate in systematic theology at Humboldt Universität zu Berlin.

Lauren R. E. Larkin is an MDiv and STM graduate of Trinity School for Ministry and is pursuing doctorate options in the area of systematic theology.

Jonathan A. Linebaugh is an assistant professor of New Testament at Knox Theological Seminary, Fort Lauderdale, Florida.

Contributors

Jürgen Moltmann is Professor of Systematic Theology Emeritus in the Protestant Faculty of the University of Tübingen, Germany.

Heinz-Dieter Neef is Professor of Evangelical Theology in the Protestant Faculty of the University of Tübingen, Germany.

Ashley Null is research fellow, German Research Foundation's Thomas Cranmer Project, Theological Faculty, Humboldt University of Berlin.

Raymond C. Ortlund Jr. is pastor at Immanuel Church in Nashville, Tennessee.

Dylan D. Potter is Senior Lecturer in Theology at TCA College in Singapore.

Justyn Terry is dean, president, and Professor of Systematic Theology at Trinity School for Ministry in Ambridge, Pennsylvania.

Tullian Tchividjian, is pastor of Coral Ridge Presbyterian Church and author of *Glorious Ruin: How Suffering Sets You Free*, and *One Way Love: The Power of Unconditional Love in A Conditional World*.

Jonathan Wong, is a doctoral candidate in systematic theology at Wycliffe College, University of Toronto.

Simeon Zahl is Junior Research Fellow in Theology at St. John's College at the University of Oxford.

Foreword

TULLIAN TCHIVIDJIAN

PAUL ZAHL SAVED MY life. Well, more precisely, God saved my life through Paul Zahl. Let me explain. Like most people who grew up in the Evangelical subculture, I had always assumed that the gospel was simply what non-Christians must believe in order to be saved, but then after God saves us we advance to the deeper, more practical waters of "discipleship." I learned this, for the most, in bible believing churches and Christian schools. Because I heard more about what I needed to do for Jesus than what Jesus had already done for me, I naturally concluded that the focus of the Christian faith was the life of the Christian. So I went to work. It wasn't long, however, before my "Christian" life became all about me.

Martin Luther defined sin as "mankind turned inward." And sadly, the way I had come to understand Christianity became terribly narcissistic. I was spending all my time thinking about how I was doing: if was learning everything I was supposed to be learning, whether I was doing it right or not, pondering my failures, and brooding over my momentary spiritual successes. My exclusive focus became the pursuit of personal holiness. What I discovered is that the more I focused on my need to do, the less I actually did. The more I fixated on my need to get better, the worse I actually got—I became neurotic and self-absorbed. I was learning the hard way that when the goal becomes conquering our sin instead of soaking in the conquest of our Savior, we actually begin to shrink spiritually. Preoccupation with my performance over Christ's performance was making me increasingly self-centered and morbidly introspective—the exact opposite of how the Bible describes what it means to be sanctified.

Weary and worn out by the "do more, try harder" message I had subscribed to, a trusted friend turned me on to Paul Zahl. I listened to his sermons, read his books, and wondered why I had been in church my whole life and never heard this stuff. The truth I heard from Paul set me free. Contrary to what I had heard and believed, Paul helped me to see that Christian growth is not, "I'm becoming stronger and stronger, more and more competent." Rather, Christian growth is coming to the realization of just how weak and incompetent I am and how strong and competent Jesus continues to be for me. I started to realize that when we stop narcissistically focusing on our need to get better, that is what it means to get better! That when we stop obsessing over our need to improve, that is what it means to improve!

It was Paul who helped me to see that because of Christ's finished work on my behalf, I had nothing to prove or protect. I could stop pretending. I could take off my masks and be real. The gospel set me free from trying to impress people, appease people, measure up for people, or prove myself to people. The gospel granted me the strength to admit that I'm weak and needy and restless—knowing that Christ's finished work has proven to be all the strength and fulfillment and peace I could ever want, and more. Since Jesus is my strength, my weaknesses don't threaten my sense of worth and value.

Since I was first told about Paul Zahl a number of years ago, he has become a dear friend—a friend who saved my life by helping me to see that

- Because Jesus was strong for me, I'm free to be weak;
- Because Jesus was Someone, I'm free to be no one;
- Because Jesus was extraordinary, I'm free to be ordinary;
- Because Jesus succeeded for me, I'm free to fail;
- Because Jesus won for me, I'm free to lose.

Introduction

Zahl & Gospel

The Saving Grace of Paul F. M. Zahl

Todd Brewer and John D. Koch Jr.

For the many people who have ever heard a sermon by Paul Zahl, this was likely their first introduction to Paul and the great themes of his life. To these unsuspecting listeners, Paul's great themes would become their own and possibly change their life. For many, it was their first encounter with a preacher whose sermons broke through that elusive barrier between heart and mind, between thought and action, between theory and life. Paul Zahl is a preacher and theologian who foregoes the vague spiritual platitudes and saccharine sentimentality that permeates so much of modern conversations about religion and spirituality. He instead wades into the depths of a human existence that is marked by fear, uncertainty and despair, offering words of comfort, mercy and hope in such a way that many who have listened to him or have learned from him may not be able to articulate why, but—like people who were present when Dylan went electric—they know that things were not going to be the same anymore.

This is not to say that Paul Zahl preaches a hidden, secret, or in any way "new" Gospel message, but that he actually goes all the way with it, he does not shy away from the agony of the anguished Apostle Paul in Rom 7:24 who cries out "Wretched man that I am, who will deliver me from this body of death?" any less than the triumphant cry of that same anguished person a few verses later who exclaims "there is, therefore, now no condemnation for those who are in Christ Jesus" (Rom 8:1). In other words, Zahl—following the Apostle Paul—understands that Christians and non-Christians are separated only by one all important, life changing thing. Christians are those who know that in the midst of their guilt, fear and shame, there is one who has shown mercy, there is one who has in the words of the great Samuel Crossman hymn, "love to the loveless shown."

This conviction goes deeper than a theological category or idea and is for Zahl, quite simply, "*vox ipissima Christianismi,* the true voice of the Christian religion."[1] He explains the importance of this in the introduction to his book *Grace in Practice,* where he writes:

> The message of God's grace, or one-way love, has captivated me for as long as I can remember. It saved my life during my early twenties, restored my marriage in my middle twenties, then created in me a father loved by my children. Grace remade my ministry and made possible my contact with sufferers as well as with prodigals . . . One way love is the heart of Christianity. It is what makes Christianity Christian.[2]

Based upon this fundamental conviction, throughout his career, Paul Zahl has been a passionate exponent of a view of human existence that would be unbearable without the message of God's mercy and grace. It is this single fact of human history—the crucifixion of Jesus Christ for the "ungodly" (Rom 5:8)—that acts as a tether on his thought, a lifeline bound to that great expression of God's redeeming love that allows for limitless exploration of the depths of human weakness and despair.

On account of this deep conviction that human existence, at all times and in every place, consists of the relationship between sin, mercy and God, i.e., the relationship between the law and the Gospel, he has been free to engage with many different forms of art and culture, seeing all human expression as being driven by this core relationship. Consequently, Zahl's wide interests have resisted the traditionally sharp division between academic disciplines. With books in church history, biblical studies, ethics, systematic theology and pastoral care, he has demonstrated an unusual scholarly breadth. Whether it is in the writings of Plato and Aristotle, the artwork of the Reformation, or the music of the Beach Boys, Paul has been able to bring to light the human condition that underlies it all; in

---

1. Paul F. M. Zahl, *Grace in Practice: A Theology of Everyday Life* (Grand Rapids: Eerdmans, 2007), ix.

2 Ibid.

other words, he has brought theology to life. Whether it be women in the English reformation, the depths of systematic theology, or the teaching of the historical Jesus, Zahl has employed a wide variety of instruments to create a symphony of grace.[3]

The reason that Paul Zahl's academic career has had such a pastoral impact is because he, like few others, evinces a personal engagement with the subject matter that elicits a similar response from his hearers and readers. In this way, one could say that Zahl is truly an incarnational theologian since the concepts and ideas he speaks about are no idle thoughts; rather, they are ideas from which he derives his very being. What has been the triumph of his career is that he has been able to bridge the emotional response to this message and its intellectual concerns in a way that truly speaks (to borrow a well-worn phrase) to both the head and the heart.

The scope of this book is meant to reflect a bit of this theological unity and disciplinary diversity, with scholars from a variety of fields of study contributing toward his common themes of sin, grace, and grace-in-practice. Much like all of Zahl's publications, it seeks to be engaging on both an academic and pastoral level because at his heart, Paul F. M. Zahl—gifted and renowned theologian—is fundamentally a preacher of Jesus as the friend of sinners. Whatever else one could say about his prolific career, the thread that runs throughout his work in widely divergent academic disciplines is the conviction that the words of the Apostle Paul to Timothy constitute the central core of the Christian message: that Christ Jesus came into the world to save sinners, the "comfortable words" of absolution and forgiveness.

The first section, "Free Will—Not!" covers issues of sin and anthropology. The opening essay by Susan Eastman explores the question of theodicy from the perspective of the book of Romans and its view of sin, evil, and the gospel. Paul's dual account of evil ascribes it to both human action and cosmic forces which co-opt human agency. The gospel as God's active working with humans against these destructive forces is then the only answer to the problem of theodicy. The next essay by Jonathan Wong engages the contemporary debate on the issue of free will in defense of Martin Luther's concept of the bound will. He then offers several implications of this for the practice of preaching. In the final essay of this section, Todd Brewer examines the portrayal of the disciples in the Gospel of Mark and its implications for anthropology. Through their failure to comply with Jesus' conditions

---

3. Although long a staple theological category within Lutheran and some Reformed circles, the distinction between Law and Gospel has a less obvious—but nevertheless powerful—pedigree within the Anglican tradition, the tradition to which Zahl has served for over thirty years. Cf. Ashley Null, *Thomas Cranmer's Doctrine of Repentance: Renewing the Power to Love* (Oxford: Oxford University Press, 2000).

for discipleship, the disciples exemplify the inherent limitations of human agency to fulfill the demands of obedience.

If Part One describes the human *plight* of brokenness and sin, then Part Two, "One-Way Love" concerns the divine *solution* to this problem. Who will deliver us from our bondage? Noting modern apprehension to notions of substitutionary atonement, Justyn Terry reaffirms the indispensability of this doctrine to the Christian understanding of forgiveness and grace. Forgiveness and grace both demand a substitution which is only found in Christ's work on the cross. Jonathan Linebaugh compares St. Paul with Pseudo-Solomon and their understandings of grace. While Pseudo-Solomon believes that God bestows grace justly to the worthy recipients, for Paul God's grace is specifically directed to the unworthy, ungodly. Next, Heinz-Dieter Neef surveys the Old and New Testament appearances of angels. Throughout a variety of accounts, angelic manifestations demonstrate God's merciful relationship with human beings. In opposition to Aristotle's anthropology, Lauren Larkin utilizes the work of Eberhard Jüngel to explicate an anthropology defined by the doctrine of justification. If justification by faith is an event which creates-out-of-nothing, then personhood is then not defined by who we are, but by our being in Christ. The following essay by John Koch similarly explores the issue of Christian ontology in contemporary theology, arguing that the distinction between law and gospel, properly understood, articulates an extrinsic ontology which avoids the accusation of subjectivism. C. FitzSimons Allison investigates the New Testament usage of three words: *dikaiosunē, logizomai,* and *parakaleō* with a specific eye toward pastoral care and the proper preaching of the gospel. The penultimate essay in this section by George Carey examines recent ecumenical developments on the doctrine of justification, contending that this new unity represents a de-valuing of the doctrine of justification and betrays a foundational difference in the understanding of the Church. Finally, Jürgen Moltmann suggests that justification is for both the sinner and the godforsaken and therefore must involve both forgiveness of sin and restitution for the victims of sin. This requires an honest confession of sin and humiliation before God and man and the overcoming of evil with good.

The next section, "Strength in Weakness," broadly outlines the *effect* of God's grace and what grace actually looks like in practice in everyday life. The first essay, by Simeon Zahl, champions a justification for Paul Zahl's frequent utilization of analogy on the basis of the ubiquity of the Holy Spirit. This grounds all of human experience within the instrumental activity of the Spirit, thereby enabling one to generously discern God's activity within all of life. With an eye toward contemporary Christianity, Mark Mattes utilizes Luther's "Theology of the Cross" as the hermeneutical key to both theology and a life lived before God. God is not actively found by humanity; rather the passive sinner is killed, graciously raised by God, and freed to serve the neighbor. Then, Justin Holcomb describes the effect of one-way love to victims of sexual assault. Where there is shame, a loss of identity, guilt, despair or anger the gospel brings peace and healing. In his essay, "Gospel Doctrine, Gospel Culture," Ray Ortlund investigates Paul's pastoral response to the Galatian church, suggesting that the proclamation of the gospel must occur both in the pulpit and in the gracious culture of the church. Just like Peter in Antioch, if the church fails in either, the effectiveness of its message is compromised. Geiko Müller-Fahrenholz, underscoring the power of humiliation and the need for it to be addressed by Christian theology, outlines a three-step process for the healing of humiliation through an apology, the granting of forgiveness and a covenanting between the respective parties which ease the burdens of those who are wronged. The next essay, by Dylan Potter, maintains that anxiety and stress in ministry are themselves a sign that the gospel has been abandoned in favor of some form of the law. Instead, the peace promised in the gospel also applies to ministers themselves, the fruit of which is a relaxation and leisure. In his thorough essay, Ashley Null researches the liturgical reforms of Thomas Cranmer and his introduction of the "Comfortable Words" following the absolution of sin. For Cranmer, these compact articulations of the gospel were formulated as the divine instrument to allure the hearts of believers to Christ. In the last essay, James Dunn examines Paul's pastoral response to the controversy over dietary and social practices in the churches of Corinth and Rome. Paul navigates difficult compromises, affirming the concerns of all parties while calling for mutual respect. One's conduct is only accountable to God's approval and is not grounds for denunciation of either party.

In the final chapter, "Guard of Honor: *Envoi* and Epilogue," Paul Zahl offers a retrospective of his scholarly history, his influences and themes, as well as a reflection on how he has since changed his mind. After recounting the overarching themes of this book and reaffirming their significance, Zahl wishes to also account for what he believes to be the unreal nature of life in a way reminiscent of the final words of his great teacher, Martin Luther, whose final written words were *Wir sind Bettler, Hoc est verum*: we are beggars, this is true.

This book is intended to be both a celebration of the life and work of Paul Zahl as well as an introduction to not only his thought, but to the ways in which this great truth—that God has definitively and conclusively shown his mercy to sinners by the Cross—has shaped and oriented people's thinking. In it diversity, it represents the freedom of the Gospel itself by illustrating the intellectual freedom and creativity that is born out of a confidence of God's mercies having quieted the fear of judgment and condemnation. In this way, its diversity is also a testament to its consistency, because under that freedom echoes the constant refrain—one that Paul Zahl has firmly implanted into the hearts of countless people—that God's one-way love has come into the world to seek and save the lost. In a day when too few pastors are theologians and too few theologians are pastors, Paul Zahl has stood proudly in the historic Anglican tradition as one who has endeavored to preach the Gospel in all of its intellectual and emotional fullness, resting on the conviction of Jesus's own words, that "my sheep will hear my voice."

PART 1

Free Will—Not!

1

The "Empire of Illusion"

Sin, Evil, and Good News in Romans[1]

SUSAN GROVE EASTMAN

IN 1977, THE NOVELIST Walker Percy published a best-seller called *Lancelot*.[2] It made quite a splash, not least because of its stunning exposé of the moral poverty of a society with no language for evil. The main character, Lancelot Andrews Lamar, is locked up in a psychiatric ward after killing his wife, his wife's lover, and their friends, by blowing up his New Orleans home during a hurricane. The novel consists of his retrospective, disjointed account of those events, as told to a priest who visits him. He tells of his disgust with the superficial "niceness" and profound duplicity of his wife's friends and lovers, all directors and actors who were filming a movie at his antebellum home. Lancelot sees his own horrific actions as a quest to get at the heart of evil, and to name human responsibility for it. He says:

> "Evil" is surely the clue to this age, the only quest appropriate to the age . . . God may be absent, but what if one should find the devil? Do you think I wouldn't be pleased to meet the devil? Ha ha, I'd shake his hand like a long-lost friend . . . In times when nobody is interested in God, what would happen if you could

---

1. The title of this essay is taken, not without irony, from Hedges, *The Empire of Illusion*. I say "not without irony" because Hedges lumps Christianity in the category of "illusion."

2. Percy, *Lancelot*.

prove the existence of sin, pure and simple? Wouldn't that be a windfall for you? A new proof of God's existence! If there is such a thing as sin, evil, a malignant force, there must be a God![3]

Lancelot is fascinated with the problem of evil, trying to get to the heart of it, because he has given up on the existence of God. But, he claims, if one could identify "sin"—a real, honest-to-god sin—one would know there is a God also.

I was reminded of Lancelot while reading Andrew Delbanco's searing book, *The Death of Satan*, which explores the demise of belief in, and language for, personal evil within American society.[4] The book links the loss of a language for evil with a loss of religious faith.[5] Although Delbanco himself does not consider religious belief in any sort of transcendent deity to be a live option, he asks whether an adequate account of evil is possible without such belief. From his self-professed "secular" viewpoint, he sees only two alternatives. One might revive the religious conception of evil as an "alien invader," but absent any notion of transcendence, this revival devolves into "the blamable other—who can always be counted on to spare us the exigencies of examining ourselves." Or one might opt for a privative notion of evil, as does Augustine, but excised of Augustine's belief in a transcendent, gracious God; here, Satan is, in Delbanco's words, "a symbol of our own deficient love, our potential for envy and rancor toward creation." Delbanco adds that this "latter way—evil as privation—is much more difficult to grasp. But it offers something that the devil himself could never have intended: the miraculous paradox of demanding the best of ourselves."[6]

The theme of this essay is the apostle Paul's treatment of sin and evil in his letter to the Romans. Percy and Delbanco brilliantly set forth the issues that arise in any contemporary attempt to talk about evil: questions of its source (or sources), scope, relationship to human agency, and relationship to God. Within the bounds set by secular rationality, answers to the first three questions come to rest on human institutions, and above all, on human

---

3. Ibid., 144–46, 54.

4. Delbanco, *The Death of Satan*.

5. Ibid., 220. Despite acknowledging the millions of people who do believe in a transcendent divine presence, Delbanco claims "it is the central and irreversible fact of modern history that we no longer inhabit a world of transcendence." He leaves those who do profess religious faith out of the book because his focus is the "relentless . . . advance of secular rationality in the United States," and the concomitant loss of an adequate language for evil.

6. Ibid., 234–35. Delbanco does not seem to recognize that the understandings of human agency in both accounts are changed in fundamental ways when they are divorced from their Christian settings.

individuals, and the issue becomes simply this: do we locate evil in others, demonizing them, or in ourselves? Hence Delbanco writes, "The essential modern evasion was the failure to acknowledge evil, name it, and accept its irreducibility *in the self*."[7] For Paul, however, living as he does in a cosmos that is transcendent as well as personal, such an evasion is of what we might call second order importance; the essential *primal* evasion is the failure to acknowledge *God*, name *God as God*, and accept that God cannot be reduced to the self. Once that fundamental evasion occurs, everything else becomes, to quote another critic of the American scene, an "empire of illusion."[8]

In what follows, I shall attempt to show that Paul's account of both sin and evil (which are not precisely the same) provides resources for naming human accountability for evil, the necessity and limits of judgment, and the larger reality of sin as that which deceives us and co-opts even the "the best of ourselves" for its death-dealing ends. Furthermore, in Paul's vision, the transcendent and personal operation of divine grace creates the conditions in which such naming is possible, and corporately constitutes human agents with the hope of victory over evil. I will begin with an overview of Paul's language about "evil" and "sin" in the structure of Romans, in relationship to two overlapping but distinct depictions of the human predicament. Then I will suggest some ways in which this complex, layered and paradoxical picture of human existence may enrich our own discourse about evil and sin, and illuminate the radical good news of Paul's gospel.

EVIL AND SIN IN THE STRUCTURE OF ROMANS

I approached this project with the expectation that evil and sin would be roughly equivalent in Paul's discourse, as signifying a personified, malevolent power. Such, however, is not precisely the case. Evil is the object of active verbs; sin, almost always in the singular, is the acting subject.[9] Furthermore, the terms cluster in different sections of the letter: "evil" occurs primarily in chapters 1–3 and the paraenesis of chapters 12–14, resurfacing in the final exhortation of 16:19; "sin" dominates chapters 5–7, although it does appear a few times earlier in the letter. The terms come together in 7:19–21.

---

7. Ibid., 197, italics added.

8. Hedges, *The Empire of Illusion*.

9. Paul always uses the Greek word *harmartia* and its cognates to denote "sin." "Evil" here covers a range of human actions, as in the vice list of Rom 1:28–30. The Greek word *kakos* is Paul's most common word for evil (Rom 1:30; 2:9; 3:8; 7:19, 21; 12:17, 21; 13:3, 4, 10; 14:20; 16:19).

Evil

We begin with evil, because that is where Paul begins. A survey of his language yields four intriguing observations:

First, we hear a fair amount about "evil" before we hear the term "sin." In Romans 1–3, *evil is what humans do*. It is the object of somewhat interchangeable action verbs: *kartargazomai*—to bring to pass, to accomplish, to put into effect (2:9); *poieō*—to do (3:8); and *prassō*—to bring about, to accomplish (1:32; 2:1–3). Evil attributes also accrue to human character, first appearing in an extensive vice list that characterizes human beings who have been handed over (by God) to an "unreasoning mind" (*adokimon noun*) and improper conduct, precisely because they did not "see fit" (*edokimasan*) to acknowledge God (1:28–30): "They were filled with every kind of wickedness, evil, covetousness, malice. Full of envy, murder, strife, deceit, craftiness, they are gossips, slanderers, God-haters, insolent, haughty, boastful, inventors of evil, rebellious toward parents, foolish, faithless, heartless, ruthless" (1:29–31).

Second, in these first three chapters Paul traces a link between distorted cognition, false speech, and evil acts, all of which occur *within* human beings. Beginning with the apocalypse of the wrath of God against the ungodliness (*asebeia*) and wickedness or unrighteousness (*adikia*) of human beings who suppress the truth—that is, as Paul quickly makes clear, the truth that God is the creator who alone must be worshipped and served (1:18)—the depiction of evil culminates in a catena of scriptural quotations that paint a bleak and horrifying picture of humanity's attitudes and actions "under the power of sin" (3:9–18):

> as it is written: 'There is no one who is righteous, not even one; there is no one who has understanding, there is no one who seeks God. All have turned aside, together they have become worthless; there is no one who shows kindness, there is not even one.' 'Their throats are opened graves; they use their tongues to deceive.' 'The venom of vipers is under their lips.' 'Their mouths are full of cursing and bitterness.' 'Their feet are swift to shed blood; ruin and misery are in their paths, and the way of peace they have not known.' 'There is no fear of God before their eyes.'

We note in particular here the loss of understanding, the proliferation of what Beverly Gaventa has aptly called "toxic speech," and the violent breakdown of human relationships.[10] The theme of deception runs through this narrative, from the suppression of the truth of God, to the vices of deceit, malignity, whispering, and slander (1:29–30), to duplicitous violence.

---

10. Gaventa, "From Toxic Speech to Doxology."

Third, after chapter three the terminology of "evil" drops out of Paul's vocabulary, until it reappears in 7:19–21, but now in tandem with "sin," and again in the context of deception. What is most striking is that, whereas in chapters 1–3, "evil" is what humans do, in 7:19–21, evil is what "sin" does, *counter* to the wishes of the self. Sin now performs the actions previously ascribed to human beings: *kartargazomai* (7:17, 20), and *poieō* (7:20–21).

Finally, in 12:17–21, a new situation has come into being, in which Paul confidently commands, "Do not be conquered (*nikō*) by evil, but conquer (*nika*) evil with good." Thereafter, "evil" occurs in the context of Pauline exhortation within the community of faith as something to be avoided, and as the opposite of loving service and of the good (13:3, 10; 14:20; 16:19). The final appearance of "evil" is in Paul's closing exhortation: "I would have you wise as to what is good and guileless as to what is evil. And the God of peace will soon crush Satan under your feet" (16:19b–20a). Here, precisely in regard to evil, the apocalyptic hope of God's victory over Satan grounds Paul's exhortation to the Romans.

Sin

We expect Paul to talk a lot about sin, and he does, but in surprising, counterintuitive ways. Again, I note four intriguing observations:

First, the terminology of "sin" occurs very little in the first three chapters of Romans. In verbal form, it describes what all human beings do: "All who have sinned without the law will also perish without the law, and all who have sinned under the law will be judged by the law" (2:12); and: "all have sinned and fall short of the glory of God" (3:23). Human beings are also described as "sinful" or "sinners" (3:7; 5:8, 19; using the substantive *hamartōlos*). And Paul briefly introduces "sin" as a singular noun denoting a power *over* human beings: "all, both Jews and Greeks, are under sin" (3:9).

Second, by far the thickest cluster of *harmartia* language occurs in chapters 5–7, beginning with sin's "entrance" into the cosmos through the trespass of the one man, Adam. Here sin is the singular subject of active verbs: sin came into the cosmos and death came with it (5:12); sin increased (5:20); sin reigned (*ebasileusen*) in death (5:21). Sin is a realm of existence (6:1–2), like a household over which it rules as a slavemaster (6:6–11). Sin lords it over mortal bodies (6:12–13), exercising lethal bondage and repaying its slaves with death (6:16–17; 20–21, 23). Sin uses the law of God as a military staging area (*aphormē*) from which to launch its attacks on humanity, specifically by using the law to generate covetous desires (7:8), and to deceive and kill (7:11).

Sin uses "the good," which is both the law itself and the human yearning for the life promised by the law, to accomplish death (7:13).

The human actor recedes curiously into the background here, particularly in regard to the performance of evil. The falsehood and violence previously attributed to human beings are now the province of sin itself (7:11). Whereas in the first account human beings are "sinners," now *sin* is the surpassing "sinner" (7:13). And whereas in 1:30 human beings are "inventors of evil," now indwelling *sin* itself accomplishes evil through its *unwilling* human minions (7:14–20). "I" want to do the good, serving it with "the law of my mind." But sin wrests the good law, the law of God, to its own purpose of death, making it "the law of sin and death" (7:22–25; 8:2).

Third, therefore, we note the complex interaction of sin and the law of God. In 3:19–20 the law holds all humanity accountable before God, by giving the knowledge of sin. But in 5:12–13 and 7:8–9, that knowledge is also the energizing of sin. At first, sin's activity appears to *rely* on the law. But like a monstrous creation in an old sci-fi movie, once it is brought to life sin *uses* the law to deceive and to kill (7:11). No wonder Paul hastens to clarify that the law is good, by putting the blame for evil squarely on sin. In effect, Paul says: "Don't blame the law for evil! Blame sin!"

Fourth, after chapter 7, sin ceases to be the subject of active verbs. Its demise is described in 8:3: "sending God's own Son in the likeness of sinful flesh and for sin (*peri hamartias*), God condemned sin in the flesh, in order that the just requirement of the law might be fulfilled in us, who walk not according to the flesh but according to the Spirit." Thereafter Paul's focus shifts from the death worked by indwelling sin, to the life given through the indwelling Spirit: "If the Spirit of the one who raised Jesus from the dead dwells in you, the one who raised Christ from the dead also will give life to your mortal bodies through his Spirit which dwells in you" (8:10–11). After this, the only references to sin are in 11:27, where Paul quotes the promise that God will take away Israel's sins (Jer. 31:33 and Isa. 27:9), and 14:23: "Whatever is not of faith is sin." In neither case is sin an enslaving power; its shadow has shrunk down to human size.

To recap these observations about the language of evil and sin in Romans:

1. Evil is a human attribute and action that dominates 1:18—3:18, particularly in a nexus of distorted perceptions, duplicitous speech, and violent actions. After 3:18 it drops from sight, until it reappears briefly in 7:19–21 as that which "I, yet not I but sin dwelling in me," does. The next time we hear about evil is in the exhortations of chapters 12–14, as that which Christians may and must overcome. The human actor,

once weakened and subverted by "the sin that dwells in me" (7:17, 19), now has been liberated and remade by the indwelling Spirit (8:9, 11).

2. After a few tantalizing appearances in chapters 2–3, "sin" appears on the human stage in 5:12, and thereafter rampages through history until the end of chapter 7. Thereafter it ceases to function as an enslaving power, and quickly drops from sight.

3. Only in 7:19–21 do these terms occur together, with sin as the primary agent that "works," or "accomplishes," evil.

4. In Romans 1–3, the law functions to identify and judge sin (2:12–14; 3:19–20). In Romans 5–7, the law awakens and energizes sin, only to be conscripted into sin's lethal purposes.

These observations about evil and sin correlate with two depictions of the human situation and God's redemption in Romans.[11] The first account, in Rom 1:18–5:11, renders all humanity accountable (3:19) before God, being "without excuse" (2:1), without exception (3:10), and therefore rightly under divine judgment and deserving of God's wrath (1:18; 2:8; 3:5; 5:9). The judgment falls, despite the fact that humanity has been delivered *by God* into the power of its own passions and mendacity, because that deliverance into enslaving powers is also God's judgment on humanity's primal idolatry. God's redemptive activity in this state of affairs consists in Christ's death for "the ungodly," the "sinners," and the "enemies" (5:6, 8, 10), resulting in the "rectification of the ungodly" (4:5; cf. 1:18), and deliverance from the eschatological wrath of God (5:9; cf. 1:18).

In his second account (5:12—8:39), Paul retells the same story, but with an expanded cast of characters: "Therefore as through one human being (*anthrōpos*) sin came into the world and through sin, death, and death spread to all human beings because all sinned" (5:12). This second narrative takes up the themes of the first: humanity is under condemnation, and delivered from condemnation (5:12–21; 8:1–3, 33–34). But humanity also

11. In an influential and important article, "Paul and Jewish Apocalyptic Eschatology," Martin deBoer argues that these two sections of Romans follow two distinct "tracks" in Jewish apocalyptic thought. The first section, Rom 1:18—5:11, displays what deBoer calls "forensic apocalyptic eschatology . . . characterized by the fact that human beings willfully reject or deny the Creator, who is the God of Israel, thereby bringing about death and the perversion or corruption of the world. Adam and/or Eve are the primal ancestors who set the pattern for all subsequent human beings." 4 Ezra and 2 Baruch provide examples of this kind of eschatology. In Rom 6:1—8:39, "cosmological apocalyptic eschatology" dominates Paul's argument. This track highlights the existence of "evil angelic powers [that] have, in some primeval time . . . come to rule over the world." 1 Enoch in particular provides an example of this pattern of apocalyptic discourse. In Rom 5:12–21, the two tracks completely overlap. DeBoer, "Paul and Jewish Apocalyptic Eschatology."

is held captive by sin as a hostile cosmic power, from which it needs deliverance (5:21—6:14; 8:18–39). God's liberating action involves Christ's union with humanity in incarnation, death, and resurrection, humanity's participation with Christ in death (through baptism), and the proleptic power of resurrection life mediated through the Spirit of God who raised Christ from the dead (6:1–14).

These two accounts present a simplified picture of a complex text. The first account is anthropological in focus, emphasizing human responsibility; the second is cosmological in scope, emphasizing human enslavement. But already in chapter 1, Paul nuances his depiction of human agency in regard to evil; we are precisely *not* free agents who simply choose evil over good; rather, we sin because God has delivered humanity over to distorted passions and a debased mind (1:24–28; 3:9). The two accounts overlap completely in 5:12–21, where deliverance from condemnation leads directly to the liberating reign of grace (5:17, 21). This combination of judicial and cosmological motifs returns in Rom 8:1, 33–34, where God's redemption encompasses both deliverance from condemnation, *and* victory over hostile cosmic powers.

What might these overlapping accounts contribute to contemporary conversations about evil? I suggest that the first narrative, with its focus on culpability and judgment, explores the connection between evil and the lie, and sets before us both the necessity and the limits of judgment. The second renders a complex, "participatory" depiction of human agency in relation to sin, on the one hand, and the liberating power of the indwelling Christ, on the other.

EVIL, THE LIE, AND THE NECESSITY AND LIMITS OF JUDGMENT

Paul depicts evil-doing as a web of falsehood and violence accompanied by a corresponding suppression of human capacities for perception and cognition. In Paul's words, human beings "were made futile in their thinking, their senseless (*asunetos*) hearts were darkened." Their self-knowledge became distorted: "Claiming to be wise, they became fools." Thus their ability to recognize truth was compromised, whether in relationship to themselves, to their surroundings, or to others—let alone God.

This cognitive and perceptual impairment has important implications. It means that the difference between "truth" and "falsehood" is not located in the *intentions* of the individual, but in the difference between an accurate ("truthful") or distorted ("false") orientation to the fundamental reality of God's creation and rule in the cosmos. Deception thus goes deeper than consciously false speech; it concerns, rather, the idolatry that creates and maintains an alternative, counterfeit personal reality. In contemporary terms we see this idolatry in many forms: virtual reality, "life on my terms," "personal truth," "it doesn't matter what you believe as long as you're sincere," and so forth. People consciously lie, and people also unconsciously act out the implications of living in a lie; this too, for Paul, is evil. Thus the common excuses, such as "I didn't mean to do it"; or "well, that's what I said, but I didn't mean it," or "I didn't know what I was doing," are simply irrelevant to questions of human culpability and divine judgment. Intentions are slippery if not impossible to pin down. At least here in Rom 1:18—5:21, Paul does not try to do so.

Here Paul's account gives us a way to talk about moral accountability for evil, and the urgent necessity of acknowledging human complicity in interlocking systems of lies and violence, in a world in which responsibility for evil is notoriously elusive. It speaks to the necessity of judgment. Illustrations are not lacking in our day. One thinks, for example, of the use of propaganda to engineer the genocide in Rwanda. The complicity of post-colonial powers, the distribution of lies about Tutsis combined with a systematic habituation in violence, and the use of the radio to incite and direct the killing, can all be narrated, their logic analyzed, and their perpetrators named. In his haunting book, *We Wish to Inform You that Tomorrow We Will be Killed with Our Families: Stories from Rwanda,* Philip Gourevitch writes: "In 1994, Rwanda was regarded in much of the rest of the world as the exemplary instance of the chaos and anarchy associated with collapsed states. In fact, the genocide was the product of order, authoritarianism, decades of modern political theorizing and indoctrination, and one of the most meticulously administered states in history."[12] In such a state, must not the cries for some kind of accountability, truth-telling, and judgment be honored? Gourevitch quotes a survivor, whose siblings all were murdered: "People come to Rwanda and talk of reconciliation . . . It's offensive. Imagine talking to Jews of reconciliation in 1946."[13] Another man named Giramahatzu, who murdered his neighbors, tries to make excuses: "We were just pawns in this. We were just tools."[14] But the relatives of the people whom he killed say, "[This] man is responsible for what he did."[15] So judgment on the evil that human beings

12. Gourevitch, *We Wish to Inform You,* 95.

13. Ibid., 240.

14. Ibid., 307.

15. Ibid., 305.

do, including the slander that fosters violence and the lies that attempt to evade responsibility, is indeed necessary. Like the psalms of imprecation, Rom 1:18—5:11 gives voice to this cry for divine judgment.

At the same time, however, this depiction of evil recognizes the *limits of human judgment*. As a corollary of humanity's debased mind (1:29) and universal bondage to sin (3:9), Romans 2–3 fosters a profound suspicion of one's own capacity for judging others rightly, and offers an exposé of self-deception. Paul is scathing: "You have no excuse, whoever you are, when you judge another; for in passing judgment upon others you condemn yourself, because you, the judge, are doing the very same things" (2:1). There is no human judge who stands in a neutral place in which to see fully and correctly–that place is reserved to God. Romans 14 displays the social embodiment of this argument against human judgment, as Paul repeatedly exhorts the Roman Christians not to judge one another (14:3–22). As in Romans 1–3, this rejection of human judgment is based on the certainty of divine judgment on oneself as well as on the other: "Why do you judge your brother? Why do you despise your brother? For we all will stand before the judgment seat of God" (14:10).

In Rom 1:18—5:11, then, the first account of evil as something human beings do offers at least three contributions to discourse about evil and ethics: it explores the intimate connections between distorted perceptions, falsehood, and violence; it honors the necessity of human accountability; and it recognizes the limits of human judgment.

It has, however, one significant shortcoming. The shortcoming is this: where does the responsibility for evil finally come to rest? Recalling the stories from Rwanda, we ask whether responsibility falls fully and completely on the man who murdered his neighbors, or on the "evil regime." What of the international powers who made money by supplying weapons to the killers? What of the other nations who chose to ignore what was happening? As one ascends the organizational ladder, the responsibility is always just one or two steps higher. And finally, in an atrocity of such proportions, where does one begin? As Gourevitch says, the ideal genocide is one in which everyone takes part in the killing, because "if everyone is implicated, then implication becomes meaningless."[16]

Furthermore, whenever the ultimate source of evil is located in human beings, violence will continue to be justified, precisely in the name of ridding the world of evil. To get rid of evil, get rid of the source, wherever, or in whomever, one finds it. This is the very logic of genocide. Gourevitch observes:

16. Ibid., 96.

And strange as it may sound, the ideology—or what Rwandans call "the logic"—of genocide was promoted as a way not to create suffering but to alleviate it. The specter of an absolute menace that requires absolute eradication binds leader and people in a hermetic utopian embrace, and the individual—always an annoyance to totality—ceases to exist.[17]

As long as human beings are seen as the source and agents of evil, the human response will be to demonize and eradicate them.[18] The cycle is never-ending. To this day, the aftermath of the Rwandan genocide rages on in East Africa.

It seems, therefore, that this first account of evil, as a human attribute and action, is necessary and important, but ultimately inadequate. It provides a partial diagnosis of the human situation, but lacks the power to change it. So we turn to Paul's second account, in which sin becomes a dominant actor on the stage of human history, and in which the power that overcomes sin is none other than Christ's incarnation, death, and resurrection. In the progression of Paul's argument, this second narrative circumscribes and re-frames the first. The result is a layered, somewhat inconsistent but accurate and liberating picture of humanity's relationship to evil, and God's transformation of that relationship. That picture creates a space for naming the untidy realities of both the human perpetration of evil speech and deeds, and humanity's suffering and bondage to evil.

BONDAGE AND LIBERATION

What does this space look like? I begin with a closer look at the conjunction of "evil" and "sin" in Rom 7:15–20:

I do not understand my own actions. For I do not do what I want, but I do the very thing I hate. Now if I do what I do not want, I agree that the law is good. But in fact it is no longer I that do it, but sin that dwells within me. For I know that nothing good dwells within me, that is, in my flesh. For the willing of the good is close at hand (*parakeitai*), but not the accomplishment of it. For I do not do the good I want, but the evil I do not want is what I do. Now if I do what I do not want, it is no longer I that do it, but sin that dwells within me. So I find it to be a law that when I want to do what is good, evil lies close at hand (*parakeitai*).

17. Ibid., 95.

18. The alternative, according to Delbanco, is to focus on ourselves as the locus and source of evil. But is this an adequate safeguard against the violent impulse to eradicate evil, or does it simply turn that impulse inwards in self-destructive ways?

Paul drives home the point by repeating verbatim, "it is no longer I that do it, but sin that dwells within me." What is going on here?

It is important to hear what Paul does *not* say here. He does not say, "Even when I do the good, my desires are selfish or sinful." He does not say, "I want to do the good, but am powerless to act because my will is enslaved." He says, "I act, but find, to my horror, that even when I think I am doing the good, what I accomplish is evil. So it must not be me doing it, but sin dwelling in me." Paul does not search for evil in human wants and desires. He continues rather to locate evil in the *results* of human actions, but now he has introduced a new actor called "sin," who comes between the person's wish for the good and the evil outcome. Not only does Paul distinguish between sin and God's law here; he also distinguishes between sin and the "I." Both the law that promises the good, and the self that seeks the good, have been commandeered by sin as a hostile agent.

The effects of this new development are profound. By inserting "sin" between the person's wish and its outcome, for the first time Paul opens up the question of intention. I noted earlier that Paul does not limit falsehood to conscious intentions, precisely because we are so prone to self-deception and being deceived. What is striking here is that when he does speak in terms of human wants, he speaks in such a positive way. "The best of ourselves" wants the good, intends the good, but now—deceived by sin (7:11)—accomplishes evil. Nothing in the text says that Paul here is only talking about believers or unbelievers, regenerate versus unregenerate humanity, or any other re-inscription of a divide between "godly" and "ungodly." Rather, this "I" who wants the good, but finds even that desire for the good exploited by sin, is all humanity "in the shadow of Adam."[19]

Thus, although deception continues to play an integral role in the production of evil, now sin is the deceiver, and the person is "the deceived." We recall Paul's description: "For sin, seizing an opportunity in the commandment, deceived me and through it killed me" (7:7b-11). Here sin plays the role of the serpent in the garden, which deceived Eve and thereby brought death into the world.[20] The inadequacy of limiting falsehood to merely human intentions is abundantly clear. So also is the importance—and impossibility—of a full perception of "sin's" lethal attack on the human race.

Much is gained by this way of talking, which is admittedly foreign to many of our modern sensibilities. In the first place, Paul's cosmic language acknowledges the way the enormity of some forms of evil quite simply

19. Hofius, "Der Mensch im Schatten Adams." See also Meyer, "The Worm at the Core of the Apple."

20. Paul uses the same verb for "deceive" in 2 Cor 11:3 to speak of the serpent deceiving Eve. See also 1 Tim. 2:14. See Hofius, "Der Mensch im Schatten Adams," 118.

defies the human capacity for perception and hence evaluation. Gourevitch says his book on Rwanda is "about how people imagine themselves and one another—a book about how we imagine our world."[21] But then a bit later he describes visiting a former school filled with the bodies of the genocide victims, and trying to see what was in front of his eyes, but at some level being unable to do so because "it was still unimaginable. I mean, one still had to imagine it."[22] The world has become "unimaginable"—"un-image-able." We see, but we cannot perceive. And in our lack of perception, we allow, and sometimes we replicate, the very evil we abhor.

Second, standing before this mystery of evil, we recognize the limits and dangers of attempts to explain it. If the enormity of evil that is committed by human hands can at the same time defy our capacity for perception, it also defies *explanation*. In his memoir entitled *The Book and the Sword: a Life of Learning in the Shadow of Destruction*, David Weiss Halivni reflects on his own experience of the Holocaust, saying: "[E]ven raising the theological question of why there was a Shoah—implying that there exists a satisfactory answer—is objectionable . . . When it comes to explanations, we should be careful, lest we justify what happened."[23] The reason for this is that any attempt to find a reason must locate those responsible, and who, in the end, will that be? So Halivni continues:

> Sometimes the line between explanation and justification is very thin. Any logical explanation will accuse the victim, increase the burden of guilt, and add to the victim's suffering. The very suffering is that we don't know why we suffered, we can't explain it, we can't conceivably say that God wanted children to be gassed. We can't attribute that to God; nor can we attribute it to sin, even though we believe that everything comes from God . . . One can know God's ways, but not God's reasons. So it is incumbent upon us to know every nuance of the suffering; but in the end, it must remain suspended in mystery.[24]

Note the logic here. If we try to explain such evil in terms of human responsibility, the guilt keeps circling around and lands on the wrong people, the victims. But if we push beyond, believing, as we must, in a God who is sovereign, then finally we must place the explanation and responsibility on God's doorstep. But this we cannot do. So the explanation "must remain suspended in mystery."

21. Gourevitch, *We Wish to Inform You*, 6.

22. Ibid., 16.

23. David Weiss Halivni, *Book and the Sword*, 154–56.

24. Ibid., 156.

When we turn back to Romans, what do we hear? I noted earlier that Romans 1–5 demonstrates both the necessity and limits of human judgment in response to culpability for evil. To this, Romans 7 contributes the further idea of "sin" as a power that uses even the best of human intentions for lethal ends. But we must be clear that neither of these moves *explains* evil, precisely because, like Halivni, Paul claims that everything ultimately comes from God. The question becomes, not whether evil can be understood, let alone rationalized, but whether God can be trusted in the midst of it, both to be present and ultimately to defeat evil. Paul's conviction and hope is that through the crucifixion God takes even evil into the divine life, paradoxically by entering into the suffering and death of humanity as both culpable and victim (8:3). And that leads to my third point.

Because the cumulative effect of the cosmological account of sin is to compromise human agency in relationship to "sin" as a hostile, suprahuman power, Paul's language here provides resources for aligning the gracious presence of God *with* the human agent who wants the good, over *against* the malign, destructive forces that would work evil. There is a complex, participatory picture of agency at work here. Paul says, "The evil I do not want is what I do . . . it is no longer I doing it, but sin dwelling in me." This is the exact inverse of Gal. 2:20, where Paul says, "I have been crucified with Christ. It is no longer I who lives, but Christ who lives in me." In both cases, the linguistic pattern is "I, not-I." We see two acting subjects here, and in my view Paul depicts both as operative simultaneously. That is, the self is qualified both in relationship to sin, which is simultaneously "other" and "indwelling," and in relationship to the indwelling Spirit of the God who raised Jesus from the dead (8:10). But it is the Spirit of God who holds the future.

Now it seems to me that this way of talking has tremendous power in addressing some forms of the human experience of evil. I have in mind the ways in which persons and communities may be entrapped by distorted images of reality, self-destructive addictions or compulsive behaviors, memories whose hold on the present seems intractable, and so forth. These also are forms of sin as an enslaving power, although its lethal effects may more often be turned inward than outward. Yet they also work death. Paul's way of talking, with its overlay of subjects and its image of God in Christ, through the Spirit, entering into the human situation, both affirms the agency and good intentions of persons who suffer thus, and answers their need for help from an external advocate. The image is one of God graciously allied with human beings over against the sin within and among them.

Finally, this alliance of God *with* human beings, *against* evil, takes place, in Paul's vision, in a community that refuses to answer evil with evil.

It is no accident that when "evil" resurfaces in Romans 12, it is in the context of Paul's exhortations to the church as a whole, and specifically in his encouragement to resist the desire for retribution: "Bless those who persecute you . . . Repay no one evil for evil . . . never avenge yourselves, but leave it to the wrath of God . . . if your enemy is hungry, feed him; if he is thirsty, give him drink . . . Do not be conquered (*nikō*) by evil, but conquer (*nika*) evil with good" (12:14–21). That is, the nurturing of human agents who now *can* overcome evil happens in a communal life that replicates Christ's grace towards all humanity: "ungodly, weak, sinners, enemies of God" (Rom 5:6–10).

CONCLUDING REFLECTIONS

In Romans 1–8 Paul gives us two distinct narratives of the relationship between human beings, sin, and evil. Subsequent interpretations of Paul's gospel can be delineated by the relative weight they place on these two narratives. In the first, human beings are culpable "sinners" in need of forgiveness, and redemption consists of deliverance from the justly deserved wrath of God, which falls on Christ rather than on us. In the second, human beings are enslaved and deceived by sin as a hostile power that co-opts even the best human endeavors, and redemption consists of deliverance from that enslaving power through union with Christ. As E. P. Sanders put it: "Here is a distinction that will not go away. In brief, it is the distinction between saying that Christ dies *for* Christians and that they die *with* Christ, between saying that Christians are sanctified and justified from their past transgressions and that they have died with Christ to the power of sin, between saying that they should live 'blamelessly' and that they live 'in the Spirit.'"[25] Can these two narratives be reconciled? Clearly in Paul's view they can; as Sanders adds, "These two series were not distinct in Paul's mind."[26] In the structure of Romans, the two come together in 8:1: "There is therefore now no condemnation for those who are in Christ Jesus." The promise of "no condemnation" implies deliverance from judgment, answering the plight of Adam's heirs in 5:16: "the judgment following one trespass brought condemnation." "In Christ Jesus" is the language of participation, building on the language of union with Christ in Rom 6:1–11. It would be tempting to think that Paul says one is justified, or delivered from condemnation, by a human action of participating

25. Sanders, *Paul and Palestinian Judaism*, 520., emphasis original. To be sure, however, Paul never says "Christ dies for *Christians*"; Christ died for all, without distinction.

26 Ibid.

in Christ.[27] But this is not exactly the case. Rather, as Rom 8:3 makes clear, we are not delivered from condemnation through *our* participation in Christ, but rather through *Christ's* full participation in the bondage and condemnation that fell on Adam's heirs: "For God has done what the law, weakened by the flesh, could not do: sending his own Son in the likeness of sinful flesh and for sin, he condemned sin in the flesh." Our deliverance from condemnation and life in Christ are the outcome of Christ's experience of condemnation *for* us, and participation *with* us.

Paul's ways of talking about sin and evil derive from this stunning good news; it is the event of Christ's union with humanity to the death—death on a cross—that reveals the depth and power of sin countered by the even greater depth and power of God's love. As J. Louis Martyn put it, using the language of "invasion" to denote the sending and death of Christ, "God would not have to carry out an invasion in order merely to forgive erring human beings. The root trouble lies deeper than human guilt, and it is more sinister. The whole of humanity—indeed, the whole of creation (3:22)—is, in fact, trapped, enslaved under the power of the present evil age."[28] The good news entails liberation from this power.

Yet human experience also includes both culpability and condemnation for evil-doing; we are simultaneously perpetrators and victims of sin, both culpable for the evil we do, and unable to break free of that evil. Paul's rich description of the human predicament requires that we name ourselves as both. If we find this illogical or inconceivable, perhaps that is the result of the pervasive and persistent illusion that we are autonomous individuals, self-directed, freely choosing our actions, and hence solely responsible only for what we choose. Perhaps it also is the result of our focus on intentions rather than actions as the locus of culpability and judgment. As we have seen, however, Paul does not think in terms of individual autonomy, nor does he focus on intentions as the object of divine judgment.

We can push these observations further; Paul's discourse not only requires us to name ourselves as both perpetrators and victims, but Paul's gospel also makes it possible to do so. Deceptive and deceived, in sin's "empire of illusion," we are unable rightly to name our wrong. Paradoxically, even the law, which should show us our wrong, becomes a tool of deception in sin's hands. And the condemnation pronounced by the law only intensifies the enslavement exercised by sin, because the effect of condemnation in human beings is to kill hope and trigger defensive self-justification. But as

27. This indeed is what Sanders does say: "The normally juristic, forensic or ethical language of righteousness is forced to bear the meaning of 'life by participation in the body of Christ.'" Ibid., 504.

28. Martyn, *Galatians*, 105.

Stanley Hauerwas rightly claims, "the recognition of evil is possible because God never leaves us without hope. That is, hope makes possible the ability to take the next step necessary to discover that we are not condemned to live out our past. We discover that we are only able to name our sins on the way to being free from them."[29] In other words, "no condemnation" opens the door to a truthful naming of our human faults and frailty. To paraphrase Rom 5:6–10, because Christ died for us and reconciled us to God, *now* we can say "while we were still weak . . . while we were yet sinners . . . while we were enemies."

Finally, the structure of Romans 1–8, with its dissimilar accounts of evil and sin, leaves us with a question as to the ultimate character of sin. In the last analysis is sin a characteristic of human beings, or is it a hostile and fundamentally alien cosmic power? And if the latter, which seems implied by the way in which Rom 5:12—7:25 reframes the earlier narrative, then is Paul not ascribing an agency and power to "sin" that borders on a Manichean view of the cosmos? Two concluding reflections may help our reflection on this question.

First, as noted earlier, sin drops out of the vocabulary of Romans after 8:3, except for two places (11:26; 14:23). In neither of these does sin have the agency which it exercises in chapters 5–7. It is as if sin, having been dealt with through the flesh of Christ (8:3), ceases to have power over those who are "in Christ." The indwelling power of the Spirit is far greater (8:9–11). This is certainly not to say that Christians do not sin; if that were the case, Paul would not have needed to write all those letters! Rather, Christians exist in two competing realms: the "present evil age," which is under the dominion of sin and death, and in which, short of the eschaton, we are complicit simply by virtue of being Adam's heirs; and the new creation, proleptically present in the body of Christ. It is the second that holds the future, in which Christ reigns as Lord over all creation. And thus it is the second that for Paul is the mode of Christian life, even though at present that life is hidden in the midst of conflict, suffering and death. This is why, in Rom 12:21, Paul can confidently tell the Romans to overcome evil with good. And note in what this victory over evil consists: precisely the refusal to repay evil with evil or to presume to usurp God's role as judge (Rom 12:17–20).

Second, in Rom 11:32 Paul announces, "God has consigned (*sunekleisen*) all to disobedience, so that he might have mercy on all." This supremely counter-intuitive claim parallels Gal 3:22, where Paul claims, "the scripture consigned (*sunekleisen*) all to sin." Remarkably, here

---

29. Hauerwas, "Seeing Darkness, Hearing Silence," 39.

imprisonment under "sin" or its human expression, "disobedience," is precisely in accordance with God's will to exercise mercy on behalf of all humanity through Christ. Sin, the terrifying slave master that in 5:12—7:25 ruled through the law and death, now is revealed as simply a bit player in God's drama of salvation. It rules for awhile, and its rule is terrible, but at the last it is only "a poor player that struts and frets his hour upon the stage, and then is heard no more."[30]

> When the perishable puts on the imperishable, and the mortal puts on immortality, then shall come to pass the saying that is written: "Death is swallowed up in victory." "O death, where is thy victory? O death, where is thy sting?" The sting of death is sin, and the power of sin is the law. But thanks be to God, who gives us the victory through our Lord Jesus Christ (1 Cor. 15:54–57).[31]

BIBLIOGRAPHY

DeBoer, Martin. "Paul and Jewish Apocalyptic Eschatology." In *Apocalyptic and the New Testament: Essays in Honour of J. Louis Martyn*, edited by Joel Marcus and M. L. Soards, 169–90. JSNTSup 24. Sheffield: JSOT Press, 1989.

Delbanco, Andrew. *The Death of Satan: How Americans Have Lost the Sense of Evil*. New York: Farrar, Straus & Giroux, 1995.

Gaventa, Beverly. "From Toxic Speech to Doxology." In *The Word Leaps the Gap: Essays on Scripture and Theology in Honor of Richard B. Hays,* edited by J. Ross Wagner, C. K. Rowe and A. K. Grieb, 392–408. Grand Rapids: Eerdmans, 2008.

Gourevitch, Philip. *We Wish to Inform You That Tomorrow We Will Be Killed with Our Families: Stories from Rwanda*. New York: Farrar, Straus & Giroux, 1998.

Halivni, David Weiss. *Book and the Sword: A Life of Learning in the Shadow of Destruction*. New York: Farrar, Straus & Giroux, 1996.

Hauerwas, Stanley. "Seeing Darkness, Hearing Silence." In *Naming Evil Judging Evil*, edited by R. W. Grant, 35–52. Chicago: Chicago University Press, 2006.

Hedges, Chris. *The Empire of Illusion: The Loss of Literacy and the Rise of Spectacle*. New York: Nation Books, 2009.

Hofius, Otfried. "Der Mensch Im Schatten Adams." In *Paulusstudien II*, 104–54. WUNT 143. Tübingen: Mohr/Siebeck, 2002.

Martyn, J. Louis. *Galatians: A New Translation with Introduction and Commentary*. Anchor Bible 33A. New York: Doubleday, 1997.

Meyer, Paul. "The Worm at the Core of the Apple." In *The Word in This World: Essays in New Testament Exegesis and Theology,* 57–77. Louisville: WJK, 2004.

Percy, Walker. *Lancelot*. New York: Farrar, Straus & Giroux, 1977.

---

30. Shakespeare, "Macbeth," Act 5, Scene 5.

31. I am delighted to dedicate this essay to Paul Zahl, a passionate advocate of the grace of God and its power to break the bonds of condemnation.

Sanders, E. P. *Paul and Palestinian Judaism: A Comparison of Patterns of Religion.* Minneapolis: Fortress, 1977.

Shakespeare, William. "Macbeth."

2

Born Free?

Recovering the Doctrine of the Bound Will for the Sake of Preaching in the Church

JONATHAN WONG

INTRODUCTION

PREACHING IS NO LONGER in favor. It has lost its luster in contemporary society, and the word "preach" often carries a negative connotation (e.g. "Don't preach to me!"). This is not surprising considering what passes as preaching in many pulpits on Sunday mornings. Most of what is heard from the preacher is either an exhortation to do better (or think better, or feel better, etc.), or an attempt to entertain those who come so that they feel that they get their money's worth. It is a sad state of affairs that the church finds itself in. What are truly rare are pulpits that bring comfort to those who are weary and heavy laden. Church is the last place people go to for "comfortable words." Is it any wonder that people are leaving the church in numbers?

How can we change this approach to preaching? What is it that has led to the situation where preaching now afflicts the afflicted and comforts the comfortable? Would it be too bold to suggest that it is because we have not taken Luther's insight into the human condition to heart, and have neglected the doctrine of the bondage of the will? This leads us to believe that either people are all capable of changing themselves, and that all they need is "a little help from my friends" (Lennon and McCartney) or a swift kick up the rear end. In the introduction to their fresh translation of Luther's best work, *The Bondage of the Will*, J.I. Packer and O. R. Johnston point out that the "recovery [of this doctrine] will involve something of a Copernican revolution in our outlook on many matters."[1]

This essay is an attempt to recover this doctrine by trying to clarify Luther's understanding of the bound (or un-free) will, with a little help from some (theological) friends. This will be done by examining (and hopefully refuting) the criticisms leveled against the doctrine, while seeking to defend theologically the un-free will. This essay will also make some suggestions in regards to an approach to preaching that might be more helpful in terms of how to reach the average person in the pew with the "comfortable words" of the Gospel.

SOME BACKGROUND

The first time I encountered Paul Zahl was for one of my first classes in seminary. It was a Spiritual Formation class (incidentally his alternate title for the course was "Whatever Gets You through the Night"). One of the key objectives he had in the class was to answer the question, "What is the Gospel?" He laid out the implications of the grace of God with regards to how it applies to life, and how it should shape and form us as Christians. There were many things that Dr Zahl brought up that were challenging (understatement) but in particular the hardest pill to swallow was when he dealt with the doctrine of the bondage of the will. Having grown up in the environment of a Charismatic-Evangelical Anglican home and church community in Singapore, I was very unfamiliar with this aspect of theological anthropology. I was in fact convinced that free will was absolutely non-negotiable for what it means to be human. If I had been asked at that point, I might have even been quite willing to admit that I was an Arminian, or at least had Arminian leanings in my theology. Paul, however, pointed out that we are bound and are not able to help ourselves. He said, "The natural man hates this message. Anything is better than not being in control. We have a huge resistance to not being in control of our destiny. We cringe at 'Wretched man that I am, who will deliver me from this body of death?'" That was certainly my experience sitting in that class. Yet as I examined the readings assigned, read Scripture again with fresh eyes, and reflected on my own life experience, I could not help finding myself slowly moving towards a new appreciation of the un-free will.

1. Luther, *The Bondage of the Will*, 60.

Since that time, in my own ministry in different parishes, I have found that this concept of the bound will continues to be a difficult one for people to accept. Everyone is happy to hear the message of God's unconditional grace towards us as sinners. Many agree with the insight of the effects of original sin. But very few are able to accept the concept of the bound will. Yet the fact remains that unless we accept that our wills are bound, and in need of the grace of God to free us, we will always find ourselves struggling to try to force a compassionate response upon ourselves towards fellow sinners, and to be able to avoid the ever-present danger of either falling into despair or a self-righteous disposition as ministers of the gospel.

THE CASE FOR FREE WILL

The defense for free will from an Evangelical perspective has mostly come from Arminian theologians.[2] It should be pointed out that Arminianism has often been mislabeled as being primarily concerned with the belief in free will. Roger Olson, in his defense of Arminianism points out that it is a myth that has been promulgated (and at times even believed by those who would consider themselves Arminians) that Arminian theology "begins with and is controlled by belief in freedom of the will."[3] He insists that for Arminius, and Arminianism as a whole, "The controlling belief is not free will but God's good character, which is manifested in love and justice. Free will enters in only because without it God becomes the all-determining reality, who is necessarily the author of sin and evil, whether directly or indirectly."[4]

The primary concern for Arminians, therefore, is to safeguard God's character in our theologizing. If there were no free will, then this would necessarily lead us down a path towards a kind of divine determinism, that will ultimately lead to a God who is the source of evil and sin. The argument put forward is that "Arminians believe in free will because they see it everywhere assumed in the Bible, and because it is necessary to protect God's reputation."[5] The objection raised towards those who insist on the denial of free will is that this would mean God controls all human choice and action, which logically leads to the conclusion "that this would make God the

---

2. This is not to say that there are not others who also have much to say on the matter. Roman Catholics are also proponents of this position, but as I am approaching this from a Protestant Evangelical perspective, the Arminian view of free will is most common in that context, and is thus presented here.

3. Olson, *Arminian Theology*, 97.

4. Ibid., 114.

5. Ibid., 98.

author of sin and evil . . . [And] this makes God at least morally ambiguous and at worst the *only* sinner."[6] This "exhaustive divine determinism" can only result in a God whose goodness is suspect. It also opens the possibility that God sins by "willing others to sin" or by being the very cause of sin.[7]

Furthermore, the insistence on the lack of free will runs counter to the biblical witness of a God who is love, which is revealed in Jesus Christ.[8] This does not mean that Arminians deny that God directs the affairs and actions of humankind. What they reject is "that God controls all human choices and actions."[9] "God is love, and therefore expresses his power, not by having to control everything like an oriental despot, but by giving humanity salvation and eternal life under the conditions of mutuality."[10] This "mutuality" requires for there to be some place for human free will to operate, otherwise we are no longer free autonomous beings, but robots who can only act as programed. And of course, there is no such thing as robot love (with apologies to WALL-E). For real love must be freely offered. Love that is forced, or determined, by someone else cannot truly be love. "God's love is the inner content of all doctrines of Christianity. It is what they are all *about*."[11]

The concern to protect "God's good character" is admirable. Any doctrine that can call into question the goodness of God or causes one to stumble should be treated with suspicion. However, the concerns expressed by those who advocate free will are in themselves problematic. Firstly, the insistence on free will being "everywhere assumed" in Scripture is a stretch. Clark Pinnock points to the fact that this "theological shift" from "determinism" came about "because of a fresh and faithful reading of the Bible in dialogue with modern culture, which places emphasis on autonomy, temporality, and historical change."[12] If one looks at many of the biblical arguments they make, the question that arises is whether the zeitgeist of human autonomy inclines the modern Arminian theologian to elevate statements in Scripture that carry even the slightest whiff of free will to confessional status, while ignoring other more explicit statements of the un-free will. The danger therefore is that such readings of the Bible may place a greater emphasis on being "fresh" rather than "faithful."

6. Ibid., 99.

7. Ibid..

8. John 3:16; 1 John. 4:9

9 Olson, *Arminian Theology*, 99.

10. Pinnock, ed., *The Grace of God, the Will of Man*, x.

11. Fitz Guy, "The Universality of God's Love," in ibid., 35.

12. Ibid., 15.

Second, the question must be asked as to why there is a need to "defend" God? Luther pointed out that there is a hiddenness to God, what he called *Deus absconditus*.[13] In his work *Heidelberg Disputation* (1518), he said in thesis 19, "That person does not deserve to be called a theologian who looks upon the invisible things of God as though they were clearly perceptible in those things which have actually happened."[14] In trying to "protect God's reputation," one becomes susceptible to the danger of making God less than He is, and in essence denying what He has actually revealed in His Word. The insistence on limiting God's sovereignty (even though they call it "self-limitation") goes against the witness of Scripture. The Bible says that God "hardens the heart of whomever he chooses" (Rom 9:18b). Yet Paul says, "Is there injustice on God's part? By no means!" (Rom 9:14). What we are left with is a conundrum, a paradox as to how God's apparent "evil" action is not unjust. However, are we in any position to question God's actions and measure them against our standard of "good and evil"? Luther pointed out that, "God is He for Whose will no cause or ground may be laid down as its rule and standard; for nothing is on a level with it or above it, but it is itself the rule for all things."[15] After all, God said, "my ways [are] higher than your ways and my thoughts than your thoughts" (Isa 55:9). God alone is the standard by which we know right and wrong, or good and evil. Luther says, "What God wills is not right because He ought, or was bound, so to will; on the contrary, what takes place must be right, because He so wills it. Causes and grounds are laid down for the will of the creature, but not for the will of the Creator—unless you set another Creator over him!"[16]

We are called to believe this by faith. Not a blind faith. Rather it is a faith rooted in the revelation of God through his Word. Luther points out:

> there must be room for faith, therefore, all that is believed must be hidden. Yet it is not hidden more deeply than under a contrary appearance of sight, sense and experience. Thus, when God quickens, He does so by killing; when He justifies, He does so by pronouncing guilty; when He carries up to heaven, He does so by bringing down to hell . . . Thus God conceals His eternal mercy and loving kindness beneath eternal wrath, His righteousness beneath unrighteousness . . . If I could by any means understand how this same God, who makes such a show of wrath and unrighteousness, can yet be merciful and just,

13. Latin for "the hidden God."

14. Forde, *On Being a Theologian of the Cross*, 72.

15. Luther, *The Bondage of the Will*, 209.

16. Ibid.

there would be no need for faith. But as it is, the impossibility of understanding makes room for the exercise of faith when these things are preached and published; just as, when God kills, faith in life is exercised in death.[17]

Finally, the case could be made that the Arminian proponents of free will have not fully understood what it means to have an un-free will. They appear to equate the bondage of the will with God controlling "all human choices and actions."[18] The fear is that wills that are bound lead to automatons rather than free, autonomous beings. This is not what is being said in the doctrine of the bound will.

OUR WILLS ARE BOUND

There is no denying that the bondage of the will is a problematic doctrine. It smacks of determinism and cuts against grain of the human desire for independence and autonomy. Yet this is unmistakably the biblical view, and it is also something that is seen in the experience of everyday life. However, to hold a theology that the will is bound is to find oneself "swimming upstream against the surrounding culture."[19] The case for the bound will is going to be made by first explaining what it is not, before outlining what it is. This will then be rounded out by working out the implications of this doctrine for the practice of preaching in answering the question at the end: "So what?"

Critics of the un-free will often mistake it for determinism. For instance, Olson in his defense of Arminian theology used the term "determinism" as the counterfoil to the Arminian commitment to free will.[20] This, however, is a misconception. In speaking of the bound will, Barth says, "It has nothing whatever to do with the battle between determinism and indeterminism. It is not a decision for determinism . . . It does not consist at all in the fact that man cannot any longer will and decide, i.e., that he is deprived of *arbitrium*,[21] that he has no will at all. If this were the case, he would no longer be a man; he would only be part of a mechanism moved from without."[22]

---

17. Ibid., 101.
18. Olson, *Arminian Theology*, 98.
19. Zahl, *Grace in Practice*, 103.
20. Olson, *Arminian Theology*, 97–98.
21. Latin for "will."
22. Barth, *Church Dogmatics*, IV/2, 494.

The very fact that critics of the bound will use the term "determinism" as a synonym for the bondage of the will, raises the question as to whether they have understood Luther's insight into human nature, or his theological anthropology. He does not deny that humans can exercise their will. However to imagine that the will is "free" in the sense that we are completely autonomous, is mistaken. He likened human will to an animal, which stands between two riders. The will is either ridden by God, going where God wills; or it is ridden by Satan, and goes where the enemy wills.[23] This is a crude illustration. On the surface, it can sound very much like a sort of determinism. However Luther clarifies this by saying, "The will, whether it be God's or man's, does what it does, good or bad, under no compulsion but just as it wants or pleases, as if totally free."[24] What he means is that what we naturally want is always contrary to what God wants. So the will is never some neutral, undecided force. It is always autonomous. But that is the crux of the problem. It never chooses to subject or submit itself to God. It can only choose what it wants, what the human being desires—self-autonomy. Never what God wills or desires.

This means that the will is bound, not because we as humans are like puppets on string, dancing to the machinations of a divine (or satanic) puppet master. The reality is that we are bound because of the corruption of original sin, of human depravity. Forde says, "The bondage of the will means that we find ourselves in a situation where we simply cannot do what is asked of us, and we cannot do it because we will not."[25] We exercise our wills to choose what we want. We can do no other. "No one is forced. It is something more like an addiction. We all do what we want to do! That is precisely our bondage."[26] It is the nature of our condition. In this way, we as human beings are apparently "free." Barth says, "He has not ceased to be a man. He wills. He is a Hercules, the *arbiter*[27] of what he does. But he does what he does in the corruption of his will. He does not, therefore, do it *libero*[28] but *servo arbitrio*[29]."[30] So the reality is that as human creatures,

---

23. Luther, *The Bondage of the Will*, 103–4.

24. Ibid., 81.

25. Forde, *Theology Is for Proclamation*, 44.

26. Forde, *The Captivation of the Will*, 37.

27. Latin for "judge."

28. Latin for "with a free will."

29. Latin for "with a will in bondage."

30. Barth, *Church Dogmatics*, IV/2, 495.

"we have no remaining choice, not because we are supposedly forced into something, but because we have already made it."[31]

A note on Karl Barth as an aside is probably appropriate here. He has sometimes been viewed as a critic of Luther, and there are widespread impressions that Barth assessed Luther negatively.[32] George Hunsinger, one of the foremost interpreters of Barth, disagrees. While he was vigorous in his polemic (not only of Luther), Barth's indebtedness to Luther is immense. "The Luther of *The Bondage of the Will* and similar writings made a profound impression on Barth's mind . . . What separated Barth here from the main tendencies of the Reformed tradition while aligning him squarely with Luther was the deep inner connection Barth discerned between unconditioned grace, human incapacity, and the doctrine of *simul iustus et peccator*."[33]

Luther's *simul iustus et peccator* "meant that grace came to faith in three basic modes: once for all, again and again, and more and more—in that order of significance."[34] While Calvin placed emphasis on the once-for-all and the more-and-more aspects of grace, Barth retrieved the pointedness of Luther's doctrine by bringing into focus the again-and-again aspect of grace, and "conspicuously reinstated" it in his soteriology, where "grace is new to us as sinners each morning . . . [and] comes to us again and again in the perfection of the finished work of Christ."[35] Barth believed that "the grace that was unconditioned by anything other than itself was the very grace by which our ongoing human incapacity as sinners was overcome—not more and more, but again and again—by the gift of faith."[36] This grace that comes "again and again" is key for preaching. It means that preachers should never stray from the gospel because we constantly need it again and again due to our "dual" nature. We will look at this again a little later in the essay.

In many ways, the objections to the un-free will are entirely understandable. They are a "defense mechanism" that the human person reflexively deploys when under threat. We cling to our autonomy like a drowning man to a piece of flotsam. Even when rescue is offered, we will not let go. It is why it is only an act of grace that saves us! In essence we say, "God I cannot trust you with my destiny, therefore I must claim at least enough freedom

31. Forde, *Theology Is for Proclamation* 46.

32. Hunsinger, *Disruptive Grace*, 280.

33. Ibid., 301. *Simul iustus et peccator* is Latin for "simultaneously justified and sinful."

34. Ibid., 299.

35. Ibid., 299–300.

36. Ibid., 301.

to control it myself."[37] This is ultimately the reality of the human condition, as an effect of the fall.

Forde points out that calling the event in Genesis 3 "the fall" is actually misleading. Depravity (or original sin) is not about a downward move on our part, about our choosing to wallow in the gutter of human existence. It is rather the movement towards the temptation offered in the garden that "you will be like God" (Gen. 3:5). The problem of sin is that we want to be gods. Forde says that what happened in the garden should be more accurately termed an "upward fall." "It is not a downward plunge to some lower level in the great chain of being, some lower rung on the ladder of morality and freedom. Rather, it is an upward rebellion, an invasion of the realm of things 'above,' the usurping of divine prerogative."[38]

This is why the bound will is so difficult to accept. We struggle with it for it seems to go against our notions of what is good and right. It undercuts our notions of freedom, and it undercuts our self-asserting desires. Barth says, "[this doctrine] cannot be either proved or disproved by empirical findings or a priori reflections."[39] It must be derived and defended Christologically. It has to be a faith statement. For Barth's dogmatics:

> Any claim to know in advance what 'the good' consists in is misguided. The human problem is precisely that we *do* construct notions of 'the good', and that they are more often than not corrupted or even demonic. Breaking the closed circle of human certainty requires that we attend to what God is saying, not 'normalizing' the commandment by assimilating it to what we already know, but allowing our moral imaginations to be stretched. The good is never simply 'the natural', but must be *learned*, and that through an encounter with the Word that the Word itself makes possible.[40]

Therefore it is only by revelation that we can know what is "good." This too is Luther's assertion. "God does many things which He does not show us in His Word, and He wills many things which He does not in His Word show us that He wills . . . we must keep in view His Word and leave alone His inscrutable will; for it is by His Word, and not by His inscrutable will, that we must be guided."[41]

---

37. Forde, *Theology Is for Proclamation*, 46.

38. Ibid., 48.

39. Barth, *Church Dogmatics*, IV/2, 494.

40. Mangina, *Karl Barth*, 147.

41. Luther, *The Bondage of the Will*, 170–71.

SO WHAT?

So what are the pastoral implications of the bound will? This understanding of the human condition should cause us to re-think evangelism, pastoral care, and even Christian education in their current forms. However, the area that this essay is concerned with is that of preaching in the church. Packer and Johnston pointed out that accepting the principles that Luther drew out in *On the Bondage of the Will* ought to lead to "a radically different approach to preaching."[42] This is because the preachers will see their congregation as a gathering of people whose wills are bound, instead of a gathering of people who have wills that are completely free. "The presupposition for proclamation is not the free choice of the will, but the bondage of the will."[43]

The upward fall has left us in a predicament. In our quest for self-determination, we end up either deifying ourselves, or we seek to make gods of something (or someone) else which we can control, leading to us becoming Calvin's proverbial "idol factories." "In defiance of God we claim to be free. Such "freedom," of course, is only faith in ourselves over against God—our defense mechanism against God."[44] The result of this is that we lose our faith and trust in God. This is where preaching comes in. It is only through the preached word that faith is restored. For "faith comes from what is heard, and what is heard comes through the [preached] word of Christ" (Rom 10:17). The people that fill our pews are in desperate need. They have come because they are "weary and heavy laden" (Matt 11:28). Yet instead of rest they receive an additional burden of what they ought to do, or be, or become. This is because the preacher assumes that their wills are free, and they assume that the hearers must exercise their free will to help themselves, of course with the help of grace, like a power pellet, to give that extra boost to get over the rough patches. The reality, however, is that they are sinners whose wills are bound, and they cannot act on the exhortation, because they will not. As Forde points out, "The will will will what it will!"[45] Therefore the hearers, "need deliverance, not a helper merely but a Saviour."[46]

What is the form of this proclamation that the preacher makes to un-free wills? In his book *Positive Preaching and the Modern Man*, P.T. Forsyth says:

42. Ibid., 60.
43. Ibid., 42.
44. Ibid., 46.
45. Forde, *Theology Is for Proclamation* 47.
46. Forsyth, *Positive Preaching and the Modern Mind, 1907*, 2.

the gift to men in Christianity is the Gospel deed of God's grace in the shape of forgiveness, redemption, regeneration . . . By grace is not here meant either God's general benignity, or His particular kindness to our failure or pity for our pain. I mean His undeserved and unbought pardon and redemption of us in the face of our sin, in the face of the world-sin, under such moral conditions as are prescribed by His revelation of His holy love in Jesus Christ and Him crucified. And by the Gospel of this grace I would especially urge that there is meant not a statement, nor a doctrine, nor a scheme, on man's side; nor an offer, a promise, or a book, on God's side. It is an act and a power: it is God's act of redemption before it is man's message of it. It is an eternal, perennial act of God in Christ, repeating itself within each declaration of it. Only as a Gospel done by God is it a Gospel spoken by man. It is a revelation only because it was first of all a reconciliation. It was a work that redeemed us into the power of understanding its own word . . . The gift of God's grace was, and is, His work of Gospel. And it is this act that is prolonged in the word of the preacher, and not merely proclaimed.[47]

The Gospel alone is our proclamation. It is a word of absolution that comes, not from human speech, but from the divine act of God. The actual forms of the sermon can vary, but the content must always be "the Gospel deed of God's grace." As the apostle Paul said in his letter to the Corinthian church, he sought to bring the message of the Gospel "through the foolishness of our proclamation" (1 Cor. 1:21). He says, "When I came to you, brothers and sisters, I did not come proclaiming the mystery of God to you in lofty words or wisdom. For I decided to know nothing among you except Jesus Christ, and him crucified" (1 Cor. 2:1–2).

The common misconception is that the Gospel is only needed at the beginning of the Christian life. It is something preached only to non-believers, or those who have just come to faith. The perception is that the normal Christian needs to move on from there, to progress to "higher things." Yet if we view the grace of God, as Barth pointed out, as coming in the two modes of once-for-all and again-and-again, then we see that this cannot be so. This idea that the Gospel is only required at the start is viewing grace only as once-for-all. Yet the need we have is for it to be "new every morning" (Lam. 3:23). Therefore grace must also come to us again and again. We can never "graduate" from the Gospel. This is why preaching must be categorical, or unconditional. As Forde says, "Proclamation

47. Ibid., 3.

that gives forgiveness to sinners on account of Christ alone is the only solution for all our problems with God."[48]

CONCLUSION

James Nestingen in his introduction to *The Captivation of the Will*, quotes Forde: "If you begin with the assumption of freedom, the preoccupation is always how to keep freedom in check, how to bind; But if you begin with the assumption of bondage, the preoccupation is always how to set out the word that frees."[49] The irony is that the preacher who assumes free will has to lay down boundaries to protect and prevent his hearers from wandering off the reservation; while the preacher to un-free wills freely preaches a word of grace and absolution, a word that sets those born in captivity free.

The renewal of an understanding of human anthropology in the light of Luther's bound will has tremendous importance for the church today. It will transform not only the preaching but also the preacher. It will help to prevent the Monday morning blues that inevitably results from the realization that most people have not, and cannot, do what was asked of them in the sermon. It lifts the burden from the preacher, and relieves the resentment that inevitably comes when the congregants who are assumed to have free wills, never seem to change. A deep understanding of the bound will also transforms the preacher by allowing him to feel a deep compassion for fellow sufferers. He will begin to understand Christ who says that, "Those who are well have no need of a physician, but those who are sick" (Mark 2:17) —that the church is a hospital, whose mission is to heal the sick.

BIBLIOGRAPHY

Barth, Karl. *Church Dogmatics.* Translated by G. W. Bromiley. Edited by G. W. Bromiley and T. F. Torrance. Vol. IV/2. Edinburgh: T. & T. Clark, 1958.

Forde, Gerhard O. *The Captivation of the Will: Luther vs. Erasmus on Freedom and Bondage.* Edited by Steven Paulson. Grand Rapids: Eerdmans, 2005.

———. *On Being a Theologian of the Cross: Reflections on Luther's Heidelberg Disputation, 1518.* Grand Rapids: Eerdmans, 1997.

———. *Theology Is for Proclamation* Minneapolis: Fortress, 1990.

Forsyth, P. T. *Positive Preaching and the Modern Mind, 1907.* 1st Austrian ed. Coromandel East: New Creation Publications, 1993.

Hunsinger, George. *Disruptive Grace: Studies in the Theology of Karl Barth.* Grand Rapids: Eerdmans, 2000.

---

48. Forde, *Theology Is for Proclamation* 78.

49. Forde, *The Captivation of the Will,* 21.

Luther, Martin. *The Bondage of the Will.* Translated by J. I. Packer and O.R. Johnston. Grand Rapids: Fleming H. Revell, 1957.

Mangina, Joseph L. *Karl Barth: Theologian of Christian Witness.* Louisville: Westminster John Knox, 2004.

Olson, Roger E. *Arminian Theology: Myths and Realities.* Downers Grove: IVP Academic, 2006.

Pinnock, Clark H., editor. *The Grace of God, the Will of Man: A Case for Arminianism* Grand Rapids: Academie Books, 1989.

Zahl, Paul F. M. *Grace in Practice: A Theology of Everyday Life.* Grand Rapids: Eerdmans, 2007.

3

The Un-Free Will and the Markan Depiction of Jesus' Disciples[1]

TODD BREWER

IT IS THE PURPOSE of this article to demonstrate that, through its depiction of Jesus' disciples, the Gospel of Mark espouses a view of human nature analogous to what later came to be called "the un-free will." Mark's presentation of the disciples is a well-worn path in New Testament studies, with the predominant paradigm for this assessment being a measurement of the disciples' capacity to understand Jesus' teaching and actions. On the basis of the so-called secrecy theme, the Gospel of Mark is construed as a gradual unfolding of the revelation of Jesus. This description of unfolding revelation has taken different forms in recent scholarship. Rudolf Bultmann believed that the messianic secret was invented by Mark to harmonize Mark's own Hellenistic, Pauline Christianity with traditions of Jesus' life and to demonstrate that Jesus' Messiahship is only recognized through faith in his resurrection.[2] Timothy Weeden suggested that the Gospel is structured to correct a mistaken *theios anēr* mythological conception of Jesus in favor of the

---

1 This essay is dedicated to Paul Zahl with deep appreciation for his ministry and teaching, from which I first learned to think theologically through the issues of anthropology, grace, law and Gospel. The following is inspired by a passing comment Paul once made in class noting that the historical infidelity of the disciples demonstrates a "low anthropology."

2. Bultmann, *Theology of the New Testament*, 1:32.

crucified Messiah.[3] Finally, William Telford highlights the contrast between the nationalistic, Jewish "son of David" and the more Hellenistic "son of God" Christology.[4] All of these different theories are variations on a similar theme: what is at stake in the gospel of Mark is the differentiation between true and false Christologies. The characters of the Gospel are meant to portray this grappling over Jesus' identity. To the degree that characters rightly *understand* Jesus' identity they are held as exemplars for the reader, while misapprehension is admonished.

This general approach sheds a great deal of light on the mysterious meaning of the Gospel of Mark. It may account for Jesus' puzzling demand for secrecy (Mark. 1:44; 5:43; 7:36; 8:30; 9:9, etc.) as well as the strategic placement of Christological confessions (3:11; 5:7; 8:30; 9:7; 15:39). However, a paradigm which privileges understanding as the hermeneutical key to the Gospel has some key limitations when it comes to the disciples. First, it seems odd that Mark would cast peripheral characters as positively demonstrating full understanding while the disciples—those to whom Jesus has given the secret of the kingdom of God (4:11)—would somehow escape full understanding. Moreover, a characterization of the disciples' understanding as either positive or negative fails to account for the varied depiction of the disciples themselves. A categorical characterization of the disciples on this basis also overlooks both their occasional moments of brilliance and stubborn obliviousness. One can only conclude that the disciples demonstrate various levels of understanding. But most of all, proper understanding of Jesus is not the only prerequisite needed for one to be called a disciple. In addition to proper understanding, Jesus also places concrete conditions upon the disciples if they are to truly become *Jesus'* disciples and enter into the kingdom.[5] Obedience or disobedience to the commands results in the gain or loss of status as a disciple of Jesus.

The following will examine Jesus' most explicit command regarding discipleship and outline the subsequent actions of the disciples as the narrative unfolds. It is from this final vantage point that it may be possible to

3. Weeden, "The Heresy that Necessitated Mark's Gospel [1968]."

4. "By both employing and correcting the emphases of these separate traditions, by a discriminating use of Christological titles, and, above all, by means of the secrecy motif, Mark has presented these traditions in such a way as to leave his readers in no doubt as to the significance that ought to be attached to the historical figure of Jesus, namely, that he is the supernatural 'Son of God.'" Telford, *The Theology of the Gospel of Mark*, 54. See also Dunn, "The Messianic Secret in Mark."

5. Put positively, this indicates that Mark's concept of faith/belief encompasses both proper understanding of Jesus and a proper response which encompasses the entirety of one's being. This comes close to the Pauline conception of faith which is simultaneously obedience (Rom 1:5) and a response to the word (Rom 10:17).

make a comprehensive assessment of the disciples, toward the proposal of a Markan anthropology. It will be shown that, on the one hand, the disciples are both able to understand Jesus and what he requires of them. Yet for all their willfulness, the failure of the disciples to obey Jesus' command is part of a larger theme demonstrating the totality of human failure.

WHO ARE JESUS' DISCIPLES?

Jesus' call to his first disciples contained the simple exhortation that they follow him (*akoloutheō*). Jesus is always on the move, preaching wherever he sees fit, and the simple task of the disciple is to follow behind him. Initially, the invitation to discipleship is given indiscriminately to all with no condition beyond spatial proximity. Of course, this demand to follow Jesus implies one's leaving their existing circumstances of life, though such an implication is not the same as a required precondition. Jesus' disciples are those unrighteous sinners (2:17) who have done the will of God, namely to follow Jesus (3:35).[6] In this way, Jesus' initial followers were largely self-selected and the composition of the followers was determined only by their willingness to travel.[7] It is only at Mark 8:34–38 that Jesus begins a series of teachings that specifically outlines the requirements to be his disciple. His new teaching occurs immediately after the first of three passion predictions (8:31) and marks an abrupt turn in Jesus' self-disclosure. While Jesus has faced opposition from Jewish leaders who wish to kill him (3:6), there has been little indication that this desire would result actually result in Jesus' death.

The new reality of Jesus' impending death therefore prompts a similar change for his disciples. Jesus states that those who want to follow behind him must lose their lives (8:43). The discipleship imagery is striking, with a clear emphasis on movement. Jesus does not say "be crucified and then follow," but "take up your cross and follow," the implication being that crucifixion lies ahead of the disciple at the end of the one's journey with Jesus.[8] Therefore the decision to become a follower demands the acceptance of a premature death on a cross.

---

6. See Shiner, *Follow Me!*, 194–98.

7. While Jesus appoints twelve apostles to be with Jesus, preach, and cast out demons (Mark 3:14–15), beyond this missionary vocation there is little distinction between "the twelve" and the disciples who have elected to follow Jesus (compare 4:10 with 4:34). See also Best, *Disciples and Discipleship*, 157.

8. The implication of a future death by crucifixion seems the most straightforward reading of this passage, especially in light of Jesus' own predicted death. *Pace* Gundry, who sees Jesus' call as a metaphor pertaining to public ridicule. Gundry, *Mark*, 435–36.

For the disciples, the seamless transition from Jesus' passion prediction to the similar requirement for discipleship enables the disciples to understand themselves and Jesus as travelling parallel paths bound for the same destination.[9] The disciples understand that if Jesus' way ultimately leads to death, those who claim to be his disciples must likewise follow him to their own crucifixion. Yet in the same way that Jesus' death will paradoxically lead to a resurrection on the third day, the disciples can believe that their death will also somehow lead to a new resurrected life. Jesus and his disciples are inseparably bound together. By contrast, the crowd has not been made aware of Jesus' prior passion prediction. It remains unaware that this ultimate requirement for discipleship will also be assumed by Jesus himself. He is not their messianic co-sufferer, but their demanding teacher. While the disciples may have understood that their salvation was somehow related to Jesus' own resurrection, the crowd hears only a faint suggestion that their death will have a salvific end.

The introduction of the crowd in 8:34 primarily suggests both the limitless nature of Jesus' call to discipleship and the comprehensive scope of divine retribution. Failure to become a disciple and follow Jesus will have vast consequences. When paired with both verses 8:34–35 and 38, the wisdom sayings of 8:36–37 take on the form of a warning. One who fails to give up his life will forfeit his soul, a thing infinite value. The value of heavenly life is contrasted with the worthlessness of earthly life. To accept Jesus is to deny oneself through the acceptance of death. But this general statement concerning the state of the world and its relation to the eternal things of God takes on the character of eschatological warning when juxtaposed with 8:38. What appears to be a wisdom saying about life and death is instead shown to be the judgment of God upon those who, out of shame, fail to follow the Son of Man. Jesus himself will be the arbiter of judgment. Positively, this threat of future judgment states as clearly as possible that obediently following Jesus to death is the only way to find salvation *beyond* death. However paradoxical it may sound, the choice is supposed to be obvious to the disciples.

Jesus demands of his disciples no less than their lives. The command is absolute without any exceptions and applies to all people. The disciple who follows Jesus to their death will be rewarded with a future salvation. More importantly for this study, those who fail to follow Jesus to the end will reap for themselves divine judgment far worse than any earthly death. This conditional either/or between faithfulness and apostasy underlies Jesus' description of discipleship. As Morna Hooker has said, "the crucial divide

---

9. Hooker, *The Gospel according to Mark*, 207.

is not between those who acknowledge Jesus as the Messiah and those who do not, but between those disciples who are prepared to follow him on the way of suffering and those who are not."[10] Much like Moses on the plains of Moab in Deuteronomy 28, Jesus conditionally offers life or death to those who either follow him into death or reject his call and fall away.

Given a discipleship that is dependent upon the faithful obedience of the disciple, there are many possible avenues of understanding available to the interpreter. One could push behind the text backward to the prophetic task of the historical Jesus[11] or forward to the "anti-enthusiastic temper" of the Markan community.[12] However, these questions are premature unless they consider the Mark 8's construal within its narrative context. The continuation of the narrative outlines the subsequent actions of the disciples, thereby functioning as an extended commentary on the teaching and its effect. An account of Mark's understanding of discipleship must move both forward and backwards between the giving of the command and its reception as both mutually interpret one another. It is important to note that, unlike Jesus' first passion prediction, there is no mention of the disciple's response to Jesus' teaching. There is no indication that the disciples accept, reject, or misunderstand Jesus' teaching.

ACCEPTANCE OF JESUS' CALL TO DISCIPLESHIP

Despite the intensifying of Jesus' impending tragedy in each successive conflict with Jewish leaders and Jesus' repeated predictions of his death, the attitude of the disciples to this tragedy is not directly reported until it is prompted by Jesus in 14:27–31.[13] This section bears a striking similarity to 8:31–33,[14] both in form and content, suggesting that it is meant to be a commentary and continuation of Jesus' previous teaching. Peter speaks several times throughout the Gospel, but these are the only two times Jesus directly contradicts Peter's misunderstanding. Jesus addresses his disciples and declares "You all will fall away (*skandalizō*), because it is written: 'I will strike the shepherd and the sheep will be scattered.'" Similar to 8:32, Jesus' prediction is emphatically disputed by Peter, who claims he will be loyal to

---

10. Ibid., 208.

11. Wright, *Jesus and the Victory of God*, 183.

12. Käsemann, "Sentences of Holy Law in the New Testament," 78.

13. A reference could be implied at 14:19, with the disciples freely admitting the possibility that they could betray Jesus, though this seems to have more to do with the force of Jesus' accusation than it does with the disciples' self-understanding.

14. So Marcus, *Mark 8–16*, 973.

Jesus—"Even if everyone else falls away." And as in 8:33, Peter's impetuous response is corrected by Jesus. Yet the similarities between these passages are meant to heighten their differences. Whereas in 8:31–33 Peter is disputing the necessity of Jesus' death, Peter now contests Jesus' low assessment of his loyalty. In the former instance Peter's opposition to Jesus is the work of Satan, while the latter is an expression of Peter's devotion.

If Peter previously failed to understand that the mission of Jesus and his followers necessitates their deaths, Peter now fully understands exactly what is required of him and correctly declares his willingness to follow Jesus to his own death. While Peter's confession of faith occurs in opposition to Jesus' own prediction, this must not obscure that Peter here vows to fulfill the requirements of discipleship previously outlined in 8:34. Peter even understands his death to coincide with Jesus' own death, "If it is necessary that I will die *with you*" (14:31), indicating a confidence in his own future resurrection as promised by Jesus in 8:35.[15] Moreover, Peter also speaks on behalf of the disciples as a whole: "and they all were saying the same" (14:31). Peter's confession, and therefore his understanding of Jesus and discipleship, is mirrored by the rest of the disciples.[16] The disciples appear to have obediently learned from Jesus exactly what is demanded of Jesus' followers and demonstrate an unyielding resolve to act accordingly. Given this profession of faith, it seems questionable whether a negative portrayal of the disciples is warranted on the basis of their ability to understand Jesus.

THE DISCIPLES FORSAKE JESUS

In the face of Jesus' prediction that his disciples would all fall away, Peter and the rest of the disciples declare their enduring allegiance to Jesus even in the face of death. Yet Jesus did not command that his disciples must simply be willing to die, but that they would persevere with him to the point of death. As Jesus goes, so too must the disciples follow him. So when Jesus is arrested at the hands of the chief priests, the disciples must likewise be arrested with him. Instead of accepting this commission as disciples of Jesus, they all abandon Jesus and flee (14:50). At the precise moment when persecution comes and Jesus is in most need of his followers, they all abandon him to face his end alone.

15. For the link between salvation offered in 8:35 and Jesus' own resurrection mentioned in 8:31, see above.

16. The suggestion that this confession by the disciples represents a "lack of self-knowledge" under the assumption that "humans *could* be faithful to God under their own steam" is certainly be true retrospectively, but there is no indication at this point in the narrative that this is the case. Marcus, *Mark 8–16*: 973.

As illustrated by the young man who flees naked, the "all" who abandon Jesus implies more than just "the twelve" disciples, and perhaps even includes those, like Bartimaeus, who have begun following Jesus "on the way" (10.52).

But the "all" mentioned here does not yet include Peter, who "followed Jesus from afar" (14:54). The narrative ensues in the exact order suggested by Peter's own declaration in 14:29: all have fallen away, but will Peter remain? This ambiguity is reinforced through the spatial description of Peter's following of Jesus, but only from afar. He has not yet forsaken Jesus, but his standing is far from certain. Jesus is then led to the high priest and interrogated by the chief priests, elders and scribes. This questioning of Jesus sharply contrasts Peter's own interrogation by a servant of the chief priest. While Jesus willingly accepts, if not orchestrates, his own death sentence, Peter denies his affiliation with Jesus in increasingly unequivocal terms. In his third denial, Peter "began to curse [Jesus? the questioner?] and swear saying, 'I do not know this man of whom you speak" (14:71). Were Peter to affirm his affiliation with Jesus, he too would be obediently put to death alongside his Lord. Instead, he takes his place next to Judas Iscariot and among the other disciples as those who have fled and abandoned Jesus.

Within the Markan narrative, these are the last recorded actions of the disciples. No mention is ever made of a reconciliatory return to Jesus' side to tragically die with their Lord. Instead, the Gospel of Mark ends with the disciples having forsaken Jesus to die alone. In accordance with Jesus' own words in 8:34–38, this failure stipulates that the disciples will die forsaken by Jesus. Just as he commanded, those who save their lives will lose them "when the Son of Man comes in the glory of his Father with the holy angels." By their actions, the disciples have forsaken their call as disciples and instead deserve divine judgment.[17] Within the Markan portrait of the disciples, this is the final and decisive word. The dividing line between disciples and apostates is drawn with the disciples on the outside looking in.

TOWARD A MARKAN ANTHROPOLOGY

What reasons does the Gospel of Mark give for the disciples' failure? Why do they flee from Jesus when he is arrested? One may suggest that the disciples abandon Jesus because they do not anticipate the resurrection. If only they had understood that they too would be raised then they might not have fled from death so decisively. Or it could be postulated that the disciples flee because they have stubbornly failed to grasp the sheer necessity of Jesus'

---

17. Tannehill, "The Disciples in Mark," 188.

crucifixion. In their eyes, a crucified messiah is a failed messiah.[18] These possibilities may seem plausible as an imaginative reading of the disciples' motives, but they are not the answer suggested by the narrative itself. As shown above, it would be wrong to construe this failure as a misunderstanding of Jesus and the necessity of his death and resurrection.

Instead, Mark provides his own explanation for the disciples' failure within their peculiar portrayal during Jesus' prayer in the garden of Gethsemane. It is often noted that Jesus' exhortation to the disciples to stay awake takes on metaphorical meaning beyond the physical ability to resist sleep.[19] The scene in Gethsemane occurs immediately after the disciples vow not to fall away on account of Jesus and just before Jesus' arrest. In reverse order from Jesus' prediction of the disciples' abandonment, Jesus first addresses Peter directly before then admonishing the rest of the disciples. In this context, the metaphorical meaning of sleep is correlated to the question of disciples' fidelity to Jesus.[20] The failure to stay awake and keep watch corresponds to their obligation to take up their crosses and follow Jesus to their death. Therefore Jesus' statement "the spirit indeed is willing, but the flesh is weak" (14:38) refers to the disciples struggle to remain faithful to Jesus in the face of coming persecution. Mark employs the very Pauline antithesis between spirit and flesh, though it carries a different meaning. The "spirit" does not reference the Holy Spirit,[21] but represents one's being as it relates to perception (2:8) and emotion (8:12).[22] The description of one's spirit as eager, or willing, strongly resembles Peter and the disciples' dedication to Jesus. But the willingness of one's spirit is immediately contrasted with the weakness of the flesh.[23] The emphasis here is not on the intervention or

18. As Achtemeier suggests, "Time and again, despite private explanations . . . They betray their inability to grasp what is going on about them . . . They say things that show their total lack of comprehension of what Jesus tried to tell them (e.g., 8:32; 10:38), and they confirm their failure when in the critical moment they all desert him. They have thus not only misunderstood, they have rejected what they have seen." Achtemeier, *Mark*, 93.

19. Kelber, "Mark 14:32–42: Gethsemane: Passion Christology and Discipleship Failure; Collins, *Mark*, 681. This type of figurative reading is also found in Mark 8:22–26, where the blindness of the man corresponds to the "blindness" of the disciples.

20. So Wiarda, "Scenes and Details in the Gospels."

21. As it does for Schweizer, *The Good News according to Mark*, 314.

22 When Mark wishes to describe the action of the Spirit, he almost always designates this as the *Holy* Spirit, with the exception of the obvious context of Jesus' baptism (Mark 1:10, 12). Conversely, these are the only occasions where the word is modified by a possessive pronoun, indicated that a spirit is something which people have. This concept of "spirit" bears a strong resemblance to the western concept of the will, especially as it relates to the unity of the intellect and passions. For further treatment of the unified will, see: Thomas Aquinas, *Summa Theologica*, III vols., vol. II, IaIIae. q6–48.

23. For Mark, "flesh" does not carry any explicitly negative connotations, but refers

influence of apocalyptic forces acting on humanity;[24] instead, humanity and its own ability or inability is in view. For all their desire to accomplish what is required of them, the disciples suffer from a frailty which thwarts their intentions. This frailty does not simply result in a proclivity to sin; instead this weakness results in the failure of the disciples. Jesus addresses disciples who have already fallen asleep, hypothetically asking, *"Are you not able to keep watch one hour?"* This question of capability has already been anticipated by Jesus' prayer, where Jesus asks his father what is possible (*dunatos* 14:35, 36) according to his will. Though the disciples fully intend to follow Jesus to their deaths, knowing that this is what is required of them, they are fundamentally *unable* to do so.

For Mark, the gap between the disciples' willing and doing is both particular to the disciples and universal of all people. It is particular in that their failure is specifically occasioned by Jesus' command and the circumstances of the disciples' lives. The command to "take up your cross" is addressed to a particular audience at a specific point in time within his narrative. It would render Mark a disservice to dislocate this command from its narrative context and apply it universally as a mandate to martyrdom for all people at all times. Yet Mark himself intends for his portrait of the disciples to demonstrate the universal problem of human ability. As the narrative continues beyond the abandonment of the disciples it becomes clear that this abandonment has expanded beyond the disciples to also include all the other main characters in the story. Having previously rejected Jesus' call to discipleship, the Jewish leaders sentence Jesus to death and the once loyal crowd now ridicules him. The women followers of Jesus are recorded as having witnessed the crucifixion, but just like Peter in courtyard, they do not take up their crosses, but look on "from afar" (15:40).[25] They do not approach Jesus' tomb with anticipation of his predicted resurrection, but with burial spices. They fearfully leave the tomb and in defiance of the angels' command "said nothing to anyone" (16:8).[26] One could possibly find

instead to human corporality. The term cannot mean "the seat of the human propensity to sin," as Joel Marcus infers on the basis of 1QH 12[4]:29–32 and 7[15]:24–25 (Marcus, *Mark 8–16*, 979.). This would make Jesus' description of the weakness of the flesh redundant, since this weakness would already be implied by the term "flesh." Marcus also overlooks the internal Markan evidence, which contains two other instances of the term "flesh." The first (10:8) is a citation of Genesis 2:24, and the second (13:20) refers to humans in general as the object of God's salvation.

24. Cf. ibid., 988.

25. Munro, "Women Disciples in Mark?"

26. "The seed has fallen on rocky ground once again, as fear, not faith motivates their actions. Like the Twelve before them, the women too flee in silence." Tolbert, *Sowing the Word*, 295. See also Miller, "They Said Nothing to Anyone." The failure of

positive demonstrations of faith from characters such as Bartimaeus' following of Jesus "on the way" (10:52), Simon of Cyrene's taking up of Jesus' cross (15:21), or the confession of the centurion (15:39). However, these judgments are premature. At noted above, Bartimaeus deserts Jesus with the rest of the disciples. And while Simon of Cyrene "takes up" *a cross*, this cross is not his own, but Jesus'. Rather than a compassionate act of loyalty to Jesus, Simon aids the Romans in Jesus' execution. Finally, while the centurion at the cross may properly confess Jesus' identity, an overall positive evaluation overlooks the concrete demands of 8:34–38.[27] These examples enlarge the bleak portrayal of the disciples to include all humanity.

It may seem rash or unjust to make such an absolute categorization concerning all the characters of the Gospel of Mark. How could it be that the disciples who have traveled with Jesus for so long are as guilty as Jesus' enemies? It is true that the disciples never demonstrate a hostile desire to kill Jesus; this designation is reserved exclusively for the Jewish leaders. But the command of Jesus does not allow for any gradations of guilt or innocence that would exonerate the disciples from their ultimate failure.[28] Instead, the conditional demand applies to all without any exceptions. Whether it is Peter or Judas, all are under the same judgment. Jesus does not die surrounded by his devoted followers, but without any comrade. His cry of dereliction at the cross expresses both his divine and human forsakenness as he faces his enemies alone. The Gospel concludes[29] on a bleak, open-ended note with no positive depiction of human faithfulness.

The resultant portrait of human ability is both varied and starkly pessimistic. On the one hand, the disciples demonstrate a remarkable capacity to understand Jesus and his teachings. Fallen human nature is not without rational capabilities, oblivious to perceiving the requirements of discipleship and the truth of Jesus' identity. Peter and the rest of the disciples genuinely understand the necessity of Jesus' death/resurrection and the requirement of a disciple to accept a similar fate. One the other hand, the Gospel also expresses the limitations of rationality and human action. The "should" of life always lies beyond the feeble limits of human capability.[30] Accord-

---

the women also calls into question Bultmann's suggestion that the resurrection itself is the key to unlock genuine faith.

27. *Contra* Tannehill, "The Disciples in Mark."

28. Cf. Martin Luther: "For with God there is nothing intermediate between righteousness and sin, no neutral ground, so to speak, which is neither righteousness nor sin." Luther, *Luther's Works: Volume 33*, 264.

29. This assumes that the longer ending of the Gospel (16:9–20) is a later addition, as testified by the overwhelming textual evidence.

30 Cf. Luther, "by the words of the law man is warned and instructed as to what he

ingly, knowledge of what is required itself is not enough to actually produce what one willfully desires to accomplish. Despite our rational faculties, the problem of disobedience cannot be overcome by a rationalistic appeal to didacticism and an enlightened maturity, as envisioned by thinkers such as René Descartes or Immanuel Kant.[31]

Moreover, the gap between the disciples' proper knowledge and their failed actions also implies the further fracture between willing and doing. They failed even though they vowed to do otherwise. There lies an inescapable gap between the desire to obey and the ability to actually obey.

The human condition is marked by an inevitable failure on account of its own inherent limitations. The will is not free to obey of its own accord, but it is bound and unable to accomplish its desires. The disciples as models of humanity demonstrate that human existence is split by an unaccountable frustration of its desires. As Paul Zahl has repeatedly insisted throughout his ministry, "Human beings are not as free to act as they like to think they are. They are more hemmed in, more constrained by outward circumstanced and forces within, than they wish to concede . . . we often do what we do not want to do, and do not do what we want to do."[32] While it was Sigmund Freud who popularized this idea in the twentieth century,[33] Christian theology has traditionally named this rupture within the self "original sin" or the "un-free will." The Markan portrait of the disciples perfectly demonstrates this unbridgeable gap between the "ought" of divine demands and human inability to obey. The human condition is marked by an inevitable failure on account of its own inherent limitations. It is a picture of a flawed and sinful humanity standing before God in dire need of mercy from the One who gave his life as a ransom for many.

---

ought to do, not what he is able to do." Luther, *Luther's Works: Volume 33*, 127.

31. Cf. "But is man by nature morally good or bad? He is neither, for he is not by nature a moral being. He only becomes a moral being when his reason has developed ideas of duty and law." Kant, *Kant on Education*, V. 102; p. 08.

32. Zahl, *Grace in Practice*, 104.

33. Cf. "Mental processes are in themselves unconscious and only reach the ego and come under its control through incomplete and untrustworthy perceptions . . . *the ego is not the master in its own house.*" Freud, *The Complete Psychological Works of Sigmund Freud*, 143. But unlike in Freud's atheist analysis, for the Gospel of Mark the division between willing and doing is principally occasioned by the divine command. This provides a distinctly theological orientation to Markan anthropology, since it is God who determines the conditions by which one's life is found. All humanity is accountable before God and therefore one's activity must ultimately be directed toward Him. In accordance with the stipulation of God's commands, the relationship between God and humanity must principally be articulated in negative terms.

BIBLIOGRAPHY

Achtemeier, Paul J. *Mark*. Proclamation Commentaries. Philadelphia: Fortress, 1975.

Aquinas, Thomas, Saint. *Summa Theologica*. 3 vols. Vol. 2. New York: Benziger, 1984.

Best, Ernest. *Disciples and Discipleship: Studies in the Gospel according to Mark*. Edinburgh: T. & T. Clark, 1986.

Bultmann, Rudolf. *Theology of the New Testament*. Translated by Kendrick Grobel. 2 vols. New York: Scribner, 1951.

Collins, Adela Yarbro. *Mark: A Commentary*. Hermeneia. Minneapolis: Fortress, 2007.

Dunn, James D. G. "The Messianic Secret in Mark." In *The Messianic Secret*, edited by C. M. Tuckett, 116–31. Issues in Religion and Theology. Philadelphia: Fortress, 1983.

Freud, Sigmund. *The Complete Psychological Works of Sigmund Freud*. Translated by James Strachey. Vol. 17. London: Random House, 2001.

Gundry, Robert Horton. *Mark: A Commentary on His Apology for the Cross*. Grand Rapids: Eerdmans, 1993.

Hooker, Morna D. *The Gospel according to Mark*. London: A. & C. Black, 1991.

Kant, Immanuel. *Kant on Education*. Translated by Annette Churton. Boston: Heath, 1900.

Käsemann, Ernst. "Sentences of Holy Law in the New Testament." In *New Testament Questions of Today*. Translated by W. J. Montague. New Testament Library. London: SCM, 1969.

Kelber, Werner H. "Mark 14:32–42: Gethsemane: Passion Christology and Discipleship Failure." *Zeitschrift für die neutestamentliche Wissenschaft* 63 (1972) 166–87.

Luther, Martin. *Luther's Works: Volume 33*. Translated by E. Gordon Rupp et al. Edited by Jaroslav Pelikan et al. Minneapolis: Fortress, 1972.

Marcus, Joel. *Mark 8–16: A New Translation with Introduction and Commentary*. Anchor Bible 27A. New Haven: Yale University Press, 2009.

Miller, Susan. "'They Said Nothing to Anyone': The Fear and Silence of the Women at the Empty Tomb (Mk 16.1–8)." *Feminist Theology* 13/1 (2004) 77–90.

Munro, Winsome. "Women Disciples in Mark?" *Catholic Biblical Quarterly* 44 (1982) 225–41.

Schweizer, Eduard. *The Good News according to Mark*. Translated by Donald H. Madvig. London: SPCK, 1971.

Shiner, Whitney Taylor. *Follow Me! Disciples in Markan Rhetoric*. Society of Biblical Literature Dissertation Series 145. Atlanta: Scholars, 1995.

Tannehill, Robert C. "The Disciples in Mark: The Function of the Narrative Role." In *The Interpretation of Mark*, edited by William R. Telford, 169–96. 2nd ed. Studies in New Testament Interpretation. Edinburgh: T. & T. Clark, 1995.

Telford, William R. *The Theology of the Gospel of Mark*. New Testament Theology. Cambridge: Cambridge University Press, 1999.

Tolbert, Mary Ann. *Sowing the Word: Mark's World in Literary Historical Perspective*. Minneapolis: Fortress, 1996.

Weeden, Theodore J. "The Heresy That Necessitated Mark's Gospel [1968]." In *The Interpretation of Mark*, edited by William R. Telford, 63–88. Issues in Religion and Theology. London: SPCK, 1985.

Wiarda, Timothy. "Scenes and Details in the Gospels: Concrete Reading and Three Alternatives." *New Testament Studies* 50 (2004) 167–84.

Wright, N. T. *Jesus and the Victory of God*. Minneapolis: Fortress, 1996.

Zahl, Paul F. M. *Grace in Practice: A Theology of Everyday Life*. Grand Rapids: Eerdmans, 2007.

PART 2

One-Way Love

4

The Grace of God in Salvation

Substitutionary Atonement and the Forgiveness of Sins

JUSTYN TERRY

THE THEOLOGY OF GRACE advocated by Paul Zahl is a theology of the cross, and one of its many strengths is that it takes seriously the substitutionary work of Christ crucified. Zahl recognises the importance of this much disputed doctrine, for without it he can see no source for the abundance of grace that sinners need.

> The atonement of Christ on the cross is the mechanism by which God's grace can be offered freely and without condition to strugglers in the battle of life. Grace is not offered by God as a fiat. We all wish that the innocent had not had to die for the guilty. We wish that a different road, a road less travelled in scars, had been taken. But we have been told that this was the necessary way by which God's law and God's grace would be resolved. It had to be resolved through a guilt-transfer, making it "possible"—the idea is almost beyond maintaining—for God to give the full scholarship to the candidate least qualified to receive it.[1]

Mysterious as it may be, the sinless Christ's dying in the place of sinful humanity is the indispensable means by which God could justly justify sinners and

1. Zahl, *Grace in Practice*, 117–18.

impute his righteousness to them. By making this claim, and by developing his thinking in terms of the blood of sacrifice and the justice of the courtroom,[2] Zahl stands against a widespread rejection of substitutionary atonement that may be largely attributed to the criticisms made of it by Immanuel Kant. Kant objected to the idea that an innocent third-person could suffer the punishment for the sins of guilty persons. The effect of that objection is surprisingly significant. What might at first glance appear to be the elimination of just one possible option amongst many regarding the atonement turns out to be the loss of an essential active ingredient in any fully developed exposition of Christ's saving work. If it is lost much else will also be lost with it, as Friedrich Schleiermacher, the father of modern liberal theology, found after first rejecting substitutionary atonement when he was at seminary.[3]

In this paper I shall argue in support of Zahl's view that Christ died as the substitute for sinful human beings as an act of sheer grace. I shall begin by examining Kant's objection to the doctrine before seeing how those concerns might be properly countered. After that I shall show that substitution is an inevitable aspect of forgiveness, and so the gospel of the forgiveness of sins is unavoidably a gospel that rests on substitutionary atonement. In conclusion we shall see that Zahl has a crucial point to make that must not be lost if we are to faithfully hear, live, and proclaim the salvation of Jesus Christ.

KANT'S OBJECTION TO SUBSTITUTIONARY ATONEMENT

In his *Religion within the Limits of Reason Alone* (1793), Immanuel Kant attempted to present a version of Christianity that could be accepted on the rational principles of the Enlightenment and thereby overcome many of the objections it faced in the light of that movement. The inscrutable supernatural realm was not so much rejected as left alone as unknown and unknowable. This meant that the miraculous aspects of the biblical revelation were set aside as superstition.[4] Kant then reworked the Christian faith to accent its moral value. This highly innovative project required a substantial rethinking of the doctrine of atonement.

Kant insisted that no person can represent or "take another's place" (*Stellvertretung*) in matters of personal guilt.[5] He said,

2. Zahl, *A Short Systematic Theology*, 61ff.

3. Franke and Hill, *Barth for Armchair Theologians*, 11.

4. Kant, *Religion within the Limits of Reason Alone (1794)*, 48.

5. Ibid., 66ff.; italics original.

> [Moral evil] is no transmissible liability which can be made over to another like a financial indebtedness (where it is all one to the creditor whether the debtor pays the debt or whether some one else pays for him); rather is it the most personal of all debts, namely a debt of sins, which only the culprit can bear and which no innocent person can assume even though he be magnanimous enough to wish to take it upon himself for the sake of another.[6]

This is not, however, to suggest that sinful human beings only have punishment for their sins to look forward to beyond the grave. It is instead to relocate the atoning work from Jesus Christ to the repentant human being.

> The coming forth from the corrupted into the good disposition is, in itself (as "the death of the old man," "crucifying of the flesh"), a sacrifice and an entrance into the long train of life's ills. These the new man undertakes in the disposition of the Son of God, that is merely for the sake of the good, though really they are due as *punishments* to another, namely to the old man (for the old man is indeed morally another).[7]

Not that this is to entirely exclude the work of Christ. As Kant goes on to explain,

> And this [new] moral disposition which in all its purity (like unto the purity of the Son of God) the man has made his own—or, (if we personify this idea) this Son of God, Himself—bears as vicarious substitute the guilt of sin for him, and indeed for all who believe (practically) in Him; as savior He renders satisfaction to supreme justice by His sufferings and death; and as advocate He makes it possible for men to hope to appear before their judge as justified. Only it must be remembered that (in this mode of representation) the suffering which the new man, in becoming dead to the old, must accept throughout life is pictured as a death endured once for all by the representative of mankind.[8]

So Jesus Christ retains a place in this reconciliation, but it is as the personification of an idea, rather than as the irreplaceable divine-human mediator, giving the "idea" priority over the person himself. Colin Gunton takes Kant to task for this, saying it, "translates Christianity into its opposite"[9] by wrest-

---

6. Ibid., 66. Here and in subsequent quotations we shall retain the translator's gender specific language. The reader is invited to amend it to contemporary usage.

7. Ibid., 67.

8. Ibid., 69.

9. Gunton, *The Actuality of Atonement*, 8.

ing the saving work away from Jesus Christ and giving it instead to human-ity. Since Kant employs Christian categories to make this reversal (vicarious substitute, savior, advocate etc.), Gunton then asks, "[C]an this be a rational or reasonable way to read the foundational texts [of Christianity]?"[10] In the end, can this attempt to confine the Christian religion within the procrus-tean bed of reason alone truly claim to represent biblical Christianity?

Kant was wrestling with the vital question of how it could be just for the innocent to suffer for the guilty. This is surely the very essence of injus-tice. Even if someone were willing to do so, how could their punishment make any difference to another person, namely, the offender? Kant also asks the question of what it would mean for the dignity of human actions if such a transaction could even be countenanced.[11] By so doing Kant raises the classic questions about grace and forgiveness. Can it indeed ever be just to forgive someone an offence? Does it not inevitably belittle the pain and damage caused by the action that is being forgiven? And will it not always be a problem when someone acts graciously, if grace means what Kant says it means, "a superior's decree conferring a good for which the subordinate possesses nothing but the (moral) receptivity" for it"?[12]

But the problem with Kant's position is not merely that he stresses justice over mercy, but that he sees Jesus Christ as an innocent third party. Innocent, he is; third party he is not, since he is the incarnate God against whom sinners sin. It was God who was in Christ reconciling the world to himself (2 Cor. 5:19). So there is no third party in this picture; there is just the sinner and the sinned-against united in the person of Jesus Christ. Al-lowing Christ to be treated as an external benefactor in the debtor analogy runs the risk of incorporating an Ebionite Christology that denies his divin-ity, which is an inevitable result of the Enlightenment project.

If we revisit the debtor analogy that Kant offers and see it in terms of two parties rather than three, the question of substitution takes on an en-tirely different perspective, enabling us to overcome the moral objection that he very properly levels at the tripartite scheme. When one person forgives another they decide not to hold the injury they have suffered against their offender any longer. They surrender their rights to repayment or compensa-tion. So the king who forgives his servant a debt of ten thousand talents (Matt 18:21–35) chose to accept the loss; it becomes his bad debt. As such it is a costly act, as forgiveness generally is, since this action substantially

10. Ibid.

11. Paul Tillich described Kant as the great prophet of human dignity in connection with just this point. Tillich, *The Shaking of the Foundations*, 157.

12. Kant, *Religion*, 70 n.

depletes his assets. It is, however, only through that gracious generosity that his servant could be forgiven.

Forgiveness is always substitutionary. What was once the debt of the servant is now the bad debt of the king. What was once a word I should not have spoken or an action I should not have taken is now the insult borne or the pain absorbed by somebody else when they forgive me. On each such occasion one person suffers for the wrongdoing of another. As Mennonite scholar Myron S. Augsburger puts it: "True forgiveness means that the innocent one resolves his wrath occasioned by the sin of the guilty one and liberates the guilty person in freedom. Self-substitution is always the cost in forgiveness."[13]

When we say that on the cross Jesus died for the sins of the world we mean that he bore the cost of forgiving sins. Our sins are no longer held against us but carried by him. As the Apostle Peter puts it, "He himself bore our sins in his body on the cross" (1 Pet. 2:24). Sin led to death as divine justice demands (Gen. 2:17; Rom 6:23), but it led to Jesus' death rather than ours as divine mercy desired. Understood in this way, the language of debt does not call into question the substitutionary nature of atonement, but instead is seen to require it.

Forgiveness of sins is, of course, one of the doctrines of the Nicene Creed—"we acknowledge one baptism for the forgiveness of sins"—and as such held by Trinitarian Christians all around the world. Each time we make that confession, we are, I believe, acknowledging substitutionary atonement since forgiveness is always substitutionary.

THEOLOGICAL SUPPORT FOR SUBSTITUTIONARY ATONEMENT

The importance of substitutionary atonement has been stressed by many theologians down the centuries. Rather than trace out its historical trajectory, let us take note of two of the theologians who have been particular inspirations to Paul Zahl, Martin Luther and Karl Barth, beginning with the man to whom Zahl may owe his greatest theological debt: Martin Luther.

Luther spells out the vicarious character of Christ's work in his commentary on Galatians. When he discusses chapter 3 and verse 13, ("Christ redeemed us from the curse of the law by becoming a curse for us—for it is written, 'Cursed is everyone who is hanged on a tree'"), he says:

> And this, no doubt, all the prophets did foresee in spirit, that Christ should be the greatest transgressor, murderer, adulterer,

13. Augsburger, "Justice in Forgiveness," 5.

53

> thief, rebel, blasphemer etc. that ever was or could be in all the world. For he, being made a sacrifice for the sins of the whole world, is not now an innocent person and without sins, is not now the Son of God born of the Virgin Mary; but a sinner, which hath and carrieth the sin of a Paul, who was a blasphemer, an oppressor and a persecutor; of Peter, which denied Christ; of David, which was an adulterer, a murderer, and caused the Gentiles to blaspheme the name of the Lord; and briefly, which hath and beareth all the sins of all men in his body, that he might make satisfaction for them with his own blood.[14]

There is no hesitation to ascribe to Jesus the full burden of sin and to say that he died under the condemnation it deserved, and Luther does so in a way that draws out its pastoral implications. Those implications are further developed when he then applies the benefits of this sacrifice of Christ to the believer's life in terms of the "happy exchange." In The Freedom of the Christian (1520), he writes:

> So Christ has all the blessings and the salvation which are the soul's. And so the soul has upon it all the vice and sin which become Christ's own. Here now begins the happy exchange and conflict. Because Christ is God and man who never yet sinned, and his piety is inconquerable, eternal and almighty. So, then, as he makes his own the believing soul's sin through the wedding ring of its faith, and does nothing else than as if he had committed it, just so must sin be swallowed up and drowned.[15]

When a sinner is justified by faith, Jesus receives the sins of the sinner and the sinner receives the righteousness of Christ. It is indeed a happy exchange, which both reveals and supplies God's grace.

These are some of the teachings from which Kant was seeking to distance himself in order to refine the Christian faith for a modern audience. It is striking to notice, however, how Kant's endeavour to raise the dignity of the human being has just the opposite effect. In setting aside the grandeur and significance of Christ's atoning work, Kant lost the astonishing dignity that is conferred to human beings in that their God would countenance such a rescue for them.

Since Immanuel Kant, many notable theologians from the Lutheran tradition, including Friedrich Schleiermacher, Albrecht Ritschl, Rudolf Bultmann, and Robert Jenson, have found little, if any, space for substitutionary atonement. However, two important contemporary Lutherans have

14. Luther, *A Commentary on St. Paul's Epistle to the Galatians*, 269.

15. Quoted in Lohse, *Martin Luther's Theology*, 226.

wished to stress its significance: Eberhard Jüngel and Wolfhart Pannenberg. In an essay entitled, "The Mystery of Substitution," Jüngel places special emphasis on Mark 10:45, ("For even the Son of Man came not to be served but to serve, and to give his life as a ransom for many") and states that this verse expresses the view that, "one person has done or suffered something on behalf of, that is in place of, other persons."[16] He then goes on to state: "In the person of Jesus Christ God took our human place."[17] Wolfhart Pannenberg explains his position in his Systematic Theology:

> In the condemnation and execution of Jesus, God "made him to be sin [for us] who knew no sin, so that in him we might become the righteousness of God" (2 Cor. 5:21). In this situation of condemnation and execution, Jesus (whom, through the resurrection, God showed to be innocent) bore death as the consequence of our sin, thereby effecting representation in the concrete form of a change of place between the innocent and the guilty.[18]

Pannenberg sees this as part of the biblical revelation about the atonement, especially in the teaching of the apostle Paul in texts like Gal 3:13; 2 Cor 5:21; and Rom 8:3 ("For God has done what the law, weakened by the flesh, could not do. By sending his own Son in the likeness of sinful flesh and for sin, he condemned sin in the flesh").

> As Paul saw it, God himself by means of human judges not only made Jesus to be sin but also had him bear in our place (and not merely in that of his Jewish judges or the whole Jewish people) the penalty that is the proper penalty for sin because it follows from its inner nature, i.e., the penalty of death as the consequence of separation from God.[19]

Both Jüngel and Pannenberg affirm in their different ways that vicarious atonement has a firm biblical basis and is of considerable theological importance.

Another theologian to whom Zahl pays close attention is Karl Barth. Writing after the First World War, this Swiss theologian was struggling to overcome the limitations of Kant, Schleiermacher and Ritschl that had so influenced his theological education, especially under Wilhelm Herrmann. Barth found in Luther and Calvin theologians who took the Bible as their starting point for theology and could help him develop his own thinking in the light of the word of God. With their help Barth came to affirm

16. Jüngel, *Theological Essays II*, 152.

17. Ibid., 155; italics original.

18. Pannenberg, *Systematic Theology*, 427.

19. Ibid., 426.

that Christ died as a substitute for sinners.[20] He could answer the question "What has in fact taken place in Jesus Christ?" with the reply, "We will first give the general answer that there has taken place in Him the effective self-substitution [*selbsteinsatz*][21] of God for us sinful men."[22] Barth sees it as a repeated theme of the Gospels, perhaps most clearly seen in the trial of Jesus when Pilate releases Barabbas.

> The Jesus who was condemned to be crucified in the place of Barabbas (Mark 15:6–15) stands on the one side, and Barabbas who was pardoned at the expense of Jesus stands on the other; for he was not crucified, nor did he really contribute to his own liberation which came about when sentence was pronounced on that other.[23]

Jesus exchanged his own position as the obedient Son of God for that of this particular disobedient son of Adam. But it was not just for this one man that he did it but for the sinners of the whole world. So Barth says: "It was to fulfill this judgment on sin that the Son of God as man took our place as sinners. He fulfils it—the man in our place—by completing our work in the omnipotence of the divine Son, by treading the way of sinners to its bitter end in death, in destruction, in the limitless anguish of separation from God, by delivering up sinful man and sin in His own person to the non-being which is properly theirs, the non-being, the nothingness to which man has fallen victim as a sinner and towards which he relentlessly hastens."[24]

The judgment of God in Jesus Christ is thus the judgment of the sin of all in the one who was without sin but who took it upon himself to be the one great sinner and to be judged in the place of all. This is the means by which forgiveness of sins may be offered to the world.

Forgiveness of sins is the very essence of God's grace for Barth; indeed he virtually equates the two: "What does not pass over this sharp ridge of forgiveness of sins, or grace, is not Christian."[25] Since grace is such a central

---

20. This situation is complicated by the fact that the German word '*Stellvertreter*' may be translated "representative" or "substitute." G. W. Bromiley himself notes this ambiguity in his preface (IV/1, vii) and generally translates it as "representative." At times he translates *für uns* as "substitute" (e.g., IV/1, 230 of the English edition, 252 of the German edition). This may simply mean "for us" in the sense of "on our behalf," as our representative, rather than "in our place," as our substitute. As we will see, however, Barth's use of the concept of substitution is not dependent on the translation of either of these terms.

21. Literally "self-insertion."

22. Barth, *Church Dogmatics*, IV/1, 550.

23. Ibid., 230.

24. Ibid., 253.

25. Barth, *Dogmatics in Outline*, 152.

category for Barth, so is the forgiveness of sins. "The way of the Christian is derived from the forgiveness of sins and leads to the resurrection of the body and eternal life."[26] "[I]t is always the case that when the Christian looks back, he is looking at the forgiveness of sins."[27] And "What in retrospect we know about ourselves can always only be that we live by forgiveness."[28]

Barth defines forgiveness as "my sin not reckoned to me."[29] This clarifies several important aspects of divine forgiveness. Firstly, it means that to forgive is not to excuse. There is no need of extenuating circumstances to which appeal may be made. The sinner is genuinely culpable, but in forgiving us God is not reckoning our sin to us because Christ has taken it to himself. Forgiveness does not mean "any mitigation of the severity with which sinful man is rejected by God. Rather it speaks of the fulfilment of that rejection."[30] Secondly, it means that to forgive is not to condone. There is no indication that what was done was all right; it was not. It was a transgression of God's law and a deviation from God's good purposes. "The word 'forgiveness' speaks of a judicial act in which God has maintained His glory in relation to man. But it does not speak of a new purpose or disposition or attitude on the part of God."[31] In forgiving someone their sin, God is not holding that sin against them, because Christ has borne the cost of forgiveness himself. So we may say that in the forgiveness of sin God brings justice (it really was sin) and mercy (but he will not seek recompense) into gracious convergence. It is not "forgive and forget," but it is "forgive and refuse to recall." Forgiveness, then, is the place where justice and mercy meet in the substitutionary death of Jesus Christ.

CONCLUSION

Forgiveness lies at the heart of God's gracious reconciling work in Christ. He died for the forgiveness of sins; and we respond in faith to that astonishing action through repentance and baptism for the forgiveness of sins. The great covenantal promise, "I will be your God and you will be my people" (Ezek 36:28), is fulfilled through Christ's costly act of atonement, and humbly received in faith by sinners. The Son of God became incarnate to bear sin to death and rise again for our justification (Rom 4:25), and we are united with him in his death and resurrection in baptism (Rom 6:4). So forgiveness

26. Ibid., 149.
27. Ibid., 150.
28. Ibid.
29. Ibid.
30. Barth, *Church Dogmatics*, IV/1, 94.
31. Ibid..

helps us to understand both the saving work of Christ and the need for a human response to that gracious action, and therefore enables us to draw together these objective and subjective aspects of salvation.

With his great concern for human suffering, it is no surprise that Paul Zahl would want to stress God's grace of forgiveness. It is genuinely good news for helpless sinners. It is also a familiar concept to the unchurched in ways that would not be true of terms like "atonement" and "justification." This is not to minimise the difficulty for someone who is truly converting to Jesus Christ. God's offer of forgiveness is a gift that needs to be received if someone is to be reconciled to the God whom we have so grievously offended. That in turn requires someone to be willing to recognise their wrongdoing as sin, to believe the offer of forgiveness as genuine, and to be willing to accept it as such. Only then can the relationship with God be restored. This is where the substitutionary death of Jesus Christ connects with the daily reality of struggle and failure of human existence, and breathes hope into despairing people. That forgiveness inevitably involves substitution, as we have seen. So if we are to maintain this central aspect of the gospel message we will, like Zahl, want to affirm substitutionary atonement.

BIBLIOGRAPHY

Augsburger, Myron S. "Justice in Forgiveness." *The Living Pulpit* 16/2 (2007) 4–7.

Barth, Karl. *Church Dogmatics*. Translated by G. W. Bromiley. Edited by G. W. Bromiley and T. F. Torrance. Vol. IV/1. Edinburgh: T. & T. Clark, 1956.

———. *Dogmatics in Outline*. Translated by G. T. Thompson. New York: Harper & Row, 1959.

Franke, John R., and Ron Hill. *Barth for Armchair Theologians*. Louisville: Westminster John Knox, 2006.

Gunton, Colin E. *The Actuality of Atonement: A Study of Metaphor, Rationality, and the Christian Tradition*. Edinburgh: T. & T. Clark, 1988.

Jüngel, Eberhard. *Theological Essays Ii*. Translated by J. B. Webster and A. Neufeldt-Fast. Edinburgh: T. & T. Clark, 1995.

Kant, Immanuel. *Religion within the Limits of Reason Alone (1794)*. Translated by T. M. Greene and H. H. Hudson. New York: Harper & Row, 1960.

Luther, Martin. *A Commentary on St. Paul's Epistle to the Galatians: Rev. And Ed. On the Basis of the "Middleton" Edition by Philip S. Watson (1575)*. Cambridge: James Clark, 1953.

Pannenberg, Wolfhart. *Systematic Theology*. Vol. 2. Translated by G. W. Bromiley. Grand Rapids: Eerdmans, 1994.

Tillich, Paul. *The Shaking of the Foundations*. New York: Scribner, 1948.

Zahl, Paul F. M. *Grace in Practice: A Theology of Everyday Life*. Grand Rapids: Eerdmans, 2007.

———. *A Short Systematic Theology*. Grand Rapids: Eerdmans, 2000.

5

Scandal and Folly
Debating and Defining Grace with Pseudo-Solomon and St. Paul

JONATHAN A. LINEBAUGH

"Without the atonement, the grace of God is a beautiful dream."

—PAUL ZAHL[1]

"To THE ONE WHO works, the reward is not reckoned according to grace." So says Paul in Romans 4:4, and so most assume. Grace, so the assumption goes, is by definition not a reward; grace is free, it is unconditioned by human work or worth, it is "one-way." The intention of this comparison of Wisdom of Solomon and Paul's letter to the Romans is twofold: first, to upset the assumption that this definition of grace is obvious, and, second, to demonstrate that this understanding of grace is distinctive because it is deduced from and descriptive of God's act of justifying sinners in Jesus Christ. Put another way, this essay is an exegetical affirmation and correlation of

---

1. Zahl, *Grace in Practice*, 114.

two theses about grace: "Grace is one-way love";[2] "Neither can the power of grace be understood except by a description of the gospel."[3]

CONGRUOUS AND CONDITIONED CHARIS: *WISDOM* AND THE FITTING GIFT

Wisdom of Solomon[4] is a sermon addressed to sufferers. While it is difficult to reconstruct the socio-historical details alluded to and addressed by *Wisdom*, the tone and content of the pastoral address indicate that whatever the specific *Sitz im Leben*, the event(s) was serious enough to generate a series of questions about the stability of the cosmos, the patterns of history, and the past, present, and future justice of God. Into this crisis—a crisis that appears to be principally defined by the present flourishing of the ungodly and the suffering of the righteous (*Wisdom* 2–5)—the author of *Wisdom* announces a word of hope: the God of illimitable love is immutably just.

For the author of *Wisdom*—regularly referred to as "Pseudo-Solomon" because he speaks with the famously wise king's voice (see 9:7–8)—the most basic of all realities is that God is just. As he sings in 12.15, "You are just and you rule all things justly." Within this song, however, justice (*dikaiosunē*) has a specific definition: God's just rule is evident in his non-condemnation of the righteous (12:15) and his "fitting judgment" of the unrighteous (12:26). Put another way, divine justice is located in the *correspondence* between the form (e.g. wrath or grace) and object (e.g. ungodly or righteous) of divine action.[5] For Pseudo-Solomon, the defining event of divine justice is the Red Sea crossing. As the account is retold in *Wisdom* 10:15–21, a bipartite humanity (*dikaioi* and *asebeis*, 10:20) encounters, respectively, deliverance and destruction: "Sophia led the righteous through deep waters, but she drowned their enemies" (10:18–19). This paradigmatic event exemplifies the theological confession that God "arranged all things by measure, number, and weight" (11:19) and it anchors the promise that the eschaton will look like the exodus: the injustice of the present will be overturned as the God who acted in the past with grace

---

2. Ibid., 36.

3. Melanchton, "Loci communes theologici, 1521," 70.

4. Hereafter, *Wisdom*. The consensus, which is probable though not definitive, places the composition of *Wisdom* in Alexandria between 220 BCE and 50 CE; see C. Larcher, *Le Livre de la Sagesse*, 1.141–61; Winston, *The Wisdom of Solomon*, 20–25; Hübner, *Die Weisheit Salomons*, 15–19.

5. Cf. Philo's insistence that justice, by definition, operates "according to worth" (*kat' axian*, *Leg.* 1:87; *Mos.* 2:9).

towards the righteous and wrath towards the unrighteous acts again in accordance with human worth (see Wisdom 2–5).

The good news according to Wisdom is thus an announcement that the end will be like the beginning; or to adapt a prayer: Wisdom preaches a sermon to sufferers that says "as it was in the beginning . . . it will be." The good news, in other words, is that God will act with his fitting judgment (*axian theou krisin,* 12:26) and so condemn the ungodly and redeem the righteous. The salvific side of this divide is what *Wisdom* calls "grace" (*charis*).[6] While grace is not synonymous with justice, neither is it antithetical: God's grace operates within the pattern of correspondence that defines God's justice and so exhibits an affinity between God's saving gifts and the worth of their human recipients. For example, in *Wisdom* 4:15, God's *charis* is directed towards "his holy ones" (*tois hosiois autou*; cf. 3:9), and in 3.14, it is the law-observant and faithful eunuch to whom God gives (*didōmi*) his *charis*. In both cases the justness of God's beneficence is displayed in the identifiable congruence between benefit and beneficiary. It is important to observe, however, that within *Wisdom's* theology, the justice of grace in no way disqualifies the graciousness of grace. In fact, Seneca, in his famous treatise on gift (*De Beneficiis* I.15.6), and Philo (e.g. *Post.* 142–47), both insist that it is the absence of a careful and discriminate matching between gift and recipient that renders a gift a non-gift. The conceptual context for *Wisdom's* discourse on grace is the social and theological realm of "gift," and as Seneca and Philo indicate, in this frame of reference gifts are properly gifts when they are carefully distributed to the worthy or fitting (*dingus* in Seneca's Latin and *axios* in Philo's Greek). Within this pattern of gift exchange, a gift is a gift because it is unearned (i.e. it is not payment or wages), but the principles of justice suggest, and in the case of divine giving require, that the beneficiary is in some sense worthy, thus ensuring that the gift-loving God, rather than being whimsical and chaotic, is stable, just, and good.

This theological concern to maintain the fundamental and unalterable justice of God shapes *Wisdom's* celebration of divine grace. For *Wisdom,* Sophia, or Lady Wisdom, is God's ultimate gift (*hē charis,* 8:21), and precisely as *charis,* Sophia operates within the parameters of the just cosmic and moral order she established and sustained (7:22). This means, in exodus-like fashion, that she avoids the ungodly (1:4; cf. 7:25) and associates with the righteous (6:12; 7:27; 10:4, 5, 6, 10, 13). As Sophia's repeated rescue of the righteous characters from Genesis exemplifies in *Wisdom's* telling (10:1–14), she "delivers from trouble those who serve her" (10.9) and, even

6. God's love (*agapaō,* 11:24) and mercy (*eleeō,* 11:23) are said to extend to the objects of God's judgment, but this mercy, rather than saving the ungodly, takes the form of decelerated destruction (12:8–11; cf. 12:2).

more basically, "seeks those who are worthy (*axios*) of her" (6:16). This single criterion of "fittingness" (*axios*) can be met by a variety of human actions directed toward Sophia (e.g. seeking [6:12, 17; 8:2], desiring [6:13, 17, 20; 8:2], requesting [7.7.; 8.21; 9.1–18], loving [6:12, 17; 8:2], serving [10:9]), but in every instance of divine benefaction there is an identifiable point of correspondence between God's gift and the worth or fittingness of the human recipient. This does not mean that saving grace is accomplished *by* human worth, but it does mean that while it is emphatically Sophia who saves (*tē sophia esōthēsan*, 9:18), her saving benevolence is *for* the worthy. In other words, while the moral, social, or intellectual fittingness of the human cannot be properly called the *cause* of grace, such fittingness is a *condition* of grace: God's grace, according to *Wisdom*, is conditioned by the necessity of correspondence—God's gifts match their objects.

This pattern is evident in the two paradigmatic moments of divine grace. First, in the case of Solomon, his attainment of Sophia came as a genuine gift (*charis*) and required an authentic act of divine giving (*didōmi*, 8:21). This gift, however, was conditioned by correspondence: Solomon was a suitable recipient of Sophia because he was good (*agathos ōn*, 8:20). Similarly, and in terms of the forthcoming comparison with Paul more significantly, *Wisdom's* narration of the Red Sea crossing depicts the objects of Sophia's rescue as a "holy people and blameless race" (*laon hosion kai sperma amempton*, 10:21) and even calls this climactic instance of grace a "reward" (*misthos*, 10:17) for their labors. This succinctly captures *Wisdom's* understanding of grace: The exodus event is an unearned and divinely given deliverance (it is grace); but because the God of the exodus is "just and rules all things justly," his rescue is reserved for the righteous—not primarily because *they* are righteous, but because *God* is righteous. It is this bedrock conviction about the goodness and ultimate justice of God that determines *Wisdom's* definition of grace: the God who is good and gracious is not arbitrary or unfair. He is just and so his grace is necessarily defined and conditioned by a correspondence between gift and recipient. Grace, for Pseudo-Solomon, is God giving to the worthy.

INCONGRUOUS AND UNCONDITIONED CHARIS: PAUL AND THE UNFITTING CHRIST-GIFT

"To the one who works, the reward (*misthos*) is not reckoned according to grace" (*charis*, Rom 4:4). Returning to these seemingly obvious words from *Wisdom's* presentation of congruous and conditioned grace, and especially from *Wisdom's* depiction of the saving grace of the exodus as a reward (*misthos*) for Israel's labors (Wis 10:17), Paul's claim can no longer be heard as contextual commonsense. To put Paul's insistence that a reward for work is not grace next to *Wisdom's* description of the gracious rescue at the Red Sea as a "reward for labor" (*misthon kopōn autōn*, Wis. 10:17) is to read Romans 4:4 as a redefinition of grace. If it is not universally agreed upon that a reward for work is not grace, and *Wisdom* demonstrates that it is not, then why does Paul make this categorical claim? If the meaning of grace articulated by Paul is not a given, where does Paul's semantic innovation come from?

One indication of an answer to this question comes in the antithesis between Romans 4:4 and 4:5. Grace is not reward for work; grace is the justification of the ungodly. But this provocation is not an *a priori*; it is not, as Dunn suggests, to "restate a theologoumenon."[7] Read in dialogue with *Wisdom's* notion of fitting grace—of grace that is conditioned by correspondence—Paul's definition of grace as the justification of the ungodly sounds, to let Pseudo-Solomon quote Paul against Paul, "scandalous and foolish" because it cuts the congruence between God's gifts and their human recipients that ensures that in grace God is just. But it is just here, at the point of tension between justice and grace, that Paul's dangerous definition of grace shows itself to be deduced from an event that compels him to identify God as the "one who justifies the ungodly" (Rom 4:5). In other words, the antithesis between Romans 4:4 and 4:5, and the new definition of grace that it announces, points behind itself to the event of grace that Paul calls "the redemption that is in Christ Jesus" (Rom 3:24).

Romans 2:1—3:20, in part, operates within *Wisdom's* theological world. Romans 2:6–10, 13 describe a judgment according to the criterion of correspondence: "God will repay each person according to (*kata* + accusative) their works" (2:6); and more specifically, "it is the doers of the law who will be justified" (2:13). For Paul, however, the revelation of unrighteousness—the reality that "all are under sin" and "not one is righteous" (3:9–10)—means that the soteriological conclusion of correspondence can only be condemnation: "by works of law no flesh will be justified" (3:20). It is out of this inevitable movement from the criterion of correspondence to universal condemnation that Paul announces the impossible: "But now, apart from law, the righteousness of God is revealed. . . . All sinned . . . and are justified freely by his grace through the redemption that is in Christ Jesus" (Rom 3:21, 23–24).

---

7. Dunn, *The Theology of Paul the Apostle*, 367. For the repeated prohibition against justifying the ungodly, see Exod 23:7; Prov 17:15; 24:24; Isa 5:3; Sir 9:12; CD 1:19.

As noted above, for *Wisdom*, the righteousness or justice of God is evident in the correspondence between the form and object of God's action: he delivers the righteous and destroys the ungodly. From this vantage point, Romans 3:21–24 sounds like a "moral outage" (Kant),[8] a proclamation that promises, in Nietzsche's phrase, "a revaluation of all antique values."[9] Rather than locating "the righteousness of God" (*dikaiosunē theou*) in the congruence between the righteous and God's declaration of righteousness, Paul announces what Alan Badiou calls "an unheard-of possibility"[10]: a righteousness that is revealed in the disjunction between sin and salvation (*pantes hēmarton . . . dikaioumenoi*).[11] This can only be read as a daring deduction: Rather than promulgating a *received* definition of justice, one which assumes the affinity and order between doing and being and which stretches from Aristotle (*Eth. Nic.* II.i.4) to Sartre,[12] Paul sees the meaning of God's justice *revealed* (*phaneroō*, Rom 3:21) in an event that effects the justification of the sinner—an event that is simultaneously the demonstration (*endeixis*, 3:25, 26) of God's righteousness and the defining moment of God's grace (*dikaioumenoi dōrean tē autou chariti*, 3:24).

The basic incommensurability between Pseudo-Solomon and St. Paul sits on this Christological fault-line. In *Wisdom* the exodus is the paradigmatic exemplification of justice and grace because it instantiates the pattern of correspondence Sophia built into the cosmos. In Romans, by contrast, the justice and grace of God are not ideas or even dispositions that can be illustrated; they are mutually-interpreting ways of describing the death of Jesus and the justification it effects. In Bultmann's words, "Righteousness . . . has its origin in God's grace—i.e. in His act of grace accomplished in Christ."[13] It is from this "act of grace"—from the incongruous giving of Jesus for the justification of the ungodly—that Paul's definition of grace in Romans 4:4–5 is derived. As Barth observed, for Paul, "Grace is the gift of Christ,"[14] and it is because this gift evinces a contradiction rather than a correspondence between benefit and beneficiary that Paul redefines grace in antithesis to reward and as the justification of the ungodly. In other words, Paul does not insist that a reward (*misthos*) for work is not grace (*charis*) because such a

---

8. Kant, *Religion Within the Limits of Reason Alone* (*1794*), 164.

9. Nietzsche, *Beyond Good and Evil*, 75.

10. Badiou, *Saint Paul*, 43.

11. Following Cranfield, *Romans*, 1.205. I take the "all" of 3:23 as the subject of 3.24.

12. Sartre, *Existentialism and Humanism*, 28.: "man is nothing else but that which he makes of himself."

13. Bultmann, *Theology of the New Testament*, 1.284.

14. Barth, *The Epistle to the Romans*, 31.

claim is true by definition (*Wis.* 10:17 shows that it is not); he cuts the connection between *misthos* and *charis* because the "Christ-gift"[15] has sinners as its incongruous objects. Romans 4:4–5, then, does not argue *from* a definition of grace; it argues *for* a definition of grace that is deduced from the disjunction declaration that Christ's cross is the enactment of God's judgment upon sin and thereby the justification of the sinner (Rom 3:25–26). This is both what Jüngel calls "the deepest secret of God's righteousness"[16] and, more to the point, what Bultmann dubs "the paradox of grace" because "it is precisely the *transgressor, the sinner,* to whom it applies."[17]

It is this paradox that Paul parades in Romans 5:6–10. The gift to which Romans 5:15–17 refers is named in Romans 5:6–10; it is the justifying (5:9) and disjunctive (5:6–8) death of Christ. Elsewhere Paul can flaunt the logically foolish and theologically scandalous content of this event (1 Cor 1:18–23), but in this context, as in Romans 3:23–24, it is the objects of grace that signal its oddity. The grammar of 5:6–8 makes this point. The explanatory *gar* that opens v.7 promises an explication of the claim of v.6, but the adversative *de* of v.8 indicates that this explanation is made by way of antithesis:[18] the grace which Paul proclaims is not self-sacrifice for the righteous and/or the good. As with Romans 4:4, however, this antithesis is not obvious. Rather than being something other than grace, the "gift of death"[19] for noble persons and righteous causes was regularly regarded as the epitome of benefaction.[20] But this is merely to raise again the question about the peculiarly Pauline definition of *charis*: if self-sacrifice for the righteous and/or good is theoretically gracious, why does Paul contrast (*de*) divine grace with this hypothetical act of heroism (5:7–7)? The answer, as above, is not that the gift of one's life for a worthy person is not a gift; the answer is that *the gift* is not a death for the righteous and/or the good. *The gift* is Christ crucified for the ungodly (5:6).

In antithesis to the fitting gift of Romans 5:7 Paul announces the utter incongruity of God's grace-in-Christ. The *kairos* of the cross—the fact that Christ died for the ungodly while they were still (*eti*) ungodly—excludes the possibility of prior human fittingness and thus, in Käsemann's words,

15. Barclay, "Grace within and beyond Reason," 17.

16. Jüngel, *Justification*, 87.

17. Bultmann, *Theology*, 1: 282 (italics original).

18. Jewett, *Romans*, 360.

19. This phrase is taken from the title of Derrida's well known essay on gift, *The Gift of Death.*

20. Jewett, *Romans*, 360 n.158. cites Isocrates, *Arch.* 107; Lycurgus, *Leoc.* 86.2; Philo, *Agr.* 3.156; Diodorus Siculus, *Hist.* 9.2.6.3; cf. Plato, *Apology* 32a; Dio Cassius 80.20; Sir 4.28; *1 Clem.* 55.1.

"Christ did his saving work at an unexpected and, morally considered, even inappropriate moment."[21] "Christ died for the ungodly," writes Calvin, "when we were in no way worthy (*dignus*) or fit (*idoneus*)."[22] Entering the "still" (*eti*) of post-Adamic history (5:12–19), the Christ-gift cannot come as a "correspondingly"; it comes as a "nevertheless."[23] Rather than locating the worthy (as Sophia, God's gift does, *Wis.* 6:16), the grace Paul announces encounters the ungodly (*asebēs*, 5:6), the sinner (*hamartōlos*, 5:8), and the enemy (*echthros*, 5:10) and re-names its beneficiaries *e contrario*: it justifies sinners (5:9a) and reconciles enemies (5:10a).[24]

The tension here with *Wisdom* is acute. Paul locates the demonstration of divine love (5:8) and righteousness (3:21) in a gift given to those whom *Wisdom* consistently depicts as the fitting recipients of divine judgment. While the righteous are rescued, their ungodly (*asebēs*, 10:20) and sinful (*hamartōlos*, 19:13) enemies (*echthros*, 10:19) are destroyed. Paul, of course, can grant the deservedness of this destruction (*ta opsōnia tēs hamartias thanatos*, Rom 6:23a; cf. 1:32), but the gift he announces does not "fit"; it is given to those whose proper payment is death, but the incongruous gift (*charis*) is eternal life in Christ Jesus (6:23b). It is thus, in *Wisdom's* terms, those who are the fitting objects of God's judgment (death) who are identified by Paul as the recipients of God's unfitting grace (life).

Pseudo-Solomon, as emphasized in the previous section, is certainly a theologian of grace, but not this grace; this is something new, a sermon for the suffering *sinner* that announces the miracle of God's contradictory and creative love rather than the commonsense of correspondence leading to condemnation. For Paul, the death of Jesus for the justification of sinners is the event of grace (Rom 3:24). The cross and the disjunction declaration it effects—the unrighteous are reckoned righteous—are thus determinative for Paul's radical rethinking of grace: he thinks from the unconditioned and incongruous giving of God's son to the definition of God's grace. As Luther might say, "*omnia vocabula in Christo novam significationem accipere.*"[25] Grace, announces Paul, is not a reward for work (Rom 4:4) or heroic

---

21. Käsemann, *Commentary on Romans*, 137.

22. Calvin, *Romans*, 195. Benefits given to those who are not *dignus* is exactly the social problem Seneca's *De Beneficiis* attempts to redress (cf. I.1.2)

23. Barth, *Christ and Adam*, 2. "In the death of Christ God has intervened on our behalf in the "nevertheless" of His free grace."

24. As Cranfield suggests, the eschatological salvation of those whom God calls righteous is "very easy" when compared to the "really difficult thing" that is the creative and incongruous gift that grounds this re-naming (Cranfield, *Romans*, 1.266.).

25. Luther, "Disputatio de divinitate et humanitate Christi (1540)," 94, 17f.

self-sacrifice (Rom 5:7); grace is that which is given to and justifies the ungodly (Rom 4:5; 5:6, 8–10). Grace is Jesus Christ.

THE GOSPEL OF ONE-WAY LOVE

I opened this essay by saying that it would affirm and correlate two theses about grace: "Grace is one-way love"[26] and "Neither can the power of grace be understood except by a description of the gospel."[27] A comparison between *Wisdom* and Romans may have appeared an unpromising approach, but it is precisely in the incommensurable understandings of grace articulated by Pseudo-Solomon and St. Paul that the two theses are forced together. E. P. Sanders' book *Paul and Palestinian Judaism* created a shibboleth: "Christianity and Judaism are both religions of grace"; or in Sanders' own words, "on the point at which many have found the decisive contrast between Paul and Judaism—grace and works—Paul is in agreement with Judaism."[28] Sanders, however, and those who have recited his mantra, have assumed that grace, by definition, is "groundless," "free," and "unmerited."[29] "One-way love," we might say, has been presupposed to be the "one and only" meaning of grace.

But this is what the comparison of *Wisdom* and Romans indicates is emphatically *not* the case. For *Wisdom*, grace is unearned, but never ungrounded; grace is not payment, but it can be called reward; grace is free, but always conditioned; grace is benevolent, but not one-way. To define grace as "one-way love" is not to state a Zen-like truth; it is to follow Paul as he daringly, and from *Wisdom's* perspective dangerously, deduces a definition of grace from the scandalous event he calls the demonstration of divine love (Rom 5:8). To merge our theses about grace, "Neither can the power of one-way love be understood except by a description of the gospel."

Barth captures this necessary rooting of grace in the gospel:

> The Christian message does not at its heart express a concept or idea . . . it recounts a history . . . in such a way that it declares a name . . . This means that all the concepts and ideas used in this message [Barth explicitly mentions grace] can derive their significance only from the bearer of this name and from his history . . . They can serve only to describe this name—the name of Jesus Christ.[30]

26. Zahl, *Grace in Practice*: 36.

27. Melanchton, "Loci communes theologici, 1521," 70.

28. Sanders, *Paul and Palestinian Judaism*, 543.

29. Ibid., 394–96.

30. Barth, *Church Dogmatics*, IV/1, 16–17.

Paul Zahl offers a definition of grace: "Grace is one-way love. That is the definition of grace."[31] But while he works to take this particular understanding of grace into "everyday life," this specific understanding of grace is not an abstraction or an *a priori*; it is, as this essay's epigram shows, anchored in the atonement: "Without the atonement, the grace of God is a beautiful dream."[32] "God's grace exists in relation to the human word" as one-way love "only because of . . . Christ's final love on the cross."[33] This is a definition of grace that *Wisdom*—and as 1 Corinthians 1:23 indicates, the whole world—will regard as scandalous and foolish; but it is a definition of grace deduced from that one thing St. Paul determined to know: "Christ and him crucified" (1 Cor 2:2).

BIBLIOGRAPHY

Badiou, A. *Saint Paul: The Foundation of Universalism*. Translated by R. Brassier. Stanford: Stanford University Press, 2003.

Barclay, J. M. G. "Grace within and beyond Reason: Philo and Paul in Dialogue." In *Paul, Grace, and Freedom: Essays in Honor of John K. Riches*, edited by P. Middleton, A. Paddison and K. Wenell. London: T. & T. Clark, 2009.

Barth, Karl. *Christ and Adam: Man and Humanity in Romans 5*. Translated by T. A. Smail. New York: Harper & Brothers, 1956.

———. *Church Dogmatics*. Translated by G. W. Bromiley. Edited by G. W. Bromiley and T. F. Torrance. Vol. IV/1. Edinburgh: T. & T. Clark, 1956.

———. *The Epistle to the Romans*. Translated by E. C. Hoskyns. Oxford: Oxford University Press, 1933.

Bultmann, Rudolf. *Theology of the New Testament*. Translated by Kendrick Grobel. 2 vols. New York: Scribner, 1951.

Cranfield, C. E. B. *A Critical and Exegetical Commentary on the Epistle to the Romans*. 2 vols. International Critical Commentary. Edinburgh: T. & T. Clark, 1975.

Derrida, Jacques. *The Gift of Death*. Translated by D. Wills. Chicago: University of Chicago Press, 1995.

Dunn, James D. G. *The Theology of Paul the Apostle*. Grand Rapids: Eerdmans, 1998.

Hübner, Hans. *Die Weisheit Salomons*. Das Alte Testament Deutsch Apokryphen 4. Göttingen: Vandenhoeck & Ruprecht, 1999.

Jewett, Robert. *Romans: A Critical and Exegetical Commentary on Paul's Epistle to the Romans*. Hermeneia. Minneapolis: Fortress, 2007.

Jüngel, Eberhard. *Justification: The Heart of Christian Faith*. Translated by J. F. Cayzer. London: T. & T. Clark, 2001.

Kant, Immanuel. *Religion within the Limits of Reason Alone (1794)*. Translated by T. M. Greene and H. H. Hudson. New York: Harper & Row, 1960.

31. Zahl, *Grace in Practice*, 36.

32. Ibid., 114.

33. Ibid., 258.

Käsemann, Ernst. *Commentary on Romans*. Translated by G. W. Bromiley. Grand Rapis: Eerdmans, 1980.

Larcher, C. *Le Livre De La Sagesse, Ou La Sagesse De Salomon*. Etudes bibliques 1, 3, 5. Paris: Gabalda, 1983.

Luther, Martin. "Disputatio De Divinitate Et Humanitate Christi (1540)." In *Weimarer Ausgabe 39. II. Band, Disputationen* Weimer: Böhlaus, 1932.

Melanchton, Philipp. "Loci Communes Theologici, 1521." In *Melanchton and Bucer*, edited by Wilhelm Pauck, 18–152. Philadelphia: Westminster, 1969.

Nietzsche, Friedrich. *Beyond Good and Evil: Prelude to a Philosophy of the Future*. Translated by R. J. Hollingdale. London: Penguin, 1973.

Sanders, E. P. *Paul and Palestinian Judaism: A Comparison of Patterns of Religion*. Minneapolis: Fortress, 1977.

Sartre, Jean-Paul. *Existentialism and Humanism*. Translated by Philip Mairet. London: Methuen, 1949.

Winston, David. *The Wisdom of Solomon*. Anchor Bible 43. Garden City, NY: Doubleday, 1979.

Zahl, Paul F. M. *Grace in Practice: A Theology of Everyday Life*. Grand Rapids: Eerdmans, 2007.

6

The Angels of God in the Bible

Heinz-Dieter Neef[1]

My paper is divided into four sections: 1. The Return of the Angels 2. The Angels of God in the Old Testament 3. The Angels of God in the New Testament 4. Concluding Thoughts.[2]

THE RETURN OF THE ANGELS

"The angels, now so rarely encountered in the proclamation of the Church, have returned. They are conquering areas of the greatest variety, even the mass media. They have a new appearance and function. Some of them have become quite worldly. Yes indeed, the angels are among us."[3] This is the conclusion drawn in the 1991 issue of the journal *Kunst und Kirche* (Art and the Church) that dealt with the topic of angels. That volume demonstrates in a very impressive manner how angels pervade our daily lives, in art, in literature, and in motion pictures.

---

1. Lecture given in March 2001 in the Sunday class/Dean's class of the Cathedral Church of the Advent, Birmingham, Alabama, USA; Dean: The Very Reverend Dr. theol. Paul F. M. Zahl. I want to thank deeply Mr. Keith Myrick for the translation from German into English.

2. All biblical quotations have been taken from the New Revised Standard Version, 1989.

3. "Engel," in *Kunst und Kirche*, 235.

We often compare children with angels or we characterize persons close to us or those with endearing personalities as "angels." We often encounter representations of angels in advertising such as in that of the Swiss company "Bell," which in 1980 and 1981 sang the praises of its food products with the aid of winged, female angels. In 1991, the Ford Motor Company advertised its cars using a male devil and a female angel.[4]

In the area of art, we even speak of an "angel boom" that continues to this very day. The person who painted the most angels in the twentieth century is the Jewish artist Marc Chagall. To him, angels were signs of God's presence in earthly life. It is known that the artist Paul Klee painted thirty-five angels in the year 1939 alone, a year of catastrophe in Europe marked by death and destruction. In his works, angels are the messengers of a world that was unknown and yet was passionately longed for. His angels are reminders of genuine humanity.[5]

In addition, the topic of angels is taken up time and time again in the areas of literature and motion pictures. We may take as an example the 1947 movie "It's a Wonderful Life," directed by Frank Capra, or the 1987 movie "Wings of Desire" by Wim Wenders. The main role in these is that of "secularized angels." They have the lowest position in the hierarchy of angels. They neither proclaim anything nor do battle. They guard neither heaven nor paradise. These angels are neither heavenly messengers nor dragon-slayers. They arrive with neither lance nor flower, but rather, empty-handed. They have no halo to signify their position, and they are not transported from place to place by a pair of wings. They are guardian angels whose mission is to save and console human beings. In literature, the theme of angels appears in narratives, poems, legends, and short stories by such diverse authors as Johan Wolfgang von Goethe, Guy de Maupassant, Edgar Allan Poe, Max Frisch, Friedrich Dürrenmatt, and many other writers of world literature.[6]

The frequent appearance of angels in anthroposophy and in the area of esoterics and the New Age movement should also be mentioned. In this case, the angels are part of a pantheistic worldview, and a personification of the forces of nature. Angels are thought to be in the forests and on mountains; they are believed to have magical and aesthetic qualities. Here, the appearance of angels leads to a strengthening of one's own spiritual power and to a greater trust in one's own thoughts.

To our world, which would appear to be so secularized, the angels have indeed returned. According to a 1995 survey, one out of three Germans

---

4. Ibid.
5. Ibid., 237, 39.
6. Ibid., 236–39, 71–73.

(approximately 25 million) believes in angels. About one thousand persons, half of those surveyed, are convinced that they have personal guardian angels. Women especially were found to believe in the existence of heavenly beings. Forty-one percent of them said that angels really do exist, while only twenty-nine percent of the men said so. Twenty-four percent pictured angels as having wings; twenty-one percent saw them as wearing white clothing.

The angel boom in our secularized world stands in contrast to a significantly growing absence of angels in the proclamation of the Church. Angels are present in the *Gloria* and *Sanctus* every Sunday when the congregation joins in with the worshipful praise of the heavenly hosts, and yet they appear to go largely unnoticed by the congregation in the liturgy, church song, and Scripture readings. Even in theology, the topic of angels is seldom expressly addressed. Schleiermacher's dictum is well-known. Schleiermacher said that the concept of angels belongs to a time in which knowledge of the forces of nature was still very limited and man's control over such was at it's lowest level, so that we cannot draw any conclusions about the present or the future from the angelic apparitions known to us, and that the discussion on angels remains totally problematic for the specific area of dogmatics. He believed that only the private or the liturgical use of this concept would be acceptable.[7]

The reasons for these reservations regarding talk about the "angel of the Lord" are certainly many and diverse, for we are dealing here with an extremely complex concept that in form and content is difficult to systematize, and for which each Bible passage must be observed and appreciated on its own terms.

THE ANGELS OF GOD IN THE OLD TESTAMENT

On the whole, the Old Testament speaks of the "angel(s) of the Lord" in a rather reserved manner. The occurrences are limited to a few chapters, among which especially Genesis 16 (the story of Hagar and Ishmael), Numbers 22 (Bileam), Judges 6 (Gideon), Judges 13 (Samson) and the book of Zechariah are worthy of mention. In many Old Testament books, for example in Leviticus, Deuteronomy, Joshua, the Prophets and most of the Wisdom Literature, no angels are mentioned.

What statements does the Old Testament make regarding the angel of the Lord, his physical features, his nature, and the locations of his appearances? He meets Sarah's handmaid, Hagar, at a water source, namely an oasis, when she is fleeing from Sarah's maltreatment into the wilderness

7. Schleiermacher, *Der Christliche Glaube*, §§42.43.

(Gen 16:7). He appears to Samson`s mother at the moment that she is sitting in the field (Judg 13:9). He peacefully sits down near Gideon while the latter is threshing wheat under a tree in Ophrah (Judg 6:11). He comes to the juniper tree under which Elijah had lain down to die (1 Kgs 19:5). The angel of the Lord also appears, however, in the enemy camp of the Assyrians and kills one hundred ninety-five thousand men, after which Sennacherib has to end the siege of Jerusalem and return to Nineveh (2 Kgs 19:35).

What conclusions can be drawn from these observations? The angel of the Lord comes to those who need him. He apparently does not turn away from them. He meets them unexpectedly in daily life. He speaks with them just as human beings speak with each other. He comforts and encourages them and occasionally promises them great things, as with Hagar to whom a son was promised. When necessary, he even touches them, as in the case of Elijah. The angel of the Lord usually appears silently and peacefully. However, he sometimes vanishes in an impressive manner. Judges 6 and 13 tell how the angel of the Lord rose to heaven in a flame of fire. Judges 13:20[8] says, "When the flame went up toward heaven from the altar, the angel of the LORD ascended in the flame of the altar while Manoah and his wife looked on." Only by this spectacle did Manoah and his wife realize that they had spoken with the angel of the Lord.

There is something else that about this that is striking: the angel of the Lord fades in comparison to the task he is to perform. When the task is completed, he disappears just as quickly and unexpectedly as he came. The person of the angel is not what is important; rather, it is his message that is prominent. The message is God`s message.

Why does he come to the men and women of the Old Testament? He appears above all in dire situations in order to accompany them in their distress and to lead them out of their dilemma! This is what the angel does in the conflict between Hagar and Sarah. He resolves the conflict by advising Hagar to return to her mistress and to endure the mistreatment (Gen 16:9). In the story of the testing of Abraham's faith (Genesis 22), the angel keeps Abraham from slaying Isaac. At the very moment that Abraham takes the knife in hand to kill his son, the angel calls out from heaven, "Abraham! Abraham! Do not lay your hand on the boy or do anything to him; for now I know that you fear God."[9] Elijah wished to die because of his sharp conflict with Jezebel. That is why he lay down under the juniper bush. While he slept, an angel touched him and said, "Get up and eat!" This so-called

---

8. In the New Revised Standard Version.

9. Neef, *Die Prüfung Abrahams.*

sacramental act is even repeated by the angel. The angel seeks salvation for God's servant. For Israel, he is a protector.

In this connection, the places that speak of the Exodus out of Egypt and the crossing over into Canaan should be mentioned. In these cases, it is said that this all happened under the guidance of an angel. We read in Exod 23:20–21, "I am going to send an angel in front of you, to guard you on the way and to bring you to the place that I have prepared. Be attentive to him and listen to his voice; do not rebel against him, for he will not pardon your transgression; for my name is in him."[10]

Here, the angel is the leader and protector of Israel. It is his task to go before the people and guard it along the way so that it will reach the place that God has chosen. Because God's name is in him, he is the visible representative of God, to whom Israel is required to demonstrate respect by doing what he says so that it may dwell in peace in the face of its enemies. The angel of God is there at the beginning of Israel's wilderness wanderings, and he is also present at the end when Israel enters the Promised Land. There, he admonishes Israel to make neither any covenant with the inhabitants of the Land nor to adopt their religion (Judg 2:1–5).

Before we turn our attention to the presentation of the angel of the Lord in the New Testament, I would like to take a quick look at the so-called "interpreting angel" in the prophet Zechariah and in Daniel. In Zechariah, the angel appears in connection with Zechariah's visions. In Zech 1:8, we read, "In the night I saw a man riding on a red horse! He was standing among the myrtle trees in the glen; and behind him were red, sorrel, and white horses. Then I said, 'What are these, my lord?' The angel who talked with me said to me, 'I will show you what they are.'" So it goes, from one vision in the night to the next. Here, the angel is the interpreter of the heavenly language.

In Daniel's visions, we find the same thing as in Zechariah. In Daniel 7, Daniel's visions are described, upon which he becomes very troubled. He cannot understand what he has been shown: "I approached one of the attendants to ask him the truth concerning all this. So he said that he would disclose to me the interpretation of the matter" (Dan 7:16).

In Zechariah and Daniel, the angel has the same function as an interpreter of the visions of a human seer. This angel is clearly distinguished from the heavenly beings. He now no longer has the task of bearing messages, but rather he now has to explain them. He is no longer on the earth in order to show people the way; instead, he belongs to the world that he interprets.

---

10. Exod 23:21. Cf. Neef, "'Ich selber bin in ihm' (Ex 23,21)."

In the Bible, this interpreting angel is a sign that the distance between God and man has grown. The direct reception of God`s word is no longer possible. The interpreting angel appears exactly there where the era of pre-exilic prophecy ends. Here, we find ourselves at the point of transition from the prophetic to the apocalyptic. In the prophetic, the word has priority; in the apocalyptic, the vision is emphasized. The vision has to be interpreted. The task of interpreting is taken on by the interpreting angel. In the final analysis, he alone is in a position to inform someone of God`s counsel. Man becomes cognizant of his own guilt and sees that the judgement foretold by the prophets has come to pass. From this vantage point, it becomes clear how radical a change the coming of Christ was. A well-known German Christmas song says: "Today, he opens the gate to beautiful Paradise; the cherub no longer stands before it; to God be praise, glory, and honor!" In Jesus, the direct link with God is re-established. He doesn`t need an interpreting angel to explain the Father`s word to him. The interpreting angel has been made unnecessary. With this, we already find ourselves in Part Three of our outline.

THE ANGELS OF GOD IN THE NEW TESTAMENT

In the New Testament, the angel of the Lord is emphasized in only three situations:

1. At the coming of Christ to earth;
2. At his ascension; and
3. At his second coming.

The angels are not the focus of attention in the preaching of Jesus or in the letters of Paul. Christ did not come in order to reveal something about the angels. He did not bring a certain teaching about angels. But what significance do the angels then have?

In the stories of Jesus' birth the connection with the Old Testament becomes apparent. In the Old Testament, we have seen that the angelic visitation is concentrated around two kinds of situations: the anguish of the barren woman; here the angel announces the birth of a child (Genesis 16); and the distress of the man; here the angel announces salvation of rescue (Elijah). Both of these motifs are mingled together in the New Testament. The birth of Jesus is the fulfilment of that which had been expected, yearned and prayed for in the midst of the hardships of mankind for thousands of years. All that the men and women of the Old Testament had expected from the angel of God comes together in the person of Jesus.

In Luke 1:28, the angel Gabriel greets Mary with the words: "Greetings, favored one! The Lord is with you . . . Do not be afraid, Mary, for you have found favour with God. And now, you will conceive in your womb and bear a son, and you will name him Jesus . . . He will reign over the house of Jacob forever." Mary answers, "Here am I, the servant of the Lord; let it be with me according to your word." Then the angel leaves her. This scene shows that the angel appeared at a time of deepest distress. With his appearing, the cause for the distress is explained and at the same time is overcome. The angel promises a good new beginning and thus victory over a desperate situation.

The angel of the Lord also appears in connection with the resurrection of Jesus in Matthew 28 and Mark 16. Immediately we notice a number of parallels between the coming of the angel and that of Jesus: 1. Like the angels in the Old Testament, Jesus comes to earth as one of us; namely, he takes on "our flesh and blood." 2. Like the Old Testament angels, Jesus directs his message to the people, in the same manner that people convey messages to each other. "He was the same as any other man, and in his gestures he was found to be a man" (Phil 2:6–11). 3. As with the angels of the Old Testament, not until his departure, namely by way of the cross and the resurrection, does it become clear who Jesus actually is. In the case of the angel, only through his vanishing does it become clear to which world he belongs, namely to the heavenly realm where God dwells. 4. The eyes of the people to whom the angel came were opened as he departed. Only then was he recognized as the angel of God. It is the same with the resurrected Christ. As the resurrected One appears to his disciples, they approach him, grasp his feet, and fall down before him. Now they recognize him as the Christ. Now they can preach.

The angel at the second coming of the Lord! Here one observation stands out. No longer does the text speak of "the angel of the Lord" in the singular, but rather of "angels" in the plural, who stand around the throne of God. It is their job to point to the majesty of God; nothing else is said about them. Their task is therefore different from that of the angel that appeared to Mary and Elizabeth. It is written in Matt 25:31, "When the Son of Man comes in his glory, and all the angels with him, then he will sit on the throne of his glory."

This speaking of a plurality of angels is intended to point to another reality, namely the reality of God. Ultimately, this reality cannot be comprehended in human terms. This kind of language about the angels is found especially in the Revelation of John. Here, the idea of the royal court of God plays a special role. The court of God as such refers to all those angels who gather around God's throne to praise and glorify him. In Revelation, all the conceptions of angels appear together. Here we find the angel of judgment that pours out the wrath of God. In Revelation 15, there is a vivid description of seven angels who carry seven golden bowls full of God's wrath. In chapter twenty, an angel is one who binds Satan for a total of one thousand years, casts him into the pit, and seals him in so that he can no longer deceive the nations. In chapter twenty-one, there are angels who stand guard at the gates and on the walls of the new Jerusalem. The whole book of Revelation can therefore be termed an "angel drama." This is the only place where this so-called angel drama is found. The angels in Revelation stand for an event that we ultimately cannot comprehend: God's final coming to earth, when everything will be new and war and suffering will be eradicated.

As in the other parts of the New Testament, there is no special teaching about angels in the Revelation of John. The angels have the responsibility of worshipping God; they themselves should not, and are not allowed to, receive worship. They are merely servants. Worship is reserved for Christ alone.

CONCLUDING THOUGHTS

When we speak of the angel of the Lord, then we are talking about God's personal encounter with human beings. As humans, we inquire with wonder and amazement. How can an almighty God, the God of Heaven, take up contact with us? How can he show himself to us, without us seeing him? The angels are the answer to these questions, because it is with his angel that God touches the world. The world is his creation, and he does not want to leave it to its own devices, but rather he wants to preserve and protect it. That is the mystery of God! In his angel, God himself steps back and takes on human semblance in order to be near his creation.

Where does the angel of the Lord appear? He appears to persons in distress, men and women in life's difficult, apparently hopeless situations. He appears in the middle of threat, betrayal, oppression, and war! In these trying situations in life, he appears, and with his appearing he changes reality. He saves from people from peril; he creates salvation in the face of danger and by doing so opens up a secure future.

When the Old and New Testament concepts of angels are compared, the following observations can be made. In the Old Testament, approximately three phases of development can be distinguished. The first phase does not distinguish between God and the angel. God appears as an angel and vice versa (Gen 16). In the second phase, there is a definite distinction between the two. The angel becomes God's representative. God is not identical with him, but God can portray himself in him. In the third phase, God and angels are separate. Here, the angel now functions merely as an interpreter.

In conclusion, I have endeavoured to show that the angel of the Lord appears at central and decisive points in the history of faith of Israel. Connected with the angel of the Lord is a theologically differentiated and well thought-out image that ultimately is intended to show that in spite of all of man's guilt, unfaithfulness, and suffering, and in spite of God's wrath over such conduct, God still does not desert his people, but rather stands by them. This is seen in the angel of the Lord. God does not act according to his wrath. God is god and no man. He intends to save and not destroy his people. This will of God is represented by the angel of the Lord. He shows the people the merciful God who is concerned about his people. It is for this very reason that the angel of the Lord should not be reduced to a footnote in theology and church, in teaching and preaching, for according to Exodus 21:31, God himself is present in him. The study of the biblical concept of angels leads us into the heart of the Christian message, namely God`s love for us. Where this happens, we turn away from all esoteric occupation with the angels as spiritual healers after the death of God and allow ourselves to be reminded of the angels as witnesses of God's love.

One final thing—what do angels look like? Are they men or women or sexless beings, or are they little, chubby children? Are they figures clothed in white gowns and bearing white wings? The Bible is silent about their appearance. Their appearance is not especially important. However, we should keep an eye on the fingers of the angels, because these always point toward God and his son Jesus Christ. This is the perspective that we can learn from the angels! Let us look to God and to his son Jesus Christ!

BIBLIOGRAPHY

Akao, J. O. "Yahweh and Mal'ak in the Early Traditions of Israel: A Study of the Underlying Traditions of Yahweh/Angel Theophany in Exodus 3." *Irish Biblical Studies* 12 (1990) 72–85.

Baumgartner, Walter. *Zum Alten Testament und seiner Umwelt: Ausgewälte Aufsätze.* Leiden: Brill, 1959.

"Engel." *Kunst und Kirche: Ökumenische Zeitschrift für zeitgenössische Kunst und Architektur* 54/4 (1991).

Hirth, Volkmar. *Gottes Boten im Alten Testament.* Theologische Arbeiten 32. Berlin: Evangelische Verlagsanstalt, 1975.

Lods, Adolphe. "L'angel de Yahvé et l'âme extérieure." In *Studien zur semitischen Philologie und Religionsgeschichte: Julius Wellhausen zum 70. Geburstag,* edited by K. Marti, 263–78. Giessen: Töpelmann, 1914.

Neef, Heinz-Dieter. *Die Prüfung Abrahams: Eine Exegetisch-Theologische Studie zu Gen 22, 1–19.* Arbeiten zur Theologie 90. Stuttgart: Calwer, 1998.

————. "Ich selber bin in ihm" (Ex 23,21): Exegetische Beobachtungen zur Rede vom 'Engel des Herrn' in Ex 23,20–22; 32,34; 33,2; Jdc 2,1–5; 5,23." *Biblische Zeitschrift* 39 (1995) 54–75.

Rad, Gerhard von. "Mal'ak im Alten Testament." In *Theologisches Wörterbuch zum Neuen Testament,* edited by Gerhard Kittel and Otto Bauernfeind, 75–79. Stuttgart: Kohlhammer, 1933.

————. "Mal'ak in the Old Testament." In *Theological Dictionary of the New Testament,* edited by Gerhard Kittel, 1:76-80. Translated by G. W. Bromiley. Grand Rapids: Eerdmans, 1964.

Röttger, Hermann. *Mal'ak Jahwe—Bote von Gott: Die Vorstellung von Gottes Boten im hebräischen Alten Testament.* Regensburger Studien zur Theologie 13. Frankfurt: Lang, 1978.

Schleiermacher, F. D. E. *Der christliche Glaube nach den Grundsätzen der evangelischen Kirche im Zusammenhang dargestellt, Zweite Auflage 1830–1831.* Edited by Rolf Schäfer. Schleiermacher Kritische Gesamtausgabe, Schriften und Entwürfe 13/I. Berlin: de Gruyter, 2003.

Stier, Fridolin. *Gott und sein Engel im Alten Testament.* Alttestamentliche Abhandlungen 12/2. Münster: Schulz, 1934.

Westermann, Claus. *Gottes Engel brauchen keine Flügel.* Stuttgart: Vogt, 1957.

————. *God's Angels Need No Wings.* Translated by David L. Scheidt. Philadelphia: Fortress, 1979.

7

The Possibility of the Gospel
The Freedom to Forgive and Be Forgiven

Lauren R. E. Larkin

The philosophical and theological relationship of the concepts of actuality and possibility, while seemingly obtuse and esoteric, are nevertheless immensely important concepts for anyone interested in developing a theological anthropology, which is a catch-all term used in reference to the question of what it means to be a human being, theologically understood. This discussion was initiated by Aristotle and continues to this day, commanding the attention of philosophers and theologians alike. This essay will examine the interaction between Aristotle's conception of this relationship and that of Eberhard Jüngel, as he attempts to recast the entire discussion in light of the doctrine of justification by faith alone. The doctrine of justification radically reverses Aristotle's chronology by beginning with the pronouncement of God's grace being the constitutive ground—the actuality—from which all subsequent possibility flows. In this way, the end of judgment and law as understood by the pronouncement of absolution is the beginning of what is truly possible, or in other words, the end of Christ is the beginning of human life by faith.

Jüngel argues (and demonstrates) that the gospel message, being the final word of God, is the "speech event" that demonstrates that possibility has priority over actuality. When possibility has priority over actuality, we can declare that not only is a person separated from their deeds and acts, but that, by the event of the cross and the proclamation of the gospel of the justification of sinners, no person is beyond hope, no person's actuality trumps their possibility; the gospel tells us that no one, *not even one* is beyond possibility.

THE DOCTRINE OF JUSTIFICATION AS AN ALTERNATIVE TO ARISTOTLE

To begin dismantling[1] Aristotle's ontological priority of actuality over possibility,[2] Jüngel starts with the doctrine of justification. The doctrine of justification is the doctrine of the activity of God toward us. The doctrine of justification is an "indispensable criterion of proper theology" and is (and remains) the *articulus stantis et cadentis ecclesiae* (the article by which the church stands or falls).[3] It is by the doctrine of justification that Jüngel, and before

---

1. Essentially, Jüngel is proposing that Christian eschatology is first *Christian,* that both Jesus' kingdom of God statements and Paul's theology of justification *change* what has occurred before; they challenge the culturally historic trends in understanding actuality and possibility. So if Christian eschatology and theology is thoroughly Christian, then this becomes, for Jüngel, the starting point in calling into question the influence of Aristotle's concept of the ontological priority of actuality over possibility. Jüngel suggests, "The *necessity* of this theological dismantling of the ontological primacy of actuality over possibility is best seen by laying bare the theological starting-points from which it could be carried out. These theological starting-points can be nothing other than the basic conditions for Christian theology. For *dismantling* can only be theologically necessary when it also accomplishes the *construction* of that which is theologically necessary" (Jüngel, "The World as Possibility and Actuality," 103). In dismantling the existing framework of ontological priority of actuality over possibility, the new framework must first be dependent on the basics of Christian theology and, second, results in the construction of that which is theologically necessary, which will be the ontological priority of possibility over actuality.

2. According to Jüngel, Aristotle gives ontological priority to actuality over possibility. It is more than merely giving first position to actuality over possibility, but that the actual is the reference point for the possible, and defines the possible. Possibility has the distinct potential of becoming actualized; it can *be* (although it currently *is not*) as long as there are no hindrances to its becoming. A chair cannot walk and does not hold the possibility of walking because it is a chair and has inherent hindrances to being able to walk. Thus, to be a *walker* one has to have the capacity/ability to walk; the possibility of walking is confirmed in the actuality of walking (or the actuality of the possibility of walking (not having any hindrances to walking). This would be clearer: "the possibility of walking is confirmed in the actuality of walking, or the actuality of the possibility of walking (not having any hindrances to walking)." Jüngel writes, "Aristotle's concept of possibility is completely oriented to that of actuality. For the possible is related to the actual as (a part of) that which is not to that which is. Being cannot properly be attributed to the possible. Only that which is actual can properly be said to be" (ibid., 99).

3. Ibid., 104.

him, Luther, can declare that the person cannot become righteous by doing righteous deeds.[4] The biblical understanding of righteousness is grounded in the fact that righteousness is not an inherent quality of the soul. Righteousness, according to the Bible, depends entirely on God's activity toward humanity rather than on humanity's actuality (act); for God imputes righteousness to those who believe, and they are the righteous by faith in God's declaration and by imputation of righteousness. Luther positively affirms and asserts the "justification of the sinner by faith in the justifying Word of God," while using the doctrine of justification to dismantle the Aristotelian understanding of the righteous person. Jüngel explains that when the Aristotelian understanding of the righteous person is called into question, so too is his understanding of actuality. Jüngel writes, "'We become just by doing just acts', declared Aristotle; here he presupposes that since ethical virtues are not innate in us by nature, they do not exist in us as a possibility before they exist in actuality. Rather, we are righteous in so far as we continue to act righteously. For 'states arise out of like activity.'"[5] Through repetition (or practice) one becomes, according to Aristotle, righteous (virtuous); according to Jüngel, this claim, for Aristotle, ties "what we do" to the person: we are what we make of ourselves. Consequently, following this line of thinking, as Jüngel presents it, the person is directly affected when she stops doing the righteous acts.

4. An important aspect of Aristotle's concept of the ontological priority of actuality over possibility is, according to Jüngel, that actuality ends in *act*. The act, Jüngel explains, is the fulfillment of the actuality; in other words, one could say that for Aristotle, actuality's teleological ordering is *act*. If there is no *act*, then the possible is never realized (thus relegating the possibility to an inferior position to actuality). In other words, the virtuous person will do virtuous acts and the person is accounted virtuous if she acts virtuously (thus, one becomes righteous by doing righteous acts). If there is possibility still present in the actuality of the act, then the act itself is not fully actualized. A fully actualized act is *free* of all possibility.

5. Jüngel, "The World as Possibility and Actuality," 105–6. Jüngel is referring to Aristotle's *Nichomachean Ethics*, "as you will become a good builder from building well, so you will become a bad one from building badly. Were this not so, there would be no need for teachers of the arts, but everybody would be born a good or bad craftsman as the case might be. The same then is true of the virtues. It is by taking part in transactions with our fellowmen that some of us become just and others unjust; by acting in dangerous situation and forming a habit of fear or of confidence we become courageous or cowardly. And the same holds good of our dispositions with regard to the appetites, and anger; some men become temperate and gentler, others profligate and irascible, by actually comporting themselves in one way or the other in relation to those passions. In a word, our moral dispositions are formed as a result of the corresponding activities. Hence it is incumbent on us to control the character of our activities, since on the quality of these depends the quality of our dispositions" (Aristotle, *The Nichomachean Ethics* 1103b8–4a. Book Two, i/7–8).

Righteousness and actuality are not permanent states; they are wholly contingent on performance and repetition of righteous acts. For the elderly and the infirm (the physically sick and the mentally handicapped), it would make sense to conclude that they have either ceased to acquire actuality and righteousness (and are perhaps in the state of losing their actuality and their righteousness because maybe they cannot perform the necessary righteous acts) or they are completely incapable in the first place of performing such acts so they remain in a state of half-being because they cannot perform and repeat the necessary righteous acts that make one righteous and actual.[6] In contrast to this, the imputed righteousness of God is permanent and independent of acts. One is declared righteous by faith in the justifying God apart from works.

THE DOCTRINE OF JUSTIFICATION AND *EX NIHILO CREATE*

If the person is not determined or actualized by her acts (that person, in fact, cannot become righteous by doing righteous acts), then it is concluded that the person needs to be changed. The unrighteous person needs to be changed into the righteous person in order for righteous acts to be actualized. The person does not have the required free will that is needed for Aristotle's belief that one becomes righteous by doing righteous deeds; I am not free to be self-determined. If this bound will is the case, then I am in need of something outside of myself to determine me; that is, I am wholly dependent on God's activity toward me, in the event of justification, to make me righteous. "As a sinner, this already unrighteous person is one whose being is the radical negation of the being of the righteous person, not simply logically but ontologically. This means, however, that there is the most radical antithesis between the unrighteous and the righteous person, which can

6. It is not synonymous to say, according to Jüngel, that because something has the possibility to do something that that thing exists; it only exists if it has been actualized. Take the example of *walking*: the possibility of my walking is possible and actualized in that I do, in fact, walk. A baby, on the other hand, has the possibility of walking (it will eventually walk being of the genus that walks), but that possibility has yet to be actualized so the baby is said not to be able to walk, though it has the possibility, being human. Thus, for Aristotle, according to Jüngel, "*esti* [to be] can only be said of those things which can also be described as fully realized, as actuality. In the end, being and actuality are identical" (Jüngel, "The World as Possibility and Actuality," 99). Thus, Jüngel makes the conclusion that if being and actuality, for Aristotle, are identical, then also for Aristotle, the possible is identical with a not-yet type of "not being"—in terms of "not yet" rather than "negative nothingness," which for Jüngel is the realm of the impossible.

only be adequately stated as that nothingness which we have to consider as the antithesis of creation. The *persona mutata* [changed person] is only properly understood as *ex nihilo create* [created out of nothing]."[7]

In the event of justification, I am brought to nothingness by being associated with Christ in His death; to be made righteous, I am brought out of this death (*ex nihilo creata*) and into new life (being accounted righteous and declared justified by faith in Christ). In this way, Jüngel relates the doctrine of justification to the doctrine of creation out of nothing; and this relation is biblical. The life out of death description is soundly biblical. Jüngel refers to Rom 4:17; 2 Cor 4:16; 5:17; in these verses (to name a few) God is described as bringing life out of death, so that the outer/old person perishes and from this perishing a justified/inner person is raised and renewed daily. "The justified person," writes Jüngel, "is linked to his or her sinful self by nothing but the creative Word of God. Apart form this Word, nothingness holds sway between the *homo peccator* [sinner] and the *homo iustus* [justified person]. Indeed, the *homo peccator* has to be lost in this nothingness, if and when God declares a person to be righteous."[8] God is the one who "destroys" and "tears down" what exists and "makes out of nothing" the person who is justified; out of death comes life (cf. Matt 10:39; 16:25; Mark 8:35; Luke 9:24; 17:33). Therefore, for Luther, and subsequently for Jüngel, God is *the* "efficient cause"[9] of justification/the making righteous of the unrighteous person.[10]

The doctrine of justification by faith and the doctrine of creation out of nothing are only readily apparent from the lens of the Cross, a lens through

---

7. Ibid., 106–7.

8. Ibid., 107.

9 This reference of Luther's "efficient cause" refers to Aristotle. Specifically, Aristotle's *De Generatione Animalum,* "There are four causes underlying everything: first, the final cause, that for the sake of which a thing exists; secondly, the formal cause, the definition of its essence (and these two we may regard pretty much as one and the same); thirdly, the material; and fourthly the moving principle or efficient cause. . . ."Aristotle, "De Generatione Animalum," 715a 2–6. And from the *Metaphysics,* "'Cause' means (1) that form which, as immanent material, a thing comes into being, e.g. the bronze is the cause of the statue and the silver of the saucer, and are the classes which include these. (2) The form or pattern, i.e. the definition of the essence, and the classes which include this (e.g. the ratio 2:1 and number in general are causes of the octave), and the parts included in the definition. (3) That from which the change or the resting from change first begins; e.g. the adviser is a cause of the action, and the father is a cause of the child, and in general the maker a cause of the thing made and the change-producing of the changing. (4) The end, i.e., walking. For 'Why does one walk?' we say; 'that one may be healthy'; and in speaking thus we think we have given the cause" Aristotle, "Metaphysics," 1013a 24–35.

10 Jüngel, "The World as Possibility and Actuality," 107.

which Aristotle was not working. That God is the "efficient cause" of the justification of the sinner is only revealed in his wrath by the judgment of the law—which itself is only revealed by the event of the cross and by faith. In the judgment of the law, God gives up sinners to themselves and their sin (this is a curse). In this handing over (or being handed over) to the judgment of the law, the sinner is left alone in a sham existence (sin). Therefore, the *being* of the sinner is not a true being but an "illusory appearance of being" because sin is the lack of relation (the sinner has been handed over—which designates a break in the relation between God and the person). The sinner is one who is without relation, specifically without relation with God and without relation with her own self (since the sinner's relation to self is a relation to death, because it lacks the relation to God, and since God has handed the sinner over to death by the Law). In order to truly "find oneself," the *self* must come from outside the self and not from the self; "the self cannot realize or actualize the self." The non-relationality, the nothingness that comes from being not in relation, is less than the negative nothingness from which God first created the world (because it leads to death and death is where there is no possibility or there is impossibility). "As the loss of relation it is as it were the more pronounced form of this *nihil negativum: nihil nihilans* [the nothingness which negates]."[11] This inability to self-actualize is not readily apparent metaphysically. My need for an-*other* to actualize myself does not make "sense" apart from revelation and proclamation.

In contrast to Aristotle's belief that I am the operating subject of my actualization, the cross event, the gospel of the justification of sinners, says that I, in fact, am not only not the subject, but even if I wanted to be the subject, I cannot be since my will is not free to do so. In addition, the "nothingness which negates" is not evident apart from faith because it is "celebrated under the illusory appearance of being"; in other words, the nothingness which negates is not revealed or witnessed to apart from the Gospel, and that only in retrospect:

> Only in the one who knew no sin and yet was made sin for us
> (1 Cor. 5:21) is the sinner revealed in relationlessness and sin.
> That Jesus Christ was made sin for us by God means that the
> *destruere et in nihilum redigere* [destruction and tearing down]
> which is enacted in and with our sin is revealed in Jesus Christ,
> as he and he alone dies the accursed death which we live. Jesus'
> death on the cross is grace, since it reveals that in the midst of
> life we are in death. He makes manifest the nothingness which
> the sinner celebrates under the illusory appearance of being. Or

11 Ibid., 108.

at least Jesus' death on the cross reveals this when we allow it to speak for itself (that is, according to the law).[12]

It is by the event of the cross that we know that we are in fact dead; the cross is the manifestation of Grace and of the fulfillment of the Law—to the fullest extent of the law, Jesus suffered and died for us. In seeing this man, who knew no sin, die for us, in our stead, we are made aware of the lack of our life, that our life is the nothingness which negates because the cross has revealed that we are in fact not in relation to God; that we have been handed over to ourselves and, thus, to death. The cross exposes the "illusory appearance of being" that is the sinner's existence. But, also, the cross is the door by which we enter into relationship with God by faith in that Jesus died for us, as a perfect propitiation for our sins (cf. Rom 3:25; Heb 2:17; 1 John 2:2; 4:10).

And the cross does not merely speak for itself, but is also the "proclamation of the lordship of the risen one."[13] The gospel is the word of the cross; in that Jesus died he also is risen; thus the gospel is the proclamation of the one who died, who is risen, and the one who is known as the one who is crucified. In this way the cross (and the gospel) is the event of the love of God. "Jesus' resurrection from the dead promises that we shall be made anew out of the nothingness of relationalness, remade *ex nihilo*, if through faith in the creative Word of God we allow ourselves to participate in the love of God which occurs as the death of Jesus Christ. In this sense, Christian existence is *existence out of nothingness*, because it is all along the line existence out of the creative power of God who justifies."[14] The event of the cross causes the sinner simultaneously to be made aware that he is a sinner but also that, by faith, he is created anew. In seeing the event of the cross and being made aware of his sham existence ("Justification") the sinner dies to the self (he cannot die to himself until he is made aware of his sham existence); also, in the event of the cross and in being made aware of this sham existence he is made to die to himself, and thus to rise anew with Christ, created out of nothing since the former existence, the former person who was brought to death. Thus, writes Jüngel, "*Media vita in morte sumus*—in the midst of life we are in death—but even more; *media morte in vita sumus*, in the midst of death we are in life."[15]

12 Ibid.

13 Ibid.

14 Ibid., 108–9.

15 Ibid., 109.

POSSIBILITY AND IMPOSSIBILITY

To further Jüngel's argument against Aristotle's emphasis of the ontological priority of actuality over possibility, and its implications for the doctrine of justification and the doctrine of creation out of nothing, there needs to be clarification about the meaning of the possible and how it relates to these two. According to Jüngel, *ex nihilo create* is held against Aristotle's understanding of actuality. From what Jüngel is saying, it seems that, according to Aristotle, the world does not contain "nothingness." In a sense, "coming to be" and "passing away" cannot, for Aristotle, contain nothingness; they must contain *being*; *ex nihilo create* is a foreign concept. So, to speak in terms of actual and possible (which can also be spoken of as "change" leading to actuality), is also to say the actual and the not-yet-actual. In the event of justification, the "absolutizing" of the world in terms of actual and non-actual is challenged because, through the resurrection of the dead, there is established by theology a dimension to the world that is "nothingness" (and not simply not-yet-actualized), for there is creation out of nothing in resurrection. "Theology must establish that the radical nothingness of Good Friday is the other dimension of the being of this world."[16] And all of this understanding of radical nothingness is to refocus the axiom on God as creator out of nothing and not an attempt to create an abstracted ontology of nothingness. To establish the radical nothingness that is explicit in the Good Friday event, theology realizes the dichotomy that exists between the possible and the impossible over and against the actual and the not-yet-actual.

It is unique to the doctrine of justification and to the doctrine of the creation out of nothing to have the distinction between possible and impossible rather than the actual and not-yet-actual. In the concept of the actual and not-yet-actual lies the possibility of something, of being (as stated above). According to Jüngel, possibility's orientation toward actuality implies *change*, which is dependent upon *being* already being present. According to Jüngel, one could say that life (creation) out of death (nothingness) is too foreign a concept for Aristotle's worldview; life comes from there being a possibility for life, not an impossibility for life (nothingness; death). In this way, Jüngel uses the terms possibility and impossibility over and against actual and not-yet-actual, and, thus, heightens the uniqueness of the gospel message and the event of the cross. The gospel speaks in terms of possible and impossible rather than actual and not-yet-actual.

16 Ibid., 110.

To explain Jüngel's concepts of possible and impossible is to also speak about God, humanity, and truth as opposed to what is *actual*.[17] In this way, the distinction between the possible and the impossible is first and foremost about the distinction between God and humanity/the world and, thus, is more fundamental in terms of the gospel message and the doctrine of justification and the doctrine of creation out of nothing. "[I]n the distinction between God and the world, we are not concerned primarily with actuality, but with truth. Of course, God and the World are not distinguished in such a way that the world is identified with the possible and God with the impossible. Rather, distinguishing the possible from the impossible is a matter for God."[18] Taken a step further, humanity cannot declare what is possible and impossible; this is left to God's judgment alone. Therefore, you and I are not the judge of when another is a "lost cause," hopeless, or if it is an impossible situation for this person to come to faith. If we follow this line of thought then it might be argued that something like the death penalty is humanity deciding when someone is beyond hope, *impossible*; this alone is not a decision for us to make, rather it belongs solely in the hands of our God. Jüngel's discussion about the possible and impossible is a discussion about what is properly God's activity toward us; *with God, anything is possible.*

In the event of justification and the event of creating out of nothing, God makes himself known to the world as distinguished from the world yet related (God's being is in his becoming), and in this event something is known about the world not yet related. By the event of the Word, the world is brought to death (nothingness) and brought into life through resurrection (out of nothingness). To this world, God has spoken a promise, and that promise is characterized as possible; that which God has deemed impossible ceases.

> Making the possible to be possible and the impossible to be impossible is the business of the *Word*; in the event of the Word, God both distinguishes himself from and relates to the world. In the face of the actuality which perpetuates that which is real and which, even in 'making the future' only changes what is actual, the event of the Word of God lets the possible become possible and hands over to perish that which has become impossible. This means: by distinguishing between the possible and the impossible, the Word of God occurs as a word of promise and judgment.[19]

17 Ibid., 111.
18 Ibid.
19 Ibid., 113.

Promise is correlated to the possible and judgment is correlated to the impossible. It might also be said in terms of "yes" and "no"; that which is "yes" is possible, and that which is "no" is relegated to the impossible and ceases.

In this way, creation is fully dependent on the creative Word of God; it exists and is because God has said "yes." In a sense, one could say that the event of the word (the event of the cross and the justification of sinners which is, simultaneously, the creation out of nothing) is the restatement of the creation of the world established in Genesis (Gen. 3:31a: "And God saw everything that he had made, and behold, it was very good"). That to which God says yes, exists; in the event of the word toward the world, he may well have said, "it is good," too.

As the world is brought into being out of nothingness by the event of the Word, it is given a history; and with a history, the world is given a future within history (a promise). "The promise which constitutes the being of the world as history implies that history is gained as it is snatched from nothingness. This means, further, that the promise stands 'in a demonstrable contradiction to the historic reality [*Wirklichkeit*]. This has its grounds in the indissoluble unity of grace and judgment manifested in Christ, according to which *ex nihilo facere* [to make out of nothing] implies *in nihilum redigere* [to reduce to nothing]."[20]

In the event of justification, the sinner is brought to nothingness (death) by the divine "No"; in that the divine "No" brings the sinner (actual) to nothingness (death), the person is brought out of nothingness into being (resurrection into life) by the creative, divine "Yes" of the event of justification. In this death into life (creation out of nothing) event of justification, lies the "justified person's" (i.e. the sinner's) hope in nothing but the Word of God because the Word of God is the *efficient cause* of the justified person's life: her history and her hope for a future.

Thus, by faith (faith in the word of the cross), believers "share" in the distinction—God's distinction—between the possible and the impossible ("All things are possible for him who believes"—Mark 9:23). Through the believer's sharing in the distinction by which God relates to the world (the distinction between the possible and impossible), "the world exists as God's creation beyond the dimension of actuality."[21] In that the world is brought to nothingness in Jesus Christ, it is brought out of nothingness (death) and into new life and is considered *creation*. (Thus, for Jüngel, to be "saved" would be to be brought into death and out of death into life.) The world is active, but as *creation* (creation out of nothing, fully dependent on the Word

---

20. Ibid., 114. Jüngel is referring to Moltmann, *Theology of Hope*, 118.
21. Jüngel, "The World as Possibility and Actuality," 115.

of God) it is indispensably and irreplaceably passive. "[W]ithout [passivity] it would not be possible 'to conform ourselves to the image and example of Christ, our King and Lord who began with the active life but whose life was consummated in passion.'"[22] But even prior to the passion, is God's love (John 3:16). Essentially, according to Jüngel, there is a very present actuality of the world that causes us to be active; however this activity, this actuality is not prior to, nor to be considered superior to, the passive. By first being passive, the world is made to be active; by first being passive, the world (including ourselves) is conformed to the image of Christ.

CONCLUSION: IMPLICATIONS

In this way, the ontological priority of possibility over actuality is demonstrated. When the possible is made possible and the impossible to be impossible, there is a starting point; it is God's love which makes that which is possible *possible*; and by creating that which is possible to be possible, that which is impossible is simultaneously made to be impossible (this would be the same thing as saying, when one says "yes" to something, that one simultaneously says "no" to something else). Thus, as Jüngel writes, "In the very concept of creation it is essential to set God's love over against his omnipotence. God's omnipotence concerns actuality, God's love concerns possibility. God's love concerns the being which is in becoming."[23] Thus, possibility cannot be defined by actuality because they are both, as has been demonstrated by Jüngel, facets of being which are dependent on the fact that God's "free" love makes that which is possible ontologically prevalent over that which is actual according to God's omnipotence. And since God's "free" love has precedence over His omnipotence, actuality is oriented toward the possible (God's love) rather than the actual. In other words, we *act* because we have been loved, and since we have been loved we love and have hope, and in having hope and being loved our actions are oriented toward Him who loved us first (cf. 1 John 4:19). Our activity is directed toward a future that has arrived out of the past; this is not so with God. God's love makes that which is possible *possible* from the outside; specifically, as is revealed in the event of the word toward which the world's actuality is directed. The event of the Word is the future colliding with us, and in that collision, we have been given a past.

Possibility having priority over actuality is the very reason why forgiveness is as powerful as it is. Forgiveness is an actual statement; yet, it is

22. Ibid., 115–16. Jüngel is quoting Luther, WA/5.166.12f.

23 Ibid., 116.

an actual statement that is oriented toward the possible. In that God has *actually* forgiven me and separated my sins from me as far as East is from West, I am given possibility (actuality is oriented toward possibility). While Jüngel himself does not directly contend with the idea that "forgiveness" is the act that is oriented toward possibility, I do believe that this is a viable aspect of this concept.

Oriented toward this possibility as it pertains to humanity is that we, in conjunction with being hearers of the Word of the gospel, are forgiven; this is something unique for what it means for you and me to be human. Animals will always behave like animals; they neither need forgiveness for their works nor do they need to be separated from them. I, however, do; we do. By Jesus' work on the Cross I am *actually* forgiven (and radically so) and those works have *actually* been forgotten, and in this, there is room and space and time that is granted to me to move and change (not of my self will, but by the movement of the Word toward me and with me). And if this is the power of God's love toward me, and if in this love I am caused to love others, then the primacy of forgiving (alongside proclamation of the gospel) is the action that is oriented toward the possible by which I give another that *chance*. (Thus, when Paul says that they will know us by our love, one could easily say, "They will know us by our forgiveness.")

Concurrently, in hearing the declaration and statement about me in the proclamation of the gospel message, I am freed *to ask* for forgiveness. Because the doctrine of the justification of sinners separates me from my works and I am no longer defined by my deeds (good or bad), I am given the freedom to say, "I was wrong," and to ask for forgiveness. The shame and guilt of my wrong-doing do not have the final word (though I may and probably will feel both shame and guilt when I harm and hurt someone else). My shame and guilt have been subjected to the event of the cross; and by that event I am declared to be apart from my deeds and misdeeds. I know that I fail (and have failed) the law and that I cannot be perfect, that I have wronged God and that I have wronged others. The gospel illuminates this reality and leads me through sure death into new life. That new life is continually marked by my seeking forgiveness when I fail and hurt another, without those misdeeds having a deleterious effect on who I am, (primarily because I am known to myself as forgiven and justified, accounted righteous by God through faith in Jesus Christ). By the proclamation of the gospel of the justification of sinners, I am free to be forgiven and to forgive.

BIBLIOGRAPHY

Aristotle. "De Generatione Animalum." In *The Basic Works of Aristotle*, edited by Richard McKeon, 655–80. New York: Modern Library, 2001.

———. "Metaphysics." In *The Basic Works of Aristotle*, edited by Richard McKeon, 752–77. New York: Modern Library, 2001.

———. *The Nichomachean Ethics*. Translated by Harris Rackham. Wordsworth Classics of World Literature. London: Wordsworth, 1996.

Jüngel, Eberhard. "The World as Possibility and Actuality: The Ontology of the Doctrine of Justification." In *Theological Essays*, edited by J. B. Webster. Edinburgh: T. & T. Clark, 1989.

Moltmann, Jürgen. *Theology of Hope*. Translated by J. Bowden. London: SCM, 1967.

8

Saving Faith Alone

John D. Koch Jr.

In his essay, "Gnosticism, Antinomianism and Reformation Theology," David Yeago writes: "The fundamental misconstrual of the coherence of Christian faith implicit in standard modern accounts of Luther's theology can be described quite simply: it is the assumption that a radical antagonism of law and gospel is the ultimate structuring horizon of Christian belief."[1] The basis for this mistake, he argues, is on account of a privileging of a theological anthropology that is reliant more on nineteenth- and twentieth-century German neo-Kantianism than Luther or the Apostle Paul.[2] The

---

1. Yeago, "Gnosticism, Antinomianism, and Reformation Theology," 38. Yeago is one of a host of Lutheran (as of now) theologians who are attempting a full-scale rejection of placing the distinction between law and gospel at the heart of theological reflection. Cf. Jenson, "God's Time, Our Time"; Root, "The Joint Declaration on the Doctrine of Justification. This argument is in part sympathetic to with the exegetical argument of the "New Perspective on Paul." And, although framed in many different ways, it is the rejection of the gospel as an answer to an existential situation (however conceived) brought about by the law that is the essential argument of the (so-called) New Perspective on Paul, the work of the Finnish Lutheran School, and their respective variants. Although there are many, these two seminal works are well known: Stendahl, "The Apostle Paul and the Introspective Conscience of the West"; Mannermaa, *Christ Present in Faith.*

2. See Yeago, "Martin Luther on Grace, Law, and Moral Life," 2, where he posits that it is the "problem of the troubled conscience" that "take[s] a particular existential situation, the situation of the penitent seeking absolution, as the exclusive interpretative context within which notions such as grace and commandment, law and gospel, are to be understood . . ."

central text supporting this critique is Risto Saarineen's thesis that twentieth century "German Lutheran" theology was unduly influenced by the transcendental philosophy of Herman Lotze,[3] a philosopher who was Kantian in his ontology because he rejected a traditional "substance ontology" in favor of a "relational ontology."[4] Subsequent German Lutherans, following Lotze developed an "ontology" that did not allow for any type of essential participation in God. These German theologians, says Robert Jenson, argue that "one should ignore all ontology found in Luther; faith is purely an act of the will with no ontological implications. Faith as volitional obedience rather than as ontological participation is all that a neo-Kantianized Luther could allow.[5]" Thus one can observe the general outline of the discussion where people are arguing for different conceptions of "ontology" based upon *apriori* theological and philosophical commitments.[6] The point of this essay is not to wade into the nuances of neo-Kantian transcendentalism vs. Aristotelian metaphysics,[7] but, rather, it is an attempt to articulate an "ontology of faith" that captures Jenson's missing "implications" while maintiaing Yeago's "radical antagonism of law and gospel." An "ontology of faith" is constituted by a radical appreciation for the soteriological relationship between anthropology and Christology. In what follows, we will examine why this relationship is necessary and how it is operative in the theology of Paul Zahl. When so conceived, theology becomes the means by which life is deconstructed and interpreted in service of bringing Christ and his mercies to bear on the lives of sinful humans. This is a conception of faith that can allow the living, breathing Apostle Paul to confess without irony, "I have been crucified with Christ"(Gal 2:15), therefore illustrating a life of living

---

3. In particular, Albrecht Ritschl, Wilhelm Herrmann, Karl Holl, Erich Vogelsang, Reinhold Seeberg, Erich Seeberg, Karl Barth, and Ernst Wolf.

4. To the classic study re: "relational ontology," cf. Joest, *Ontologie der Person bei Luther*.

5. Braaten and Jenson, *Union with Christ*, viii-xi.

6. See Bielfeldt, "The Ontology of Deification," where Bielfeldt valiantly, although unpersuasively, tries to "tries to classify and clarify some of the ontological issues connected with the assertion by the Finnish school that there is, for Luther, a 'real-ontic' presence of Christ in the believer . . . [Acknowledging that] Those outside the Mannermaa circle who either staunchly disdain or avidly embrace 'Lutheran deification' often suffer from the same malady: they are not always precisely clear on the claims made by the Finnish research" (ibid., 91). This lack of clarity continues; cf. Olson, "Deification in Contemporary Theology," who gives a good overview of the ways in which deification operates with respect to the "divine energies" in traditional Orthodox theology.

7. For some of the pertinent issues, cf. Westphal, *Overcoming Onto-Theology*; and Stanley, *Protestant Metaphysics after Karl Barth and Martin Heidegger*.

faith for the justified that operates in a way other than substance metaphysics but is, nonetheless, no less real.[8]

SQUARE WORDS FOR ROUND CONCEPTS

Theologically understood, following Luther's rejection of Aristotle,[9] Justification by Faith is not amenable to classical metaphysical nomenclature, because in order to conceive of theology along these lines the subject must remain located along a transition from a *terminus ad quo* to a *terminus ad quem*. As Gerhard Forde observed in his essay "The Law in Lutheran Theology," this is the "Systematic Problem;" the idea of this movement is comprised of: "(a) the infusion of grace, (b) a movement of the free will toward God in faith, (c) a movement of the free will in recoil from sin, and (d) the remission of sin." The result of this thinking, he argues, is that "if justification comes at the beginning of the process, the process is unnecessary; if however, it comes at the end of the process, justification is unnecessary."[10] This ultimate confusion is the logical end of a system that attempts to explicate the significance of the doctrine of Justification by Faith Alone with terms and concepts beholden to classical substance metaphysics, because there is no place for the radical discontinuity between a life of unbelief and a life of faith. This is a discontinuity that the writers of the New Testament could only describe in terms of the "transition" from death to life (cf. Col 2:13) or, following the account of Jesus' interaction with Nicodemus, as having been "born again" (John 3:7). Justification by Faith is neither the starting place *nor* the destination, but the confession of those having been brought to new life out of death. Oswald Bayer explains this relation from the standpoint of the justified:

> He is unable to establish any continuity across this divide, and in virtue of his experience, hitherto, of both world and self, he is not even able to recognize one. Rather, he is created anew and has his identity permanently outside himself, in another, a stranger: in one who has replaced him in a wondrous change and exchange of human sin and divine justice (Gal 2:19 cf.

---

8. As Gerhard Forde would explain, "For Luther the divine imputation of righteousness of Christ's sake meant shattering of all such schemes. Justification therefore does not come either at the beginning or the end of a movement; rather, it establishes an entirely new situation" (Forde, "Forensic Justification and Law in Lutheran Theology," 281).

9. Cf. Luther's "Disputation against Scholastic Theology," in *Luther's Works: Volume 31*, 9–16, among others.

10. Forde, "Forensic Justification and Law in Lutheran Theology," 281.

2 Cor 5:21). With this occurrence of the vicariously atoning death of Jesus Christ, a "canon" (Gal 6:16: referring directly to 6:14f.) of truth (Gal 2:5, 14; 5:7) is given, from whence theology can only be critically disposed toward any philosophy of substance and subject, since such a philosophy permits no thought of an ex-centric being.[11]

In other words, discussions surrounding a particular "ontology" of the Christian person are bound to obscure the radical nature of Justification by Faith because they rely on the ability successfully to articulate the ontological significance of faith on the life of a particular person—the movement from some concept of vice to virtue—rather than the ontological significance of faith itself.[12] The extrinsic nature of faith alone necessitates a new way talking about the human being other than those surrounding "ontology," because the human who is "justified by faith," is created anew in such a way that defies all philosophical rationalization—either metaphysic or post-metaphysical—and, instead, rests on a change in fundamental self-awareness that *confesses* an (as-of-yet unseen! cf. Heb 11:1; 1 Cor 13:12) eschatological reality as having ultimate present importance.

This concept of an "ex-centric being," one that is so crucial to any construal of the Doctrine of Justification by Faith, rests on a distinction between law and gospel, because it is only in this distinction that one can distinguish between the *opus Dei* (the work of God) and *opus hominum* (the work of humans).[13] When these two works are confused, as they are in any theology that does not properly distinguish between law and gospel, then there can be no qualitative discontinuity between the person of unbelief and the person of faith, no "new creation."[14] Instead, the life of faith is understood to be a quantitative move from vice to virtue, from uncleanliness to cleanliness, from the profane to the holy, and this devalues the salvific action of Christ on the Cross by minimizing both the depth of human need on account of sin and the heights of God's love in "sending his only begotten son," to die. Theologically understood, few modern theologians have grasped this es-

11. Bayer, "The Word of the Cross," 47.

12. Cf. Bayer, "The Doctrine of Justification and Ontology."

13. Indeed, writes Christoph Schwöbel, this distinction lies at the heart of Martin Luther's rejection of the medieval Catholic penitential system. Cf. Schwöbel, "A Quest for an Adequate Theology of Grace and the Future of Lutheran Theology," 26. "Luther's general criticism of the medieval doctrines of grace and of the way in which the question of grace is dealt with in the practice of the church is that the distinction between God's work and human work has become blurred and that therefore their relationship cannot be adequately perceived."

14. Cf. 2 Cor 5:17.

sential soteriological relationship between anthropology and Christology as
has Paul F. M. Zahl, to whose work we will now briefly turn.

PAUL ZAHL AND THE GOOD NEWS
OF COMPLETE HELPLESSNESS

In Paul Zahl's *Short Systematic Theology,* he recounts the story of a seminarian
who, when asked to comment on the book *I'm OK, You're OK,* draws a stick
figure of Christ on the cross saying, *If I'm OK and you're OK, then what am I
doing up here?* "The student failed," writes Zahl, "but in the broader view he
passed with flying colors."[15] This anecdote illustrates the intrinsic connection
within the theology of Paul Zahl between anthropology (the doctrine of human beings) and Christology (the doctrine of Christ),[16] because for him, the
two terms are inextricably related not merely on a conceptual level, but on a
confessional level: to say something about either is, for Zahl, something tantamount to a confession of faith. In the interaction between these two concepts
lies the Christian confession of God. He explains:

> We go wrong from the beginning if we start with God in any
> other sense than as known in concrete engagement with uni-
> versal human vulnerability. We go wrong if we start from a god
> who exists detached from our experience of relentless, arbitrary,
> even cruel nature. God cannot exist apart from the Lisbon earth-
> quake of 1755 or Hurricane Mitch in 1998. We also go wrong in
> starting with God in any metaphysical or ontological remove
> from the empirical lives we live in the world. This is because of
> the existence of sin within these empirical lives. *The theme of
> sin, and its verifiability among all sorts and conditions of men and
> women, through all moments of recorded history, prevents us from
> positing a God who exists in any state of his existence apart even
> for a moment or an atom from the problem of sin.*[17]

15. Zahl, *A Short Systematic Theology,* 53–54.

16. Cf. Zahl, "Last Signal to the Carpathia," 2. "If the anthropology is flawed, then
inevitably the soteriology is flawed. If "God don't make no junk," then what need is
there for a Savior? Why did Christ have to die on the Cross, if the need of the human
race were not rooted in our paralysis and inability to help ourselves? The result of an
overly high anthropology is an overly low soteriology. The result of an overly low soteriology is a weak Christology. [emphasis and italics added] If Christ is not a Savior in the
full and plain sense of the word, then He did not have to be God. The whole encounter
of Jesus with the Pharisees in Mark, Chapter Two, when he made a connection between
his divine authority and the forgiveness of sins, ceases to mean anything. High anthropology means low soteriology means inadequate Christology."

17. Zahl, *A Short Systematic Theology,* 6 (emphasis added).

In other words, for Zahl, the relationship between anthropology and Christology must be understood *soteriologically,* meaning that God is *only* known by what he has done in Christ for the world by the cross. Therefore, theology, for Paul Zahl, if it is to be uniquely Christian, is neither metaphysics[18] nor anthropology[19] but, rather, soteriology. Despite the fact that his theology rests on an admittedly anthropocentric base, namely, human self-awareness, it, nevertheless, avoids the pitfalls of anthropomorphizing God or unduly existentializing theology on account of his radical doctrine of Original Sin.[20]

Not only does Zahl stand on the shoulders of Luther in this assertion, his remains a model of how theology is rightly conducted, namely, neither from the "top down or bottom up,"[21] but, rather, emanates out from the Cross alone.[22] According to this perspective, the question posed by the Apostle Paul at the end of Romans 7, "Who will deliver [us],?"[23] is a

18. Cf. Westphal, *Overcoming Onto-Theology*; and Stanley, *Protestant Metaphysics after Karl Barth and Martin Heidegger*.

19. For the classic exposition, cf. Feuerbach, *Essence of Christianity*, 7.

20. These two critiques, i.e., over anthropomorphizing and existentalizing theology, are the common arguments against any theology or theologian that posits a radical discontinuity between the law and gospel. For a seminal example of this critique, cf. Yeago, "Gnosticism, Antinomianism, and Reformation Theology." For a response (and further clarification) cf. Mattes, "The Thomistic Turn in Evangelical Catholic Ethics."

21. Cf. Zahl, *A Short Systematic Theology*, 7. "Christian theology is rightly described as being 'from the bottom up' rather than 'from the top down.' The usual contemporary meaning of the phrase 'from the bottom up' is theology from the vantage point of human experience, through which, partly by observation and partly by analogy, we are able to build up a picture of God, layer by layer. On the other hand, the usual contemporary meaning of the phrase 'theology from the top down' is theology that starts from revealed statements about God from God. God from the top down is over and above and also prior to human experience."

22. For the classic studies, cf. von Loewenich, *Luther's Theology of the Cross*; Forde, *On Being a Theologian of the Cross*.

23. The exegetical arguments surrounding this famous passage are, to my mind, wholly determined by a priori theological commitments, hence the widely divergent views on the issue. For a good overview of the issue, cf. Middendorf, *The "I" in the Storm*; and Dunn, "Romans 7:14–25 in the Theology of Paul." Also, see Koch, *Theological Presuppositions and the Hermeneutics of Romans 7*. As for Zahl, his position is central to this entire theological program. He writes, "we should not accept the popular notion that Romans 7 concerns the 'pre-Christian' human being or 'pre Christian' Paul rather than the 'Christian' human being and the 'Christian' Paul. That particular exegesis, which came back in Protestantism like a scorpion's tail about eighty years ago, does not square with the experience of Christians everywhere and in all times . . . If Paul *cannot* in Romans 7 be softening his over-all teaching on grace—that is, it would be extremely unlikely to believe that he suddenly switched paradigms, not to mention be untrue to life—then he *must not* be softening his teaching here. So Romans 7 has got to concern the Christian as well as the non- or pre-Christian" (Zahl, "Lex Rex," 77).

question forced on every person—Christian and non—and has only one definitive answer.[24] Here we begin to see the relation between Christology and anthropology being worked out with respect to human self-deception and intractable self-destructive narcissism or, in other words, Original Sin. Thus, Thesis I of his *Systematic* reads: Theology is Christology. He explains:

> A theology that is Christology before it is anything else is a theology from the bottom up. It begins with the existence and ministry of Jesus in his own time and space, and it states that it is *entirely agnostic* concerning anything other than what he has given us to know of the essential attributes of God. We do not know God, nor have we seen him. Even Moses, the Law-giver, saw him only "from the back" (Exodus 33:23). Our own subjective visions of God, our personal stories and experiences, are simply whatever they are. They are all tarred by the fact of universal self-interestedness, that is, sin, and by the capricious catastrophes of life that we have experienced. We cannot know God from nature or, most especially, from human nature.[25]

This sin, or "universal self-interestedness," argues Zahl, is what theologians have termed "Original Sin,"[26] and equally affects everyone who has ever lived. Therefore, he explains, this sin is "not an action. This is because sins, sinful actions, spring from sin."[27] On account of this default state of the human being, the subconscious, powerless subjugation to the "psychogenetic characteristic of sin,"[28] we are all "creatures in bondage to sin (i.e., the universal defect of nature), the law (i.e., God's just judgment upon the sins that arise from sin), and death (i.e., the universal judgment upon all, all men and women, who cannot exist in the unmediated presence of God, to die)."[29] Like the Apostle Paul, it is the relationship between these three tyrannies—sin, the law, and death[30]— that drives the soteriological emphasis. The interaction of these two theological concepts—law and sin—with respect to Christ is what shapes his theology as soteriology.

---

24. That this is an enduring theme in Zahl's work is attested to by his first book, *Who Will Deliver Us?*

25. Zahl, *A Short Systematic Theology*, 8.

26. For a study of the history and development of this idea, see Jacobs, *Original Sin*.

27. Zahl, *A Short Systematic Theology*, 54.

28. Ibid.

29. Ibid.

30. Cf. 1 Cor 15:56–57 RSV: "The sting of death is sin, and the power of sin is the law. But thanks be to God, who gives us the victory through our Lord Jesus Christ."

This idea would be further expounded in a 2003 essay for *Anglican Theological Review* titled "*Lex Rex*," in which he writes, "The relation of law and grace, or better, the relation of law, sin, and grace, is a core theme in Christian theology . . . [this relation] constitutes, at least for me, the central subject of message of theology."[31] In this essay, he articulates themes that, while particularly familiar to those theologians within the Lutheran tradition, are notably absent from serious theological discourse within his own Anglican tradition. The glaring lack of substantive engagement with any of his theological points in a response by Kelly Brown-Douglas[32] in the same issue is a case-in-point. Needless to say, this affinity with Luther has something to do with Zahl's doctoral research on Ernst Käsemann under the supervision of Jürgen Moltmann in Tübingen; however, and unlike the "response" by Brown in the same issue of *Anglican Digest*, the provocative nature of Zahl's argument rests in the fact that he maintains that the theology he expounds is not "Lutheran," but, rather, the actual message of the gospel itself. That Luther articulates something similar is due, one would imagine Zahl arguing, more with the fact that they both correctly understand the "central subject or message of theology" than it does with subscription to a particular theological school. For Zahl, as for Luther, it is this relationship between law, sin, and grace that requires the entire subject matter of theology to be framed in soteriological terms. As Oswald Bayer has observed, the subject of theology proper is not the general "study of God," or even, as Calvin so framed it, "the knowledge of God and knowledge of ourselves," but rather, the living relationship between the *deus iustificans et homo peccator*—the justifying God and the sinful human.[33]

It is not the coupling of human self-awareness with the knowledge of God that is unique to Luther's insight, but his addition of what Bayer terms the "intolerably narrow" verbal adjectives of "justifying" and "sinful." It is not merely that the knowledge of God and the knowledge of the self stand in dialectical reciprocity, but that God is *known* and confessed in relation to the *sinful* human as the *justifying* God.[34] With this, Luther was unearthing an insight into Original Sin that sees it fundamentally as unbelief, as "sup-

31. Zahl, "Lex Rex," 75.

32. Cf. Brown-Douglas, "A Response to Paul F. M. Zahl, Lex Rex."

33. Compare the two statements concerning the *subiectum theologiae*: Luther: "*Et ita cognitio dei et hominis, ut referatur tandem ad* deum iustificantem et hominenm peccatorem, *ut proprie sit subiectum Theologiae homo reus et perditius et deus iustificans vel salvator*," WA 40 II 327f. And Calvin: *Tota fere sapientiae nostrae summa, quae vera demum ac solida sapientia censeri debeat, duabus partibust constatat*, Dei cognitione et nostri." Inst. I, 1, 1. (emphasis added) quoted in Bayer, *Theologie*, 163–64.

34. Ibid.

pression of the truth" as the Apostle Paul would write in Romans (cf. Rom 1:18–23). Therefore, Original Sin is not something external to the human condition, as if it could be quantified by degree, but, rather, is something qualitative, an *intrinsic* condition of the heart from which flows human action (cf. Matt 5:17–18). In his preface to the book of Romans, Luther explains: "And the Scriptures look especially into the heart and single out the root and source of all sin, which is unbelief in the inmost heart. As, therefore, faith alone makes a person righteous, and brings the Spirit and pleasure in good outward works, so unbelief alone commits sin, and brings forth the flesh and pleasure in bad outward works, as happened to Adam and Eve in paradise, Genesis 3."[35]

In other words, for Luther, it is no surprise that people do sinful things, because it is by nature, from the heart, that actions flow; therefore, a determining factor in coming to an awareness of sin is first coming not to an awareness of God, but, rather, to an awareness of self. This way of formulating theology has a necessary subjectivistic character, but it is not *essentially* subjectivistic, because the two subjects of theology, humans and God, stand in a reciprocity that exists within set parameters, namely, one in which one is the justifier and one is in need.

We began this essay with a brief discussion of the contemporary arguments against a "radical antithesis between law and gospel" that views a rejection of "ontological participation" as hopelessly subjective. However, as we have argued, this concern, while valid, is not necessarily the case when one views the theological task as the reflection on the relationship between sin, law and grace. In this light, the "ontological change" becomes the objective confession of the awareness of genuine need, which, while not relying on participation, is nevertheless quantitatively real in that human identity is now conceived of as extrinsic rather than essential; it is extrinsic to oneself by the confession of Christ alone. Paul Zahl, with his unwavering commitment to the total inability of human beings to save themselves, has modeled a way forward in which the purity of the gospel proclaimed for sinners, and

---

35. Luther, *Luther's Works: Volume 35*, 369. This idea is echoed in his commentary on Genesis: "It is true that Eve picked the fruit first; but before she did this, she sinned through her idolatry and fell from the faith. As long as faith is in the heart, it rules and directs the body; but when it has departed from the heart, the body is the servant of sin. Therefore the fault does not lie in the sex but in the weakness common to both woman and man" (*Luther's Works: Volume 2*, 30). This "remarkable definition" of Luther's, argues Lubomír Batka, "is necessary for the proper understanding of the Bible and the successful study of theology. Already here becomes clear also the practical impact of doctrinal thinking. Weak teaching on original sin not only leads to weak teaching on justification, but it also makes impossible the understanding of Scripture." Batka, "Original Sin," 2. See also: Batka, *Peccatum radicale*.

only for sinners, actually takes those who would never, by their own natural faithlessness, confess such a thing and turns them into those whose new and darker ontological awareness evokes a confession of saving faith in the God who justifies the ungodly.

BIBLIOGRAPHY

Batka, Lubomír. "Original Sin: A Comparison of Luther and Melanchthon." Evanjelická teologická fakulta Univerzity Komenského.

————. *Peccatum radicale: Eine Studie zu Luthers Erbsündenverständnis in Psalm 51* Frankfurt: Lang, 2004.

Bayer, Oswald. "The Doctrine of Justification and Ontology." *Neue Zeitschrift für systematische Theologie und Religionsphilosophie 4* 43/1 (2001) 44–53.

————. *Theologie.* Handbuch systematischer Theologie 1. Gütersloh: Gütersloher, 1994.

————. "The Word of the Cross." *Lutheran Quarterly* 9 (1995) 47–55.

Bielfeldt, Dennis. "The Ontology of Deification." In *Caritas Dei: Beiträge zum Verständnis Luthers und der Gegenwärtigen Ökumene: Festschrift für Tuomo Mannermaa zum 60. Geburtstag.* Helsinki: Luther-Agricola-Gesellschaft, 1997.

Braaten, Carl E, and Robert W. Jenson. *Union with Christ: The New Finnish Interpretation of Luther.* Grand Rapids: Eerdmans, 1998.

Brown-Douglas, Kelly. "A Response to Paul F. M. Zahl, Lex Rex." *Anglican Theological Review* 85 (2003) 83–86.

Dunn, James D. G. "Romans 7: 14–25 in the Theology of Paul." *Present Truth Magazine* 31/8 (1977) 41–54.

Feuerbach, Ludwig. *Essence of Christianity.* New York: Harper, 1957.

Forde, Gerhard O. "Forensic Justification and Law in Lutheran Theology." In *Justification by Faith: Lutherans and Catholics in Dialogue,* edited by H. George Anderson, T. Austin Murphy and Joseph A. Burgess, 278–303. Minneapolis: Augsburg, 1985.

————. *On Being a Theologian of the Cross: Reflections on Luther's Heidelberg Disputation, 1518.* Grand Rapids: Eerdmans, 1997.

Jacobs, Alan. *Original Sin: A Cultural History.* New York: HarperOne, 2008.

Jenson, Robert W. "God's Time, Our Time—an Interview with Robert W. Jenson." *The Christian Century* 123/9 (2006) 31–35.

Joest, Wilfried. *Ontologie der Person bei Luther.* Göttingen: Vandenhoeck & Ruprecht, 1967.

Koch, John. *Theological Presuppositions and the Hermeneutics of Romans 7.* Trinity School for Ministry, 2007.

Loewenich, Walther von. *Luther's Theology of the Cross.* Minneapolis: Augsburg, 1976.

Luther, Martin. *Luther's Works: Volume 2.* Edited by Jaroslav Pelikan and Daniel E. Poellot. Luther's Works. St. Louis: Concordia, 1960.

————. *Luther's Works: Volume 31.* Edited by Harold J. Grimm and Helmut T. Lehmann. Philadelphia: Fortress, 1957.

————. *Luther's Works: Volume 35.* Edited by E. Theodore Bachmann. Philadelphia: Fortress, 1960.

Mannermaa, Tuomo. *Christ Present in Faith: Luther's View of Justification.* Edited and introduced by Kirsi Stjerna. Minneapolis: Fortress, 2005.

Mattes, Mark C. "The Thomistic Turn in Evangelical Catholic Ethics." *Lutheran Quarterly* 16 (2002) 65–100.

Middendorf, Michael Paul. *The "I" in the Storm: A Study of Romans 7*. St. Louis: Concordia Academic, 1997.

Olson, Roger E. "Deification in Contemporary Theology." *Theology Today* 64 (2007) 186–200.

Root, Michael. "The Joint Declaration on the Doctrine of Justification: A Lutheran Systematic Theological Perspective." In *Rereading Paul Together: Protestand and Catholic Perspectives on Justification*, edited by David E. Aune, 60–76. Grand Rapids: Baker Academic, 2006.

Saarinen, Risto. *Gottes Wirken auf Uns: Die Transzendentale Deutung des Gegenwart-Christi-Motivs in der Lutherforschung*. Stuttgart: Steiner, 1989.

Schwöbel, Christoph. "A Quest for an Adequate Theology of Grace and the Future of Lutheran Theology: A Response to Robert W. Jenson." *Dialog* 42/1 (2003) 24–31.

Stanley, Timothy. *Protestant Metaphysics after Karl Barth and Martin Heidegger*. London: SCM, 2010.

Stendahl, Krister. "The Apostle Paul and the Introspective Conscience of the West." *Harvard Theological Review* 56 (1963) 199–215.

Westphal, Merold. *Overcoming onto-Theology: Toward a Postmodern Christian Faith*. New York: Fordham University Press, 2001.

Yeago, David S. "Gnosticism, Antinomianism, and Reformation Theology: Reflections on the Costs of a Construal." *Pro Ecclesia* 2/1 (1993) 37–49.

———. "Martin Luther on Grace, Law, and Moral Life: Prolegomena to an Ecumenical Discussion of *Veritatis Splendor*." *The Thomist* 62 (1998) 163–91.

Zahl, Paul F. M. "Last Signal to the Carpathia." *Anglican Theological Review* 86 (2004) 647–52.

———. "Lex Rex." *Anglican Theological Review* 85 (2003) 75–82.

———. *A Short Systematic Theology*. Grand Rapids: Eerdmans, 2000.

———. *Who Will Deliver Us?: The Present Power of the Death of Christ*. New York: Seabury, 1984.

9

Three Essential Words

C. FitzSimons Allison

When the writers of the Greek New Testament explained the Gospel, they used three essential words: 1) *dikaiosunē* (righteousness) "what God does for us"; 2) *logizomai* (reckon) "how he has done it"; 3) *parakaleō* (encourage) "how we are empowered to respond." Although these three make clear the fact that the Gospel, the good news, is that God is for us, it is nevertheless almost universally misunderstood, even by church people. This claim may seem extravagant, but all we have to do is to look at the dictionary meanings of the words "preach" and "sermon" to see how distorted God's offer of a relationship with him has become in modern minds—Christian and non-Christian alike.

"Sermon" is defined as: "A discourse (spoken or written) on a serious subject, containing instruction or exhortation. Also *contemptuously*, a long or tedious discourse or harangue."[1] "Preach" is defined as: "To utter a serious or earnest exhortation, esp. a moral or religious one. Now usu. *derogatory*: to give moral or religious advice in a self-righteous, condescending, or obtrusive way."[2] Now lexicographers do not themselves establish what words mean. They merely record how words are actually used and understood in society. Yet, it is virtually impossible to find a single definition that leads one to believe that the preaching of a sermon would be a life-giving

1. *Oxford English Dictionary*, "Sermon, n.".
2. Ibid., "Preach, v."

104

event warmly welcomed by the hearers. Native Americans in Quebec call the wooden stick they use to club salmon to death a "priest." Could there be a more dire judgment on Christian churches than this? Clearly we have failed to teach the good news of the Christian faith and have, rather, reduced the expression of Christianity to tedious scolding. Whose soul does not shrivel up in the absence of the good news?

DIKAIOSUNĒ: WHAT GOD HAS DONE BY HIS RIGHTEOUSNESS

A proper understanding of the biblical word "righteous" can be of immense help in putting the good news back into Christianity. God's righteousness is not merely an aspect of who God is. No, contrary to popular perception, God's character does not set some universal standard for goodness which we then must strive to achieve within us while God passively looks on to see if we can accomplish it. The biblical understanding of the righteousness of God is different. It's not about what we have to do to please God; it is all about what God has done, is doing, and will do for us. In scripture, God's righteousness is the outer, dynamic expression of God's unique inner character. It's the sharing of who God is with us. And who is he? The one by whose actions all things are set right with him and with one another, just as he is right within himself. In Christ, God makes people right, who are not right—not right with him, not right with others, not right with themselves. In Christ, God justifies the ungodly (cf. Rom 5:6).

A young woman once told me that she credited her conversion to hearing a sermon which made clear that God's righteousness was not a passive attribute but a costly and effectual activity. The preacher had used a simple but singularly apt illustration. We would never call a woman a clean housewife because she is so fastidious that she stands aloof from any mess and condemns it as filthy. No, we would call her a clean housewife because she cleans up any dirt and tidies up every mess, even if she has to dive into its very dregs to get rid of it, even if she has to get rather dirty herself as the price of getting her house completely clean. To this young woman, this was nothing short of a life-changing revelation. She had spent all of her life as a conventional church-going person and had only heard about a righteous God who clearly condemned sin but never deigned to be smudged by it himself. She sat absolutely astonished as she realized that God's righteousness is the very opposite of condemnation. Her whole grim picture of God turned right side up, revealing to her God's graciousness to sinners.

Previously, the duties and obligations (laws) of being a wife, mother, and primary school teacher were burdens so increasingly heavy that she was at the point of despair. No matter how hard she tried, she just could not seem to fulfill the many expectations all of these obligations entailed. Yet during the sermon she experienced what Paul wrote in 2 Cor 3:9: "If the ministry that condemns men is glorious, how much more glorious is the ministry that brings righteousness." Paul knew that when Moses introduced the law to the Israelites, his face still glowed with the glory of God, for the law was "holy, righteous, and good" (Rom 7:12). Yet, its ministry was to show the people that they were not like the law, that they were not holy, righteous and good. Their knowing the meaning of just, right, and good does not mean they could act accordingly. They needed more than just information. They needed a change in the very people they were. They needed a savior who would make them right. As Paul put it, the law served as "a schoolmaster to bring us into Christ that we may be justified (righteous) by faith" (trust) (Gal 3:24 KJV).

As the preacher explained to this young woman the true righteousness of God, this young woman found the veil over her eyes being lifted (2 Cor 3:16). At last, she saw the glory of God for who he really was—the God whose very nature is to justify sinners. Now she no longer could stand aloof from him, because she realized God had refused to stand aloof from her. She warmly and willingly entered into a relationship with him.

Sadly, the popular understanding of the words "sermon" and "preach," to say nothing of the Native American priest's club, reminds us that Paul's warning still rings true. Even to this day the same veil remains over the Gospel, and untold numbers of people still do not know the glory of the righteousness of God, which is the very opposite of condemnation. They still think we can earn salvation by their behavior.

LOGIZOMAI: GOD HAS DONE IT

When the law, which has made a veil over our eyes, is lifted and we see the glory of active, operative righteousness received and known by trust in his Son, Jesus Christ, we are now reckoned as righteous. When we perceive and trust that we are seen, treated, and regarded as righteous by almighty God our hearts begin to change and our confidence in his goodness increases. Hence, we can boldly say, "Who is he that condemneth? It is Christ Jesus who died—more than that, who was raised to life—is at the right hand of God and is also interceding for us" (Rom 8:34 NIV). The recognition of this action by God gives us the confidence to trust that "there is now, therefore, no condemnation" (Rom 8:1). Trusting that we have a gracious God is the transforming goodness we know as the Gospel, and it is remarkably different from what the lexicographers tell us is preached in sermons today.

Historically, this gracious reckoning is called imputation, one of the great watchwords of the English Reformation. Richard Hooker (1554–1600) has succeeded in stating the most succinct and economical description of Anglican soteriology. "The righteousness whereby we shall be clothed in the world to come, is both perfect and inherent. That whereby here we are justified is perfect, but not inherent. That whereby we are sanctified, inherent, but not perfect."[3] The perfect righteousness of Christians in this world is the righteousness of Christ imputed, reckoned, regarded, or worded to us. These various English words used to translate *logizomai* have too often obscured the deeper meaning of the term. *Logizomai* is a derivation of the verb form of the Greek word *logos*, which is most recognizable from the prologue to the Gospel of John where John writes, "In the beginning was the Word (*logos*) and the Word was with God and the Word was God . . . And the Word was made flesh, and dwelt among us . . ." (John 1:1–14 KJV). In Christ, God has reckoned us righteous—he has *worded* us—that we may begin to become righteous.

Although clearly set out in scripture, this doctrine has been criticized and rejected by those whose minds are blinded and remain under the veil (cf. 2 Cor 3:14). It is rejected by those who rely on their obedience to the law and labor under the ministry of condemnation. An outrageous example is the article on imputation in the first two editions of *The Oxford Dictionary of the Christian Church*. The entry is as follows:

> IMPUTATION (from Lat. *imputare*, Gk. *logizomai*). In theology, the ascription to a person, by deliberate substitution, of the righteousness or guilt of another. The idea plays an important part in the Lutheran doctrine of Justification by Faith, which asserts that a man is formally justified by the imputation of the obedience and righteousness of Christ without becoming possessed of any personal righteousness of his own. By a legal fiction God is thus held to regard the sinner's misdeeds as covered by the imputation of the sanctity of Christ. This doctrine seeks support in certain passages of St. Paul (notably Rom 3:21–30; Gal. 3:21 f.) and also from St. Augustine. It is opposed both to the traditional Catholic teaching, acc. to which the merits of Christ are not imputed but imparted to man and produce a real change from the state of sin to the state of grace, and to the doctrine of Liberal theologians to the effect that our highest

---

3. Hooker, *Of the Laws of Ecclesiastical Polity, Book 5*, 684.

vocation consists in the following of Christ who is our supreme example.[4]

The article is inexcusably incorrect concerning the Lutheran doctrine that one is justified without becoming possessed of any personal righteousness of his or her own. The Lutheran teaching clearly teaches that the justified do produce good works but before the absolute righteousness of God (*Coram Deo*) those works are as filthy rags. The article also reflects the Roman Catholic accusation that the doctrine of imputation is a legal fiction, meaning that under the Reformation conception of imputed righteousness, those reckoned righteous are only fictitiously so. However, according to the Scriptures, the real legal fiction is the claim of the Council of Trent, and subsequent Roman Catholicism, that at baptism one is infused with inherent, imparted righteousness that is now our own and perfectly satisfies the righteousness of God. So wrote Cardinal Robert Bellarmine of the position of the Council: "We are truly to be made and constituted just by obtaining of inherent righteousness absolute and perfect."[5]

In contrast to the Council of Trent, the Anglican bishop, John Davenant, pointed out that saints have never claimed such righteousness, but on their deathbeds have invariably asked for mercy. "None of them speak of their own inherent righteousness before the divine tribunal, but they fly full of fear to the mercy and acceptance of God in Christ. But if they were willing to stand by their doctrine, they must either depend upon this formal cause, or give up hope of salvation."[6] Fortunately, the revised third edition of the *Oxford Dictionary of the Christian Church* (1997) was able to lift this veil that had for forty years obscured this teaching. The entry reads:

> Imputation. A central aspect of classical Protestant theologies of justification according to which the righteousness of Christ is imputed or reckoned to the believer, despite being extrinsic to his person in order that he may be justified on its basis. This is contrasted with the teaching of the council of Trent, that the believer is justified on the basis of an imparted or infused righteousness, intrinsic to his person. According to classical Protestant theology, the justification of the believer on account of the 'alien righteousness of Christ' is followed immediately by a process of renewal and growth in personal righteousness.

---

4. "Imputation," in Cross and Livingstone, eds., *The Oxford Dictionary of the Christian Church*.

5. De Just. lib. 2 cap.3. quoted in C. FitzSimons Allison, *The Rise of Moralism*, 7.

6. Davenant and Allport, *A Treatise on Justification*, 128.

Support for this doctrine is found in certain passage of St. Paul (notably Rom 4; Gal. 3:21f).[7]

For the church, the most serious issue, one that Richard Hooker highlighted, is the question over which doctrine—imputed or infused righteousness—is the real legal fiction. The teachings of the Council of Trent acknowledge that there are venial sins in regenerate people but they do not have the formal nature of sin.[8] A mortal sin, however, excludes a person from a state of grace and this state can only be restored through the sacrament of Repentance. It follows in this teaching that sin and grace are mutually exclusive and cannot exist together because having been made righteous in baptism, one is sinless until a mortal sin is committed. This claim that Christians are no longer sinners after baptism is, to say the least, an awkward conceit to carry into the New Testament.

Most of the Epistles deal with the issues of Christian sinners. The frictions between Paul and Peter and Barnabas and Silas were no mere academic matters but sin stemming from the yet imperfect righteousness of these early leaders. What's more, the failure to acknowledge that regenerate and justified people are still sinners creates the necessity of an elaborate scheme of rules by which one's innocence can be assured. One of these rules is that only those things done in full knowledge and consent of the will are technically sinful; ignorance, in this case, is sinless bliss. Dom Victor White, a Roman Catholic Dominican, shows us something of the consequences of this teaching.

> This idea of "unconscious sin" is often a difficult one for the moral theologian to grasp. Especially if he has been brought up in the traditions of Post-Reformation Catholicism (after the Council of Trent) he may find it particularly hard to square with his correct notions that mortal sin must be voluntary, performed with full knowledge and consent. But it is a fact that the psyche is much less indulgent to unconscious breaches of its own laws and demands . . . and will revenge itself for their disregard.[9]

He appends this valuable observation: "The exclusive emphasis of later theologians on "full knowledge and consent" can have the unfortunate result of putting a certain premium on unconsciousness, irresponsibility and infantilism."[10] As an obedient Roman Catholic, White must put "unconscious

---

7. "Imputation," in Cross, *The Oxford Dictionary of the Christian Church.*

8. Cf. the fifth session in: Council of Trent and Henry Joseph Schroeder, *Canons and Decrees of the Council of Trent.*

9. Mairet, *Christian Essays in Psychiatr,* 165.

10. Ibid.

sin" in quotation marks because it seems to conflict with the correct notions that, since Trent, mortal sins must have full knowledge and consent. But clearly he feels quite unhappy with this restraint under which spiritual directors and psychiatrists must work to stay in accord with the Church's teaching.

This denial that regenerate Christians are yet sinners leads to many distortions of the gospel. The human condition to which God's reckoning (imputing) is addressed is human bondage. We are not born free. We are born in bondage to our self as center of the world. We use the term "freedom" to mean at liberty, not bound or constrained. But given our self-centeredness, setting us free from any constraints leads not to liberty but to bondage. If a child is set free from the constraints of a playpen, falling down the stairs is a greater bondage. When an adult has no restraints, either external or internal in the form of conscience, he or she becomes a monster. Similarly, any free society without checks or boundaries, rules, and laws, which restrain the wills of individuals and parties, will produce the bondages of anarchy or despotism. The human will is not free, nor will it be, without restrictions, restraints, and rules. Certainly, we all know individuals who, by sudden fame or fortune, have been released from the restraints of hard work or the restrictions of monogamy, yet have entered into even greater personal bondage.

We are doubtless often more free within the limits of duty and rule than in their absence. One of the tasks of parenthood is the domestication of children, and it is not an easy job. Yet, even if successful, domestication is not the same as redemption (freedom). Our natural inclination is to see Christianity as an endeavor to domesticate while losing sight of the hope of true freedom. The domesticators in church history are correct about the need to obey the rules and do what we ought, but rules and laws are themselves unable to change hearts. The bottom line is that we are not free when all restraints are removed, and we are not free while restraints and rules are in place. In biblical language, we are not free without the law nor are we free with the law.

The Gospel speaks to this condition. God has so worded us right by the sacrifice of Christ that our love and gratitude begin to flow from this act. Freedom, according to scripture, argues C.K Barrett, is "nothing other than a synonym for salvation."[11] But the condition which the Gospel addresses is characterized by those whose eyes are yet covered by the veil, who yet believe their freedom, their salvation, lies in obedience to the law, and who fear those who seek freedom from the law. This latter fear produces enmity toward anyone proclaiming the impotence of the law to change our

11. Barret, *The Gospel according to St. John*, 285.

hearts or to bring salvation. Paul Zahl's ministry is an example of the hostility evoked by his conviction that exhorting and rebuking sinful people is vain. Knowing they are in bondage, that they are enslaved, veiled people, he appeals to that grace which alone frees sinners from bondage.

When the words from the pulpit come from one whose eyes are still veiled, they become exactly what the dictionary definitions give us concerning "sermon" and "preach." When pastors and preachers believe that the parishioners who are not behaving as Christians should are free and able to do so, they fail to see their condition as those bound and enslaved and, exhortation, fussing, rebuking, and condemnation follows. The picture of the old revival minister who thus instructed his people by reminding them "Hell ain't full. There's room for you!" is surely correct. That truth may produce fear, but it is impotent until it leads like a schoolmaster to Jesus Christ; while we were yet bound and enslaved sinners, Jesus died for us.

Richard Hooker wisely taught us in the sixteenth century that we cannot possibly forsake sin unless we first begin again to love. In his *Laws of Ecclesiastical Polity*, he wrote, "I therefore conclude, that fear worketh no man's inclination to repentance, till somewhat else have wrought in us love also."[12] This "somewhat else" is nothing less than *logizomai*, the reckoning us just by the righteousness of Christ which he does in order to free (save) us from sin.

St. Paul has another way of putting this grace of freedom (salvation), in Galatians chapter 3. In effect, he is asking, "who came first—Abraham or Moses?" He addresses the still-veiled Judaizers and points out that those who believed and trusted in God as Abraham did were heirs of the promise by him who came centuries before the law came with Moses. Therefore, the law's obedience comes after the promise: Abraham came before Moses. This reckoning (imputation) that sinners have received is the continuing work of Christ.

PARAKALEŌ:
THE EMPOWERMENT OF ENCOURAGEMENT

We now come to the third essential word in the Christian good news: *parakaleō*. It is especially important in translating Isa 40:1, "Comfort ye my people," 2 Cor 1:3–7, where it is used ten times in five verses, and in Second Corinthians, where it is used five times in four verses. In addition to these important passages, it appears throughout the Gospels and is especially significant in Acts 9:31, which reads, "so the church throughout all Judea and

12. Hooker et al., *The Works of Mr. Richard Hooker*, vi, iii,3.

Galilee and Samaria had peace and was built up and walking in the fear of the Lord and in the comfort of the Holy Spirit it was multiplied." For this Greek word, various translations use the English words: advocate (New Living Translation) comforter (KJV), and counselor (RSV and NIV), but the word, as used throughout the New Testament, always has the connotation of encourager or comforter.

The Epistle to the Romans is a unique illustration of the importance of properly understanding the meaning of this word and its implications for St. Paul's pattern of ministry. As demonstrated by the dictionary definitions above, Christianity is often perceived as starting in the 12th chapter where there are some 43 exhortations in only 21 verses. However, one can never forget that these exhortations follow 11 previous chapters that contain only three exhortations (Rom 6:11–13). The remainder of the first 11 chapters of Romans amounts to simple declaratory assertions: statements about God, his Son Jesus Christ, the Gospel, the righteousness of God revealed from faith to faith, the judgment against sin, none is righteous, no condemnation for those in Christ Jesus, and God has consigned all men to disobedience that he may have mercy on all.

Only after exhausting the proclamation of what God has done for the world in Christ does he write, "I appeal to you therefore . . ." and begins the many exhortations that were remarkably absent in the first eleven chapters. Starting with chapter 12, rather than chapter 1, logically assumes we are free to fulfill the exhortations without the prior grace of knowing we have not a God of condemnation but a gracious God of encouragement and comfort, the Holy Spirit among us. Even the first verse of chapter 12 has the word *parakaleō* translated appeal (RSV), plead (NLT), urge (NIV, beseech (KSV). A better translation might be, "I encourage you therefore . . ." We have seen that *parakaleō* can sometimes be translated exhort and, of course, some exhorting can be encouraging, but that English word can too easily slip into hortatory demands rather than true encouragement.[13]

It is from God the Father that we learn that the righteousness of God (*dikaiosunē*) is not passive but is his action in making us right. It is God, the Son, whose reckoning applies the noncondemning righteousness to us. And it is God, the Holy Spirit, who encourages and enables us to respond. This is the Holy Spirit whose very name is Paraclete, who works as the living spirit of the Triune God. The active effective righteousness of God, the opposite

---

13. To change the mood of *parakaleō* from declaratory to imperative is, in the grammatical sense, to change the spirit from Gospel back into Law, to a law that we are unable to obey and by which we are yet in condemnation. Cf. "The exhortation is distinguished from a mere moral appeal by this reference back to the work of salvation as its presupposition and basis," Schmitz, "*parakaleō*," 795.

of condemnation, is the work of the Father; the reckoning that is saving us from sin is by Christ; and the encouragement that enables our response is the Holy Spirit. Embodied in her very Gospel message, there is no Christian church that is not a Trinitarian church.

The power of the Spirit can be seen all around us. In organizations such as Alcoholics Anonymous, people are encouraged, not with their own comfort, but with the comfort with which they themselves were comforted. This is especially true of an endeavor called "Compassionate Friends." Some have had terrible experiences like losing a child through leukemia or suicide. As they had been encouraged by the Holy Spirit by the care and comfort of others to trust again, to hope again, they were then able to comfort others in a similar way. Any minister who has never been addicted to alcohol or lost a child to suicide needs the ministry of such compassionate friends to help him or her see inside the pain of those who are so afflicted. This, above all, in infinite wider circles of encouragement, is the very nature of the church.

Too often we miss the need of encouragement all around us, especially in our leaders. St. Paul would have seemed too tough-skinned to need encouragement, having suffered through shipwrecks, stoning, beatings with rods, etc.; nevertheless, he writes, "Our flesh had no rest, but we were troubled on every side, without were fightings, within were fears" (2 Cor 7:5 KJV). Then he tells of God's comfort to him through Titus who had been comforted by the congregation at Corinth. The encouragement he received from Titus was not merely Titus' comfort but that which Titus, himself, had received. It should be no wonder that John's Gospel names this comfort the "Holy Spirit."

During my first year as Rector of Grace Church in New York, the city went bankrupt and half of my vestry moved uptown or out of town and I spent a great deal of time in a New York hospital. Thankfully, and by God's great mercy, I had a Paul Zahl as a Titus, who though a curate, was an incomparable encouragement to me. He has gone on in his ministry with a compassionate eye toward human bondage, in the knowledge that what enslaved people need is not scolding, but the constant, gentle, and consistent encouragement with which he has been encouraged.

BIBLIOGRAPHY

Allison, C. FitzSimons. *The Rise of Moralism*. New York: Seabury, 1966.

Barret, C. K. *The Gospel according to St. John*. London: SPCK, 1956.

Cross, F. L., editor. *The Oxford Dictionary of the Christian Church*. Oxford: Oxford University Press, 1997.

Cross, F. L., and Elizabeth A. Livingstone, editors. *The Oxford Dictionary of the Christian Church*. London: Oxford University Press, 1974.

Davenant, John, and Josiah Allport. *A Treatise on Justification*. London: Hamilton, Adams, 1844.

Hooker, Richard. *Of the Laws of Ecclesiastical Polity, Book 5*. Cambrige, MA: Belknap, 1977.

Hooker, Richard, John Gauden, Izaak Walton, and Walter Travers. *The Works of Mr. Richard Hooker*. London: Printed by Thomas Newcomb for Andrew Crook, 1666.

Schmitz, Otto. *"parakaleō."* In *Theological Dictionary of the New Testament*, edited by Gerhard Kittel and Gerhard Friedrich, 5:773–99. Translated by G. W. Bromiley. Grand Rapids: Eerdmans, 1967.

Mairet, Philip. *Christian Essays in Psychiatry*. New York: Philosophical Library, 1956.

Oxford English Dictionary. Oxford University Press.

Trent, Council of, and Henry Joseph Schroeder. *Canons and Decrees of the Council of Trent: Original Text with English Translation*. St. Louis: Herder, 1941.

10

Justification by Faith
A Radical Doctrine

GEORGE CAREY

IN SEVERAL ARTICLES ON the Internet in 2005, Fr. Alvin Kimel, a former Anglican priest who became a Roman Catholic, stated his admiration of Dr. Paul Zahl, yet also his antipathy to his theology.[1] He narrates why now, as a Catholic, he is no longer able to agree with Paul's theology of justification by faith and in the course of his examination speaks of a "Zahlian iconoclasm." By this he means Dr. Zahl's rejection of church, sacraments, and incarnation as key elements in the story of salvation. Now, the Paul Zahl I know is easily able to stand up for himself and to show that this is not correct. But it was the word "iconoclasm" that seized my attention. It is obviously the wrong word. The man I have known for over thirty-five years has never been an iconoclast, but he has been, and is, a radical theologian and teacher. Through his scholarship, his interest in art, in modern music, and in penetrating comments on writers as diverse as Stephen King and Proust, he has followed the trail of justification down to the roots of human behaviour and lost-ness. In this tribute to a man whose friendship I value, I also want to see where justification by faith leads us when we trace its impact on people and church structures today.

---

1. Pontifications. However, in 2011 Fr. Alvin left the RC Church to become an Orthodox priest.

We must begin by reminding ourselves what is at stake here. The story did not start with Martin Luther, important though he undoubtedly was, but with the gospel itself. St. Paul puts it magisterially: "I have been crucified with Christ and I no longer live, but Christ lives in me. The life I live in the body, I live by faith in the Son of God, who loved me and gave himself for me. I do not set aside the grace of God, for if righteousness could be gained through the law, Christ died for nothing" (Gal 2:20).

In that verse, echoed by so many others in the New Testament, St.Paul asserts the forgiveness of salvation by faith through the grace of Jesus Christ and the worthlessness of human endeavour to save oneself. However, it was in the late medieval period that justification by faith was codified as a doctrine that, consequently, rent Europe asunder.

For Martin Luther, this doctrine was the *articulus stantis et cadentis ecclesiae* of the church itself: justification by faith was the absolute center of the Christian faith on which everything else in theology and church depended. Overturned at once was the entire structure of medieval Christianity with its indebtedness to the intrinsic goodness of human beings through grace given at baptism as an "habitus" which was the basis of men and women earning merit. Luther's verdict was stern and uncompromising—there was nothing good in human beings. The Fall affected our lives and natures so fully that we can contribute nothing to our salvation. Through Christ we are saved and we have nothing to boast about. We are *simul iustus et peccator*, at the one and same time righteous and sinners. What Martin Luther and the Reformers started was completed by Pope Leo X on January 3rd 1521 in his bull *Decet Romanum Pontificem* in which Luther and those who identified with him were excommunicated.

At a stroke the unity of Western Christianity was destroyed and the church divided into warring factions. Heirs to this legacy include all Protestant churches. The Thirty Nine Articles of the Church of England puts it clearly: "We are accounted righteous before God, only for the merit of our Lord and Savior Jesus Christ by faith, and not for our own works or deservings."[2]

Over four hundred years have to pass before the matter is considered again in terms and in scholarship compatible with the seriousness of the issue. Hans Küng's doctoral thesis, *Justification: The Doctrine of Karl Barth and a Catholic Reflection*,[3] was to set the ecumenical world alight. As the title suggests, Küng's aim was to investigate the Catholic tradition, and especially that of the Council of Trent's teaching on justification, in the light of Karl Barth's theology. Küng came to the conclusion that "there is a funda-

2. Article 11.

3. Küng, *Justification*.

mental agreement . . . between Karl Barth's position and that of the Catholic Church in regard to the theology of justification seen in its totality."[4] Karl Barth himself was dumbfounded and wrote admiringly to Küng, confessing that he agreed with the conclusion.

Hans Küng's book *Justification* was the start of a fresh inquiry into the doctrine of justification and gave rise to a series of ecumenical studies in which Otto Hermann Pesch's comparison of Martin Luther's doctrine of grace with that of Thomas Aquinas was also groundbreaking. Pesch concludes that, although both theologians have special theological approaches—Luther's is considered "existential" and Aquinas's "sapiental"—there are no substantial differences.[5]

With such substantial studies as that of Küng and Pesch, the stage was set for consideration of theological convergence following the Second Vatican Council, which showed an entirely new Catholic face to other churches and to the world. Absent was the former insularity of Rome and its negativity towards other ecclesial communities. The tone of Vatican II documents was conciliarity, warm and positive. A new dawn beckoned.

It was not long before official delegations representing Reformed churches, with the full authority of their churches behind them, settled down to serious dialogue with the Roman Catholic Church. Four dialogues in particular are noteworthy.

1. The Evangelical Lutheran/Roman Catholic Malta Report (1972) is of significance because, for the very first time, both sides claim that a "consensus" has been reached. From the Catholic side the verdict is given that no conditions are attached to the saving gift of God for believers. On the Lutheran side there is a broadening out of justification by faith, so that the event of justification is not limited to the individual forgiveness of sins, and is no longer seen as a purely external declaration of the sinner as righteous. Rather, through the message of justification, the righteousness of God realised in the Christ event is transferred to sinners as a reality resulting in the foundation of the new life of believers. In this sense justification can be understood as the overall expression of the saving event."[6] In this bold statement the "extrinsic" nature of Lutheranism—beloved by Luther—is laid aside.

2. The Joint Ecumenical Commission of the Evangelical Council in Germany and the German Conference of Bishops (1986) asked the

---

4. Ibid., 277.

5. Pesch, *Theologie der Rechtfertigung*, 948.

6. "Malta Report," par. 27.

question: "Do Doctrinal Condemnations Divide the Churches?" The focus of this joint study was the reciprocal condemnations of the sixteenth century. The answer given is "no" because "the reciprocal statements of repudiation in the sixteenth century no longer apply to today's partner in such a way to divide the Church."[7] We are told that the reason for this conclusion is that both sides have learned to listen to the other in a self-critical way, laying aside the distortions that are often the fruit of bitter conflict.

The document makes a powerful judgement, however, that in my opinion has not been fully considered. It states: "Therefore the doctrine of justification, which takes up this message (the message of God's saving action in Christ) and explicates it, is more than just one part of Christian doctrine. It stands in an essential relation to all truths of faith, which are to be seen as internally related to each other. It is an *indispensable* (italics, mine) criterion which constantly serves to orient all the teaching and practice of our churches to Christ."[8] It is surprising that the radical implications of these sentences have not been explored.

3. The Second Anglican–Roman Catholic International Commission (ARCIC II). This Agreed Statement acknowledges the debt it owes to the Malta Report but it conveys a more distant and cooler attitude towards justification by faith. "The matter played a less crucial role in the English Reformation," we are told. However, that would certainly have not been Cranmer's conclusion as set out in his correspondence with Henry VIIIth.[9] Of greater discomfort for me are statements concerning the word "justification" that I find little support for in Anglican theology of the Reformation period. The Report acknowledges correctly that the Reformers gave this a "declarative" meaning—to "pronounce" righteous, whereas Catholics took it to mean "make righteous." Then, without examining which interpretation is the correct one, the two are elided together with the conclusion that "Justification and sanctification are two aspects of the same divine act (1 Cor 6:11)." This, of course, the Reformers refuted strongly time and again.[10] The paragraph ends: "By pronouncing us righteous, God also makes us righ-

---

7. "Joint Declaration on the Doctrine of Justification," par. 17.

8. Ibid., par. 18.

9. MacCulloch, *Thomas Cranmer*, 208–10.

10. So Carl F. H. Henry writes: "By speaking of justification and sanctification as two aspects of one and the same divine act, [Catholic writers] cloud the fact that the two are clearly distinct and that they are not effected [*sic*] simultaneously" (Henry, "Justification," 60).

teous. He imparts a righteousness which is his and becomes ours."[11] There we have it! Four hundred years of separation of churches and of deep hostility expressed in martyrdom and suffering on both sides— done and dusted so calmly! John McEnroy's cry rings out "You can't be serious!" However, the title of the Report gives it away: *Salvation and the Church*. The moment the Church is put on the same plane as salvation we have an idea where we shall be taken. To this point and its consequences we shall return later.

4. The Joint Declaration on the Doctrine of Justification by the Lutheran World Federation and the Catholic Church (1999). If *Salvation and the Church* disappoints, JDDJ, as I shall call it, is the real thing. It is a thorough consideration of the issues and, for that matter, of far greater significance than its Anglican sister. Paragraph 5 of the Statement summarises: "JDDJ shows that on the basis of their dialogue the subscribing Lutheran churches and the Roman Catholic Church are now able to articulate a common understanding of our justification by God's grace alone through faith in Christ; it does not cover all that either church teaches about justification; it does encompass a consensus on basic truths of the doctrine of justification and shows that the remaining differences in its explication are no longer the occasion for doctrinal condemnations."

This is welcome and encouraging news and, indeed, a close consideration of the document reveals its thoroughness. However, there is an issue concerning the methodology behind the Report that has aroused some concerns. We read: "By appropriating insights of recent biblical studies and drawing on modern investigations of the history of theology and dogma, a 'notable convergence' on justification has occurred between Lutheran and Roman Catholics."[12] Intriguingly, we are never told of what such "insights" consist and can only assume they refer to fruits of biblical scholarship, such as agreement on the meaning of words such as "justification" itself as embodying a forensic meaning.

The Most Rev. Richard Sklba, the Roman Catholic co-Chair of the American national Lutheran–Catholic dialogue, offered the view, "We've found not only a profound sense of agreement on something at the heart of who we are as Christians, but we've also developed a methodology that seems to have worked." He enlarged on the methodology by saying, "We've

---

11. Again, this statement is an elision of Protestant and Catholic formulations in the sixteenth century.

12. "Joint Declaration on the Doctrine of Justification," par. 7.

come to feel comfortable with a statement that says when one group affirms this—whatever the "this" may be, depending on the topic under discussion—that's not necessarily to deny what the other group may be saying about a slightly different approach to the same topic."[13] That worries me somewhat. I can visualize, for example, a married couple disagreeing over a major matter that threatens their marriage and, instead of having a bitter argument again, they agree to disagree, with the conclusion, "Well, you have your way of seeing the problem and I have my way—so let's interpret it as we will." If this is the kind of methodology we might conclude that, in reality, there is little progress in understanding at all. Fortunately, the methodology is a little stronger than that! The report speaks of a common listening to each other in honest reflection and joint worship. There does seem to be sufficient agreement between the two sets of representatives to convince me that a real breakthrough has occurred, and that the JDDJ represents a thorough rapprochement between two Churches which had been estranged for over four hundred years.

But here I must declare my puzzlement and the crux of my argument. Justification by faith was the cardinal doctrine that divided the Western church, so why has not the healing of the Church led to a fast track on the pathway to full, visible unity? There can only be one answer to that—it is the cardinal importance the Roman Catholic Church places on the doctrine of the Church, to the detriment of everything else.

I believe that Hans Küng saw this long ago. Perceptively he wrote: "Through the Church, in faith the individual shares in universal justification. So justification as it has taken place in Christ's death and resurrection has an essentially ecclesiastical character."[14] I have not read anything in Hans Küng's writings following his impressive debut as a theologian in *Justification* that suggests a logical link between justification and church was conscious in his thought, but so it appears from the striking number of books on ecclesial subjects that followed its writing. On my shelves are to be found: *The Council and Reunion* (1960), *Structures of the Church* (1962), *The Living Church* (1963), *Truthfulness, the Future of the Church* (1968), *Infallible? An Enquiry* (1970), *Why Priests? A Proposal for a New Church Ministry* (1971), *On Being a Christian*, and *Signposts for the Future* (1980). In these books, Küng shows himself as the *enfant terrible* of the Catholic Church as he criticizes his own church's ecclesiology in the light of Scripture. The trajectory of Küng's thought suggests that, rather than the doctrine of the

13. ECLA News-Service, "Joint Declaration Affects U.S. Lutheran–Roman Catholic Dialogue."

14. Küng, *Justification*, 225.

church determining all other doctrines, justification by faith—as the center of God's work in Christ—was the interpreter for ecclesiology and everything else.[15] There is little wonder that the Magisterium has been so profoundly unhappy with Küng. While some may argue that it is Küng's liberalism that is the reason for its concern, the real basis is most likely his determination to provide a solid biblical foundation for all ecclesiastical statements, particularly in the area of papal ministry. Here, Küng finds the sole justification for the ministry of the pope in a "Petrine" ministry of service.

If this is an accurate interpretation of the link between justification by faith and the church in the writings of Küng, we have an implied criticism by one of the Roman Catholic Church's greatest theologians of his own Church's theology. It is almost as if for the Catholic Church, the doctrine of justification by faith is merely one of many doctrines among others and has little to do with ministry, the sacraments, and the life of faith. This is indirectly attested by the opening words of JDDJ where we read "the doctrine of justification by faith was of central importance for the Lutheran Reformation of the 16th century." Was it not of crucial importance also to the Catholic Church? Hardly, it seems, as the second sentence reads: "the doctrine of justification was particularly asserted and defended in its Reformation shape and special valuation over against the Roman Catholic Church and theology of that time."

There we have it. The doctrine was crucial to the Lutherans but not so to the Roman Catholic Church because it was not seen to be a church-dividing issue by the latter church. Thus, once unity on the matter is satisfactorily completed, it can be tucked away and put in its place in the church's compendious store of doctrines.[16] I have been struck how Fr. Hubert Jedin, one of the greatest Catholic theologians of the twentieth century, interpreted the data. In 1969, in an article in *L'Osservatore Romano*, he correctly noted that Luther's protest struck at the heart of all that Rome stood for: "The cause of the tragic confrontation consisted in this: Luther not only broke with human traditions, or human propositions as he called them, but he rejected the obligatory character of the ecclesiastical magisterium, the vehicle of the

---

15. In *Why Priests?* Küng states that "where there is no trace of the liberating spirit of Christ, despite all institutional claims, there is no genuine ministry and no true leadership" (*Why Priests?*, 65).

16. This is perceptively pointed out by Avery Dulles, who argues that the Roman Catholic's Official Response to JDDJ "contests the Lutheran view that the doctrine of justification is the supreme touchstone of right doctrine. It asserts, on the contrary, that the doctrine of justification must be integrated into the 'rule of faith'" (Dulles, "Two Languages of Salvation").

sacra tradition."[17] A year later, Jedin wrote these words: "In the past twenty years I have often said and written that in my view the gulf which divided Catholics and Protestants from one another did not lie in the doctrine of justification but in the sphere of the concept of the church."[18]

This is echoed in the writings of another Roman Catholic theologian, Johannes Brosseder, who asserts that Küng's theology entered "new theological territory" (through *Justification*) and "thus has taken a powerful ecumenical step forward."[19] What is the nature of this step forward? Brosseder advances the idea that in Küng's thought the church is seen as "pure instrumentality."

Pure instrumentality? Eyebrows will be raised at this somewhat reductionist view of the church, which is in Christian thought the mystical bride of Christ. But further reflection will give this definition some validity. On the same basis of Thomas More's thinking in *Utopia* that there will be no lawyers in heaven, we may conclude that when God's kingdom comes, the church has fulfilled its purpose and will no longer exist. The church, after all, is that part of the kingdom of heaven which awaits its consummation and, when all is completed, will have discharged its duty to manifest, however imperfectly, the true nature of God's kingdom. On earth, it is the place where God's grace is known and where the sacraments are made valid. It is not, and can never be, the focus of God's salvific events in Christ. It has no existence on its own as a reality separated from the pilgrim people of God. It is an *instrument* of those salvific events in which God's grace in Christ is manifest to others. The moment it blocks the movement of God's love to the world, or regards itself as the primary focus of God's mission, its boasting will be of itself and not in its Lord.

It is here that Brosseder's support for Küng's emphasis upon instrumentality leads him to conclude that his own church has not quite grasped what the apostolicity of the church means for its mission. Brosseder gives the example of the ordination of women where, if the church is seen as pure instrumentality, "the criteria of the article of justification cannot accept any reason for excluding women from access to the ministries of the Church."[20] In a devastating broadside, Brosseder concludes: "Anyone who allows ecclesiology to be the criteria of the reconciliation or non-reconciliation of churches and refuses this role to justification by faith has not begun to take

17. Jedin, "Crises in the Church."

18. Quoted in Brosseder, "The Significance of the Dispute over Justification Today," 146.

19. Ibid., 145.

20. Ibid., 148.

part in the human work of the restoration of the communion of Christian churches by removing obstacles which have been put, and are still being put, in the way of communion."[21]

Thus, when we ask "thirteen years on from agreement between the World Lutheran Federation and the Roman Catholic Church, what has been achieved?," the answer is that, apart from the Agreement itself, nothing has been settled; the churches are still going on their own ways. The same goes for the Anglican Communion and the Roman Catholic Church after the agreement *Salvation and the Church* in 1985. The illusion is that such pivotal consensus is bringing us closer. But, in reality, we are divided as much as we have ever been. Why is this? It is because we differ on our understanding of the church.

As a former Archbishop of Canterbury, I have nothing but gratitude for the way that I and my predecessors and successor have been treated by Pope John Paul II and Pope Benedict XVI. Since Vatican II relationships between our churches have been warm, cordial, and constructive. Deep personal friendships have been built up at senior levels that have added to constructive theological engagement. Theological progress has been made and will continue to be made. But am I the only non-Catholic leader to be deeply offended by the oft-repeated statements that the goal of unity is not a journey of different bodies from where they once were to a new body enriched by one another, and therefore new, but a journey back to Rome? According to Vatican II, the aim of dialogue is that estranged Christians may be brought "into that unity of the one and only Church . . . this unity we believe subsists in the Catholic Church as something she can never lose."[22] *Lumen Gentium,* a landmark document of Vatican II, informs us that the Catholic Church "subsists in" the Roman Catholic Church: "This Church constituted and organized in the world as a society, subsists in the Catholic Church, which is governed by the successor of Peter and by the Bishops in communion with him."[23] To be sure, the phrase "subsists in," acknowledges that other churches also embody graces and attributes found within the Roman Catholic Church. Yet, this is the same church which has set forth a number of doctrines since the Reformation, such as the infallibility of the Pope, and the Marian dogmas, which have but a tendentious link with the foundation documents of the church! How outrageous, then, to claim that it is "more" church than the rest of us! And yet, in our dialogues we go along

21. Ibid., 149.

22. "Unitatis Redintegratio," par. 4.

23. "Lumen Gentium," par. 8. "*Haec Ecclesia, in hoc mundo ut societas constituta et ordinata, subsistit in Ecclesia catholica, a successore Petri et Episcopis in eius communione gubernata*"

with this assertion by Rome, putting up with the explicitly stated superiority that blocks our attempts to reach a full unity—a unity that can only be made possible by a common recognition that all of us have failed and that includes our churches also. Each of us is *simil justus et peccator*, in need of God's grace. None can boast.

That is why justification by faith is a radical doctrine, and that is also why we need theologians like Hans Küng and Paul Zahl to help us unlock its full potential in our lives and in our churches.

BIBLIOGRAPHY

Brosseder, Johannes. "The Significance of the Dispute over Justification Today." In *Hans Küng: New Horizons for Faith and Thought*, edited by Karl-Josef Kuschel and Hermann Häring. London: SCM, 1993.

Dulles, Avery. "Two Languages of Salvation: The Lutheran–Catholic Joint Declaration." *First Things* (December 1999) 25–30.

Henry, Carl. F. H. "Justification: A Doctrine in Crisis." *Journal of the Evangelical Theological Society* 38 (1995) 57–65.

Jedin, Hubert. "Crises in the Church." *L'Osservatore Romano*, January 30, 1969.

"Joint Declaration on the Doctrine of Justification." Lutheran World Federation and the Catholic Church, 1999.

Küng, Hans. *Justification: The Doctrine of Karl Barth and a Catholic Reflection.* Translated by Thomas Collins, Edmund E. Tolk and David Grandskou. London: Burns & Oates, 1965.

———. *Why Priests?: A Proposal for a New Church Ministry.* Translated by Robert C. Collins. Garden City, NY: Double-day, 1972.

"Lumen Gentium." Vatican II, 1964.

MacCulloch, Diamaid. *Thomas Cranmer: A Life.* New Haven: Yale University Press, 1996.

"Malta Report." Joint Lutheran–Roman Catholic Study Commission, 1972.

News-Service, ECLA. "Joint Declaration Affects U.S. Lutheran–Roman Catholic Dialogue." 2000.

Pesch, Otto Hermann. *Theologie der Rechtfertigung bei Martin Luther und Thomas von Aquin: Versuch eines Systematisch-Theologischen Dialogs.* Walberger Studien der Albertus-Magnus-Akademie, Theologische Reihe 4. Mainz: Grünewald, 1967.

"Salvation and the Church." Second Anglican–Roman Catholic International Commission 1985.

"Unitatis Redintegratio." Vatican II, 1964.

11

We Believe in the Forgiveness of Sins, but Who Justifies the Victim?

Jürgen Moltmann[1]

For my friend Paul Zahl, for his 60th birthday. During his time in Tübingen, Paul immersed himself deeply in Ernst Käsemann's Doctrine of the Justification of the Ungodly. This text concerns the Justification of the Godforsaken [Gottverlassenen].

In 2010, instances of sexual abuse by members of the Roman Catholic Church in the Odenwald School and other educational institutions were brought to light. Today, we in the churches and in the public know how to deal with the perpetrators, but we are speechless in light of the suffering of the victims. The victimizers are called out by name while the victims (and their sufferings) remain mostly anonymous. We speculate and wonder how the perpetrators could have committed such ignominious acts, but, for fear of bringing their shame and disgrace to light and thus further injuring them, the victims are left alone. Thus, in our general public, the nature of our society is that we remember the perpetrator and forget the victim (*täterorientiert und opfervergessen*).

The Reformation doctrine of justification by faith developed out of the medieval sacrament of penance because, at their core, they are both intimately concerned with the forgiveness of sins. When we speak of "sin" we

---

1. Translated by John D. Koch Jr.

are talking about the power of evil, and today we speak of the forgiveness of sins through the grace of God by faith alone. This is altogether correct; however, it is only a half-truth. While the forgiven "sinner" is the perpetrator of evil, the question remains: what about the victims? In the justification of the sinner we have only our trespasses for which we pray in view, but where is the sacrifice for the victim before whom we are guilty? Both the Lutheran and Roman Catholic doctrines of justification and grace concern only the perpetrator of sin and not his or her object; they concern only the victimizer and not the victim. The Roman sacrament of penance and the Reformation's doctrine of justification are, like Roman law itself, uniquely oriented towards the perpetrator.

This is already the case in the Apostle Paul's teaching on sin and grace. In Romans 7, he formulates it so: "For I do not do the good I want to do, but the evil I do not want to do—this I keep on doing. Now if I do what I do not want to do, it is no longer I who do it, but it is sin living in me that does it . . ." (Rom 7:19–20).[2] Why is he not concerned with those whom his unwanted evil has harmed and to whom he has failed to do the wanted good? Why is he so concerned with himself? Comparing his statement—"the sin that dwells in me"—with the Jesus of the gospels, it is important to note that when he first sees the multitudes of the sick, the poor, and the outcasts he, "had compassion for them, because they were harassed and helpless . . ." (Matt 9:36). He did not see sinners and perpetrators, but rather victims of injustice and violence. To these victims, he brings the message of the Kingdom of God, that it belongs to them and heals them and accepts them as part of his community [*Gemeinschaft*]. To those who have no future place "in good company," he opens the expanses of God [*den weiten Raum Gottes*]. Therefore, the Gospel of Jesus initiates a wholesale reevaluation of values, a revolution that was presaged by Mary in the Magnificat, "He has brought down rulers from their thrones, but has lifted up the humble" (Luke 1:52).

When we read the Old Testament Psalms, we see that God's justice is always on the side of the poor and the weak, the victims of injustice and violence. "The LORD works righteousness and justice for all who are oppressed" (Ps 103:6). God's justice is a kingdom of creative justice. God's kingdom is not limited to establishing conceptions of good and evil. It is not one that operates on a generally accepted system of retributive justice. Rather, God's kingdom creates justice where injustice is revealed. First and foremost, he focuses on the victims of sin and frees them from their humiliation, and only then will his justice for the perpetrators be rightly

---

2. All biblical references are from the NIV.

established; justification means the creation of justice first for the victims of evil and only then for the perpetrators.

We will want to keep this relation in mind as we seek a more accurate picture of victim and perpetrator. We will begin with the perpetrators, not because they are more important, but because there exists a well established, timeworn ritual for addressing their crimes, but none such ritual exists for the justification of the victim. This ritual involves three steps by which the perpetrators of sins—the transgressors—will be brought to justice through the sacrament of penance and the forgiveness of their sins.

1. The first step takes place through the confession of sins of both com-mission and omission, both committed and allowed: *confessio oris*, the confession of the mouth. This first step is always the step out of the darkness of repression and concealment into the light of truth. Whoever confesses his sins to another stands over those sins and takes away the power of that sin that "dwells in him" and which had domin-ion over him. This is not easy, because the public recognition of guilt always comes with humiliation. For the perpetrators, for the mur-derers and torturers—as was seen in the South African Truth Com-missions—there is no way of avoiding this. They need, therefore, a sheltered place—a sanctuary. This can be the confessional and its sac-ramental seal, but it must in any case be a place where the forgiveness of sins by God is assured. Only on account of the assured forgiveness of God can the sinner confess his or her sin; without this forgiveness, there is only self-destruction. This is the great Protestant insight: we recognize our sins through the law and confess them honestly in light of the gospel. However, because both perpetrators of evil and those who fail to do good have short memories, they easily forget. Therefore, on account of their forgetfulness, they must be reminded of the effects of their sin through the eyes of their victims in order to bring about true self-awareness. Victims, on account of the scars on their souls and the wounds on their bodies, do not easily forget.

2. The second step is the change—*contritio cordis*—the movement away from the ways that have allowed the perpetration of evil or omission of the good and towards the love of life and the doing of good. Today, the personal aspect of this movement is also very important, because only a changed person can (and will) change a bad situation. Today, know-ing that we cannot live at the expense of the poor, we can affect a break with the dictatorial systems that perpetuate evil and injustice in the world. We know that we can no longer enjoy our lives at the expense

of our planet and weaker fellow creatures. This new orientation of the heart affects a change in both our personal and political lives.

3. Lastly, if all of the pain and damage has been addressed, the third step is the restoration of the perpetrator to a new and rectified community with his or her victim. This is called "restitution"—*satisfactio operum*. Nonetheless, it must be said, we all know that nothing that has been done can ever be truly undone. One can "deal with" his past evil, but nothing that has been destroyed by injustice and violence can be fully restored anew. But every act of restitution is the realized and hoped for beginning for a new and righteous community between perpetrator and victim, a community that must be always sought after and established by good deeds. In criminal justice, this is known either as "perpetrator-victim-compensation" [*Täter-Opfer-Ausgliech*] or, more commonly, "restorative justice."

For the sinner, the Roman Catholic Church developed the sacrament of penance. To the sinner, the Reformation proclaims the forgiveness of sins in justification by faith. Each way complements the other, but both are oriented towards the perpetrator. What happens to the victims of these sins? We have a ritual and a sacrament for the justification of sinners; what we need is something similar for the justification of the sinner's victims.

A PROPOSAL:

1. The first step. The victims of injustice and violence must not only bring to light their pain, but even more so the humiliation they have endured. For the victims of sexual violence, the shame and desecration they have endured silences them; it forces them into hiding where all they want is to forget and remain anonymous. Therefore, they need freedom and acceptance in order to cry out about what was done to them. They need open ears to hear their cries, because this will allow them first to rediscover their self-worth. While the guilty plea of the perpetrator can help give this back to the victims, they do not have to wait for this confession in order to be freed from their bondage. In God, the one who "executes justice for the oppressed" (Ps 146:7a), they can rediscover their indestructible self-worth which no one can corrupt or steal. Those who have not been victimized must learn not only to hear the confession of the perpetrators, but also to take seriously the cries of the victims so that their tongues will be loosed and they will be freed from their unbearable memories. Therefore, they need a

protected space of great love in order to hear and be heard. "'Break the shackles of your shame!' 'What you have endured has not affected your soul!' 'Forget any public or secret self-pity!' 'The sharing with and the participation of others is the first step into the light of truth.'" Only the truth can free the victim. These victims of the aforementioned sexual abuse by members of the Roman Catholic Church endured over thirty years of oppressive silence before even the first word was uttered.

2. The second step then, is the lifting up of the humiliation itself and offering it to God. But not only the humiliation—the victims themselves need a reversal where their own humiliation is brought out of the depths of shame and into the affirmation of life. This is the experience of a life that is loved rather than one experienced as oppression and pain.

3. The third step may then lead to a situation where the evil is not repaid with the same evil, but rather the evil is overcome by good. This is difficult, but liberating. Each person who has suffered injustice has dreams of revenge. "The one who is inflicting this pain on me," he thinks, "will someday experience the same and then we will be even, and poetic justice will be served." We think that it does not matter whether we call this revenge, retaliation, or justice, because as long as the offender is punished, we are happy; however, this type of "justice" realized often leaves a stale taste.

The Apostle Paul was right when he said, "Do not be overcome by evil . . ." (Rom 12:21), but also do not repay evil with evil: Get rid of the evil! Get rid of the humiliation and shame you have experienced! Do not lower yourself to the same level as those who have harmed you! He or she who repays evil with evil does not experience anything more sublime than do other perpetrators of evil. The person who murders a murderer is himself a murderer. Free yourself from that evil that has unwillingly invaded your life.

"But overcome evil with good," continues the Apostle Paul. When we forgive "those who trespass against us," we do not only forgive them, but also we do something good for ourselves. We overcome that evil that has invaded our lives. Forgiveness allows not only the perpetrator to turn from his or her sins, but also frees his or her victims. Forgiveness frees a person from hate; it frees the victim from the need for revenge and the shame that forces him to incessantly dwell on those who have committed evil against him.

It should be pointed out, however, that the forgiveness of sins that have actually been committed is not a form of self-help, as is the case with much modern psychotherapy. There can be healing benefits to forgiveness, and that healing can be understood as a way of grace, but self-help is not the primary goal of the forgiveness of sins. If it were, then the victim would be trapped in a closed circle of his or her own self and would not be free. On the contrary, the victim's freedom rests on the forgiveness of the sins of those who have trespassed against them; the freedom for the victim is in the forgiveness of his or her victimizer. But this forgiveness must not be understood as a sign of weakness, but of strength, because it is the exercise of sovereignty over the pitiful slaves of evil. Whoever is sovereign does not react but, rather, creatively acts and makes the first step. One can learn this type of sovereignty by studying the example of Martin Luther King's "Letter from a Birmingham Jail," which called upon the descendants of slavery to have compassion on the souls of their hateful, fearful white neighbors. Also, one can learn from Nelson Mandela, who spent more than twenty-five years in prison on Robben Island and, nevertheless, returned to South Africa with a free and sovereign soul and helped free his country from the evil of apartheid.

Just as the sacrament of penance has proven cathartic and healing for those who have committed sins, so we need a similar sacrament for the victims of injustice and violence, one that rests on the resurrection of Jesus, himself the crucified victim of injustice and violence. Then, the one-sided orientation towards the perpetrators in our justice system will be changed in favor of one that is concerned with the justification of the victims of crime. So far, judges can sentence the perpetrators to psychological help, but there is only private help like "the White Ring," or "Innocence in Danger" for the victims. Justice is not served by perpetuating a system that leaves the victim alone and privileges the perpetrators—a system in which the perpetrators can hope for amnesty, but not the victims. These people are not only victims of evil, but of public forgetfulness.

PART 3

Strength in Weakness

12

Truth and Love

The Many Instruments of the Spirit's Work

SIMEON ZAHL

Therefore anything by which the human heart recognizes the mercy of God is a word of life.

PHILIPP MELANCHTHON[1]

[F]or God alone baptizes with the Spirit, and he himself chooses how and when and to whom that baptism will be administered.

HULDRYCH ZWINGLI[2]

THROUGHOUT HIS CAREER, IN his books, essays, and sermons, Paul Zahl has given stories and analogies from literature, popular culture, and day-to-day human experience a key role in his approach to theological communication. What may appear from the outside as a sort of charming idiosyncrasy on Zahl's part—unexpected references to flying saucer movies or to Tolstoy short stories in the middle of an exposition of the doctrine of justification—is

1. Melanchthon, "Loci communes theologici, 1521," 97.
2. Zwingli, "Of Baptism," 133.

in fact a key engine behind his remarkable ministry and influence, theological as well as pastoral, over many decades.[3] There are a number of reasons why we might say this strategy is so successful—for example the fact that he often uses his examples as a source of defense-lowering irony and humor—but in what follows I want to focus on one reason in particular, a theological assumption or claim that is implicit in Zahl's use of such references and data, and which is also more or less explicit in his theological writings. The claim is perhaps not particularly controversial to those familiar with the history of theology, but it can be very controversial indeed in the more conservative American theological circles where Zahl has often been best known and where his influence has perhaps been greatest. It is this: that the redemptive and transformative activity of God through the Spirit can take place through many means and instruments, and is not the exclusive prerogative of Scripture or of the sacraments (what Luther called the "external Word"), or of the church.

In failing to recognize this fact, many theologians, ministries, and preachers cut themselves off from some of the best and most effective resources available to them, and end up presenting a picture of Christianity that can be overly removed from day-to-day human experiences and realities. In what follows, I want to provide a brief theological justification, grounded in the doctrine of the Holy Spirit, of this claim that implicitly animates much of the integrating power of Zahl's theology.

Before I begin, however, a quick word on method. Part of what lies behind this essay is an empirical observation, drawn from my own experience[4] and that of many others: that Zahl's method, which aims to help people to connect with the action of God in their lives through diverse and unusual means, *works*. This is a pragmatic assumption to make in an argument, and it is in keeping with a certain pragmatism in Zahl's own theology. That is, it is usually a mistake, in his view, when we stray too far in our thinking from what William James would call the "cash-value"[5] of pastoral effectiveness and of obvious empirical observations about the human struggles and

---

3. This feature of Zahl's "style" is so ubiquitous as to make it unnecessary to demonstrate from examples—simply read five pages of his writings, or listen to any of his sermons (on www.adventbirmingham.com and www.mbird.com) or his podcasts (PZ's Podcasts, on iTunes). That said, the index at the end of what many consider his magnum opus, *Grace in Practice*, is instructive. A quick sampling of entries includes: Lucas Cranach, Roald Dahl, Benedict Spinoza, T. S. Eliot, William Cowper, Cheap Trick, Ernst Käsemann, T. D. Jakes, Wilhelm Wrede, George Whitefield, Katherine Anne Porter, and Prince.

4. As Zahl's youngest son, I grew up with his sermons and books and observed firsthand the effect of his ministry on many, many people over the years.

5. James, "Pragmatism," 509; James, "The Meaning of Truth," 823.

experiences all around us.[6] In my view, perhaps the best way to make sense of what Zahl is up to is by interpreting it in terms of the doctrine of the Holy Spirit. So in asking the question: "Why is Zahl's theological and homiletic use of material, data, and ideas from across the wide spectrum of human experience, both religious and secular, so effective?" I answer: "Because the Spirit works through many means and many instruments."

I also engage at several points below with the theology of Martin Luther. This is first because Luther's views are quite relevant here, though in some cases only as the most compelling version of the view being disagreed with. The second reason is that Zahl has been a life-long advocate of key insights of Luther's theology, and it is not always remembered that his advocacy is not an uncritical one. It may therefore be of use to those interested in his thought to be aware of some places, alongside the many affirmations, where Zahl does not follow Luther.

THE SPIRIT'S WORK NOT LIMITED TO SOTERIOLOGY

Perhaps the best-known and most important work of the Spirit, especially in Protestant traditions, is to convey, apply, and make real to us the salvation accomplished in Jesus Christ. As Otto Weber puts it in his classic dogmatics, the Holy Spirit "appropriates to us the work of Jesus Christ"[7] with the result that "God's reconciling act in Jesus Christ within this world is made concrete in us through the Spirit."[8] What this means is that the Spirit completes the saving work of Christ by making it true for us in particular—for example by bridging the historical and metaphysical gap between Christ's atoning death (both in history and *coram deo,* "before God") and what happens in our own particular lives and experiences.[9] For Protestants since Luther, the primary—and for some, exclusive—instruments by which the Spirit does this are God's "exter-

---

6. For an example of this pragmatic method in Zahl, see his discussion of the doctrine of the Trinity in *Grace in Practice*. While acknowledging and affirming the truth of the doctrine without reservation, he argues persuasively that "To employ the doctrine of the Trinity as the starting block for anthropomorphic speculation and extreme metaphor is to cut away from real life . . . From the side of plain human experience, it is necessary to affirm that theological anthropology, soteriology, and Christology override in importance *from our side* any doctrines—intellectually satisfying as they may be—which concern the being of God in himself" (Zahl, *Grace in Practice,* 128–29; emphasis original).

7. Weber, *Foundations of Dogmatics,* 243.

8. Ibid., 246.

9. Zahl makes precisely this point about the Spirit in *A Short Systematic Theology,* 30.

nal Word" of Scripture and the scripturally-sanctioned sacraments of baptism and communion. That is, it is through these means that the Spirit brings alive and makes real to us Christ's salvation. In Luther's view, God chose these particular means in order to give us something secure and unchanging on which our faith could rest and our consciences be at peace, and also to combat the enormous power of human self-deception.[10] Although not all Protestants have gone so far as Luther in this direction, his general privileging of the biblical Word over all other instruments of the Spirit remains the touchstone for all Protestant pneumatologies.

What Luther is talking about here, however, is only the work of the Spirit in salvation. Theology has long recognized that the Spirit's work is not limited to this particular dogmatic locus—Weber is right to speak of the "many-sidedness which is characteristic of the work of the Spirit."[11] For example, there is overwhelming biblical support for the connection between the Spirit and creation, above all in the giving of life.[12] Indeed, everything that God does in the world is in some sense done through the Spirit. As Jürgen Moltmann puts it, ". . . all divine activity is pneumatic in its efficacy. It is always the Spirit who first brings the activity of the Father and the Son to its goal."[13]

10. Insightful and helpful as this view is—it points us in no uncertain terms and for wise reasons to the central and most important instruments of the Spirit's work—it is simply too narrow to say that the Spirit reliably works *only* through these particular means. Some of the reasons for this will be demonstrated later in this essay.

Elsewhere I have argued the same point at some length, though on slightly different grounds, in critiquing aspects of Luther's rejection of "enthusiastic" pneumatologies. Very briefly, the strongest argument in favor of Luther's view that the Spirit restricts its redemptive work to oral preaching of the biblical Word and to the sacraments is that it combats the great propensity in human beings, including Christians, towards projection and self-deception by making God's saving instruments external to us and therefore "objective" in their efficacy. In my view, Luther's theology of the cross adequately addresses the inescapability of self-deception on its own and does not require the addition of a problematically narrow pneumatology of the external Word. For more on this, see S. Zahl, "Rethinking 'Enthusiasm'"; S. Zahl, *Pneumatology and Theology of the Cross in the Preaching of Christoph Friedrich Blumhardt*, chapter 7.

11. Weber, *Foundations*, 2:243.

12. Key biblical texts include Rom 8:2 ("The Spirit of life") and Ps 104:29–30; various instances of God's life-giving breath and Spirit (Gen 1:30; Ezek 37:5, 14; John 20:22), as well as the plausible interpretation of Gen 1:2 in pneumatological terms, not least since the other two persons of the Trinity are already deeply involved in creation (Genesis 1; John 1; Col 1:16–17). For more on this, see Levison, *Filled with the Spirit*, 14–33; Kärkkäinen, *Pneumatology*, 23–27.

13. Moltmann, *God in Creation*, 9. In this sense, the doctrine of providence, too, with all the instruments God in his providence has at his disposal to bring about his will in the world, falls under the domain of pneumatology.

Despite what he seems to be saying in his main discussions of pneumatology,[14] Luther himself affirms this presence of God in all creation, "even in the tiniest tree leaf": "It is God who creates, effects, and preserves all things through his almighty power and right hand . . . [N]othing can be more truly present and within all creatures than God himself in his power."[15] Although Luther prefers in such instances to talk of God's "power" instead of God's Spirit, restricting Spirit-talk primarily to the efficacy of Word and sacrament, he is nevertheless happy to quote Psalm 139:7 as his single strongest proof-text concerning God's sustaining power: "Whither shall I go from thy Spirit? Or whither shall I flee from thy presence?"[16] Clearly the work of God's Spirit, like Christ's (Col. 1:16–17), is not limited exclusively to soteriology in the way that Luther seems at first to imply with his strict limitation of the Spirit's work to the "external Word."

But what of the many modes of the Spirit's work described in the New Testament that do not fall straightforwardly or exclusively under either of these headings—that consist neither simply in the making "concrete" of "God's reconciling activity in Jesus Christ" (Weber), nor in the general sustaining presence of the Spirit in all life and all creation? It is here, in the spaces between salvation and creation and at their edges, that our question about the means through which the Spirit can and does work becomes most interesting. In what follows, I wish to focus on just two such "spaces": the Spirit's connection to truth, and the Spirit's connection to love. These brief sketches of common areas of the Spirit's work and presence are not intended to be exhaustive. The topics of truth and love are chosen not least because they seem to cover much of the ground assumed in Zahl's particular use of analogies, data, and ideas from sources outside of the Bible and other obvious Christian sources, and because Zahl draws on them at some length in his theological work.

THE SPIRIT IN ALL TRUTH

One of the favorite names for the Holy Spirit in John's Gospel and in 1 John is "the Spirit of truth."[17] First and foremost, for John, there is a fundamental and intentional connection here with Christ, who elsewhere in the Gospel is himself called "the truth" (John 14:6). When Jesus tells the disciples "you

---

14. See Luther, "Against the Heavenly Prophets," 144–49; Luther, "The Smalcald Articles, 1537," 322–23.

15. Luther "That These Words of Christ," 57–58.

16. Ibid., 58.

17. John 14:17, 15:26, 16:13; 1 John 4:6.

will know the truth, and the truth will set you free" (8:32), here, too, the primary referent is Jesus himself: this freedom will come when they "continue in my word," and a few verses later the Son is described as having the same freedom-granting power that truth has (8:36). For John, the deepest, most profound, and most important "truth" of all is unquestionably that found in Jesus Christ, who is the Truth.

At the same time the scope of "truth" here is not exhausted solely through explicit reference to Christ and to his work in salvation.[18] Take, for example, a more general biblical truth, such as the many sobering reminders in the Bible that human beings are mortal and one day will die. In Genesis we are reminded that "you are dust, and to dust you will return" (Gen 3:19b). In Ecclesiastes, the Teacher urges us to "Remember your creator in the days of your youth, before the days of trouble come . . . and the dust returns to the earth as it was, and the breath returns to God who gave it" (Eccl 12:1, 7). He also reminds readers at length of their insignificance in light of inevitable death: "a generation goes, and a generation comes, but the earth remains forever" (1:4). In Isaiah, we are reminded that "All flesh is grass . . . The grass withers, the flower fades, when the breath of the Lord blows upon it" (Isa 40:6–7; cf. 1 Pet 1:24, and the resonances in Matt 6:30). Few would deny that the communication of this truth, this broad and profound truth about death and about the futility of merely human activities and strivings in light of death, falls under the remit of the Spirit of truth, despite the fact that it does not immediately or *directly* reference Christ or his work. Indeed, even for Luther, the reality of death is an important form of how God's law, in its "theological use," is preached—the reminder of human mortality and futility can pave the way powerfully for the good news of resurrection and new life in Jesus Christ.[19]

But what about when human beings are reminded of their mortality outside of the context of these particular verses in Genesis, Ecclesiastes, and Isaiah, or related ones in the Bible? What about when a person comes to be struck very deeply indeed by the fact that death mocks vain human strivings, but the experience happens not to take place in a church or during a

18. This is evident first in the simple fact that the word "truth" was chosen in these instances instead of the equally plausible "me" in order to emphasize to some degree the broader category of truth. If the intention had been narrower, the verses could easily have just read "You will know me and I will set you free" or "This is my Spirit, whom the world cannot receive."

19. For Luther, death and the threat of death are part of God's "alien work" that prepares the way for his "proper work" of love. For an explanation and many references, see Althaus, *The Theology of Martin Luther*, 169–78, 405–10. This is one area in which Luther's wider theology demonstrably does not fully follow through on the strict pneumatological boundaries articulated in his main explicit discussions of the Spirit.

sermon? Consider the extraordinary line from T. S. Eliot's "The Lovesong of J. Alfred Prufrock": "I have seen the moment of my greatness flicker / And I have seen the eternal Footman hold my coat, and snicker / And in short, I was afraid." Here, too, the relativizing of human achievement and effort in light of the inevitability of death is communicated with poetry and power.[20] Does the Spirit of truth not work through this truth about death simply because it is in a poem that is not explicitly about Christianity or deliberately patterned on Jesus' life, death, and resurrection? Can a person not be crushed by this law, and advanced along the pathway of the Gospel, through these lines from "Prufrock" being read in a high school classroom, or on a subway train, or in an armchair at home?

If still we want to insist that "No, the Spirit only works in this way through the *verbum externum*"—or, better, that God will not ever speak his "external Word" to us apart from the instruments of Scripture and sacrament—then we are forced into absurdities like these: "Perhaps if Eliot had quoted Ecclesiastes directly in the poem, then the Spirit of truth could work here, but not as it stands"; or "Yes, the Spirit could work through 'Prufrock' to prepare the way for the Gospel, but only if the relevant lines are quoted in the larger context of a biblical sermon to a gathering of at least two or three people"; or "How much of a direct biblical echo is necessary in a text before the Spirit can work through it? Is just the word 'vanity' enough, or do we need the whole line, 'Vanity, vanity, all is vanity' (Eccl 1:2b)? But what about just the two words 'Vanity, vanity'—can the Spirit work through a highly shortened quote or reference? What about a merely implied one?" And so on *ad absurdum*. The obvious answer is to such questions is that the final presence or not of the Spirit in a given instance is determined by whether or not God freely chooses, through his Spirit, to use the particular instrument or verse, not through subtle analysis of shades of relative "Biblicism."

If instead we accept the point—which once we think it through is really quite obvious and straightforward—that the remit of "truth" with which the Spirit is connected can extend to non-biblical references to truths also referred to in the Bible, such as the above about mortality, then further questions are raised. What about an experience like almost getting hit by a car, or recovering from a near-fatal disease, or the death of a loved one? As any Christian minister knows, these, too, can be used—presumably by the Spirit—to teach of us our mortality and to pave the way for turning to God.

Stepping further back, what about non-controversial scientific truths from physics and biology—say, the Law of Thermodynamics, or the double-helix structure of DNA, or the science behind antibiotics or hospital

---

20. Another classic example would be the famous rumination on death and mortality, "Out, out, brief candle!," in Shakespeare's *Macbeth*.

sanitation—are these not also truths of God in some sense and therefore formally connected to some aspect of the work of the Spirit of truth? If they were not, there would have to be, *contra* traditional Christian doctrines of God and creation, some independent, neutral truth "out there" that is disconnected from God but which explains how electric lights work and the effectiveness of the germ theory of disease. Likewise, information from psychology and other social sciences can be enormously informative about human nature, and it would be strange indeed to say that the creator God is not even potentially connected to such truth.[21] If God's Spirit animates and sustains the universe God created, the remit of the Spirit of truth must also include creation in all its aspects and workings.

An important assumption behind Paul Zahl's tireless search for profundity and insight across the whole range not just of the Bible and the Christian theological tradition, but also of human history, ideas, art, literature, music, and culture—and his ability to transmute these materials into instruments for communicating about God and the Gospel—is that any real truth about the world or about human nature is also God's truth. Such truth is in no way in competition with Biblical truth, or with the truth communicated in and through the life and work of Jesus Christ, who called himself the Truth. The insights of "The Lovesong of J. Alfred Prufrock," or of James Gould Cozzens' depiction of subtle dynamics in relationships between men and women in *By Love Possessed*,[22] can and should be seen, in the Spirit, not as competitors of biblical truth but as formidable potential allies. Indeed, subject to the free work of the Spirit, they can be real instruments for communicating God's truth to human beings in all their stubbornness and hard-heartedness.[23]

For Zahl himself, this freedom to engage with the whole of human experience and culture as potentially a place of God's work as the Spirit of truth is grounded in the principles of self-criticism and forgiveness. He makes the point clearly in *A Short Systematic Theology*'s extraordinary

21. The argument of course is not that every current scientific hypothesis is necessarily correct; it is simply that insofar as they are actually true, as so many unquestionably are, then they are by definition connected to the truth of God.

22. *By Love Possessed* is one of Zahl's favorite novels precisely because of its insight into and effective communication about difficult truths of human nature.

23. The general point that we can trust God to be present wherever the truth is to be found was communicated to me first by my father in a conversation at the outset of my academic career that I have never forgotten. He told me that the key to doing good academic work as a Christian is believing, as Ernst Käsemann once taught him, that the truth can and must be followed wherever it leads. Christians, Zahl told me, never have anything to fear from the truth, and this is as true in academic study as it is in pastoral work or in relationships.

"Thesis 21": "The method of theology grounded in self-criticism and in the confidence of forgiveness from God produces freedom. *This freedom fosters the inductive study of all ideas and all phenomena.*"[24]

THE SPIRIT IN ALL LOVE

In Zahl's pneumatology, articulated most clearly in *A Short Systematic Theology*, the most reliable locus of the risen Christ's presence in the world as the Spirit is in "the works of love." This locus is more reliable than the church, icons, charismatic experiences, and even the Bible itself.[25] The strongest argument, in his view, against the various approaches that connect the Spirit's work in a *strict* or *exceptionless* way to particular means, objects, and events, is that these rapidly fall prey to a human desire to "summon the Spirit on command." Such a desire can never be squared with the unconditional freedom of the Spirit. This doctrine of the Spirit's freedom is grounded above all on that unconquerable fortress of a "proof-text," John 3:8: "The *pneuma* [wind or Spirit] blows where it chooses, and you hear the sound of it, but you do not know where it comes from or where it goes. So it is with everyone who is born of the Spirit." In Zahl's view, there is good reason for this freedom: "God could not allow this [summoning of the Spirit on command], ever, for then he would be ours and not we his." At the same time, there is a strong empirical or pragmatic argument to be made here as well, drawn for Zahl not least from his decades of pastoral experience:

> The fact is that one Sunday's mass may be deeply meaningful to me, the next Sunday's wan and lifeless. One day's Bible study may knock me flat and demolish my complacency, the next day's may leave me cold. It is not quite so capricious within the common experience of Christian people, but the Spirit has never performed on command.[26]

However, there is an exception of sorts. As Zahl puts it, "There is only one 'form' of the unseen presence of [Christ's] absence that persists in every age and time. The form of his absent presence is the form of love."[27] This principle, too, is grounded both in pastoral experience and in one of the most extraordinary sequences in the whole of Scripture, the fourth chapter

---

24. Zahl, *A Short Systematic Theology*, 82 (emphasis added).

25. Ibid., 37 (Thesis 6); see the whole section, 24–38.

26. Ibid., 30.

27. Ibid., 37.

of 1 John, where the close connection between the Spirit and love is made abundantly clear.[28]

First John 4 gives two criteria to aid us in the discernment of the Spirit. The first is christological—if a spirit "confesses that Jesus Christ has come in the flesh" then it is certainly from God, and spirits that oppose Jesus are not from God (1 John 4:2–3). That which opposes Christ is not of the Spirit, and that which confesses him (presumably confesses him in some sense "truly," unlike the false kind of confession of Christ described in Matt 7:21–23) is of the Spirit. The second criterion addresses the basic dilemma in discerning the presence of God's Spirit, that God is not *visible*. "No one has ever seen God" (4:12). As Augustine puts it in his famous sermon on this passage, God "is a thing invisible; [therefore] he must be sought not with the eye but with the heart."[29] Given this, the way that God becomes "visible"—the way we can come to recognize his presence in the Spirit—is through the criterion of love. "[L]ove is from God; everyone who loves is born of God and knows God. Whoever does not love does not know God, for God is love" (4:7–8). The source and shape of love is always God's love for us in Jesus Christ: "We love because he first loved us" (4:19). And yet the form this takes in practice is the mundane day-to-day love—or lack thereof—between human beings. "Those who say, 'I love God,' and hate their brothers or sisters, are liars; for those who do not love a brother or sister whom they have seen, cannot love God whom they have not seen" (4:20). Love here is a grounding principle that roots both abstract theologizing and navel-gazing subjective experiences of God (neither of which is in fact problematic *per se*) in inescapable "horizontal" human realities.[30]

Just as the Spirit can be present to creation as its sustaining power without necessarily entering immediately into questions of salvation, so we can say, with Zahl, that the Spirit is present in all true works of love (above all, "when such human love resembles [Christ's] love when he was here"[31]) without immediately addressing questions of how such love relates to justifying righteousness or salvation. Luther, of course, would want to say that the greatest good works, including works of love, are really evil works when performed apart from justifying faith, but he means this entirely with respect to the particular issue of justification. When he argues that "Although

---

28. Cf. Ibid., 37–38.

29. Augustine, "Homily on the First Epistle of John," 170.

30. The connection of such love to the Holy Spirit is quite clear from context, but Augustine further underlines the connection with reference to Rom 5:5: "God's love has been poured into our hearts through the Holy Spirit that has been given to us." Cf. ibid., 169.

31. Zahl, *A Short Systematic Theology*, 38.

the works of man always seem attractive and good, they are nevertheless likely to be mortal sins," the context is whether such things can "advance man on his way to righteousness."[32] As regards righteousness before God, works of human love are every bit as inadequate as Luther claims, but that does not mean the Spirit is not present in all (true) love. One evidence of this is the fact that, if we were instead to apply Luther's principle more rigidly, to all possible works of love in the world regardless of context or intent, we would end up in the rather perverse position of saying for example that the love of non-Christian mothers for small children is evil, or that secular charity work that brings food to the starving is a "mortal sin," or that freely giving one's life for another is wicked unless the parties involved have received Christian baptism[33]—and so on, once again *ad absurdum*.

There is a remarkable statement in the first edition of Philipp Melancthon's *Loci communes*, unfortunately removed in later editions. Writing in the period just before Luther had fully firmed up his strict pneumatology of the external Word, Melanchthon developed a rather more flexible principle: "*Therefore anything by which the human heart recognizes the mercy of God is a word of life.*"[34] In context, his point is simply that we can see the grace and mercy of God at work in the Bible not just in explicit discussions of forgiveness, but also in examples of God providing for, say, the physical needs of his people. But the principle also expresses more broadly the connection between the Spirit and love which we discover in 1 John 4 and which serves as a lovely summary of Zahl's view, as expressed explicitly in his theology and implicitly in the effectiveness of his pastoral and homiletic practice. If we follow through on this principle, we are free, with Zahl, to see *potential* instruments of God's Spirit all around us, wherever Christ-like love is revealed or expressed—in "horizontal," day-to-day human realities as well as, potentially, across the whole range of human culture and experience, regardless of any explicit "Christian" reference or intention on the part of its source.

32. Luther, "Heidelberg Disputation, 1518," 39.

33. Particularly damning to over-rigid application of Luther's principle like this is the fact that each of these examples bears obvious analogy to "[Christ's] love when he was here" (Zahl, *A Short Systematic Theology*, 38): his love for us as his children (Matt 23:37), his provision of food for the hungry both physically and spiritually (Luke 9:10–17, etc.; cf. John 6:35), and of course his sacrifice of his life for others.

34. Melanchton, "Loci communes theologici, 1521," 97 (emphasis added).

CONCLUSION

There are several other areas, beyond truth and love, where we might fruitfully discuss the particular presence of the Holy Spirit outside of and in addition to traditional forms like church, sacrament, charismatic experience, and Scripture. Unfortunately, there is no space here to do more than draw attention to them very briefly. One area might have to do with God's doing of the "impossible" or miraculous (in the sense of Matt 19:26, Mark 10:27, and Luke 18:27), especially when such miracles are patterned on love—e.g., the rescue of an addict from a life-destroying addiction, or the revitalization of a dead marriage, or the renewal of peace where there is a long history of war and conflict. Another might be in true creativity, whether in art, in ministry, or aesthetics—in other words in what is sometimes called "inspiration" in the creative sphere.[35] A third would be in the area of "constructive integration," wherever dividing walls are brought down (Eph. 2:14) and false distinctions are undone, and wherever penultimate distinctions are broken down and underlying unities in God are brought to the fore.[36]

The consequence of what has been said here, especially about truth and love, has been to broaden, in biblically, theologically, and pastorally grounded ways the potential remit of the Spirit's work beyond traditional means and instruments only. The Spirit's ability to work beyond and in addition to such instruments is in no way in competition with such instruments—the Bible, the preaching of the Christian gospel, and the church in various forms remain the most common and effective instruments of all.[37] Nevertheless, the freedom of the Spirit renders every account of its work through particular means finally provisional. In this sense—taken on its own terms and read without prejudice due to his controversial and often-misrepresented sacramental views—we must be able to say, with Zwingli, that "God alone baptizes with the Spirit, and he himself chooses how and when and to whom that baptism will be administered."[38]

35. For Zahl, perhaps the archetypical example of such Spirit-connected creativity, to which he returns again and again in sermons and podcasts, is the extraordinarily innovative 1960s British music producer Joe Meek.

36. This can take place in theology, in life, and even, we can hope, in politics. Perhaps the clearest New Testament example here is Paul's doing away in Christ (Gal 3:28) and in the Spirit (1 Cor 12:13) with penultimate distinctions in human identity such as race, class, and gender. Later in his career, Zahl's theology has moved in a direction that more and more emphasizes this underlying unity in God in light of the overwhelming falsity and idolatry of human distinctions.

37. This is a point demonstrable even just on empirical or "pragmatic" grounds, as Zahl is quick to affirm.

38. Zwingli, "Of Baptism," 133.

Many examples described here are about the Spirit's use of many means to achieve its work of connecting us with the truth of God's reconciliation in Christ. In other words, they are connected to the providential work of the Spirit in salvation. But certain others—the Spirit's presence in creativity and in truths about the natural world, for example—need not fall under that heading, and connect more closely to the Spirit's sustaining presence and power in and to all creation. Overall, the impulse here, building on Zahl's own theology, is to err on the side of generosity and creative openness in the discernment of the Spirit rather than boundary-drawing. This generosity must be grounded in both the equalizing principle of self-criticism and the liberating principle of forgiveness in Christ, as Zahl notes.[39] It is also grounded not least in the ultimate relativizing of all theological knowledge, all religious experience, all ethics, and all power before the face of love, as described with such poetry and force in 1 Corinthians 13.[40] Seeing the Spirit in this way—as capable of working through many means and many instruments, including in its soteriological work of applying divine reconciliation—opens up the world to us, helping Christians to avoid idolatrous compartmentalizations, on personal, pastoral, and cultural levels.[41] Paul Zahl's life's work is long empirical demonstration of the power and the truth of this approach.

BIBLIOGRAPHY

Althaus, Paul. *The Theology of Martin Luther.* Translated by Robert C. Schultz. Philadelphia: Fortress, 1966.

Augustine. "Homily on the First Epistle of John." In *The Holy Spirit: Classic and Contemporary Readings*, edited by Eugene F. Rogers Jr., 166–73. Grand Rapids: Eerdmans, 2009.

Ford, David F. "In the Spirit: Learning Wisdom, Giving Signs." In The Holy Spirit in the World Today, edited by Jane Williams, 42–63. London: Alpha International, 2011.

James, William. "The Meaning of Truth: A Sequel to 'Pragmatism.'" In *Writings: 1902–1910*, edited by Bruce Kuklick, 821–978. New York: Library of America, 1987.

39. Zahl, *A Short Systematic Theology*: 82.

40. For a persuasive and relevant discussion of the freedom of the Spirit to transgress boundaries as a fundamental feature of biblical pneumatology, see Ford, "In the Spirit."

41. Among Zahl's most significant theological contributions, deserving of most serious continuing attention from theologians and directly relevant to this theme, is Part III of *A Short Systematic Theology*, "The Method of Theology and the Method of Life: *Libertas christiana*" (*A Short Systematic Theology*, 79–89).

In terms of the constructive undoing of unhelpful compartmentalizations, perhaps the single most effective ministry in American Christianity today is that of Mockingbird Ministries (www.mbird.com), and it is no coincidence that Zahl has been a key influence on their approach.

———. "Pragmatism: A New Name for Some Old Ways of Thinking." In *Writings: 1902–1910*, edited by Bruce Kuklick, 479–624. New York: Library of America, 1987.

Kärkkäinen, Veli-Matti. *Pneumatology: The Holy Spirit in Ecumenical, International, and Contextual Perspective.* Grand Rapids: Baker Academic, 2002.

Levison, John R. *Filled with the Spirit.* Grand Rapids: Eerdmans, 2009.

Luther, Martin. "Against the Heavenly Prophets in the Matter of Images and the Sacraments, 1525." In *Luther's Works, Vol.* 40, 79–223. Philadelphia: Muhlenberg Press, 1958.

———. "Heidelberg Disputation, 1518." In *Luther's Works,* Vol. 31, edited by Harold J. Grimm, 39–70. Philadelphia: Fortress, 1957.

———. "The Smalcald Articles, 1537." In *The Book of Concord,* edited by Robert Kolb and Timothy Wengert, 297–328. Minneapolis: Fortress, 2000.

———. "That These Words of Christ, "This Is My Body," Etc., Still Stand Firm against the Fanatics, 1527." In *Luther's Works,* Vol. 37, edited by Robert H. Fischer, 3–150. Philadelphia: Muhlenberg, 1961.

Melachthon, Philipp. "Loci Communes Theologici, 1521." In *Melanchthon and Bucer,* edited by Wilhelm Pauck, 18–152. Philadelphia: Westminster, 1969.

Moltmann, Jürgen. *God in Creation: An Ecological Doctrine of Creation.* Gifford Lectures, 1984–85. Minneapolis: Fortress, 1993.

Weber, Otto. *Foundations of Dogmatics.* Translated by Darrell L. Gruder. Vol. 2. Grand Rapids: Eerdmans, 1983.

Zahl, Paul F. M. *Grace in Practice: A Theology of Everyday Life.* Grand Rapids: Eerdmans, 2007.

———. *A Short Systematic Theology.* Grand Rapids: Eerdmans, 2000.

Zahl, Simeon. *Pneumatology and Theology of the Cross in the Preaching of Christoph Friedrich Blumhardt: The Holy Spirit between Wittenberg and Azusa Street.* London: T. & T. Clark, 2010.

———. "Rethinking 'Enthusiasm': Christoph Blumhardt on the Discernment of the Spirit." *International Journal of Systematic Theology* 12 (2010) 341–63.

Zwingli, Huldrych. "Of Baptism." In *Zwingli and Bullinger,* edited by G. W. Bromiley, 129–75. Louisville: Westminster John Knox, 2006.

13

The Theology of the Cross Speaks Today

Mark C. Mattes

In today's world, Luther's theology of the cross (*theologia crucis*) is often badly misunderstood as solidarity with victims.

It becomes tantamount to "I feel your pain." As compassionate as many are, such sentiment is fraught with self-righteousness: "God feels your pain and, *like God*, I too can feel your pain." And, whenever self-righteousness is involved, one is able to think, "I'm better than others because I feel their pain." Such an interpretation of the theology of the cross offers a sentimental and co-dependent theology: Christ is a victim and we can sympathize with him and all other victims.

The context of Luther's development of a theology of the cross was that he was called by his mentor Johann Staupitz, the vicar of the German Congregation of Augustinian Eremites, to explain his new approach to theology. This followed on the Indulgence Controversy in which Luther, on behalf of the spiritual and temporal well being of common people, protested the sale of indulgences, and in the process challenged Albrecht of Mainz, John Tetzel, and papal authority in general. Luther prepared twenty-eight theological and twelve philosophical theses for disputation for the Augustinians meeting in Heidelberg on April 26, 1518. The resulting Heidelberg Disputation,[1] presenting Luther's theology of the cross, provides not only

---

1. Luther, "Heidelberg Disputation, 1518." We will focus solely on the theological theses in this paper and it will be quoted freely.

a research program opposed to the scholastic theology of the day—what Luther terms a "theology of glory"—but also an outlook in which the Christian life is not something that we do but instead is something that is done to us. The Christian life is less about our progress in holiness and more about God's work of making us to be people of faith.

Today's misreading is different from a genuine theology of the cross because the suffering described in the theology of the cross is due to our being at odds with God. The cross is God's work of breaking down our defenses so that we can freely live sustained by God's forgiveness, mercy, and love. As Luther put it, the cross tests all things (*crux probat omnia*).[2] However, where there is brokenness, there is also grief. God's mercy provides a safe footing for us on which to grieve. And such grief cleanses us of the false illusions of old defenses, and opens us to new life, change from the inside out. It leads us into life as God intends us to live, a full, abundant life (John 10:10). Gerhard Forde used to emphasize that the gospel is for those who are burnt out on religion. This truth has few witnesses better than the theses of the Heidelberg Disputation.

THE HEIDELBERG DISPUTATION

At its core, the Heidelberg Disputation is an assault on the late medieval view of salvation taught by Gabriel Biel, among others, which affirmed that God does not withhold his grace from those who do their very best (*facientibus quod in se est Deus non denegat gratiam*).[3] Biel's view is challenged directly in thesis 16: "The person who believes that he can obtain grace by doing what is in him adds sin to sin so that he becomes doubly guilty." In Biel's theology, God has established a covenant (*pactum*) with humanity promising that he would give his saving grace to those who do their very best. In this perspective, the law and good works are understood to help the sinner become a pilgrim or *viator* who, trying his or her hardest, in cooperation with God's grace, will eventually be a *comprehensor* in paradise, one enjoying the beatific vision of seeing God face to face.

In most basic terms, Luther calls this theology a "theology of glory," focused on the Christian life as an agenda that we do. In contrast, the theology of the cross is God's program to us. In order to remake us to be people of faith, God smashes and destroys our most treasured defenses and convictions. Hence, God reveals himself, but paradoxically as concealed in the cross: God's wisdom is granted in foolishness, his power in weakness, his

---

2. Luther, *Weimarer Ausgabe 5. Kritische Gesammtausgabe*, vol. 5, 179, 31.

3. See Obermann, *Forerunners of the Reformation*, 123–44.

glory in lowliness, and his life in the death of his Son. Not surprisingly, Luther describes his theses as "theological paradoxes,"[4] carefully designed to "attack and vex scholastic theology."[5] In a word, the flipside of God's gracious generosity is our painful exposure to our own powerlessness and impotence, an experience that we neither want to admit nor endure. God's grace does not come to us therapeutically like Carl Rogers' "unconditional positive regard." God's business is not in salvaging neurotics, but in re-making sinners—sideswiping their quest for control and spaciously allowing them to trust God's promise and thus live.

More than anything, Luther believes that his theological approach is true to scripture. Luther's attack on Scholasticism was due less to his studies in Humanism or the theology of St. Augustine and more to his intense work in Bible. When Moses requested to see God's own glory, God granted Moses nothing other than God's own backside (*posteriora dei*) (Exod 33:18ff.), for no one can see God's glory and live. Similarly, following St. Paul in Romans 1:20ff., knowledge of God on the basis of God's works in nature does not catapult us into the inner workings of divine mystery, but instead condemns us as self-centered, failing to give God his proper due. While sometimes seen (anachronistically—as if Luther were in league with the early Karl Barth of the *Römerbrief*) as a contribution to epistemology, offering a critique of "natural theology," the Heidelberg Disputation is primarily focused on soteriology—*where* (not how) do we find a gracious God?[6] And the answer lies in the cross of Christ in which God demonstrates his love for us by carrying away our sin and bestowing his favor on us sinners. That said, there is an epistemology embedded in the Heidelberg Disputation, one which, as we shall see below, thwarts analogical reasoning as a route into the divine life. Analogical reasoning, however, remains for Luther as an important way of reasoning in temporal, penultimate matters, such as science and politics.

STRUCTURE OF THE HEIDELBERG DISPUTATION

The theological theses move from a discussion about God's law (thesis 1) to one of God's love (theses 28). The overall outline of the theses examines (a) the nature and worth of human works over against the question of sin (theses 1–12), (b) the impotence of human free will to avoid sin (theses 13–18), (c) the divide between the theologian of the cross and the theologian

4. See Becker's discussion on Luther's view of paradox in *The Foolishness of God*, 119–39.

5. Forde, *On Being a Theologian of the Cross*, 21.

6. Dieter, "Why Does Luther's Doctrine of Justification Matter Today," 191.

of glory (theses 19–24), and (d) God's love in Christ as a creative act that brings believers into being (theses 22–28).[7] In contrast to the widely held *pactum* theology, Luther contends that sinners misunderstand the role of human works and God's work. In our judgment, human works are splendid and good (thesis 3), while God's works are deformed and bad (thesis 4). But Luther asserts that, in truth, human works are "mortal sins" (thesis 3), while God's works are "immortal merits" (thesis 4). Hence, it is clear for Luther that appearance and reality do not correspond with respect to our potentiality. In light of God's work, one's identity is not based on actualizing one's potential *coram deo*, but on God's claiming the sinner, the ugly, the despised, and (especially) what is nothing. The paradox of God's love—in contrast to our love—is that God loves the unlovable, is attracted to what is ugly, and desires the worthless. As Theses 28 reads, "The love of God does not find, but creates, that which is pleasing to it. The love of man comes into being through that which is pleasing to it."

Luther thus unmasks a theology of glory as suffering a severe slippage between appearance and reality. God's law appears to be a means to advancement, but in reality threatens the *viator* (thesis 1). Human works appear attractive, but in reality are mortal sins (thesis 3). The works of God appear unattractive, but in reality are eternal merits (thesis 4). The will appears to be free and potent, but in reality is mortal sin (thesis 13). It would appear that if God gives us such directives as are enshrined in the law, then that must entail that we are able to fulfill them. In reality, the law proves to be un-do-able in thought, word, and deed. It thwarts us. Hence, righteousness in the presence of God is something that we cannot obtain by doing righteous deeds. Instead, the righteousness that saves is something we receive through the advocacy of our defender, our Lord Jesus Christ.

Given that thesis 28 states that God's love creates that which is pleasing to it, we are certainly dealing with a "passive righteousness" *coram deo* (before God). Luther's contention is that his reformation discovery was that of a passive righteousness, in contrast to the Aristotelian-inspired, Scholastic views of righteousness in which right deeds lead to righteous habits and thus ultimately produce a righteous character.[8] While such reasoning about an active righteousness is appropriate, beneficial, and necessary in civil matters,

---

7. See Forde, *On Being a Theologian of the Cross*, 22.

8. "This is our theology, by which we teach a precise distinction between these two kinds of righteousness, the active and the passive, so that morality and faith, works and grace, secular society and religion may not be confused. Both are necessary, but both must be kept within their limits. Christian righteousness applies to the new man, and the righteousness of the law applies to the old man . . ." See "Lectures on Galatians" (1535) in Luther, *Luther's Works: Volume 26*, 7.

Luther claims that it has no bearing on one's standing before God. Scholars debate about when Luther's evangelical breakthrough happened. While it is possible that a fully developed view of what the later Reformation tradition would term forensic justification is not present in the Heidelberg Disputation, there can be no question that Luther's argument here is a crucial step on the way to this insight. A brief reflection on Luther's mature view merits our review. Robert Kolb describes Luther's mature outlook on justification as grounded in the etymology of the German word *rechtfertigen*:

> 'Justify' or 'render righteous'—meant 'to do justice to: that is to inflict punishment, 'judicially' on the basis of a conviction, and thus to execute the law's demands', or 'to conduct a legal process as an activity of a judge', 'to execute, to kill'. From early on, Luther spoke of God's killing and making alive as he described justification, for he presumed that sinners must die (Rom 6:23a) and be resurrected to life in Christ.[9]

Suffering and the cross would appear to be bad, but are in fact the way that God breaks down self-centeredness so that we can actually rely on

---

9. See Kolb, *Martin Luther: Confessor of the Faith*, 126. Kolb builds on the work of Werner Elert. Elert notes that "When an accused person—in today's sense—justified himself we read that he 'proves his innocence', or he 'exonerates himself', or 'he is able to prove himself innocent of the misdeed of which he is accused'. The word 'justification', on the other hand, which also occurred frequently, conveyed an entirely different meaning. It designated either the criminal law suit in which hide and hair or life and limb were at stake, or—and most frequently that—the execution of a sentence, especially a death sentence. For example, as late as the seventeenth century the Saxon penal code listed the hangman's fees and other expenses incidental to the execution of bodily punishment under the caption '*Unkosten der peinlichen Rechtfertigung*' (expenses incidental to penal justification). It speaks of the '*Körper der mit dem Schwert Gerechtfertigten*' (the body of the person justified by the sword). The same linguistic usage is found also in Hans Sachs. Thus it was not confined to the speech of jurists, which was foreign to the people in general . . . Justification does not imply that man ex-culpates himself, but it means that the executioner 'must mete out justice to the transgressor'. Thus Luther conceives of it as the secular execution of punishment . . ." See Werner Elert, *The Christian Faith: An Outline of Lutheran Dogmatics*, trans. Martin H. Bertram and Walter R. Bouman (Columbus: Lutheran Theological Seminary, 1974), 299–300. Elert concludes: "Justification by faith is judgment on 'the old man.' Justice has been done him. He receives death. That is the mortification carried out in repentance. And that is not to be understood figuratively, but very realistically. The man of faith is an other than the man of sin. To be sure, a final identity of the I remains. But it is the identity of the stalk of wheat with the seed-grain, which first had to be buried (John 12:24). As the sinner becomes a believing sinner, the enemy of God which he was but no longer is as soon as he receives forgiveness, dies. As our Confessions teach, justification is forgiveness of sin. However, forgiveness is not an exoneration for the 'old' man. It is, rather, his end. The declaration of righteousness is his justification because he is receiving justice. It is death for the sinner and resurrection for the believing sinner." Ibid., 305.

God for our life and well-being. Gerhard Forde notes that the correlate of a theology of the cross is not one of glory, but instead resurrection.[10] It is because God raises the dead that we can be confident in entrusting our lives into God's good care. Because God raises the dead, we are permitted to be completely honest with ourselves about ourselves in God's presence. Such complete honesty, and not a sanative approach to justification, is the best means for any healing from sin or pain that we can hope for in this life. All this is premised on the great divide that Luther summarizes in Theses 19–24 and which I will quote at length starting from thesis 18:

18. It is certain that man must utterly despair of his own ability before he is prepared to receive the grace of Christ.

19. That person does not deserve to be called a theologian who looks upon the invisible things of God as though they were clearly perceptible in those things which have actually happened [Rom 1:20].

20. He deserves to be called a theologian, however, who comprehends the visible and manifest things of God seen through suffering and the cross.

21. A theology of glory calls evil good and good evil. A theology of the cross calls the thing what it actually is.

22. That wisdom which sees the invisible things of God in works as perceived by man is completely puffed up, blinded, and hardened.

23. The law brings the wrath of God, kills, reviles, accuses, judges, and condemns everything that is not in Christ [Rom 4:15].

24. Yet that wisdom is not of itself evil, nor is the law to be evaded; but without the theology of the cross man misuses the best in the worst manner.

To despair of our own ability (thesis 18) is nothing that our free will would ever choose. Instead, the will is captivated by its own power (theses 13–15). Few theologians have understood the dynamics of a bound will as well as has Paul Zahl. Zahl notes:

> The point for theology is that we are not subjects; we are objects. We do not live; we are lived. To put it another way, our archaeology is our teleology. We are typically operating from drives and aspirations generated by our past. What ought to be free decisions in relation to love and service become un-free decisions anchored in retrospective deficits and grievances. This is the

---

10. Forde, *On Being a Theologian of the Cross*, 1.

message of tragic literature. It is the message of diagnosis that
sees into the animating engine of the unconscious.[11]

Zahl further states that "Free entities are subjects. Un-free entities are objects. Christ Jesus, the body of God on earth, was free. The world to which he came was un-free. It is un-free still. There is therefore only one subject in the world today, and he is surrounded by countless beleaguered objects."[12] As a sanative approach to justification would emphasize, there is a sense in which we are properly ordered to the divine, but it is not the path of exercising virtues which then establish habits leading to a good character, ultimately deifying us. Rather, it is the result of God's alien work (*opus alienum*) which breaks down our defenses such that we can live by faith, and thus be opened (*Ephphatha*[13]) to God as our good and restored to this creation as created good. It is the foolishness of preaching which accomplishes this divine ordering.[14]

As Forde so rightly says, a theology of glory leaves the will in control.[15] Far from being free, the will is addicted to the self;[16] it seeks its *own* in all things, including "spirituality" or ethics.[17] So, while we as theologians of glory believe that we are doing good deeds, fulfilling the law, acquiring merit, and the like, in fact our good is less for our neighbor, but instead to secure our *own* status before God. Hence, sinners do not seek God for God's own sake, but instead seek God to fulfill their own needs.

What does it mean to be a theologian of the cross? Surely it means to be a believer. But can we be more specific about such saving faith? Paul Althaus notes that "to believe means to live in constant contradiction of empirical reality and to trust one's self to that which is hidden. Faith must endure being contradicted by reason and experience; and it must breakthrough the reality

---

11 Zahl, *Grace in Practice*, 113.

12. Ibid. Zahl follows up this last sentence with, "St. Paul famously wrote, 'Faith, hope, and love abide, these three; and the greatest of these is love' (1 Cor. 13:13)." I would describe an obverse trio this way: original sin, total depravity, and the un-free will abide, these three; and the root of the thing is the un-free will" (114).

13. On "ephphatha," see Bayer, *Martin Luther's Theology*, 106–12. See also Mattes and Darge, *Imaging the Journey*, 50–51.

14. For an excellent resource on the relation between justification and preaching see Paulson, "Categorical Preaching."

15. Forde, *On Being a Theologian of the Cross*, 9.

16. Ibid., 17.

17. Following Theodor Dieter's interpretation of Luther, we can say that sin is nothing other than to seek one's own in all things. See Dieter, "Why Does Luther's Doctrine of Justification Matter Today," 194.

of this world by fixing its sights on the word of promise."[18] Here Luther's view is clearly more accurate with respect to the New Testament witness to the cross where Jesus suffered and died because *no one* identified with him. Indeed, according to scripture, he was crucified "outside the camp" (Heb 13:13). Or as Marc Lienhard notes, the fact that God is strong in weakness, gives life by destroying, and grants grace by judgment is all tantamount to the fact that God imposes suffering on sinners in order to dislodge them from their own self-trust and let them live from trust in God[19]—to let them flee from God (as wrath) to God (as mercy).[20] Said colloquially, sinners must "hit bottom" before they can receive this grace. When we live by grace—apart from any manipulation of the law—we honor God for his own sake by letting God simply "be God." To be human is to live by faith. The question is whether we will place our trust in an idol or the true God.

CONTRADICTION NOT ANALOGY

For Luther, the reality of God is given to humanity paradoxically, under the sign of its opposite.[21] As such, it is a threat to all analogical reasoning with respect to God as indicated in theses 19 and 22 and, thus, to theological reasoning as is usually done.[22] As Vítor Westhelle notes, the Scholastics believed that reason provides an infrastructure for faith. They taught that faith fulfills reason and brings it to perfection by means of analogy.[23] By contrast, Luther provides an ironic deconstruction of analogy in theology and thereby frees theology from the dominant modes of rationality of his time, influenced primarily by Aristotle as they were. For Luther, Aristotle should not be the norm for theological reasoning, and analogy no longer is to rule in theology. Luther permits the use of analogy in philosophy and politics, insofar as they are limited to temporal, earthly matters, but reason should not be granted permission to norm God's word.[24]

This is not to say that Luther was an irrationalist. One certainly reasons both outside theology as well as within it. But reasoning in theology is accountable to the incarnation and God's paradoxical work of redeeming

18. Althaus, *The Theology of Martin Luther*, 34.

19. Lienhard, *Luther: Witness to Jesus Christ*, 98.

20. *Ad deum contra deum confugere* ("to flee from [God] and find refuge in God against God"). See Westhelle, *The Scandalous God*, 155.

21. McGrath, *Luther's Theology of the Cross*, 160.

22. See von Loewenich, *Luther's Theology of the Cross*, 11.

23 Westhelle, *The Scandalous God*, 45.

24. Ibid., 51–53.

sinners, claiming sinners as righteous. Reason is accountable to the gospel narrative in which God chooses "what is low and despised in the world, things that are not" (1 Cor 1:28). Indeed, for the mature Luther, faith obtains a kind of knowledge, even if it is starkly different from knowledge that would accrue from the law: "But Christ is grasped, not by the Law or by works but by a reason or an intellect that has been illumined by faith. And this grasping of Christ through faith is truly the 'speculative life,' about which the sophists chatter a great deal without knowing what they are saying."[25] But faith is not circumscribed *a priori* by the categories of what the Aristotelian tradition defines as rational. Indeed, the gospel transcends such circumscription.

It is true, as Denis Janz notes, that analogy builds into its structure both similarity and dissimilarity between the related matters (*relata*).[26] Christians however disagree on the nature of proposed analogous talk about God. Should we affirm Thomas Aquinas' "analogy of being," which adheres to the dissimilarity between God as uncreated and the world as created, in spite of God's imprint built into everything he has made? Or, should we instead emphasize with Eberhard Jüngel that due to the incarnation the gospel as analogous talk establishes a "still greater similarity" in the midst of such great dissimilarity between God and the world?[27]

Jüngel raises this question as a strategy to undermine the Roman Catholic scholar Erich Przywara's view of analogy, developing the results of The Fourth Lateran Council of 1215: ". . . between the Creator and the creature so great a likeness cannot be noted without the necessity of noting a greater dissimilarity between them." For Przywara, the relation between God and the world reflects a greater dissimilarity within so great a likeness between the Creator and the creature. For Jüngel, such a view is incompatible with the incarnation, God's "identifying" with the man Jesus. He proposes instead an "analogy of advent" in which God, as an "event," comes within language, incorporating parables such as the waiting father (Luke 15) which indicate the nature of God's love. God's mystery is not in the claim that God is unthinkable to the human, but rather in the triune narrative of God's generosity to humanity.

Both views of analogy, either that of "being" (Aquinas, Przywara), or that of "advent" (Jüngel) are undermined by Luther's teaching. For one thing, if the incarnation is true, we would have to say that there is truly *univocal* talk about God: that God is a specific man, Jesus of Nazareth, is no analogy

25. Luther, *Luther's Works: Volume 26*: 287.

26. Janz, "Syllogism or Paradox: Aquinas and Luther on Theological Method."

27. See Jüngel, *God as the Mystery of the World*, sec. 18, 281–98.

but univocally true. More to the question, while Janz is right to emphasize that analogy includes an element of dissimilarity, accentuated more in the Roman Catholic tradition of Przywara and the Fourth Lateran Council, and accentuated less in the Barthian tradition of Jüngel's "analogy of advent," paradox is based less on dissimilarity between two *relata* and more on the opposition between two propositional truths (which semantically refers to realities in Luther's way of thinking). That is, in analogous thinking, similarity parallels dissimilarity and vice versa, regardless of which of the two that we emphasize in the polarity. However, opposition, with which we deal in paradoxes, pits sameness against its opposite. The pairings aligned with the theology of the cross—"strength in weakness," "granting life through death," "giving grace through judgment"—present not merely dissimilarities but oppositions. Such oppositions, encountered in the gospel's claim of sinners, confound reason's ability to develop analogies and put reason on a different track as an instrument accountable to what God has actually done. Later, in his *Lectures on Galatians* (1535), Luther noted that law and gospel are not only distinct but are "separated as more than mutually contradictory."[28]

Now, the concept "sameness" is a different matter than that of "dissimilarity." Sameness and its opposite incorporate conflict, even incompatibility, which the polarity of similarity and dissimilarity does not. The polarity of similarity and dissimilarity may transcend commensurability as one-to-one correspondences that can be compared and contrasted. But it carries a more neutral tone than that of sameness and difference.[29] In the latter case, we are dealing with matters that are incompatible. In the case of the theology of the cross, it is the incompatibility between life and death, whose opposition thwarts any attempt at systematic synthesis, especially that of Hegel's. In a sense, seen abstractly, the same is the opposite of its opposite, while the opposite of the dissimilar is harder to establish since the similar includes an element of difference with respect to that to which it is compared, and vice versa. Here, there is more than mere incommensurability, but instead an incompatibility built into the structure of the relationship itself. Only if God re-creates new life out of death can some thread of a relationship be maintained. As Luther later put it in the *Bondage of the Will*, such opposition between God's proper work and alien work is so that faith will remain faith: "Hence in order that there may be room for faith, it is necessary that everything which is believed should be hidden. It cannot, however, be more deeply hidden than under an object, perception, or experience which is

28. Luther, *Luther's Works: Volume 26*: 337. In spite of such contradiction between law and gospel, Luther says that they "are nevertheless very closely joined in experience."

29. See Richard Bernstein's discussion of comparability, compatibility, and commensurability in *Beyond Objectivism and Relativism*, 86ff.

contrary to it. Thus when God makes alive he does it by killing, when he justifies he does it by making men guilty, when he exalts to heaven he does it by bringing down to hell . . ."[30]

A NEW ANTHROPOLOGY

One thing is always clear when we deal with Luther: he has a distinctive outlook on anthropology, the question of what it means to be human. For Luther, human life is a result of suffering the unconditional and absolute working of God upon us in all things. Luther is a "God-intoxicated" man. He cannot conceive of life in a secular way, as if there were some kind of "naked public square" either in society or even within oneself. While temporal matters are to be distinguished from eternal ones, they are no less *God's* affairs. This is an earth and cosmos that God claims as his own. For Luther, God is active and at work, "masked," in anything and everything, always addressing us. Of course, God is not everywhere active for our welfare. Much of what we experience in life is not God's mercy, but his wrath or his hiddenness. But, in Luther's mind, no human can experience life apart from God, whether that person honors God or not. Similar to H. R. Niebuhr's ethical aphorism that "God is acting in all actions upon you. So respond in all actions upon you as to respond to his action,"[31] Luther would re-evaluate this directive as: "God is acting in all actions upon you. So trust that God is remaking you to be a person of faith in this way." It is not that Luther has no place for ethics. Far from it.[32] But in his mind, our action—our works—are on behalf of our neighbor and the world. After all, God does not need our works. Our neighbor does.

Most belief systems, whether religious or secular, affirm the dictum to "develop your potential." We can see such an affirmation in the various religious traditions of Augustinianism, the "negative theology" of mysticism, Thomism, much of Calvinism, Anabaptism, mainline (liberal) Protestantism, Hinduism, and Buddhism. Even secular approaches, such as Capitalism, Marxism, Humanism (even Nietzschian *Übermensch* nihilism) all affirm that we need to develop our potential! "Be all you can be!" is not far from *facere quod in se est*. Luther parts company with them here:

30. Luther, *Luther's Works: Volume 33*, ed. Jaroslav Pelikan, et al., trans. E. Gordon Rupp, et al. (Minneapolis: Fortress, 1972), 62.

31. H. Richard Niebuhr, *The Responsible Self*, 25.

32. See "Luther's 'Ethics'" in Forde, *A More Radical Gospel*; Lazareth, *Christians in Society*; Elert, *The Christian Ethos*; Pearson, "Luther's Pragmatic Appropriation of the Natural Law Tradition."

Our potential is not to be developed for ourselves, for some benefit that we might receive now, in the future, or in eternity. Instead, if our potential is to be developed at all, it should be for the sake of our neighbors, serving them as "little Christs," not for our own merit before God or whatever we consider ultimate.

In contrast to all these theologies and philosophical systems that require our active participation, in Luther's theology of the cross, God renders us passive. We suffer the sovereign workings of God in all our affairs. And, in contrast to a "purpose driven" approach to faith matters, much of God's work is painful. This is because there is so much that God must tear down before he can build up. Few have expressed this better than the Kierkegaard translator, the late Edna Hong:

> Our God has chosen to become involved in the divine failure—humanity. Our Savior chose to share with us the pain, punishments, and penalties of being imperfect humans. And God's Secret Agent of Reform chooses to help us imperfect creatures respond to the terrible call to be new creatures in Christ. For it is a terrible call, and it is a long, long, painful journey. For there is so much to tear down before the Holy Spirit can build up. There are so many fake props to knock down. And the end of the painful road is not perfection, but perfect humility. Not morbidity and self-loathing, but a humble and contrite heart.[33]

Luther called this God's "alien work." This is God's work of rending our self-righteous defenses so that God can do his "proper work" (*opus proprium*) of nurturing us in faith. This is the truth of thesis 18: we must utterly despair of our own abilities. Said colloquially, we must let go of being our own "higher power" for ourselves and instead trust in the true God who proves his goodness in raising Jesus from the dead, and raising us in Jesus as well. Some might wish to flee to God in order to avoid pain. But the only God we will ever encounter is the one who leads us into pain. God pains us, indeed kills us, as old beings due to the fact that it is very painful for us to let go of ourselves as controlling people, those who wish to be their own gods for themselves.[34] The end result of God's work is to lead us through pain and make us new creatures, truly free.

---

33. Hong, *The Downward Ascent*, 50–51.

34. "Man is by nature unable to want God to be God. Indeed, he himself wants to be God, and does not want God to be God." See "Disputation against Scholastic Theology" (1517), thesis 17 in Luther, *Luther's Works: Volume 31*, 10.

DECIPHERING THE ERA

It is commonly thought that our age is no longer driven by a sense of guilt consciousness. We are far more apt to dismiss guilt as an objective reality—a violation of God's commands—and speak subjectively instead of guilt "feelings," as if our guilt could be therapeutically worked through or denied outright. And, if that is the case, perhaps Luther's (and the classical Reformers') concern about guilt is no longer relevant. It has long been said that our society wrestles not with guilt but meaninglessness, that is, contemporary people are no longer haunted by guilt but by anomie. We do lots of things but we lack an ultimate purpose that gives meaning to all the things we do. Of course, we might respond, "Who is responsible for this?," and ignore the fact that we ourselves are complicit in this culture of anomie. In light of this, Alan Jones, an Episcopal Dean in San Francisco, several years ago noted that we live in an age when everything is permitted and nothing is forgiven.[35] But our not being alarmed by our guilt hardly means that we are innocent. People are not less sinful than they were years ago. We simply have more tricks to let ourselves off the hook and not feel so guilty.

In that light, one might listen carefully to preaching of late. At one time, preachers condemned sin outright from their pulpits. The pulse now seems to be, if you accept Jesus as your Lord and Savior, everything will be just fine. This type of preaching might be popular, but is it true to Christian discipleship? Is it true to Jesus, who told us that we too have a cross awaiting us (Mark 8:34–35)? Does it not render religion into the very trivial thing for which the classical atheists, such as Ludwig Feuerbach, Karl Marx, and Sigmund Freud ridiculed religion—that faith is a kind of sugar pill? At some level, perhaps, the atheists have some insight into some forms of so-called Christianity.

In days of yore, Lent and the confessional service were taken with great seriousness. During Lent, before receiving the sacrament at any time of year, people actually were asked to examine themselves, in thought, word, and deed, along with their confessor in light of the Ten Commandments. This was not due to some kind of self-loathing, but instead to the desire to be really honest about oneself before God. What we Christians no longer seem to be doing has been taken up by people seeking recovery from addictions. There one needs to do a "fourth step" in which one does a "searching moral inventory" of one's life. This process becomes the basis for a "fifth step" in which one confesses this moral inventory to oneself, another, and one's "higher power." Even to this day; this process is a standard procedural step

---

35. See "Speaking the Gospel Today," in Forde, *The Preached God*, 179.

in programs of recovery. We Christians seem to have forgotten what people in recovery know.

Even so, one might quickly object to Luther's line of thinking. After all, who tries to do good works to earn salvation? This objection might have a point. Perhaps quite untrue to Luther, we hardly see God as a judge anymore. However, our failure to acknowledge God as judge or our denial of it will not abate his judgment. Indeed, we will be judged for failing to acknowledge him as the ultimate judge (Matthew 25). In spite of this, with our secularistic outlook neither does our failure mean that we are relaxing more. It is fair to say, at least for Americans, that our workaholism is killing us. Even those of us who ignore the need for a gracious God can hardly find a gracious workplace. Our own lack of civility in the workplace comes around to bite us. Evidence indicates that the chief thing that American workers complain about is not poor salaries and benefits, but their fellow workers.

And few of us escape what a therapist might call an "inner critic," often an inner abuser, for whom none of our works measure up. On top of that, no therapy or drug seems to be able to silence this inner critic or abuser. In a world hell-bent on glory, we need a word of grace. As Luther reminds us, "The law says, 'do this,' and it is never done. Grace says, 'believe in this,' and everything is already done" (thesis 26).

Abandoning the biblical God, the one who judges the quick and the dead, will not free us from theology, at least a theology of glory. For that theology is the perennial theology of a fallen race. Even those of us for whom God as working in all things is absent still face critique from co-workers, fellow students, parents, our "inner critic," and a whole host of things which trigger such self-critique. Ultimately, whether we believe it or not, it is God who will critique us. Our (Gnostic[36]) centering of ultimate matters in ourselves and relegating matters with God as penultimate will be found wanting. As Luther says in Thesis 11, "Arrogance cannot be avoided or true hope be present unless the judgment of condemnation is feared in every work." Hence, our unbelief and our workaholism might be nothing other than a defense—against God our ultimate and truthful judge and critic. Few thinkers have understood such self-defense as well as the late anthropologist Ernest Becker, who in his book, *Denial of Death*, claimed that we humans use symbols in order to gain a sense of an ultimate worth in view of the pervasive death that erodes such confidence.

> But man is not just a blind glob of idling protoplasm, but a creature with a name who lives in a world of symbols and dreams and not merely matter. His sense of self-worth is constituted, and his

36. See Bloom, *The American Religion*; Lee, *Against the Protestant Gnostics*.

cherished narcissism feeds on symbols on an abstract idea of his own worth, an idea composed of sounds, words, and images, in the air, in the mind, or paper. And this means that man's natural yearning for organismic activity, the pleasures of incorporation and expansion, can be fed limitlessly in the domain of symbols and so into immortality. The single organism can expand into dimensions of worlds and times without moving a physical limb; it can take eternity into itself even as it graspingly dies.[37]

In Becker's mind, such quests to secure self-worth fail us. The cross is un-avoidable and inevitable, no matter who one is or whether one seeks to honor the creator or not. For Luther, the cross is a particular event—the death of Jesus of Nazareth. But it has bearing upon all people in all times. Its point is that self-justification—the very reason why we put Jesus on the cross—will do us in. And, ultimately, it is God who is doing every sinner in, rendering them all quiet and passive, so that he might do his work in them. There is no better response to the charge of quietism leveled at practitioners of the theology of the cross than that eventually we'll all be quite quiet, six feet under. Hence, for Luther: *CRUX sola est nostra theologia,* "the cross alone is our theology."

TO MAKE ALL THINGS NEW

In her book, *Bright Valley of Love,* Edna Hong describes the dark days of Hitler and how they bore upon the epileptic colony of Bethel, sponsored by the German Church and led by Pastor Fritz von Bodelschwingh. Hitler's goal, of course, was to liquidate all epileptics. At Bethel, hope was given to a cripple, Gunther, who lived with his epileptic friends. One Advent Pastor Fritz, following up on Gunther's inquiry, asked the children why Christmas was so great. Gunther's friends struggled for a response, but it was specifi-cally Lena who provided the answer:

> Lena, who had covered her face with her hands and laid it on the table in perfect imitation of her Uncle Pastor, beat and cudgeled her brains. Why, oh why did God send his Son at Christmas? And finally in that dim brain box a great light burst. Leni climbed from her chair to the table. "Because," she shouted triumphantly, "Because everything has a crack!"
>
> Pastor Fritz strode to Lena's side and gathered her into his arms. From that lofty perch she could kiss the top of his head ecstatically. Pastor Fritz knelt beside Gunther's chair. Their eyes

37. Becker, *The Denial of Death,* 3.

met. By the same path that pain had sped from one to the other, a radiant trust returned.

"It is true, Gunther, that there is a crack in everything. God sees the crack better than we do, and the crack is ever so much worse than we think it is. That is why God sent his Son from the heavenly home to our earthly home. Not to patch up the crack, but to make everything new. That is why Christmas is so great, Gunther."[38]

To make everything new! This is what God is about in raising the dead. As noted above, resurrection is the other side of the cross. A theology of resurrection is the complement to the theology of the cross. And, it is something that only God can do. But that means that God refuses to work with zombies. We really do need to die to playing god for ourselves. And it is that death from which God raises us. Because God has raised Jesus from the dead, God makes good on his promise. And this promise is given to us in the very words of absolution: Your sins are forgiven.

In faith we are united with Christ and his goodness; we receive his gifts. But we share in Christ's goodness only because he was willing to become the "greatest thief, murderer, adulterer, robber, desecrator, blasphemer, etc., there has ever been anywhere in the world,"[39] bearing our sin and that attack which is heard in his cry of dereliction, "My God, my God, why have you forsaken me?" While our theorizing about the atonement is appropriate in order to keep us in the true faith, we need to keep in mind that the atonement cannot be reduced to a theory. Ultimately, the atonement is God's action to save us in Jesus' cross and resurrection. It is a scriptural truth. But just for that very reason this truth must be delivered in the word of promise—the gospel—in public preaching.

CATEGORICAL GIFT

For Luther, our earthly and worldly reality is not to be seen as a mere portal to the eternal, our desire to rest in God and to live comfortably to God. The "wise" (wisdom of the world) see in beautiful things an opportunity to ascend to beauty itself. As noble as that ascension sounds, it does not free us from ourselves. Our will remains in control. Hence, Luther notes in thesis 14, "Free will, after the fall, exists in name only, and as long as it does what it is able to do, it commits a mortal sin." Again, God's attitude about beauty is so very different from ours. He "does not find, but creates, that which is

38. Hong, *Bright Valley of Love*, 60–61.
39. Luther, *Luther's Works: Volume 26*: 277.

pleasing to it" (thesis 28). God deems us sinners as beautiful because he sees us as his creatures—and as redeemed.

In light of what has been said, it seems that with your defenses or guard up, you never see the world as it actually is. You only see it through the broken lens of self-protection at every corner. God's proper work permits us to see the way things really are, permits us to experience the world as creation, as sure and pure gift (and not as the starting point for heavenly ascent) or a project whose perfection is our task. In contrast to the German philosopher Immanuel Kant's affirmation of a "categorical imperative," in which we must do those things which should be a universal law for everyone (and thus thereby fulfill our deepest human potential), German theologian Oswald Bayer proposes that God's grace is simply and nothing other than "categorical gift."[40] What more can God give you than the forgiveness that he has already given you in Jesus Christ—and with that forgiveness, life and salvation? Unlike the theology of glory, grace is not a supplement for human willpower, something by which we can perfect nature, be elevated to the eternal, or achieve a utopia of peace and justice. Rather, grace liberates nature. It sets it free from being "curved in on itself." And set free, we are free for others and this good earth, in their needs and their call to us.

In light of a theology of the cross, we can name sin for what it actually is. It is not merely misdeeds. At a deeper level, sin is a kind of addiction to self (seeking one's own in all things). In that regard we can see why Luther contends that "desire" can be extinguished.[41] Why? You have already been given the gift. What more could you be given? You have received forgiveness of sins, and where there is forgiveness of sins, there is new life, openness to creation as a gift and not as a resource for our self-development. How? Forgiveness opens you up by making your defenses go down. When your defenses are down you can live outside your skin in others and their needs. As Rowan Williams noted, "To know forgiveness in the midst of hell because of the cross of Christ is the true criterion of the Christian faith."[42]

40. Bayer, *Theology the Lutheran Way*, 119.

41. Thesis 22: "Thus also the desire for knowledge is not satisfied by the acquisition of wisdom but is stimulated that much more. Likewise the desire for glory is not satisfied by the acquisition of glory, nor is the desire to rule satisfied by power and authority, nor is the desire for praise satisfied by praise, and so on . . . The remedy for curing desire does not lie in satisfying it, but in extinguishing it. It other words, he who wishes to become wise does not seek wisdom by progressing toward it but becomes a fool by retrogressing into seeing folly. Likewise he who wishes to have much power, honor, pleasure, satisfaction in all things must flee rather than seek power, honor, pleasure, and satisfaction in all things. This is the wisdom which is folly to the world." See Luther, "Heidelberg Disputation," 54.

42. Williams, *The Wound of Knowledge*, 152.

Or, one might say, in God's eyes you are "validated." As accepted by God, as God's own, we are free.

HOW FREE?

Gerhard O. Forde once told the following story:

> A pastor friend related an interesting reaction from a teen-
> ager to *Free to Be*, a little book on Luther's Catechism by James
> Nestingen and myself. He said he didn't like the book because
> it seemed to tell him he could do anything he wanted to do!
> Now what is one supposed to say to that? The most immediate
> reaction, I suppose, would be to jump in on the defensive and
> thunder, "No! No! No!—of course not, you can't do whatever
> you want to do!

Forde responds:

> But think for a moment. Perhaps then the whole battle would
> be lost. One must sail into the storm. Should one not rather
> say "Son, you are right. You got the message. The Holy Spirit is
> starting to get to you." For now, you see, the question is: "what
> do you want to do? Who are you now that God has spoken his
> word to you?" But is that not dangerous? Of course it is! But
> God has taken a great risk to get what he wants. We can only
> follow him in that. Is it not "cheap grace"? No! It's not cheap,
> it's free! "Cheap grace," you see, is not improved by making it
> expensive, a "bargain basement" special. It's free.[43]

Such freedom is dizzying. We are all afraid that such freedom is no guar-
antee that we will not abuse our freedom. But St. Paul's point is well-taken:
how can we who have died to sin still live in it? We should not run from
gospel-freedom. After all, if the Son sets you free, you will be free indeed![44]
As self-justifying, our freedom in Christ may terrify us, but for the anxious
conscience, nothing can be sweeter. Jesus has come not for the righteous but
for the sinful and if you are at all aware of your sin, and its consequences, you
simply cannot get enough grace, enough gospel. When it comes—through a
preacher's mouth—you jump for joy and want more.

43. Forde, *Justification by Faith*, 33–34.

44. See the hymn by Danish bishop Hans A. Brorson "God's Son Has Made Me
Free"; free translation by Oscar R. Overby, put to music by Edvard Grieg (Minneapolis:
Augsburg Choral Library, 1945 and 1973).

CONCLUSION

As we are free, as we are open to this creation as God's creation; in faith, we can serve. We are offered a path indifferent to either that of antinomianism (the view that the old Adam or Eve does not need the law) or legalism (we are bound by the law). Instead, we are confident that a good tree issues in good fruit, naturally and spontaneously. At its core, even our sanctification ultimately is not our doing, not a program, but the work of the Holy Spirit. In sanctification it is God who gets more of us and not so much we who get more of God. As we are being conformed more and more to the image of Christ, we are less and less concerned about our spiritual progress and more concerned about matters at hand: how can I honor God and serve neighbor in word and deed? Growth in grace: less of oneself and more of God, and all of this due finally to God's own doing! This is our pilgrimage, our *itinerarium*. And the more sway that Christ has over me, and the less sway that the old Adam has over me, is there not more power, even more growth, in Christ-likeness . . . even if such growth defies calculation and measurement?

Our life is that of the cross and the resurrection.—none can escape the pain that life brings, especially if we seek to do what is right in the world. Yet, such painful events are not beyond God's work. God works through the crushing events of life precisely to raise the dead, to call sinners as his own, to remove them as the centers of their own universes and replace them with himself as center. God provides us a new path upon which to walk, good works which serve our neighbor, and a grateful heart from which to praise him. For this, we can be most grateful.

BIBLIOGRAPHY

Althaus, Paul. *The Theology of Martin Luther*. Translated by Robert C. Schultz. Philadelphia: Fortress, 1966.

Bayer, Oswald. *Martin Luther's Theology: A Contemporary Interpretation*. Translated by Thomas H. Trapp. Grand Rapids: Eerdmans, 2008.

———. *Theology the Lutheran Way*. Translated by Jeff Silcock and Mark C. Mattes. Grand Rapids: Eerdmans, 2007.

Becker, Ernest. *The Denial of Death*. New York: Free Press, 1973.

Becker, Siegbert. *The Foolishness of God*. Milwaukee: Northwestern Publishing, 1982.

Bernstein, Richard. *Beyond Objectivism and Relativism: Science, Hermeneutics, and Praxis*. Philadelphia: University of Pennsylvania Press, 1983.

Bloom, Harold. *The American Religion: The Emergence of the Post-Christian Nation*. New York: Simon & Schuster, 1992.

Dieter, Theodor. "Why Does Luther's Doctrine of Justification Matter Today." In *The Global Luther: A Theologian for Modern Times*, edited by Christine Helmer, 189ff. Minneapolis: Fortress, 2009.

Elert, Werner. *The Christian Ethos: The Foundations of the Christian Way of Life*. Translated by Carl J. Schindler. Philadelphia: Muhlenberg, 1957.

———. *The Christian Faith: An Outline of Lutheran Dogmatics*. Translated by Martin H. Bertram and Walter R. Bouman. Columbus: Lutheran Theological Seminary, 1974.

Forde, Gerhard O. *Justification by Faith: A Matter of Death and Life*. Philadelphia: Fortress, 1982.

———. *A More Radical Gospel*. Edited by Mark C. Mattes and Steven Paulson. Grand Rapids: Eerdmans, 2004.

———. *On Being a Theologian of the Cross: Reflections on Luther's Heidelberg Disputation, 1518*. Grand Rapids: Eerdmans, 1997.

———. *The Preached God: Proclamation in Word and Sacrament*. Edited by Mark C. Mattes and Steven Paulson. Grand Rapids: Eerdmans, 2007.

Hong, Edna. *Bright Valley of Love* Minneapolis: Augsburg 1976.

———. *The Downward Ascent*. Minneapolis: Augsburg, 1979.

Janz, Denis R. "Syllogism or Paradox: Aquinas and Luther on Theological Method." *Theological Studies* 59 (1998) 3–21.

Jüngel, Eberhard. *God as the Mystery of the World: On the Foundation of the Theology of the Crucified One in the Dispute between Theism and Atheism*. Translated by Darrell L. Guder. Grand Rapids: Eerdmans, 1983.

Kolb, Robert. *Martin Luther: Confessor of the Faith*. Oxford: Oxford University Press, 2009.

Lazareth, William H. *Christians in Society: Luther, the Bible, and Social Ethics*. Minneapolis: Fortress, 2001.

Lee, Philip J. *Against the Protestant Gnostics* New York: Oxford, 1987.

Lienhard, Marc. *Luther: Witness to Jesus Christ: Stages and Themes of the Reformer's Christology,*. Translated by Edwin H. Robertson. Minneapolis: Augsburg, 1982.

Loewenich, Walther von. *Luther's Theology of the Cross*. Minneapolis: Augsburg, 1976.

Luther, Martin. "Heidelberg Disputation, 1518." In *Luther's Works, Volume 31*, edited by Harold J. Grimm, 39–70. Philadelphia: Fortress, 1957.

———. *Luther's Works: Volume 26*. Edited by Jaroslav Pelikan, H.C. Oswald and H.T. Lehmann, Luther's Works. St. Louis: Concordia, 1976.

———. *Luther's Works: Volume 31*. Edited by Harold J. Grimm and Helmut T. Lehmann. 55 vols. Minneapolis: Fortress, 1957.

———. *Luther's Works: Volume 33*. Translated by E. Gordon Rupp, Philip S. Watson, A.N. Marlow and B. Drewery. Edited by Jaroslav Pelikan, Philip S. Watson, H. T. Lehmann and H. C. Oswald. Minneapolis: Fortress, 1972.

———. *Weimarer Ausgabe 5. Kritische Gesammtausgabe*. 121 vols. Vol. 5, D. Martin Luthers Werke. Weimar: Böhlaus, 1892.

Mattes, Mark C., and Ron Darge. *Imaging the Journey . . . Of Contemplation, Meditation, Reflection, and Adventure*. Minneapolis: University Lutheran Press, 2006.

McGrath, Alister E. *Luther's Theology of the Cross* London: Blackwell, 1985.

Niebuhr, H. Richard. *The Responsible Self: An Essay in Moral Philosophy*. Louisville: Westminster John Knox, 1999.

Obermann, Heiko. *Forerunners of the Reformation: The Shape of Late Medieval Thought Illustrated by Key Documents*. Philadelphia: Fortress, 1981.

Paulson, Steven. "Categorical Preaching." *Lutheran Quarterly* 21 (2007) 268–93.

Pearson, Thomas D. "Luther's Pragmatic Appropriation of the Natural Law Tradition." In *Natural Law: A Lutheran Reappraisal*, edited by Robert C. Baker and Roland Cap Ehlke, 39–63. St. Louis: Concordia, 2011.

Westhelle, Vitor. *The Scandalous God: The Use and Abuse of the Cross*. Minneapolis: Fortress, 2006.

Williams, Rowan. *The Wound of Knowledge: Christian Spirituality from the New Testament to St. John of the Cross*. Lanham, MD: Cowley, 1991.

Zahl, Paul F. M. *Grace in Practice: A Theology of Everyday Life*. Grand Rapids: Eerdmans, 2007.

14

Grace for Victims

Justin S. Holcomb

ONE-WAY LOVE TO VICTIMS

There is an epidemic of sexual assault, and victims need the kind of hope and help that only the gospel of Jesus Christ can provide. If you have experienced the disgrace and violence of sexual assault, this is written to you and for you—not about you. What happened to you was not your fault. You are not to blame. You did not deserve it. You are not responsible for what happened to you. Nobody had the right to violate you. You were supposed to be treated with dignity and respect. You are not worthless. You were sinned against. Despite all the pain, healing *can* happen and there *is* hope because there is grace.

Grace is "one-way love."[1] This is the opposite of the experience of victims of sexual assault, which was "one-way violence." It seeks you out even if you have nothing to give in return. Grace is being loved when you are or feel unlovable. Grace has the power to turn despair into hope. Grace listens, lifts up, cures, transforms, and heals. To the experience of one-way violence, God brings one-way love.

Disgrace is the opposite of grace, and is experienced by the numerous victims of sexual assault. It destroys, causes pain, deforms, and wounds.

---

1. Zahl, *Grace in Practice*, 64.

Disgrace alienates and isolates, making the victim feel worthless, rejected unwanted, and repulsive, like a persona non grata (a "person without grace").

God in his grace declares and promises that you will be healed of your disgrace. Contrary to the proponents of the healing benefits of self-esteem for victims, this promise does not come from within you but from outside of you. One-way love does not command "Heal thyself!" but declares "You will be healed!" Jeremiah 17:14 promises, " Heal me, O Lord, and I shall be healed; Save me, and I shall be saved, For you are my praise." God's one-way love replaces self-love and is the true path to healing. This is astonishingly good news and it highlights the contrast between disgrace and grace or one-way violence and one-way love. God heals our wounds.

THE DISGRACE OF SEXUAL ASSAULT

Defining what exactly a sexual assault is has been debated and eventually narrowed to exclude those who have been wounded. A broad definition is necessary to avert leaving out real victims who have been assaulted, and those who should be supporting. In Rid of My Disgrace, my wife Lindsey and I define sexual assault as *any type of sexual behavior or contact where consent is not freely given or obtained and is accomplished through force, intimidation, violence, coercion, manipulation, threat, deception, or abuse of authority.*[2]

The number of occurrences of sexual assaults is staggering. At least one in four women[3] and one in six men[4] are or will be victims of sexual

2. Holcomb and Holcomb, *Rid My Disgrace*, 28.

3. Hall, *Any Woman*; Koss, Gidycz, and Wisniewski, "The Scope of Rape: Incidence and Prevalence of Sexual Aggression and Victimization in a National Sample of Higher Education Students"; Koss, "Rape: Scope, Impact, Interventions, and Public Policy Responses"; Kilpatrick, "Criminal Victimization: Lifetime Prevalence, Reporting to Police, and Psychological Impact"; Kilpatrick and Seymour, "Rape in America: A Report to the Nation"; Koss and Dinero, "Discrimination Analysis of Risk Factors for Sexual Victimization among a National Sample of College Women". Tjaden and Thoennes, "Prevalence, Incidence, and Consequences of Violence Against Women: Findings from the National Violence Against Women Survey." And Sorenson, "The Prevalence of Adult Sexual Assault: The Los Angeles Epidemiologic Catchment Area Project." An estimated 20–25 percent of college women in the United States experience attempted or completed rape during their college careers: Fisher, Cullen, and Turner, "The Sexual Victimization of College Women." On college campuses, 74 percent of victims knew their assailant and nine out of ten offenders included boyfriends, ex-boyfriends, classmates, friends, and acquaintances: Hart, "Violent Victimization of College Students."

4. One study suggests the rate of abused males may be far higher, between 20–30 percent. See Briere, *Child Abuse Trauma*, 4. A 2005 study conducted by the US Centers for Disease Control and Prevention, on San Diego Kaiser Permanente HMO members,

assault in their lifetime. And these statistics are probably underestimates. Sexual assault is frequent—every two minutes someone in the United States is sexually assaulted. Sexual assault takes place in trusted relationships—80 percent of the perpetrators know the victims (a relative, spouse, dating part-ner, friend, pastor, teacher, boss, coach, therapist doctor, etc.). It occurs in 10 to 14 percent of all marriages,[5] and in families incest is experienced by 10 to 20 percent of children.[6] Not surprisingly these figures need to factor in the fact that due to the shame sexual assault brings to its victims it is one of the most underreported crimes. Of these underreported crimes males are less apt to report it due to their socialization.

Regarding the age breakdown of sexual assault, 15 percent of sexual assault victims are under age twelve, 29 percent are ages twelve to seventeen, and 80 percent are under age thirty.[7] The highest-risk years are ages twelve to thirty-four, and girls ages sixteen to nineteen are four times more likely than the general population to be victims of sexual assault.

---

reported that 16 percent of males were sexually abused by the age of eighteen: Dube, "Long-Term Consequences of Childhood Sexual Abuse by Gender of Victim." A 2003 national study of US adults reported that 14.2 percent of men were sexually abused before the age of eighteen: Briere and Elliot, "Prevalence and Symptomatic Sequelae of Self-Reported Childhood Physical and Sexual Abuse in a General Population Sample of Men and Women." A 1998 study reviewing research on male childhood sexual abuse concluded that the problem is "common, under-reported, under-recognized, and under-treated": Holmes and Slap, "Sexual Abuse of Boys: Definition, Prevalence, Correlates, Sequelae, and Management." A 1996 study of male university students in the Boston area reported that 18 percent of men were sexually abused before the age of sixteen: Lisak, Hopper, and Song, "Factors in the Cycle of Violence: Gender Rigid-ity and Emotional Constriction." A 1990 national study of US adults reported that 16 percent of men were sexually abused before the age of eighteen: Finkelhor, "Sexual Abuse in a National Survey of Adult Men and Women: Prevalence, Characteristics, and Risk Factors." Within the past few years, North American researchers have found that one out of six boys is a victim of sexual abuse. See Dorais, *Don't Tell: The Sexual Abuse of Boys*, 16; Holmes, Offen, and Waller, "See No Evil, Hear No Evil, Speak No Evil: Why Do Relatively Few Male Victims of Childhood Sexual Abuse Receive Help for Abuse-Related Issues in Adulthood?" Only 16 percent of men with documented histories of sexual abuse considered themselves to have been sexually abused: Widom and Mor-ris, "Accuracy of Adult Recollections of Childhood Victimization: Part 2. Childhood Sexual Abuse."

5 Bergen, *Wife Rape*; Finkelhor and Yllo, *License to Rape*; Russell, *Rape in Marriage*. Mahoney and Williams, "Sexual Assault in Marriage: Prevalence, Consequences and Treatment for Wife Rape."

6 Briere and Runtz, "University Males' Sexual Interest in Children"; Finkelhor et al., "Sexual Abuse in a National Survey of Adult Men and Women"; Russell, "The Incidence and Prevalence of Intrafamilial and Extrafamilial Sexual Abuse of Female Children."

7. "2004 National Crime Victimization Survey," (Washington D.C.: U.S. Depart-ment of Justice, 2004).

Victims are not just statistics, but humans created in the image of God who experience a wide range of physical, emotional, psychological, and physiological effects. The emotional effects of sexual assault are not just brain chemical and physiological responses to stimuli, but they reveal what you believe about God, yourself, your experience of sexual assault, others, and the world.

The gospel of Jesus offers new emotions to victims and how they relate to the current emotions they experience. Grace offers to victims the gift of refuting distortions and faulty thinking, and replaces their condemning, counterfactual beliefs with more accurate ones that reflect the truths about God, themselves, and God's grace-filled response to their disgrace. Some of the most prevalent responses to sexual assault include denial, distorted self-image, shame, guilt, anger, and despair. Let's look at each one and see how God applies grace to disgrace through the gospel of Jesus.

DENIAL

Sexual assault often communicates to victims that they are alone, unimportant, beyond hope, and not worthy of sympathy. It tempts victims to deny, minimize, and repress the experience of being assaulted, especially among those assaulted by someone they know. Denial and minimization are key methods victims use for lessening or coping with the pain and trauma from an assault.

Many victims do not fully acknowledge what has happened to them, or they minimize the intensity of the experience. Initially, denial can slow the process down to create a buffer or safety zone so survivors can begin to cope with difficult emotions. Denial fuels the myth that time heals all wounds. However, instead of lessening suffering, too much denial and minimization may increase the pain. They do not allow the victims to deal with the severe mental and emotional tolls, the psychological destruction, and the traumatic effects of the assault.

Instead of denying, minimizing, or ignoring what happened to you, God mourns what happened. In the person of Jesus he identifies with you, and he has compassion. Jesus "was despised and rejected by men; a man of sorrows, and acquainted with grief."[8] Christ not only suffered for his people but also suffers with them. This is primarily demonstrated at the cross of Jesus. He knows what it means to be alone, naked, bleeding, and crying out to God. He shared in absolute abandonment and the pain of sufferers, and was a victim of violence and suffered injustice. While the cross shows us

8. Isa 53:3.

that God understands pain and does not judge you for your feelings of grief, the resurrection shows you that God is active in restoring peace, that He conquered sin and is reversing its effects.

God knows your suffering. He sees, responds, and invites you to participate in the sorrow and grief He has for your situation. You can safely grieve the evil that has been done to you, name it as evil, and be assured that God is present with you even when you are alone. You are not encouraged to be silent or deny, but to feel and express your emotions, to cry or weep, to grieve the destruction you experienced. Because of Jesus, you have the privilege to confidently go to God and receive grace and mercy. Your need and your cries don't cause God to shun you or distance himself from you. Rather, he has compassion on you (Heb 4:14–16), and can sympathize with your weaknesses.

IDENTITY

Sexual assault victims not only have a tendency to deny what has been done to them, but to distort who they are. The issue of identity is a significant part of a victim's self-image. Disgrace done to victims can result in feelings of disgust toward themselves. A sense of identity confusion about "who I am" can contribute to an identity of self-condemnation or a view of the self as nothing. There are lots of people with profoundly negative self-images, which can fuel self-blame, self-hate, and self-harm. Sexual assault maligns a victim's sense of self and communicates that they are stupid, filthy, foolish, worthless, defiled, impure, damaged, gross, screwed-up, unwanted, or dirty.

Making a transition from a "victim" identity to an identity in Christ is offered in God's redemptive work through Jesus. If you are a victim of sexual assault, then that is a part of your story that you should not deny or minimize. If it becomes *the* story about you, then your identity will be founded on disgrace. But God offers the redemptive story told in scripture. The identity from that story is founded on grace in at least two specific ways.

First, if you have faith in Christ, God calls you certain things that convey value. The "people of God" is one of the most significant. This intimacy of God's concern for his people is seen clearly in the declaration that you are a child of God if you trust in Christ (1 John 3:1–2). This is, perhaps, the most remarkable thing you can be called. This new identity is rooted in being adopted into God's family. God adopted you and accepted you because he loves you. You didn't do anything to deserve his love. He loved you when you were unlovable.

Second, because of faith in Christ, you are the righteousness of God. 2 Corinthians 5:21 is an identity-altering statement: "For our sake he made him to be sin who knew no sin, so that in him we might become the righteousness of God." This is imputation, which is ascribing characteristics to someone that they do not have by nature. Imputation is the crediting in our favor, from the standpoint of God, who is the source of all judgment, of the perfect moral worth of Jesus. It also implies the humiliation of Jesus, by means of the transfer to him of the full burden of the disgraces we have done and those done to us. By faith we are "in Christ" and as such we are seen as he is. His righteousness, holiness, and blamelessness are imputed to us.

If you are in Christ, your identity is deeper than any of your wounds. It is also found in Christ and founded on Christ, who is God, so your new identity is more secure and stable than any other identity that has been attributed to you. This truth brings great relief, because you are not doomed to live as a victim. It doesn't eliminate your wounds nor silence your cry for deliverance or healing. But it does mean those wounds are not the final word on who you are. They don't enslave you and determine your life.

The difference between identity in Christ and anything else is huge. The difference is between resignation to a life as a victim and its consequences versus living secure in Christ and all the grace that comes with it. In order to have the cycle of disgrace broken we need a God before whom we can put aside the disguises. When we trust in Christ, disgrace is halted and we can step onto the firm ground of God's acceptance, love, and grace.

You can rest in the knowledge and assurance of your new identity because you did not earn it and no one can take it away from you no matter what they have done to you. It was achieved for you by God. Nothing can separate you from the love of God. You are secure in God because you are his and he cannot disown himself.

SHAME

Sexual assault is shameful for victims, and feelings of nakedness, rejection, and dirtiness are often associated with their assault. The feeling of shameful self-blame is often powerful and prominent for many victims. Jean-Paul Sartre accurately describes shame as "a hemorrhage of the soul" that is a painful, unexpected, and disorienting experience. Shame has the power to take our breath away and smother us with condemnation, rejection, and disgust. To be shamed is to be abased and dishonored, to be rejected from the community—especially when a victim isn't believed, is told to be silent, is blamed, or is not supported. To feel ashamed is to experience the pain of embarrassment, disapproval, and rejection.

Shame is a painfully confusing experience—a sort of mental and emotional disintegration that makes us acutely aware of our inadequacies and shortcomings, and is often associated with a shrinking feeling of failure. It can be particularly destructive if a victim feels stigmatized by withering, energy-draining feelings of worthlessness. Oftentimes victims will attempt to numb this pain through drugs, alcohol, sex, power, success, or whatever else enables them to stop feeling. You'll do whatever it takes to start feeling a measure of self-worth. You may even seek to overachieve religiously or morally in order to relieve the feelings of shame, but this only short-circuits and increases it.

But there is good news. God understands your shame. God extends his compassion and his mighty, rescuing arm to take away shame in the person of Christ. Jesus reveals the love of God for his people by covering their nakedness, identifying with those who feel or have been rejected, cleansing all their defilement, and conquering their enemy who shames them. He actively pursued outsiders and outcasts, those who experienced shame. Jesus purposely reached out to those who were rejected and considered "outside the camp" because they were considered "unclean"—morally, socially, or religiously. His solidarity with the shamed and excluded of his day led to the ultimate experience of shame—his crucifixion.

The purpose of the Roman cross was to expose, display, and humiliate the condemned. Ironically, God takes the weapon of evil—shame—to mock and then destroy it. Christ's resurrection interrupts the celebration of evil and triumphs over shame, by shaming shame and revealing God's love for, not rejection of, you.

On the cross, Jesus both experienced shame and took your shame on himself. Yet Jesus, of all people, did not deserve to be shamed. Still, he took on your shame, so it no longer defines you nor has power over you. Because of the cross, we can be fully exposed, because God no longer identifies us by what we have done or by what has been done to us. If we trust in Jesus, God sees us as Jesus was: pure, righteous, and without blemish. We have been given the righteousness of Christ. We can't add to it or subtract from it. In Jesus, you are made completely new.

GUILT

Many sexual assault victims feel deep guilt. This is frequently manifested in condemnation, judgment, and self-blame. Guilt is accompanied with the threat of judgment. And judgment is the root of fear, anxiety, stress, depression, chronic self-contempt, anxiety or panic attacks, self-hate, anger, and sometimes suicide. Guilt accompanies victims of sexual assault because many feel that they could have avoided it somehow.

No matter where you were, who you were with, why you were there, or what you felt when you were there the sexual assault that took place was not your fault—not at all. This realization all by itself can bring great freedom and relief. Yet as soon as you move past this roadblock, you face the reality that the sin done against you is probably not the only reason you've felt guilty. You have sinned against God and others—both prior to your assault and in response to what happened to you. You may be tempted to justify your sinful behaviors because of the harm, assault, mistreatment, loss or betrayal you've experienced, but when seen through a cross-centered lens, this is simply one self-atonement strategy among many.

The shocking message of grace is that Jesus was forsaken for us so we could be forgiven. The cross is the convergence of great suffering and divine forgiveness. Psalm 85:10 says that "righteousness and peace" will "kiss each other." The cross is where that occurred, where God's demands, his righteousness, coincide with his mercy. Jesus laid down his life as our substitute. We receive divine forgiveness, mercy, and peace because Jesus took our divine punishment, the result of God's righteousness against sin. God in Christ is submitting to God's own wrath for the sake of forgiving sinners. God turned his wrath away from you and toward Christ on the cross.

This is why the cross is the power of God to save you and forgive you. If you trust in Christ, all your sins—past, present, and future—are forgiven. All of them. Also, threat of punishment, or sense of judgment, is canceled. Because of the cross, God declares you righteous if you trust in Jesus. In addition to being declared righteous, you are also reconciled to God through the cross.

In the resurrection, God turns your eyes away from your sins and directs them to Christ. This means that the gospel is not just negatively stated—no more guilt, no more condemnation, no more wrath—but is also understood positively. In Christ you are loved, accepted, innocent. You can be honest about every sin and failure without fear because you know he is for you and will forgive you for Jesus' sake. You can have assurance and confidence in relating to God. Your guilt is gone.

ANGER

Sexual assault is unquestionably an evil, sinful act that understandably elicits anger. Deep in the hearts of victims, anger swells up against the perpetrator, their rage inflamed by suffering. Anger can be a natural and healthy response to sexual assault. While nearly all victims appropriately experience anger, most express it poorly or not at all.

It is likely that you have been discouraged from expressing your anger. Most victims feel pressure from their families, society, or religion to ignore or suppress it. But suppression does not help anger to dissipate over time. Instead, anger turns into bitterness, hatred, and revengeful obsessions. In fact, unresolved or denied anger can become a destructive force that can tear your life apart through depression, anxiety, paralyzing fear, physical ailments, or symptoms of post-traumatic stress. Anger holds you hostage and leaves you vindictive, addicted, embittered, immoral, and unbelieving.

Scripture does not always describe anger as sin. God is angry and calls you to "be angry." God is angrier over the sin committed against you than you are. He is angry because what happened to you was evil and it harmed you.

Godly anger participates in God's anger against injustice and sin. God is the only one who is perfectly angry and is never sinfully angry. Because we are sinners, we frequently distort and confuse godly anger with our own desire for vengeance or control. This is why the general message of Scripture is that anger is a dangerous emotion that is most often destructive. However, it is appropriate to be angry about the injustice, sin, violence, and evil you experienced. You are not only *invited* to be angry at evil, you are *expected* to be angry. You are invited by God to cry out for him to do what he has promised to do: destroy evil and remove everything that harms others and defames God's name.

Because vengeance is God's, you are free from the exhausting hamster wheel of vindictive behavior. Victims can trust God to make all wrongs right so they can get on with their lives and not fixate on bitterness and hatred. God's wrath is a source of positive hope for the victim. You know that God loves you and will destroy the evil that has harmed you. Because vengeance is God's, you don't have to be vengeful; you can love and forgive your enemy.

Receiving forgiveness and love from God through Christ is essential to understanding forgiveness. Because God forgave you for your sins, you are now free to forgive others. Jesus received God's anger and punishment so those guilty of cosmic treason would be forgiven. As sinners who have received mercy instead of wrath, we have the otherwise inexplicable capability simultaneously to hate wrong and to give love to those who do wrong. What God did for us becomes the power to change. God's one-way love toward us amid our sin undermines our bitterness and can prompt forgiveness of those who sin against us.

DESPAIR

Despair is the most commonly reported symptom of sexual assault. Feeling that you lost something, whether it's your innocence, youth, health, trust, confidence, or sense of safety can lead to despair. For those who have experienced the evil of sexual violence, it's likely that you've had an encounter with despair and depression.

Depression adds seemingly inescapable weight to the existential experience of despair.

For some victims, feelings of hopelessness and helplessness come and go, while for others these feelings deepen into despair. When the feelings of powerlessness are internalized, self-hatred and self-pity intensify to the point of despair. Despair deadens our hearts to the hope that we will be rescued, redeemed, and relived of suffering.

But there is hope. Rather than being simply a desire for a particular outcome that is uncertain, hope is characterized by certainty in the Bible. Hope is sure because God is behind the promise, and the hope you need right now borrows from God's faithfulness in the past and anticipation of it in the future. The basis you have for hope is the resurrection of Jesus from the dead.

Because of Jesus' resurrection, all threats against you are tamed if you trust in Christ. Jesus conquered death, so death and evil done to you is not the end of the story and you can have hope. In being united to Christ, you, too, will conquer as you look through the eyes of faith to the one who has accomplished everything on your behalf through his death and resurrection.

The resurrection of Jesus has also launched a new creation and the coming of a new heavens and new earth where disgrace will be replaced by grace, anxiety will give way to peace, and despair will be banished. In the new creation God will be with us; he will bring peace and we will be perfected. Jesus is the first of that new creation, has already given you new birth into that new creation, and promises to complete it in you, making you gloriously, perfectly like him. What about now? God has not only given us a sure hope, but sent the person of his Holy Spirit to comfort us in the despair and isolation we face in the present.

Godly despair is the groan of the Holy Spirit, and while you may see no explanation for your pain, he knows there is an answer and lovingly communicates your pain to a sovereign God who listens. Your God is strong and he, not the evil done to you, will have the final say about you. That hope animates "groans within ourselves" that everything will someday be renewed. We will be delivered from all sin and misery. Every tear will be wiped away when evil is no more.

So we groan in pain because the painful is still painful. But we also groan in hope because we know what is to come. Hope is a positive expectation for something in the future as opposed to despair that sees only pain and hardship. Biblically, hope has the power to encourage in the present because it is based on sure future expectations. Gabriel Marcel wrote, "Hope is a memory of the future." This side of glory, we will not be fully redeemed and satisfied, but sorrow opens the heart to the desire for the hope of redemption to be fully realized.

GRACE & REDEMPTION IN THE BIBLICAL STORY

It is important to address the effects of sexual assault with the biblical message of grace and redemption. Between the Bible's bookends of creation and restored creation is the unfolding story of redemption. According to the Old Testament, creation begins in harmony, unity, and peace (*shalom*) with God, other human beings, and nature, but redemption was needed because tragically, humanity sinned against God and his word and the result was disgrace and destruction—the vandalism of *shalom*. This violation of shalom was a moment of cosmic treason before God, and plunged humankind into a relational abyss. Sin wrecks the order and goodness of God's world, inverts love for God, which in turn becomes idolatry, and inverts love for neighbor, which becomes exploitation of others. Sin has defiled how things ought to be.

Sex, the very expression of human union and peace, given by God to be pleasurable, intimacy-building in marriage, and the means by which his image-bearers would be spread throughout his good world, becomes a tool for violence after the Fall. Sexual assault is one of the most frequent and disturbing symbols of sin in the Bible. It is uniquely devastating precisely because it distorts the foundational realities of what it means to be human: sexual expression is perverted and used for violence, intrapersonal trust is shattered, and disgrace and shame are heaped on the victim. Sexual assault creates in the victim's mind a tragic and perverse linkage between sex, intimacy, and shame. It can influence how victims feel about themselves, how they understand connections and boundaries with others, and ultimately, how they relate to God. But God does not leave humanity alone. Throughout the Old Testament, he promises to restore *shalom* through the promised Messiah of Israel and the hope of the world.

The Gospel of Jesus Christ occupies the central place in the New Testament, as the message of first importance. God's desire for *shalom* and his response to violence culminates in the person and work of Jesus Christ. The restoration of *shalom* is fully expressed in the life, death, and resurrection of

Jesus and its scope is as "far as the curse is found." Jesus Christ came into this violent world that was shattered by sin, and he suffered a violent death at the hands of violent men in order to save rebellious sinners, rescuing them from divine wrath, and supplying them with divine peace, mercy, grace, and love. The cross is God's attack on sin and violence; it is salvation from sin and its effects. The cross really is a *coup de grace*, meaning "stroke of grace," which refers to the deathblow delivered to the misery of our suffering. The sinless one suffered disgrace, in order to bring sinners grace. The resurrection is the vindication that shalom has been restored. Jesus is the redemptive work of God in our own history, in our own human flesh.

Trusting Jesus isn't a faint hope in generic spiritual sentiments, but is banking our hope and future on the real historical Jesus who lived, died, and rose from the dead. Grace is available because Jesus went through the valley of the shadow of death and rose from death. Jesus responds to victims' pain and past. The gospel engages our life with all its pain, shame, rejection, lost-ness, sin, and death.

So now, to your pain, the gospel says, "You will be healed." To your shame, the gospel says, "You can now come to God in confidence." To your rejection, the gospel says, "You are accepted!" To your lostness, the gospel says, "You are found and I won't ever let you go." To your sin, the gospel says, "You are forgiven and God declares you pure and righteous." To your death, the gospel says, "You were dead, but now you are alive." The message of the gospel redeems what has been destroyed and applies grace to disgrace.

BIBLIOGRAPHY

"2004 National Crime Victimization Survey." Washington DC: U.S. Department of Justice, 2004.

Bergen, R. K. *Wife Rape: Understanding the Response of Survivors and Service Providers* Thousand Oaks, CA: Sage, 1996.

Briere, J. *Child Abuse Trauma: Theory and Treatment of the Lasting Effects.* London: Sage, 1992.

Briere, J., and D. M. Elliot. "Prevalence and Symptomatic Sequelae of Self-Re- Ported Childhood Physical and Sexual Abuse in a General Population Sample of Men and Women." *Child Abuse & Neglect: The International Journal* 27 (2003) 1205–22.

Briere, J., and M. Runtz. "University Males' Sexual Interest in Children: Predicting Potential Indices of 'Pedophilia' in a Nonforensic Sample." *Child Abuse & Neglect: The International Journal* 13 (1989) 65–75.

Dorais, M. *Don't Tell: The Sexual Abuse of Boys.* Montreal: McGill-Queens University Press, 2002.

Dube, S. R. "Long-Term Consequences of Childhood Sexual Abuse by Gender of Victim." *American Journal of Preventive Medicine* 28 (2005) 430–38.

Finkelhor, D. G. "Sexual Abuse in a National Survey of Adult Men and Women: Prevalence, Characteristics, and Risk Factors." *Child Abuse & Neglect: The International Journal* 14 (1990) 19–28.

Finkelhor, D. G., Hotaling G., Lewis I.A., and Smith C. "Sexual Abuse in a National Survey of Adult Men and Women: Prevalence, Characteristics, and Risk Factors." *Child Abuse & Neglect: The International Journal* 14 (1991) 19–28.

Finkelhor, D. G., and K. Yllo. *License to Rape: Sexual Abuse of Wives.* New York: Holt, Rinehart & Winston, 1985.

Fisher, B. S., F. T. Cullen, and M. G. Turner. "The Sexual Victimization of College Women." Washington, DC: Department of Justice, National Institute of Justice, 2000.

Hall, R. *Any Woman: A London Inquiry into Rape and Sexual Assault* London: Falling Wall, 1985.

Hart, T. "Violent Victimization of College Students." U.S. Department of Justice: Office of Justice Programs, Bureau of Justice Statistics Special Report, 2003.

Holcomb, J. S., and L. A. Holcomb. *Rid My Disgrace: Hope and Healing for Victims of Sexual Assault* Chicago: Crossway, 2011.

Holmes, G.R., L. Offen, and G. Waller. "See No Evil, Hear No Evil, Speak No Evil: Why Do Relatively Few Male Victims of Childhood Sexual Abuse Receive Help for Abuse-Related Issues in Adulthood?" *Clinical Psychology Review* 17 (1997) 69–88.

Holmes, W. C., and G. B. Slap. "Sexual Abuse of Boys: Definition, Prevalence, Correlates, Sequelae, and Management." *Journal of the American Medical Association* 280 (1998) 1855–62.

Kilpatrick, D. G. "Criminal Victimization: Lifetime Prevalence, Reporting to Police, and Psychological Impact." *Crime and Delinquency* 33 (1987) 479–89.

Kilpatrick, D. G., and A. Seymour. "Rape in America: A Report to the Nation." National Victims Center: Arlington, VA, and Crime Victims Research and Treatment Center: Charleston, SC, 1992.

Koss, M. "Rape: Scope, Impact, Interventions, and Public Policy Responses." *American Psychologist* 48 (1993) 1062–69.

Koss, M., and T. E. Dinero. "Discrimination Analysis of Risk Factors for Sexual Victimization among a National Sample of College Women." *Journal of Consulting and Clinical Psychology* 57 (1989) 242–50.

Koss, M., C. A. Gidycz, and N. Wisniewski. "The Scope of Rape: Incidence and Prevalence of Sexual Aggression and Victimization in a National Sample of Higher Education Students." *Journal of Consulting and Clinical Psychology* 55 (1987) 162–70.

Lisak, D., J. Hopper, and P. Song. "Factors in the Cycle of Violence: Gender Rigidity and Emotional Constriction." *Journal of Traumatic Stress* 9 (1999) 721–43.

Mahoney, P., and L. Williams. "Sexual Assault in Marriage: Prevalence, Consequences and Treatment for Wife Rape." In *Partner Violence: A Comprehensive Review of 20 Years*, edited by Jana L. Jasinski and Linda M. Williams, 113–62. Thousand Oaks: Sage, 1998.

Russell, D. E. H. "The Incidence and Prevalence of Intrafamilial and Extrafamilial Sexual Abuse of Female Children." *Child Abuse & Neglect: The International Journal* 7 (1983) 133–46.

———. *Rape in Marriage.* Indianapolis: Indiana University Press, 1990.

Sorenson, S. B. "The Prevalence of Adult Sexual Assault: The Los Angeles Epidemiologic Catchment Area Project." *American Journal of Epidemiology* 126 (1987) 1154–64.

Tjaden, P., and N. Thoennes. "Prevalence, Incidence, and Consequences of Violence against Women: Findings from the National Violence against Women Survey." Washington, DC: US Department of Justice, 1998.

Widom, C. S., and S. Morris. "Accuracy of Adult Recollections of Childhood Victimization: Part 2. Childhood Sexual Abuse." *Psychological Assessment* 9 (1997) 34–46.

Zahl, Paul F. M. *Grace in Practice: A Theology of Everyday Life*. Grand Rapids: Eerdmans, 2007.

15

Gospel Doctrine, Gospel Culture

RAYMOND C. ORTLUND JR.

THE FIRST TIME I heard Paul Zahl teach, Isaiah 50:4 was his text: "The Lord GOD has given me the tongue of those who are taught, that I may know how to sustain with a word him who is weary." The ministry the Lord gave his messianic Servant so long ago is reflected today in his pastoral servant, the Rev. Dr. Paul F. M. Zahl. I am happy to participate in this celebration of Paul's life and ministry.

Paul Zahl sustains weary sinners with the word of gospel grace. His ministry is unmistakably marked by the good news of "one-way love," as opposed to law and judgment. But such a ministry is unusual. With so much gospel filling Holy Scripture, one might expect comfortable words to abound among us. One might even expect sinners and sufferers to be running toward our churches. They rarely do. The failure is not in the gospel. Nor is the failure in the good intentions of Christian people. But it is possible to undervalue the relational power of the gospel.

My purpose here is to clarify those social dynamics of the gospel. Grace-justification creates a humane environment for sinners, quite opposite to the ugly social dynamics of self-justification. If we assess ourselves and our ministries not only at the level of doctrinal profession, but also at the level of relational reality, we can better understand what it means to be faithful to the gospel.

This matters, because justification by faith alone is not just one doctrine among others. It is, as our Lutheran friends have rightly taught us, "the article by which the church stands or falls." Luther also taught us that justification by faith alone is hard to accept and hard to hold onto. In his commentary on Galatians, he wrote: "This doctrine cannot be beaten into our ears too much. Though we learn it and understand it well, yet there is no one who takes hold of it perfectly or believes it with all his heart, so frail a thing is our flesh and disobedient to the Spirit."[1] What I am proposing here, on the basis of Galatians, is that the gospel, and justification in particular, calls for more than doctrinal subscription in our churches; it also calls for cultural incarnation in our churches.

I am not saying it is easy to follow through at both levels. It is impossible without Christ himself, as I will assert in my conclusion, but we would be unfaithful to settle for doctrinal correctness only, even on the doctrine of grace, without also establishing a culture of grace in our churches. In other words, if justification by faith alone is the doctrine on which the church stands or falls, what does it *look like* to stand rather than fall? Is it possible to fall, while we think we are standing? The book of Galatians shows it is possible. A church can trumpet the doctrine of grace-justification while, at the same time, be crippled with the dysfunctions of self-justification. In Galatians, Paul is pressing the gospel forward at both levels—the true doctrine and the beautiful culture. He could not be satisfied if the Galatians' only response to his letter would be to reassert justification by faith alone as their official theology; it is clear from this letter that he also expects them to create in their churches social realities consistent with the grace of their theology. That two-fold pursuit defines faithfulness to Christ.

I begin with three assumptions.

1. *The classical Protestant doctrine of justification by grace alone through faith alone in Christ alone, apart from all our works, is the truth.* The Thirty-Nine Articles put it briefly and clearly: "We are accounted righteous before God only for the merit of our Lord and Saviour Jesus Christ, by faith, and not for our own works or deserving. Wherefore, that we are justified by faith only is a most wholesome doctrine and very full of comfort."[2]

   This articulation of the doctrine rightly reminds us of the objectivity, the exteriority, the out-there-ness, the Someone-Else-ness of our justification, received with the empty hands of faith alone, as John Bunyan also reminds us in his *Grace Abounding*:

---

1. Luther, *A Commentary on St. Paul's Epistle to the Galatians,* 40; style updated.

2. Bicknell, *A Theological Introduction to the Thirty-Nine Articles of the Church of England,* 199.

> One day as I was passing in the field, and that too with some dashes on my conscience, fearing lest all was still not right, suddenly this sentence fell upon my soul, *Your righteousness is in heaven.* And I thought as well that I saw, with the eyes of my soul, Jesus Christ at God's right hand. There, I say, is my righteousness, so that wherever I was or whatever I was doing, God could not say of me, John Bunyan lacks my righteousness, for that righteousness is right before him. I also saw that it was not my good frame of heart that made my righteousness better, nor my bad frame that made my righteousness worse, for my righteousness was Jesus Christ himself: the same yesterday and today and forever. Now did my chains fall off my legs indeed . . . I went home rejoicing for the grace and love of God.[3]

2. *Self-justification is the deepest impulse in the fallen human heart.* We might sincerely agree with the biblical doctrine of justification by faith alone. But down in our hearts, it isn't that simple, is it? Gerhard Forde helps us see ourselves: "The problem lies in the fact that the Old Being will not and cannot *hear* gospel no matter what one says. The Old Being will only use whatever is said as part of the protection, solidification in the *causa sui* project [the self-justifications we build], and translate it into or see it as a ratification of the legal system. That is, the Old Being will turn *whatever one says* into law."[4] We deeply desire to save ourselves, we sincerely believe we can, and we never stop trying, though our righteousness inevitably generates unrighteousness. Guilty anxiety and moral fervor must satisfy themselves somehow. Hence, the strife in our churches.

   Our mentality of blind self-justification makes Paul's letter to the Galatians endlessly relevant to believers. We do not get rid of Galatianism by embracing grace-justification. But, by embracing grace-justification, the door opens to freedom from our compulsive self-justifications. The Puritan William Fenner saw justification by faith alone as a moment-by-moment resource for sinning Christians: "As there is a fountain of sin in us, so there is a fountain of mercy in Christ . . . for every poor soul to wash in. As we sin daily, so he justifies daily, and we must go daily to him for it . . . Justification is an ever-running fountain, and therefore we cannot look to have all the water at

---

3. Bunyan, *Grace Abounding to the Chief of Sinners*, 91–92; style updated.

4. Forde, *Justification by Faith*, 92; italics original.

once."[5] Self-salvation is a human problem universally. It is a *Christian* problem. It *continues* to be a Christian problem—deeply, personally so.

3. *Gospel doctrine creates a gospel culture.* The gospel does more than re-new us personally within. The doctrines of grace also create a culture of grace, called a healthy church, where the gospel is articulated at the level of doctrine and incarnated at the level of culture and vibe and ethos and feel and relationships and community.

The doctrine of regeneration, for example, creates in a church a culture of humility (Eph 2:1–9). The doctrine of justification by faith alone creates a culture of inclusion (Gal 2:11–16). The doctrine of reconciliation creates a culture of peace (Eph 2:14–16). The doctrine of sanctification creates a culture of life (Rom 6:20–23). The doctrine of glorification creates a culture of hope (Rom 5:2). And the doctrine of God creates a culture of honesty (1 John 1:5–10). If we want these doctrines to carry persuasive force, we pastors must cultivate this humane culture in our churches. If we want such a culture to thrive, we must not take doctrinal short cuts. Without the doctrine, the culture is unsustainable. Without the culture, the doctrine appears powerless. But churches where the doctrine and culture converge bear a living witness to the truth and beauty of the gospel.

But getting a church there and keeping a church there is not easy. An example of how badly we can split doctrine and culture is the Lord's parable of the Pharisee and the tax collector: "He also told this parable to some who trusted in themselves that they were righteous, and viewed others with contempt" (Luke 18:9). The Pharisee was going to the temple, the place of substitutionary atonement, because he believed in it. But his heart was more devious than his belief. His self-justifying heart spewed out personal contempt toward the tax collector. Self-justification creates an outlook of aloofness and superiority and negative scrutiny. Though we hold the doctrine of grace-justification sincerely, our deeper thoughts and feelings can slip into functional self-justification, and it shows. Trusting in ourselves that we are righteous and viewing others with contempt always go together. When we see these negative dynamics of dismissive condescension, there is a reason. And the reason is a gospel deficit in the heart, however genuine the gospel profession in the head. We look at our doctrinal statements and our mental beliefs, and they seem to line up. But a tip-off that the gospel does not have as deep a hold on us as we wish is whenever, like this Pharisee, we start looking for a scapegoat, someone to judge, someone to whom we can

5. Fenner, *The Soul's Looking-Glass*, 109; style updated.

transfer our self-hatred. Whenever we *need* someone else to be wrong, to preserve our own cherished innocence, we are in self-justification mode and we aren't really trusting in the perfect Scapegoat God provided at the cross. What else can such thinking create but a culture of ugliness? But justification by faith alone creates a culture of acceptance and warmth and beauty and safety: "Therefore welcome one another, as Christ has welcomed you, for the glory of God" (Rom 15:7). The more clearly that doctrine is taught, and the more beautifully that culture is developed, the more powerfully a church can bear prophetic witness to Jesus as the true Friend of sinners. He will be honored, and people will come.

Those are my three assumptions. Now to Paul's letter to the Galatians, where he guides believers away from self-justification and toward grace-justification in both doctrine and culture. It goes beyond my purpose here to validate a reading of Galatians centered in the Reformation understanding of forensic justification. Membership in the people of God is also, and clearly, within the range of Paul's concerns. My reasoning below depends on it. But, as Doug Moo argues in his recent summation of the debate, there is no warrant for collapsing justification and membership into one concept.[6] With this persuasion, I will consider three brief passages in Galatians.

First, in Galatians 1:10, Paul says, "For am I now seeking the approval of man, or of God? Or am I trying to please man? If I were still trying to please man, I would not be a servant of Christ." Apparently, some had accused Paul of being a cowardly people-pleaser because of his message of grace and his ministry adaptability. Now he counters that accusation: "My anathemas in verses 8–9—is that what a compromiser would say?"

What is the gospel doctrine embedded in verse 10, and how is Paul himself demonstrating its gospel culture? The doctrine implicit in this verse is the all-sufficiency of Christ, which is entailed in justification by faith alone. We know from Philippians 3 that Paul linked in his mind the surpassing worth of knowing Christ with the righteousness that comes only through faith in Christ (Phil 3:7–9). Why trust in Christ alone for our righteousness, unless he occupies the place of ultimacy over all things? But he does. Paul is not saying in Philippians 3 that his former successes are now neutral to him. He is saying they are distasteful, compared with Christ. Paul's view of Christ is so high that his judgment is the only one that finally matters. That being so, faithfulness to him means, for us, that Christ's approval *alone* is enough forever. That gospel conviction creates a culture of courageous independence, such as we see in Paul here in verse 10.

---

6. See Moo, "Justification in Galatians," 174., where Moo also quotes Simon Gathercole: "The *content* of the doctrine of justification by faith should be distinguished from its *scope*." Italics original.

Paul cared about people too. He cared about their opinions and their feelings, and he wanted to please them. He says in 1 Corinthians 10:33, "I try to please everyone in everything I do." Paul never stopped thinking about how he could win people's hearts for Christ. He was widely adaptable, because he respected people's various ways of seeing things. He found a way to harmonize his desire to please people, on the one hand, with his deeper desire to please God, on the other. When Paul faced a choice between pleasing himself and pleasing others, he pleased others. When he faced a choice between pleasing others and pleasing God, he pleased God. He is so clear about this that he states his position as a stark either/or: "If I were still trying to please man, I would not be a servant of Christ" (Gal 1:10). He will not depart from Christ for anyone, because his justification is in Christ alone. Therefore, to Christ alone he gives himself, whatever social price he might pay. He is willing to be unpopular, even controversial. He doesn't relish it. But neither is he threatened by it. And by his example, he is calling the Galatians and us into his benevolent objectivity of mind.

The first indicator of gospel doctrine getting traction as gospel culture is the magnificence of satisfaction with Christ alone, even when people misjudge our motives. The finality of Christ does not position us to go with the Christian crowd, as if we needed human approval to stand on our own two feet. Yes, we pastors benefit from gentle accountability to one another. But more deeply, our business is with God.[7] Otherwise, we fall into an ugly culture of conformity, and we stop serving him: "If I were still trying to please man, I would not be a servant of Christ."

In his address on justification by faith alone, J. Gresham Machen called this gospel doctrine:

> an answer to the greatest personal question ever asked by a human soul—the question, "How shall I be right with God? How do I stand in God's sight? With what favor does he look upon me?" There are those, I admit, who never raise that question; there are those who are concerned with the question of their standing before men but never with the question of their standing before God; there are those who are interested in what "people say" but not in the question of what God says. Such men, however, are not those who move the world; they are apt to go with the current; they are apt to do as others do; they are not the heroes who change the destinies of the race. The beginning of true nobility comes when a man ceases to be interested in the judgment of men and becomes interested in the judgment of God.[8]

7. Calvin, *Institutes of the Christian religion*, 1.17.2.
8. Machen, *God Transcendent*, 89–90.

It is noble to serve Christ, though inevitably some will find fault. The good news of acceptance in him alone creates a culture of emotionally secure, adaptable leaders who can say, "I do it all for the sake of the gospel" (1 Cor 9:23).

Second, in Galatians 2:11–14, Paul writes: "But when Cephas came to Antioch, I opposed him to his face, because he stood condemned. For before certain men came from James, he was eating with the Gentiles; but when they came he drew back and separated himself, fearing the circumcision party. The rest of the Jews acted hypocritically along with him, so that even Barnabas was led astray by their hypocrisy. But when I saw that their conduct was not in step with the truth of the gospel, I said to Cephas before them all, 'If you, though a Jew, live like a Gentile and not like a Jew, how can you force the Gentiles to live like Jews?'"

There was nothing wrong with holiness in traditional Jewish dress. But there was a lot wrong with absolutizing that tradition, because Christ fulfilled the rituals of the Mosaic Law. When Peter distanced himself from the un-kosher Gentile believers, he was throwing redemptive history into reverse gear and ignoring the triumph of Christ crucified. He was saying, in effect, that Gentiles *had* to adapt to Jewish culture for them to be good enough for Christ—and for Peter. What an insult to the finished work of Christ on the cross. How demeaning to those Gentiles. What a violation of justification by faith alone. What a pathetic church culture.

And Peter knew better. God had taught him, "What God has made clean, do not call common" (Acts 10:15). What was driving Peter here in Antioch was not ignorance, nor a deeper insight into the gospel, but fear of church politics: "He drew back and separated himself, fearing the circumcision party." When Peter denied Jesus back in the gospels, he was panicking for his physical self-preservation. Here in Antioch he is denying Jesus again, this time panicking for his social self-preservation. Possessed by that primitive fear, Peter falsified the gospel—not at the level of doctrine but at the level of culture. He was forcing (Gal 2:14) these Gentile believers to conform to Jewish customs, in order to be acceptable to God and full members of his church. Paul twice calls it hypocrisy (Gal 2:13). Fear of human disfavor feeds hypocrisy and posturing and wanting to be perceived in a certain way or identified with certain people or riding a certain bandwagon. What is this fear, but the empty drivenness of self-justification? It is a powerful force among Christians. Peter's fearful hypocrisy was so contagious that even Barnabas was swept away. Paul alone stood up and opposed Peter openly. We can be glad he did. If Paul had caved too, the spread of the gospel would have stalled, because the gospel would have been accessible only to those few people who could embrace Judaism in addition to Jesus.

Earlier in chapter 2, Paul writes how, at another decisive moment, he took a bold stand, "so that the truth of the gospel might be preserved for you" (Gal 2:5). Both there and here in verse 14, what Paul insists on is "the truth of the gospel," that is, the gospel in its unmistakable clarity and unmixed purity and uncomplicated authority. Peter's conduct obscured the truth of the gospel, though nothing had changed at the technical level of his profession of faith. But for Paul, gospel faithfulness is more than *saying*, "Justification by faith alone is the truth." We must demonstrate the truth of the gospel, or we unsay what we say. But we might not even notice, if all we do is look at the doctrine and tell ourselves, "That's what I believe." So did Peter. Paul says in verse 16, "We [you and I, Peter] have believed in Christ Jesus, in order to be justified by faith." Peter never denied that doctrine. What he did was deconstruct the culture entailed in his own professed doctrine. Paul shows, in verses 15–21, that Peter's *behavior* betrayed the gospel. Peter was rebuilding the culture of self-justification he had torn down (verse 18). Peter was nullifying the grace of God and desecrating the cross of Christ (verse 21). And Peter was an apostle. In fact, everyone involved in this sorry episode was a Christian believer. Again, self-justification is a Christian problem. Here in Antioch it was even an *apostolic* problem. Preserving the truth of the gospel is no simple matter.

This passage prompts us to ask deeper questions. We must ask ourselves more than do we subscribe to the doctrine of justification by faith alone? We must also ask, are we keeping in step with the truth of that doctrine? Do we even see gospel faithfulness with that magnitude? Paul included *applying* the gospel within his concept of faithfulness to the gospel. He demanded that Peter and the others follow their own doctrinal vector by their practice: "I saw that *their conduct* was not in step with the truth of the gospel . . ." The gospel is more than a place to stand; it is also a path to follow, without caving to political pressure, but boldly pressing the gospel forward, because it is in the face of resistance that the grace of Christ becomes clearer.

John Stott calls Paul's confrontation of Peter "without doubt one of the most tense and dramatic episodes in the New Testament."[9] We can benefit from power encounters—but not personal rivalries—so that more gospel beauty appears among us. It was when Paul's apostolic boldness refused to satisfy an inappropriate demand that that demand could then reconsider its own intensity and see the all-sufficient Christ with greater clarity, humility and joy, and get back in step with how gracious he really is.

What then is the doctrine embedded in Galatians 2:11–14, and what kind of culture does that doctrine create? The doctrine is that everyone who

---

9. Stott, *The Message of Galatians*, 49.

simply trusts Jesus for their justification is clean before God, whatever their background. They do not need to add to the merit of Christ another layer of acceptability to man. If God declares us kosher through Christ alone, who can demand more? The culture created by that doctrine is one of openness, freedom and safety. Jesus said, "My yoke is easy" (Matt 11:30). But self-justification creates a culture of oppression—though people passionately committed to Protestant doctrine can generate it, as in fact Peter did.

The striking thing about Galatians 2:11–14 is that Paul considers gospel culture just as sacred as gospel doctrine. He fought for that culture, because the doctrine of grace-justification cannot be preserved in its integrity—"the truth of the gospel"—if surrounded by a culture of self-justification.

Thirdly and finally, in Gal 4:17 Paul writes of the false teachers, "They make much of you, but for no good purpose. They want to shut you out, that you may make much of them." And then in 5:15 he warns the Galatians themselves, "But if you bite and devour one another, watch out that you are not consumed by one another." There is no gospel here. These are the negative dynamics unleashed into a church by the mentality of self-justification. What kind of dark church culture emerges? Two observations.

First, selfish ambition. Galatians 4:17 exposes the manipulative power of exclusion: "They make much of you, but for no good purpose. They want to shut you out, that you may make much of them." "They make much of you" could be paraphrased, "They are zealous for you, they are eager to win you over, they take such an interest in you, they seem to care about you so deeply." The false teachers appeared loving and concerned, but they had an ulterior motive. It was like chapter two in *Tom Sawyer*. Tom got the other boys to whitewash the fence for him by the manipulative power of exclusion. Mark Twain called it "a great law of human action" that, "in order to make a man or boy covet a thing, it is only necessary to make the thing difficult to attain."[10] But full inclusion in the church of Christ is easy to attain. All one needs is Christ, and he gives himself away freely, on terms of grace, received with the empty hands of faith.

To accomplish their hidden purpose, the false teachers had to get Paul out of the way. So they cultivated a sense of grievance against Paul, as if he were an enemy (Gal 4:16). If the false teachers could blur the people's hyper-focus on Christ—and Paul was a barrier to that end—they could take control and reshape the religious culture of those churches more to their liking. So they defined acceptability within Galatian Christianity on their own self-advantageous terms. The people, in their weakness and insecurity, were falling for it, conforming to a culture of exclusion. Without a return to

---

10. Twain, *The Adventures of Tom Sawyer*, 20.

the gospel, the false teachers would have those churches to themselves, their own religious sandbox to play in, their ambition successful, their reign unchallenged, their claims apparently justified. John Calvin comments: "This stratagem is common to all the ministers of Satan, of alienating the people from their pastor, to draw them [the people] to themselves [the false teachers] and having, so to say, disposed of the rival, to take his place."[11] Paul is so disturbed by what the Galatians cannot see that, when he takes pen in hand at the end of the letter, he adds this: "It is those who want to make a good showing in the flesh who would force you to be circumcised . . . They desire to have you circumcised that they may boast in your flesh" (Gal 6:12–13). The false teachers wanted to use the Galatians as badges of honor, to enhance their own importance. It was self-justification by numbers of conversions—not conversions to Christ for his glory, but to their group for their own self-validation. Their behavior was the opposite of what Paul required of himself back in chapter 1, when he refused to compromise the gospel for the sake of human approval. He was a servant of Christ. The false teachers were promoters of Ego.

Second, savage destruction: "But if you bite and devour one another, watch out that you are not consumed by one another." How does an animal bite and devour its victims? By its mouth. Even so, the Galatians were in danger, from their sins of the tongue, of destroying one another. With the false claims of legalism disturbing them, tongues were aroused, even unrestrained. The Galatian churches were unstable to begin with, because the reassuring finality of "It is finished" had been eroded away. Insecurity, anxiety, fear and anger had entered in. How could it be otherwise? Self-justification *cannot* create anything but an unsatisfiable demandingness, for Christ is not its satisfying provision. No matter how well a person has been raised to be courteous, self-justification must generate finger-pointing and accusing and slandering and dividing. And whoever "wins," the gospel loses.

In 1974, I heard Francis Schaeffer lecture at the Lausanne Congress on World Evangelization in Switzerland. He proposed that, to compel the attention of the world today, our churches must be marked by two contents and two realities. The two contents are sound gospel doctrine, and honest answers to honest questions. The two realities are true spirituality, and the beauty of human relationships. Relational beauty is essential to gospel persuasion. How could it be otherwise? Jonathan Edwards taught us that beauty is "the first principle of being, the inner, structural principle of being

---

11. Calvin, *The Epistles of Paul the Apostle to the Galatians, Ephesians, Philippians and Colossians*, 82.

itself."[12] Beauty is not ornamentation on the surface of things. It is essential to who God is. But Christians who bite and devour each other are ugly. They may think they are defending God and everything sacred. But can the Beautiful One be served in such a way?

In an essay entitled "Justification and Violence," William Edgar proposes that "when classical justification, based on the propitiatory work of Christ, is absent, human beings will grasp for substitutes, often grotesque ones."[13] For example, Edgar sees the violence of the French Revolution as a bloody ritual of self-justifying atonement. The guillotine was a "counterfeit for Calvary," the way for France to be cleansed of the past, and be born again as a nation. He contends that the racially motivated lynching of the Deep South were ritual killings and blood sacrifice, displacing guilt onto a victim, to purge evil away and preserve a white self-image of honor. Why do sinners become violent, rather than penitent, when reaching for something regarded as good? The reason is, we sinners cannot bear our own shame. The unresolved guilt must go somewhere. If not onto Christ the only true Victim, violent Christians will transfer their unresolved anguish to a human substitute, denying the cross.

Church savagery is far more than a lack of personal niceness. It reveals a gospel deficit deep in a church's corporate soul. But where Jesus reigns, love reigns as "a mutual protection and kindness."[14] Paul was a man of courageous forthrightness and apolitical independence. He was also a man of love, humility, and warmth: "You were called to freedom, brothers. Only do not use your freedom as an opportunity for the flesh, but through love serve one another. For the whole law is fulfilled in one word: 'You shall love your neighbor as yourself'" (Gal 5:13–14). Strong principles and humane relationships, together simultaneously, mark a church as faithful to the gospel.

What then does it mean for a church to stand, rather than fall, by the gospel? It means that a church teaches the doctrine of grace-justification, while it also builds—and, inevitably, protects—a culture of grace-justification. In that kind of church, no one is forced to prove himself, no one is personally humiliated or pressured to conform to a human demand. Everyone is free to seek the Lord and grow in grace, in harmony with others around. At Immanuel Church in Nashville, where I serve, we think of it in this simple way: gospel + safety + time. Gospel: good news for bad people through the finished work of Christ on the cross. Safety: a non-accusing

12. McClymond and McDermott, *The Theology of Jonathan Edwards*, 93.

13. Edgar, "Justification and Violence," 131.

14. Calvin, *The Epistles of Paul the Apostle to the Galatians, Ephesians, Philippians and Colossians*, 102.

environment of sympathy and honesty. Time: no pressure, no hurry, but space for complicated people to rethink their lives. Who doesn't need that, and a lot of it? If confrontation is ever required in a faithful gospel culture, it is only "so that the truth of the gospel might be preserved for you" (Gal 2:5).

For some churches, this larger understanding of gospel faithfulness might require repentance and reformation. Our churches might not be as gospel-centered as we thought. If a Protestant church enshrines the doctrines of Christ within a culture of Ego, it effectively de-gospels the gospel, and the felt presence of the Savior of the world is diminished.

How then can we, in our weakness, bear faithful witness to the gospel today? Is it even possible? Yes, but only if we walk by the Spirit moment-by-moment: "But I say, walk by the Spirit and you will not gratify the desires of the flesh" (Gal 5:16). That is not mechanical or formulaic. It is very personal, very costly. But there is no other way. It means more than theological alertness. It means real-time dependence on God. It means putting ourselves— not others—under the judgment of his Word. It means being forgiven constantly and following Christ with daily crucifixions of our pride.

In the flesh, we will create doctrinally correct cultures of ugliness. But in the Spirit, and only in the Spirit, we can become, imperfectly but visibly, living proof of the "one-way love" of Jesus. This is the gospel faithfulness our generation must see.

BIBLIOGRAPHY

Bicknell, E. J. *A Theological Introduction to the Thirty-Nine Articles of the Church of England*. London: Longmans, 1959.

Bunyan, John. *Grace Abounding to the Chief of Sinners*. Philadelphia: Woodward, 1828.

Calvin, John. *The Epistles of Paul the Apostle to the Galatians, Ephesians, Philippians and Colossians*. Translated by T. H. L. Parker. Grand Rapids: Eerdmans, 1965.

————. *Institutes of the Christian Religion*. Translated by Henry Beveridge. Grand Rapids: Eerdmans, 1983.

Edgar, William. "Justification and Violence." In *Justified in Christ: God's Plan for Us in Justification*, edited by K. Scott Oliphant, 131–52. Fearn: Mentor, 2007.

Fenner, William. *The Soul's Looking-Glass*. London: Rothwell, 1651.

Forde, Gerhard O. *Justification by Faith: A Matter of Death and Life*. Philadelphia: Fortress, 1982.

Luther, Martin. *A Commentary on St. Paul's Epistle to the Galatians: Rev. And Ed. On the Basis of the "Middleton" Edition by Philip S. Watson (1575)*. Cambridge: James Clark, 1953.

Machen, J. Gresham *God Transcendent: Messages by J. Gresham Machen*. Edited by N.B. Stonehouse. Edinburgh: Banner of Truth Trust, 1982.

McClymond, Michael J., and Gerald R. McDermott. *The Theology of Jonathan Edwards*. Oxford: Oxford University Press, 2012.

Moo, Douglas J. "Justification in Galatians." In *Understanding the Times: New Testament Studies in the 21st Century, Essays in Honor of D. A. Carson*, edited by Andreas Köstenberger and Robert W. Yarbrough, 160–95. Wheaton, IL: Crossway, 2011.

Stott, John R.W. *The Message of Galatians*. London: Inter-Varsity, 1968.

Twain, Mark. *The Adventures of Tom Sawyer*. Toronto: Belford, 1876.

16

The Forgiveness of Sins
and the Healing of Humiliation[1]

GEIKO MÜLLER-FAHRENHOLZ

IN SOME CHURCHES, ESPECIALLY the Orthodox, the formulations of the ancient Christian creeds have an almost sacred status. They are unchangeable. I respect that. But it does not prevent me from thinking aloud about what it would mean if we were to make an amendment to the ancient texts by saying: We believe in the forgiveness of sins and the healing of humiliations. What would we gain?

I do believe that it is important to supplement the forgiving of sins by the healing of humiliations. For while it is clear that sin, if it remains unforgiven, will lead to violence, it is not so clear that humiliation is bound to end up in violence, too.[2]

---

1. This is the English version of a talk I gave at a symposium on "Remembering and Forgiving" organized by the Protestant Academy of Bad Boll on the occasion of the 85th birthday of Professor Jürgen Moltmann (April 8, 2011), Paul Zahl's and my *Doktorvate*r.

2. A word about humiliation: I use it for the German word "*Kränkung*" even though its connotations are somewhat different. *Kränkung* means that you suffer an insult or a wrong that makes you "*krank*," i.e. sick at heart. It is the enforced helplessness that damages your identity and causes feelings of mortification, outrage, or vexation.

SOME REFLECTIONS ON THE RELATIONSHIP OF SIN TO HUMILIATION

Is it not peculiar that we can use the verb "to sin" only in the active form and not in the passive? We say: "I sin." But we cannot say: "I have been sinned." It is the same in German or in the European languages based on Latin. This linguistic peculiarity says a lot about the way in which sin has been understood throughout the centuries. And this peculiarity has contributed to the fact that many women and men no longer know what to make of sin.

The traditional Christian concept of penitence is part of the problem. It is based on the "activist" understanding of sin as broken relationship between humans and God. This is a notion that Christianity shares with its Jewish origins. Hence we read in Psalm 51:4: "Against thee, thee only, have I sinned . . ." Accordingly St. Paul states: "For all alike have sinned, and are deprived of the divine splendor . . ." (Rom 3:23) Against thee only? Does this mean that our understanding of sin is linked to our understanding of God? Before God we stand as sinners. Against the Holy and Eternal One we have committed our sins. If this is the idea, then forgiveness of sins is but another word for God's justification of the sinner by grace alone.

If this soteriological interpretation is what the Apostles' and the Nicene Creeds are aiming at when they speak of the forgiveness of sins, then it makes little sense to speak of the healing of humiliations. But what happens with our concept of sin when we lose our relationship to God? For many of our contemporaries God has disappeared. So why should they think of themselves as sinners? The problem is that the reality of sin has not disappeared. We need to move beyond a purely vertical and soteriological understanding of sin. Sin also has a horizontal dimension. For the Sin (in singular) that alienates us from God expresses itself in sins, that is in acts of wrongdoing, in daily transgressions, in acts of violence and in omissions of what we ought to have done. The sins we commit concern our fellow human beings and our fellow creatures and Earth itself in its many life forms. Our sins are as diverse as are our relationships with the world around us. Our sins express themselves not simply in acts of wrongdoing; they are also embedded in our social, political and economic structures. And there is also the dimension of sin in the habits of the heart, in habitual cultural patterns such as racism or anti-Semitism.

Hence it is our creatureliness (if I may use such a word) that forces us to move beyond a mere vertical understanding of sin. And more than that, it is a Christological insight that our relationship with God reflects itself in our dealings with our neighbors. This is evident in the ways Jesus lived with and for the outcast, the lonely, and oppressed till the hour of his death. No need to quote the famous parable of the final judgment in Matthew 25:31ff. We know it by heart; or don't we? If the presence of the Messiah is to be recognized in "one of these, however humble," then we begin to see those who suffer from our deeds and omissions. And then, for Christ's sake, it matters a lot what our Sin against God means for our sins in our daily lives.

Let me remind you of the parable of "the unforgiving servant" in Matthew 18:23–35. It tells us of a man who owes his king the incredible sum of ten thousand talents. In the time of Jesus ten thousand was the highest imaginable number. The entire tax revenues of Judaea and Samaria in those days amounted to 200 "talents." And King Herod with his luxurious lifestyle had about 900 talents per year to dispose of. We read in the parable that this servant falls to his knees and promises to pay everything back. (In view of the sum, this is nothing but wishful thinking.) We read that the king's mercy is so abundant that he forgives the servant his entire debt. We are familiar with the next turn of the story. This man who has just experienced this ultimate pardon runs into a fellow servant who owes him 100 denarii, which—according to present-day situations—equals three monthly salaries. This is not nothing, to be sure, but it is a manageable sum upon which an agreement could easily be found. But not in this case. This fellow servant does not have the money ready to repay his debt upon which the other has him put in jail until the debt is paid. We know how the king deals with this unforgiving servant once he learns of his evil behavior. But what we tend to overlook is the consequence of this story that Jesus addresses to his disciples: "So also my heavenly Father will do the every one of you, if you do not forgive your brother from your heart" (Matt 18:35). So here we have a direct link between God's readiness to forgive and our own willingness to forgive. The same link is in the Lord's Prayer where we pray to God for "forgiveness of our trespasses as we forgive those who trespass against us." So the verb "to sin" does not only have an active, but also a passive form. We sin against others as others sin against us.

Jürgen Moltmann belongs to the theologians who have drawn our attention to the fact that 20th century liberation theologians have accentuated this new aspect of our understanding of sin. They have raised the issue of sin from the viewpoint of the victims and the suffering. And once we follow this perspective, our thinking about sin becomes relevant to women and men of today. For even if they may mean to not have anything to do with God, they know how it feels to be abused, slandered, defamed, exploited, humiliated. Far too many know this by heart and in their bodies. The world is full of it.

With that, our search for the forgiveness of sins takes up a fresh urgency. To the observation that English writer and theologian Brian Frost has pointed out, that every human being has a forgiveness problem,[3] I am adding: "Because every human being has a humiliation problem." Both aspects have to be considered if we want to understand what forgiveness is. Who are those who are forgiving? They are only those who have suffered abuse, persecution, humiliation. Therefore, all questions about the possibility of forgiveness are intimately linked to whether and how the humiliated are enabled to find a way out of their humiliations, whether and how those made low can be straightened up, and whether and how the pain of those who have been tortured can come to rest. Therefore: I believe in the forgiveness of sins and the healing of humiliations.

Why do I put this emphasis on humiliation? Let me start with a little story. It takes us back to 1948, to my village school. Post World War II conditions had it that our school consisted of one large room, a large play ground, and one teacher. In the mornings he would teach grades five through eight, and in the afternoons the kids in grade one through four. I must have been in grade three, my brother Enno in grade two. For reasons which I cannot reconstruct I thought that school started at 3 p.m.. But as Enno and I got there we found out that class has started at 2 already. The teacher sent my brother to his place. But of me he wanted to know why we had been late. "I thought school started at 3," I stammered. "I see," he said and came so close that my back was pressed to the wall. (My place was in the last row.) "And why did you think that we start at 3?," he pressed on. "I . . . I don't know," I tried to say. Everybody stared at me, and I felt like crying. "I see, you don't know," he said with a cynical tone and pressed me even more to the wall. Some time later, after what appeared to me to be an eternity, he turned around and resumed his teaching. I have never forgotten this incident; I could not get over the humiliation and—what was more frightening—I was amazed at the hatred that swept over me and at the suspicion with which I looked at everything this teacher did from then on.

My God, you might say, what a triviality! Such things—and much worse things—happen all the time! That is true. I mention that little story from my childhood days simply to indicate how widespread and massive experiences of humiliation are at home, in schools and universities, in offices and barracks, not to mention the prisons. I refer to my little story because it gave me a first idea of the hatred that is begotten by humiliations, and of the longing for revenge that springs from experiences of enforced helplessness.

Humiliations are damaging our sense of self. They are hurting our very being. That explains why they stick so forcefully in our memories,

---

3. Cf. Frost, *Struggling to Forgive: Nelson Mandela and South Africa's Search for Reconciliation.*

perhaps even more forcefully than our own wrongdoing. To live with humiliations is a difficult thing. Therefore, many try to store these experiences away in the chambers of denial, apathy, or a generalized distrust of everyone and everything.

It goes without saying that this applies not only to individual human beings but also to entire ethnic groups, peoples, and nations. Corporate humiliations play a significant role in the ways peoples deal with each other. To quote from an article of the Israeli writer David Grossman forty years after the end of World War II (1985): "When I think of the Holocaust the dominating feeling continues to be one of humiliation. Not anger, or feelings of revenge, neither hatred, but a bitter and disconsolate humiliation about what was done to human beings."[4] I firmly believe that the impact of humiliations in our personal lives as well as in the political realms is being gravely underestimated. Obviously, to follow on Grossman' remarks, Israel's policies of occupation with regard to the Palestinians cannot be understood correctly without remembering the bitter heritage of humiliation that so many Jewish people carry with them to their graves and carry over to the next generations. And similarly, without the legacy of humiliation that began back in 1947, the desperate terrorist attacks of Palestinians cannot be understood adequately. There is no way of understanding the policies of the Irish, the Polish, or Hungarian nations, to name but these three European peoples, without looking carefully at the history of humiliations that they have suffered over the centuries. Or to quote from an article of the Tunisian journalist Ghania Mouffok: "Living in a dictatorship is the most humiliating experiences which a human being can make. It is also this humiliation against which the Arab peoples have risen. It was an uprising of oppressed souls."[5]

These are but a few examples to demonstrate that the destructive impact of our sins in today's world becomes obvious when we see them in the perspective of their victims. The mighty shadow of guilt is humiliation, and the violent outbursts of humiliation reproduce guilt. This is the reality of the vicious circles of violence and retaliation. It follows that we need to think about the healing of humiliations if we want forgiveness of sins to have a liberating and redeeming power. There can be no forgiveness without the liberation from the bondage of humiliation. How can this take place?

4. D. Grossman: *Die Zeit*, January 27, 1985. (Translation: GMF)
5. In *Süddeutsche Zeitung*, April 6, 2011, p. 2. (Translation: GMF)

THE DYNAMICS OF PROCESSES OF RECONCILIATION: THREE STEPS

Why do I introduce reconciliation here? My observation is that forgiveness is only one step although of central importance within a wider process for which I use the term reconciliation. I hope to be able to explain this in the following part. What I have tried to say thus far leads me to conclude that each act of wrongdoing produces a twofold history of effect (*Wirkungsgeschichte*). Simply put, on the side of the perpetrator we are bound to find a history of denial—in other words, psychic maneuvers such as rationalizations, justifications, or trivializations to cover up shame and guilt.

On the side of the victims we find a history of shaming which also produces its own forms of denial. Here we come across various forms of distrust, anxiety, and/or aggressiveness. The longer these dual histories exist side by side the harder the enmity becomes. In the course of time—and in many cases such histories exist side by side for centuries—we observe ever-growing walls of mutual distrust that can easily lead to wars, and have done so in the past.

But sometimes there are within these antagonistic groups movements striving for change. For them, the enmity becomes intolerable. They are searching for peaceful solutions. Such movements are decisive, for without them processes of reconciliation do not stand a chance. By the way, it is important to really think of *processes*; for considerable time is needed to move through the necessary steps. Provided there is enough momentum to move beyond enmity we can distinguish three steps.

The first step needs to be made by the perpetrator(s) by offering an apology to the victim(s). Such an apology or plea for forgiveness must be serious, precise, and unambiguous. There needs to be a clear recognition of the wrong that has been done, and of its various aspects and consequences. And there must be a distinctive readiness to stand up to the effects of the wrong that has been done and to make amends.[6]

Such an initiative requires considerable emotional and moral sovereignty, for it contains an element of denuding oneself. Those who manage to acknowledge their guilt make themselves vulnerable and that requires a lot of courage. An example of such a courageous and unambiguous acknowledgement was the speech of Richard von Weizsäcker, President of the Federal Republic of Germany, in 1985, forty years after the end of World War II. Many representatives of nations that had suffered from that war expressed that they considered this to be an adequate and honorable apology.

6. Cf. Lazare, *On Apology.*

Whenever apologies are general and unspecific they tend to be without success. Worse still, they deepen the bitterness of the grieving side. To give here an example that also comes from my German background: when in 2010 numerous cases of sexual abuse in institutions of the Roman Catholic Church found their way into the public, the bishops offered a very general apology which provoked responses of disappointment and anger by the victims.

An apology is but the first step. To be sure, it is a crucial one because it opens up a healing process. For the perpetrator, such a "coming out" may have some salutary effect, but it is not yet the end of the way. The victims must do the second step. They need to come to terms with what has been offered to them. Will they be able to respond affirmatively to the apology? Is it adequate, so that they can respond with the granting of forgiveness? These are very real questions. There can be no automatism here. People often tend to think that to ask for forgiveness already implies the granting of it. " But I did apologize!" they will say, thereby assuming that forgiveness must be the consequence. To offer an apology is the beginning. But to respond to such a plea by granting forgiveness constitutes a painful moment for the victim side. They are forced to face what was done to them, to return, as it were, to the places of their humiliation, to move beyond their denial, to let go of their "identity" as the eternal victim.

The granting of forgiveness also signifies a high degree of emotional sovereignty. You leave the bondage of your humiliations; you become the master of your own house. And that is healing.

This is the mystery and wonder of forgiveness. When and where victims forgive they do not only liberate the perpetrators from the burden of their guilt, they also liberate themselves from the burden of their own humiliation. To forgive is to set the other free—and oneself too.[7] "

What follows is the third step. I call it the covenanting part of the reconciliation process. In the traditional Christian theology of repentance this is called the *satisfactio operum*. What does this imply?

It is a tragic fact that wrongs cannot be undone. Their effects linger on. But it is possible to soften the consequences of past wrongs, to create ways to prevent similar wrongs from happening again, to agree on practical measures, to ease the burden inflicted by the wrong, and to create cooperative projects in social, educational, political, and economic fields. (In many

---

7. It is important for victims to work on their willingness to forgive even if the wrongdoers have no intention to ask for it. As the South African Anglican Bishop Ruben Philip said to me, "In my heart I have forgiven the Apartheid people although they have not offered me their apology. But I intend not to be a prisoner of the Apartheid system. I want to be free, and at peace with myself."

cases it is not the money that makes the difference!) To offer an example: The South African Truth and Reconciliation Commission had the mandate to facilitate the first two steps, and they did this in an exemplary manner. Regarding the third step the TRC Commission set up a list of clear proposals and submitted it to the government. Unfortunately, the government took years to come up with some reparations. And this reluctance halted the healing that the TRC had begun; it frustrated the hopes of many victims and deepened their resentment.

I am not saying that reconciliation processes that successfully move through these three stages will lead to a complete forgetting of past guilt and hurt. We can only forget what is no longer hurting. And that may well take a lot of time. But what we are in fact able to do is to decontaminate our memories of wrongdoing and humiliation, thereby creating confidence among the antagonistic partners and opening up areas of cooperation. We gain a lot if we help each other to look back at our wretchedness without rage and pain and to arrive at a way of affirming our common woundedness. There is such a thing as smiling under tears.

To bring this part to a close: By taking you through these three steps I did not end up merely repeating some mediation techniques. I needed to show the reality of humiliations so we can be fixed in a number of ways, such as rediscover the salutary importance of forgiveness even to those of our contemporaries who do not believe in God. I am searching—in Dietrich Bonhoeffer's terms—for a "non-religious interpretation" of such a loaded theological concept as forgiveness. My hope is that by looking at the massive impact of humiliation this may be more effectively achieved.

FORGIVENESS IS THE LIBERATION OF THE FUTURE FROM THE CHAINS OF THE PAST

The German-Jewish philosopher Hannah Arendt, whom the Nazis forced into exile and who died in New York in 1975, mentions in her book *Vita Activa* that Jesus was "the discoverer of the role of forgiveness in the realm of human affairs."[8] Christians may like to hear that, but I do not think that it is true. Rather I believe that the possibility of forgiveness and reconciliation is a gift that God has planted into our creaturely being.

However that may be, Arendt is right in saying that in the act of forgiving we humans are unlocking the chains that bind us to the past. If we were unable to forgive we would forever remain under the dictatorship of past

8. Arendt, *The Human Condition*, 238.

deeds (and omissions) and could not undertake anything new.[9] This seems obvious, and so Arendt finds it all the more surprising that forgiving has not become a self-evident factor of our political culture. In this context she writes about the human capacity to make and keep promises as a way to make the future safe. Human beings need this capacity for two reasons. In view of the threatening openness of the future, one which Arendt calls an "ocean of uncertainty," humans need to create "islands of predictability and guideposts of reliability."[10] Therefore, she argues, this capacity has become a steady component of human affairs.

I find this convincing. But what I find astounding is the fact that Arendt does not connect these two "capacities." What she calls the "darkness of the human heart" has a lot to do with the legacies of guilt and humiliation—in theological terms, with the reality of sin—in our lives. These legacies are alive in the memories of people; they constitute the framework of their thoughts and feelings and, therefore, determine their behavior. Thus they narrow their range of action. They undermine their capacity to enter into reliable covenants, and so render the future even more incalculable than it is already.

Look at the classical Anglican marriage liturgy, for example, and you will discover the importance of an "ordered past" for the reliability of the covenant into which the couple is about to enter. Before the marriage vows are taken the priest addresses the couple and says: "I require and charge you both, here in the presence of God, that if either of you know any reason why you may not be united in marriage lawfully, and in accordance with God's Word, you do now confess it." This formulation reflects the experience that unresolved conflicts contain a dangerous virulence for any new treaty. This implies that the forgiveness of sins and the healing of humiliations are prerequisites for the success of our covenants. As this fact is often overlooked, many treaties and covenants are not worth the paper on which they are written.

With these reflections I wish to underline what I have attempted to say earlier on about the nature of burden-sharing. The idea cannot be to restore past relationships but to inaugurate more reliable ones. Bygones can never be bygone unless they are healed and initiate more steadfast links.

I wish to conclude this part by saying that the forgiveness of sins and the healing of humiliations constitute the daily opportunity to liberate ourselves from the painful memories that keep us tied to our past, and thus to open ourselves up for new options. The Lord's Prayer reflects this well. We pray for the daily bread that God may grant us and then we pray for the forgiveness of our sins as we forgive the sins others have inflicted on us. As

9. Ibid.
10. Ibid., 244.

we need the bread for our daily sustenance so we need the daily asking for and granting of forgiveness to keep going on. Hence the Lord's Prayer shows the way to understand our present not as a prolongation of the past but to get hold of their creative and innovative moments.

CONTINGENCY AND MERCY—THE SOURCES OF THE RECONCILING ENERGY

But why is it so difficult to ask for, and to grant, forgiveness? Why can we not let go of our humiliation? What if they occurred ages ago? Obviously, we lack the energy to take the necessary steps. By looking at processes of reconciliation we observe again and again that there is an intermediary force. I call it the third factor. There are conflicts with which a mediator— a person trusted by both sides—can initiate a change toward healing. Likewise, in legal or inter-ethnic conflicts mediators can at times facilitate extraordinary solutions to grave conflicts. A telling example is the mediating intervention of the Roman Catholic Community of Sant'Egidio based in Rome, in the civil war in Mozambique. In 1992, after two extremely difficult years, a peace treaty was negotiated that has been kept till today. But who empowers the mediators?

It is no accident that the Ancient Creeds place the forgiveness of sins in the Third Article deals with the workings of the Holy Spirit. The Spirit (in Hebrew the feminine *ruach*) of God is believed to be the energy that is capable of fundamentally renewing our human condition. There is a Rabbinic saying: "Before God made creation he made the *teschuba* (which is the capacity for change)." In other words, the possibility of conversion and renewal belongs to the marvels of God's creation. God's *ruach* is the power within all things. Therefore, what proceeds from God's will is not a fate that preordains everything. Nor does it follow a predetermined course. There is, in God's world, an element of contingency. Hence we may conclude that processes of reconciliation are expressions of this contingent power and reflect God's freedom. But how can this freedom become our freedom?

Let me return to the "unforgiving servant" in Jesus' parable because it struggles with just this question. In the center is the man who has received an overwhelmingly great forgiveness and yet turns around and puts a fellow servant into prison to squeeze a comparatively trifling sum of money out of him. So the King asks him, "I forgave you all that debt because you besought me; and should not you have had mercy on your fellow servant, as I had mercy on you?" (Matt 18:33) That exactly is the problem. How can God's mercy become our mercy? Evidently, the experience of mercy does not necessarily turn us into merciful people. In fact, there may even be a subtle twist that works against it. Has the experience of overwhelming mercy given the servant a feeling of impotence and, therefore, of humiliation? Perhaps it was of such an effect that he used the first opportunity to exercise some little power by throwing his fellow into jail? How, then, do we rightly deal with God's forgiveness? How can we receive it without resentment, but rather with joy and jubilation?

I suggest that we would be more receptive to God's mercy if we lived more seriously with our vulnerability. As Martin Luther said at the end of his life, "We are beggars, that is true." This is a way of acknowledging that our dependence on God is all-embracing. It starts with the air we are breathing, the clear water that we drink without much thinking. If we were more attentive we would understand that we are indebted to the Creator of heaven and earth in a way that defies all understanding. If we were to rightly meditate on the Passion of Christ we would get an idea of the mercy of God. What I mean to say is this: In order to share more consciously in the *ruach* of God and to appropriate a bit of God's mercy for our own lives, a sense of our existential receptivity is central.

This is not as easy as it sounds. The mystics, for instance, speak of the need for the soul to become empty in order to make room for God's will to live in us. In Orthodox Churches some monks have attempted to create meditative practices that would enable them to arrive at a bodily experience of the divine mercy.[11] And in the *praxis pietatis* of many Protestant Churches, many attempts have been made to respond to God's sanctity with a life of sanctification and to let God's mercy be reflected in active mercy.

Second, such receptivity must be complemented by gratitude that is far more difficult than it sounds. Gratitude means realizing our neediness, without accompanying feelings of anger and envy. In other words, gratitude is the active and joyful recognition of God's friendliness that carries us from one moment to the next. Gratitude transcends our common ways of thinking and, together with receptivity, creates the framework for imagining new possibilities.

I have often wondered why the Apostles' Creed speaks on the "holy, catholic Church" without mentioning the practical life that follows from this conception, except for one thing. Before it comes to the "resurrection of the body and the life everlasting" it mentions the forgiveness of sins. That is an indication of what the "communion of the saints" means in real life. The Communion is placed in this world to witness to the forgiveness of sins and the healing of humiliations. The communion of the saints introduces

---

11. Cf. Coakley, *Powers and Submissions*, 103ff.

initiatives of reconciliation in a world torn apart by enmities. This also explains why Christian churches must be engaged in the ecumenical movement or, differently put, in a global network that opens prisons of fear and resentment, that breaks up bottlenecks of despair, and that thus enables undreamt-of life options.

I conclude with a wonderful example: When the 19 year-old man was drafted into the armed forces he took Goethe's "Faust" with him. But in the prison camps of Zedelgam and Norton Camp the poet's beautiful words lost their meaning. A "deadening horror" filled the young man's heart over the total defeat. This horror grew deeper as he saw pictures of the Bergen-Belsen concentration camp, and with them slowly realized that in the name of his fatherland massive crimes had been committed against Europe's Jewish people. An army chaplain brought him a Bible, and in the Passion of Jesus he recognized the One who understands.

Upon the YMCA's initiative, Norton Camp was turned into a small university. The POWs were visited by famous theologians such as the Swede Anders Nygren, the Dane Niels Hansen Soe, the Dutch Willem Vissert Hooft—who was the General Secretary of the World Council of Churches (then in formation)—and the famous American missionary John Mott, the founder of the International Missionary Council. Faith in the Christ who suffers for us and with us formed the center of this ecumenical fellowship, which transcended even the highest walls of hatred.

Dutch students met with German prisoners. They did not conceal the sufferings that they and their Jewish compatriots had endured under German occupation. When the prisoners confessed the guilt of the Germans and asked for forgiveness the Dutch group responded by granting it. And they all embraced each other at the end. In captivity, liberation. Behind walls and bars a new vocation!

The young POW whose story I recall is/was Jürgen Moltmann. Since the early fifties his stupendous oeuvre has traveled around the globe. His work has touched the lives of many women and men in many lands. It has also touched my life and that of Paul Zahl. As a matter of fact, Moltmann was the *Doktorvater* for both of us, and through him we became friends. It so happened that in our professional lives both Paul Zahl and I have had to spell out in some detail what it means to cope with hurt. But, by the grace of God, we have also been helped to experience the deep liberation that comes from the forgiveness of sins and the healing of humiliations.

BIBLIOGRAPHY

Arendt, Hannah. *The Human Condition*. Chicago: University of Chicago Press, 1958.

Coakley, Sarah. *Powers and Submissions: Spirituality, Philosophy, and Gender*. Oxford: Blackwell, 2002.

Frost, Brian. *Struggling to Forgive: Nelson Mandela and South Africa's Search for Reconciliation*. London: HarperCollins, 1998.

Lazare, Aaron. *On Apology*. Oxford: Oxford University Press, 2004.

17

Ministry as Leisure

Rediscovering the Concept of Rest

DYLAN POTTER

IN HERMAN MELVILLE'S NOVEL *White Jacket,* which he wrote just prior to *Moby Dick,* one encounters a theatrical figure by the name of Cadwallader Cuticle, M.D.. Melville penned *White Jacket* to highlight the fatuitous use of physical punishment that was a staple of American naval life during the 19th century. A smallish man in his sixties, with a glass eye, false teeth, and a wig, Dr. Cuticle is the Surgeon of the Fleet and as passionate about his profession as he is peculiar to behold. Toward the end of the novel, one of the crew, a foretopman, is shot by the enemy and requires surgery to remove the bullet lodged in his thigh. Fortunately, or so it would seem, Dr. Cuticle is onboard. However, as the crowd of alarmed crewmen gather around the makeshift operating table, which was little more than a plank, Cuticle is exposed as a tadpole of a physician, all head and no heart.

The odd-looking Cuticle is by all estimates a technically brilliant physician and scientist, but his bedside manner leaves much to be desired; he personifies the callousness that was the norm among naval officers during Melville's era. He seizes the opportunity to help the wounded man, but in a bizarre act, he first lectures the crew, at some length, about the macabre and rarefied life of a surgeon. Once the speech is over he turns to his patient, but instead of undertaking the delicate procedure to extract the projectile, Cuticle opts instead for amputation and unceremoniously saws through the young man's leg. Without missing a beat, he then launches into a second lecture about human anatomy and the treatment of gunshot wounds. Shortly after he finishes the operation and his tragically ironic soliloquy, a solitary crewmember alerts the oblivious Cuticle to what his captive audience had already realized, "Please, sir," pleads the Steward, "the patient is dead."

THE PROBLEM WITH LAW

Although Dr. Cuticle is a fictitious character, he is also quite real in the sense that he represents the application of the law at moments when the gospel is desperately needed. The law and gospel are mutually exclusive values that govern all of life. By "law" I simply mean words and actions that harm persons instead of building them up; by "gospel" I mean just the opposite. Another way to describe this distinction is that the law crucifies and the gospel resurrects. In the church, the law accomplishes its mission by lecturing as incessantly about the Christian's duty to climb higher and grow deeper as Cuticle lectured his crewmates about the intricacies of medicine. The problem is not that the law is inaccurate in its estimate of human beings (Christians included) and their relationship to God, but that it is designed to be long on diagnosis and short on cure. Churches that prescribe the law as a curative agent are actually poisoning those they seek to help. It is designed to add insult to injury. This is why St. Paul wrote to the church at Corinth that "the letter kills, but the Spirit gives life," and nicknamed the law "the ministry of death" and "the ministry of condemnation" (2 Cor 3:6–9). It is not a wise course of treatment where ailing people are concerned. Unless the antidote of grace is administered to counteract the law, it will produce the same effects as Cuticle's crude procedure did on the foretopman.

THE CLERGY AND THE LAW

One indication that a clergyperson has come under the law's heavy hand is that they begin to eschew leisure in order to pursue what are perceived to be any number of sacred duties, aspirations, and ambitions. They fight rest because they are convinced that exhaustion in the name of a worthy cause is a sign of orthodoxy. However, clergy like this always die the death of a thousand cuts as they try to motivate themselves and their weary congregations to put a bit more effort into being a Christian. It takes years sometimes, but many of them, not to mention their spouse and children, implode emotionally and physically as they try to cope with the stress of juggling an endless number of responsibilities. The phenomenon of the burned-out pastor is so commonplace that The New York Times featured an article several years ago entitled "Taking a Break From the Lord's Work," which revealed that Christian clergypersons "now suffer from obesity, hypertension and depression at rates higher than most Americans. In the last decade, their use of antidepressants has risen, while their life expectancy has fallen. Many would change jobs if they could."[1] The article also found that many pastors fail to take a holiday, feeling duty-bound to work themselves to death in Christ's name. Perhaps this is why, in some denominations, the number of pastors who quit within the first five years has quadrupled. The ministry has become so wounding and painful for some clergy that they conclude with Dr. Cuticle that the only solution is to elect for full amputation, which in this context means leaving the pastorate altogether, and on occasion, the church.

One struggles to find adjectives to describe the spirit that possesses clergy and sets them on a course of self-destruction in the name of God and Christ. It is certainly not a "holy" spirit; the words "manipulating," "enslaving," and "legalistic" are better alternatives. Having given themselves over to the service of Christ and his church, a minister's year is a blur of sermons, new members, website updates, visitations, meetings, baptisms, building programs, confirmations, weddings, divorces, fundraising campaigns, funerals, church growth strategies, counseling sessions, Easters, Advents and Christmases. Who is sufficient for these things? No wonder some pastors begin to view sermons as opportunities to exhort the laity to do a better job in the week ahead; they are merely reflecting their own experience and understanding of Christianity. Perhaps their souls have grown thin because they concluded at some point that God is too busy keeping track of ecclesiastical chores to notice bruised reeds and smoldering wicks, especially when they are the one who is bruised and smoldering. Their God is a "hard man" (Luke 19:21) because nobody told them that the gospel of grace also applies to one's life after salvation, and so they keep slogging along until one Sunday morning the reed breaks in half and the wick is completely snuffed.

Not all ministers who leave the parish do so for reasons related to physical exhaustion brought on by the demands of a full schedule. Others leave because they are emotionally exhausted. It is not uncommon for a group of parishioners, or even a single parishioner, to take it upon themselves to scrutinize some aspect of the pastor's life: it may have to do with their preaching, the amount of visitation they do or fail to do, their looks or mannerisms, their compensation, or worse, their spouse or children. Fortunately, those sorts of people do not usually speak for the whole congregation, but there is always one or two in every church. The majority of

---

1. Vitello, "Taking a Break From the Lord's Work."

churchgoers are simply trying to make it through the week. They are like those in Lamentations 5:5, who cry out "With a yoke on our necks we are hard driven; we are weary, we are given no rest." Although they have genuine concerns and troubles that are as painful as was the bullet in the sailor's thigh, the burden of hearing countless sorrows is emotionally draining.

On the other hand, given that there also tends to be a good deal of positive feedback in a vocation like the ministry, it is entirely possible that pride and a need for recognition lead to compulsive work habits among clergy members. One spends hours writing a sermon because they want the congregation to like them and to say more nice things to them after the service. The attention can be intoxicating. Miroslav Volf observes, "The contemporary religion of work has little to do either with worship of God or with God's demands on human life; it has to do with 'worship' of self and human demands on the self."[2]

Moses stumbled into this trap as well, having assumed that he was the only one competent to preside over cases between his fellow Hebrews; he was corrected thanks to his father-in-law Jethro, whose counsel is as timeless as it is humbling, "What you are doing is not good. You and the people with you will certainly wear yourselves out, for the thing is too heavy for you. You are not able to do it alone." This is the essence of the message as taught and lived by Jesus: "the thing is too heavy for you." Despite the protestations of one's ego to the contrary, both ministry and life itself are too cumbersome for one to bear, either physically or spiritually. However, it appears this is not the message that pastors are hearing or sharing, nor is it perhaps what congregations want to hear if popular Christian literature is any measure of how the church thinks about this issue.

One of the most popular books on "Christian leadership" in recent years maintains that pastors must design and pursue a detailed action plan if their church is to grow numerically and spiritually. The author, a former seminary professor turned church consultant, recommends that the pastor and twenty-five to thirty leaders from the congregation should meet together every three or four weeks for a period of not less than nine months. These strategy sessions are held on Friday evenings from 6:00 to 9:00 p.m. and Saturday mornings from 8:00 a.m. to noon. This amounts to approximately 2,100 people-hours of planning time, which is more than an average American works in an entire year. These are also hours not spent with a spouse, children, and extended family; even if this fact does not explain why some are willing to subject themselves to this time-consuming arrangement, the abandoned parties will perceive the long absences as a

2. Volf, *Work in the Spirit*, 129.

veiled judgment. In short, nobody wins. One recollects Paul's words to the church at Colossae that there are many things in the world that "have indeed an appearance of wisdom in promoting self-imposed piety, humility, and severe treatment of the body, but they are of no value in checking self-indulgence" (Col 2:22–23). However, the absence of leisure is only a symptom of a deeper malaise, which is the refusal to accept vulnerability and incapacity as the point where God meets his people. Leisure is simply having grace for oneself, and when this happens, it is highly unlikely that the pastor will insist upon meeting with "star players" at the church for three-quarters of a year to talk about the playbook.

LEISURE: THE ANTIDOTE TO LAW

While I was a seminarian, it was Paul Zahl who taught me how to understand grace in the context of the parish. This one lesson has stuck with me ever since, and was itself worth the price of my entire education. This is no exaggeration. Many of my classmates have similar testimonies; it was as if the message of one-way love came to us from outer space, which is an especially fitting description for anyone who knows a little about Paul's taste in movies. What he has taught me is that there is a strong relationship between longevity (read: "survival") in ministry and one's doctrine of anthropology. It is difficult to understand how a pastor could remain the ministry very long if they believe that wounded people are in control and simply need more exhortation to get their act together. Dr. Zahl has not only survived but thrived in ministry for over three decades because he maintains a high view of Christ and low expectations for humans. When a pastor recognizes that people are less able to help themselves than is commonly assumed, they will, at the very least, make sure the last word these people hear before the service ends on Sunday is an absolving word of grace: "Be at leisure dear friends; Christ has finished his work and is seated at the Father's right hand on your behalf." This is the greatest privilege in ministry as far as I am concerned, and it is the one thing that keeps people coming back every week. Nobody leaves a grace-centered church, neither pastors nor parishioners.

Having spoken about the effects of law and gospel, labor and leisure, upon pastors, it is worth considering by way of analogy the effects upon congregations. Like the three thousand transgressors who perished after Moses brought down the Law from Mt Sinai, exhortative sermons are often received by parishioners as accusations. They become acutely aware that the pastor is speaking about their sins of omission and commission and if the only recourse offered is to stop omitting and committing, they will eventually wither and die. Likewise, when the Hebrews were confronted in their idolatry, the law pronounced them guilty but provided no remedy, "and that day about three thousand of the people died" (Ex 32:28). However, no pastor can afford to come down the mountain in this fashion if they hope to communicate the grace of God for sinners, because as lawbreakers themselves, they stand in the same need as their congregation. Conversely, the other pericope to consider deals with the day of Pentecost, when the Holy Spirit empowered Peter to preach the law of repentance, then to proclaim Christ crucified and the promised forgiveness of sins to those within earshot, as well as their children. "Those who accepted his message were baptized, and about three thousand were added to their number that day" (Acts 2:41). What followed was a season of worship, mutuality, generosity, and reverential awe among the early Christians, who enjoyed one another's company and goodwill as God continued to add to their numbers. The law slew three thousand but the gospel brought life to three thousand.

The distinction between these two approaches to ministry is captured in remarkable detail in Lucas Cranach's *Gesetz und Gnade* (Law and Grace). Cranach was something of a renaissance man and a close friend of Martin Luther, but is typically celebrated for his artistic skill. On the left side of the painting, he portrays the Fall, the expulsion from Paradise, the Ten Commandments, and Christ seated on his judgment throne. There is a young man in the foreground, a representation of humanity, who is being marched toward hell by Satan and a spear-wielding skeleton who represents death. Several austere characters in the foreground are looking at the young man and pointing to the Ten Commandments. This is the law, in all its severity. On the right side, Cranach represents the gospel. Here, Adam is standing in the foreground, together with John the Baptist. Adam is in a posture of reception, hands raised to receive the Holy Spirit who is proceeding from the pierced side of the crucified Christ, whose blood is streaming forth in a shower of forgiveness. Dividing the picture in two is a tall tree; the left side is completely barren while the right side of the tree is in full leaf, reinforcing the effects of the two approaches.

Preaching the gospel is not about delivering a message of repentance and duty—that is simply stage one—nor is it about challenging people to "live out the gospel," a command for which there is no precedent in the New Testament. That is law, and it creates turmoil and heightens anxiety. Likewise, moralism and positive thinking always fall short of the gospel, because they both put humans in the driver's seat rather than calling attention to the fact that Christ alone has "done all things well." Said Luther to Erasmus, "these words of yours, devoid of Christ, devoid of the Spirit, are colder than ice itself," and the same could be said for moralistic sermons because rather than fostering a restful stance, they urge one to intensify activity. The gospel is a word of grace and forgiveness to be received; it is a consolation. The gospel is a calming word from heaven: "Christ died for sinners." My suspicion is that moralism from the pulpit is a direct reflection that the pastor is either skeptical about grace, or not personally vested in the sermon itself, or both. In either case, such sermons are unable to act as a conduit for the love of Christ to flow to the congregation, but communicate that this love will only be dispensed after one begins to work harder at being Christian, which never actually happens.

I have suggested that for the sake of Christianity's future, the one thing hard-working ministers and congregations desperately need week after week is spiritual and physical leisure. What this means, theologically speaking, is that we all simply need to be propped up by the gospel, or held up like marionettes. There is nothing impious about being unobligated or of being spiritually and physically still; this allows God to be God for a change. Christ alone has obtained forgiveness for sinners and that is enough for people like St. Paul who "decided to know nothing among you except Jesus Christ, and him crucified" (1 Cor 2:2). Knowing Christ crucified *pro me*, or "for me," is the only thing that can cause dry bones in the parish to live again—not programs, not buzz words, not clever illustrations, trendy music, or an attractive and winsome pastor . . . only Christ who lived, died, and arose for you and me will get us through the worst life has to offer. Amazingly, when this incredible truth is held out to parishioners week upon week, it produces fruit, the very fruit pastors wear themselves out exhorting the congregation to produce.

PHYSICAL LEISURE

I am aware that some readers might find my appeal for rest to imply that if one was just to try a little harder to have some leisure, then all would be well. This is not the perception I want to give. As has already been suggested, spiritual leisure precedes physical leisure, where spiritual leisure is defined as living by faith and grace alone. As Luther pointed out in his *Commentary on Galatians*, spiritual exercises never produce true leisure: "Various holy orders have been launched for the purpose of securing peace of conscience through religious exercises, but they proved failures because such devices only increase doubt and despair. We find no rest for our weary bones unless we cling to the word of grace." Based upon Jesus' statement in Matthew 11:28–30, both spiritual and bodily leisure are part of the same gracious promise; this is a gift to be received rather than a goal toward which to work. "Come to me, all you that are weary and are carrying heavy burdens, and I will give you rest. Take my yoke upon you, and learn from me; for I am gentle and humble in heart, and you will find rest for your souls. For my yoke is easy, and my burden is light." According to the Savior, rest, like faith and salvation, is something freely given to the redeemed.

Christ responded to human restlessness in two ways. First, he sancti-fied physical rest by entering into it himself: sleeping in a boat (Mark 4:38), sitting by a well (John 4:6, 27), going to parties (Matt 9:9–13), and removing himself from genuinely needy people in order to spend time with his disciples or in prayer (John 11:6, 21; Luke 5:15–16). Perhaps the biblical writers re-corded these mundane events to highlight the humanity of Jesus, but it is also enlightening to read how his disciples found this practice slightly odd. Jesus eventually calls his disciples to try it for themselves, encouraging them to "come away to a deserted place all by yourselves and rest a while" (Mark 6:31). The second way Jesus responds to human restlessness is by ensuring a spiritual and eternal rest by way of his cross (Matt 11:28–29; John 14:1–4; Col 1:19–20; Heb 4:8–10; 1 John 3:19). His two responses provide the rationale for a minis-try of leisure, which has both spiritual and physical expressions.

Yet not everyone around Jesus approved of the way he did ministry. One reads in the gospels about the tightly-wound Pharisees who constantly lurked in the background of Jesus' ministry in the hope that they would find charges to bring against him. When they were resting on the Sabbath, Jesus did works of healing; when they thought he should be charging ahead at upholding the law, Jesus rested. Of course, Jesus did concede that ambitious do-gooders could be justified by taking a more active approach to life and salvation; he qualified it this way: "For I tell you, unless your righteousness exceeds that of the scribes and Pharisees, you will never enter the kingdom of heaven" (Matt 5:20). One just needs to outdo the religious ultra-mara-thoners. If that is not one's cup of tea, then Jesus alone will have to do. If, as Jesus suggests here, we are only ever standing still before God in terms of our justification, I would maintain that bodily leisure is just the physi-cal extension of that spiritual reality. Thus, the Christian who is at leisure spiritually will also discover leisure in the physical dimension; they are two sides of the same coin.

What Christianity says is that clergy and congregations are no longer subject to the treadmill of the law, this actually frees them to run like the wind. A vacation-less pastor has no more of God's righteousness or love credited to their account; in fact, God began lavishing it upon them from the foundation of the world. So why labor for that which cannot satisfy? Why hobble around the church like a weary, heavy-laden, soul when there is an easy yoke and a light burden to be received? Why worry or be concerned about tomorrow when God cares for dandelions and ensures that even the pigeons are fed? Christ has called you a friend, not a slave.

CONCLUSION

One wonders how many restless souls have become agnostics, if not atheists, since entering the ministry, but who stand in pulpits trying hard to believe again. May I just suggest that Christ has even died for the sectors of unbelief in every heart? I say this because Christ is not simply a partial substitute for his people. He did not fulfil *most* of the law. He is a complete substitute for sinners. He fulfilled the *entirety* of God's law on our behalf: "And when you were dead in trespasses and the uncircumcision of your flesh, God made you alive together with him, when he forgave us all our trespasses, erasing the record that stood against us with its legal demands. He set this aside, nailing it to the cross" (Col 2:13–14). Christ already took your doubts into consideration when he died for the sins of the world, an event which included the sum total of who we were, are, and will be.

Allow me to nail my colors to the mast on behalf of weary clergy and congregations: you have always been standing in the shadow of the crucified Christ. This is how you are seen by God, because to be "crucified with Christ" means that God has taken whatever accusations stand against you, and clothed you with a forgiveness that reaches into eternity past and eternity future. God is the active agent and we are utterly passive, so passive that we were not even born at the time Christ fulfilled all righteousness on the cross for our sakes. Such a thought, which is not just a nice idea, but a fact, has a way of putting compulsions, neuroses and doubts into neutral gear, at least for a moment. What can the Christian possibly add to the work and cross of Christ? What is the only reasonable reaction to God's omni-graciousness but gratitude, thanksgiving, and joy? Even if after experiencing this grace, a Christian remains restless and wanders into prodigal territory in search of a better grace, they will return—sometimes not until they rest on their deathbed—to the only one who ever held them in an unblinking gaze of acceptance. After all, God could never snub restless prodigals without becoming a hypocrite himself, since there is nothing more profligate than the cross.

Jesus was so relaxed about the use of law in his ministry that he maintained a posture of grace and forgiveness throughout, forgiving an adulterer, pardoning thieves, calling Judas "friend" after the betraying kiss, pleading for absolution of his murderers while he was languishing on the cross, and crowning his apostate friend Peter as the leader of his church. Up was down and down was up with Christ, and that is especially good news for restless and harried pastors who need their world turned inside out. "Ho, everyone who thirsts, come to the waters; and you that have no money, come, buy and eat! Come, buy wine and milk without money and without price. Why do you spend your money for that which is not bread, and your labor for that which does not satisfy? Listen carefully to me, and eat what is good, and delight yourselves in rich food" (Isa 55:2). The quickest route for restless souls to enjoy leisure is to become reacquainted with this God-man who subjected himself to Cuticle's bone saw and expects so little of you in return that he has done it all for you, whether you like it or not. This sort of sacrificial grace shocks souls who have been conditioned to think of Christianity as a prescriptive faith, but it is simply the counterintuitive fact that one has been living under the enormous umbrella of *sola fide* for nearly 2,000 years now. If Jesus was right that "it is finished," and he was, then we who enter God's rest may also cease from our labors just as God did from his.

BIBLIOGRAPHY

Vitello, Paul. "Taking a Break from the Lord's Work." *The New York Times*, August 2, 2010, A1.

Volf, Miroslav. *Work in the Spirit: Toward a Theology of Work*. 1991. Reprinted, Eugene, OR: Wipf & Stock, 2001.

18

Comfortable Words
Thomas Cranmer's Gospel Falconry

J. ASHLEY NULL

But if any man hath fallen . . . let him nevertheless hear the Word of God, so fatherly alluring us unto amendment.[1]

FOR TOO LONG NOW it has been accepted that the heart of the English Reformation was in fact the mind. For many scholars what moved the first Protestants in England was a bookish clarity of thought, an intellectual longing to be freed from the deadening hand of inherited custom and superstition—in short, the inherent power of their reason reasserting itself.[2] A.G. Dickens gave the most robust exposition of this view.[3] In contrast to what he saw as the ignorant affective ritualism of popular medieval piety, Dickens explained the English Reformation as the inevitable outcome of an increasingly educated

1. Von Wied, *A Simple and Religious Consultation*, fol. 230v. The spelling, punctuation, and diction of all early modern sources have been modernized in this chapter.

2. Although scholars today normally refer to the early English Reformers as "evangelicals," for an essay in honor of the author of *The Protestant Face of Anglicanism*, I have chosen to use the older term. For the use of the term "evangelical" in this context, see Null, "Thomas Cranmer and Tudor Evangelicalism," 226–30.

3. Dickens, *The English Reformation*.

populace encountering the "rational appeal of a Christianity based upon the authentic sources of the New Testament."[4] If Eamon Duffy and others have since soundly refuted Dickens' whiggish blindness to the normative catechetical and liturgical sinews that bound head and heart together in medieval English devotion,[5] these scholars have shown no hurry to revise as well Dickens' characterization of emerging English Protestantism as, so to speak, "head-driven." It would seem indisputable that only an ideological philistinism on par with the Chinese Cultural Revolution could account for the wholesale destruction of a material cultural as intellectually rich and aesthetically moving as that of the medieval English church. After all, amongst many others crimes against beauty, did not the reformers' myopia obliterate the cheerful company of countless angels in parish churches across the country, whitewashing their delicate blond curls and brightly colored robes just to provide a sterile canvass for the black Gothic lettering of English Bible verses. How could anyone with a heart have done something like that?

DISASSOCIATION OF SENSIBILITY?

Of course, it is absolutely true that the reformers were a people of the Book. They insisted that authentic Christianity gave priority to the plain sense of Scripture over everything else, including traditional beliefs like purgatory, pardons, and penance, and including deeply-ingrained devotional practices like praying to saints and burning lights before their images. After the sword of scriptural authority had cut away centuries of error, what remained, the reformers believed, was the simple message of salvation by faith in Christ alone. This "fervent Biblicism" was the coat-of-arms by which they presented themselves on the doctrinal battlefield and by which they recognized their comrades-in-arms.[6]

Yet despite this deep commitment to a coherent intellectual program, the fervor of the English reformers was not merely ratiocinative. Without exception, they were followers of Erasmus. His humanist approach to theology had rejected the dominance of scholasticism precisely because its turgidly technical wranglings had so little interest in and even less effect on the actual lives of ordinary people. Instead of syllogistic reasoning, Erasmus emphasized rhetorical persuasion through the power of God's Word.

4. Dickens, "The Shape of Anti-clericalism and the English Reformation," 380.

5. Duffy, *Stripping of the Altars*; Duffy, *The Voices of Morebath*; Rex, "The Role of English Humanists in the Reformation up to 1559."

6. Marshall, *Religious Identities in Henry VIII's England* (Aldershot, UK: Ashgate, 2006), 7.

Since Scripture contained the "living image of Christ's most holy mind," its message could move human affections deeply, inflaming hearts with a transforming love for God, and encouraging human wills to choose a life of practical good works which bettered themselves and their society.[7] As a result, this same affective response to Scripture lies at the very heart of the two most detailed conversion narratives from the first English Protestants.

According to Thomas Bilney, an early martyr (d. 1531), he often "felt a change" in himself "from the right hand of the Most High God" when he read Scripture. It happened for the first time while reading Erasmus's new Latin translation of the Bible. Although he had been "allured" by the edition's reputation for rhetorical eloquence rather than any interest in theology:

> I chanced upon this sentence of St. Paul (Oh most sweet and comfortable sentence to my soul!) in 1 Tim. 1:15: 'It is a true saying and worthy of all men to be embraced, that Christ Jesus came into the world to save sinners, of whom I am the chief and principal.' This one sentence, through God's instruction . . . working inwardly in my heart, did so gladdened it— which before was wounded by the awareness of my sins almost to the point of desperation—that immediately I felt a marvelous inner peace, so much so that my bruised bones leapt for joy. After this, the Scripture began to be more pleasant to me than honey or the honey comb.[8]

Katherine Parr, the widow of Henry VIII, used the same emotive language to describe her transforming encounter with Scripture:

> 'Come to me all you that labor and are burdened, and I shall refresh you.' What gentle, merciful, and comfortable words are these to all sinners . . . What a most gracious, comfortable, and gentle saying was this, with such pleasant and sweet words to allure his enemies to come to him . . . when I behold the beneficence, liberality, mercy and goodness of the Lord, I am encouraged, emboldened and stirred to ask for such a noble gift as living faith . . . By this faith I am assured; and by this assurance I feel the remission of my sins. This is it that maketh me bold. This is it that comforteth me. This is it that quencheth all despair . . . Thus, I feel

---

7. Null, "Tudor Evangelicalism," 238–40.

8. Fox, *Actes and Monuments*, 1141–43. Bilney's description of his conversion is contained in correspondence to Bishop Cuthbert Tunstall during Bilney's 1527 heresy trial. Foxe has given two versions, the original Latin and an English translation. The citations are based on Foxe's translation, but altered as needed for more precision and clarity in contemporary English against the Latin original.

myself to come, as it were, in a new garment before God, and now by his mercy, to be taken as just and righteous.[9]

"I felt a supernatural change within," "gladdened my heart," "I felt inner peace," "leapt for joy," "more pleasant than honey," "pleasant and sweet words," "I am assured," "I feel the remission of my sins." "I feel myself in a new garment": plainly, such sensuous discourse is not the patois of emotionally stunted anoraks and blue-stockings. To borrow a term from T. S. Eliot, no dissociation of sensibility held sway over the English reformers. As much late medieval Catholics as early modern Protestants, they too kept head and heart together. Or, to use Eliot's language again, the first English reformers clearly "felt their thought."[10] In fact, their conversion narratives make clear that they adopted solifidianism not as a repudiation of their late medieval piety, but precisely because they found its grace and gratitude theology much more effective in moving them to experience its true affective fulfillment.

"ALLURE"

This unity of metaphysical sense and physical sensibility can be seen in one of the reformers' favorite verbs to use in conjunction with the Gospel: "allure." According to the Oxford English Dictionary, the word is derived from the practice in falconry of casting a meat-laden lure to recall a bird of prey. Such hawking was a pursuit for gentlemen and, thus, a common recreation amongst Henry VIII's courtiers. Even Thomas Cranmer, the Archbishop of Canterbury, was a frequent falconer. He was well-known to find refreshment after long study through hawking, for his father had made sure that his son was practiced in the sport from youth as a sign of his good birth, despite their relatively modest means.[11]

The popularity of falconry amongst the societal elite meant that "allure" was often used in early modern discourse as a synonym for temptation, to draw someone into sin by baiting their baser desires. Hence, the King's Book translates James 1:14 as "but every man is tempted, drawn, and allured by his own concupiscence."[12] Yet, the idea of "allure" as appealing to the senses to attract others to something positive was equally present. In a 1539 Palm Sunday sermon before Henry VIII, Cuthbert Tunstall compared personal humility to a sweet smell hidden in a corner whose aroma allured men to seek out its

9. Parr, *The Lamentation of a Sinner*, sigs. B3v, B4v-B5r, B6r.
10. Eliot, "The Metaphysical Poets."
11. Nichols, ed. *Narratives of the Days of the Reformation*, 239.
12. Lacey, *The King's Book*, 121.

source, an apt comparison not doubt, since it was certainly as rare at court to encounter a sweet-smelling chamber as a humble courtier.[13]

Since Erasmus emphasized rhetorical persuasion over syllogistic disputation, he often used "allure" in this positive sense of drawing people towards embracing virtue. In his landmark handbook for practical piety, the *Enchiridion*, he wrote that the purpose of true learning was "to allure very many to a Christian man's life."[14] In contrast to the acerbic divisiveness of debate, because Erasmus treated the word as a synonym for persuasion, his use of "allure" carried the connotation of moving people "with courtesy, gentleness and pleasures." Therefore, nothing more succinctly summarized Jesus' mission: "The son of man came forth minding to stir up this nation to the love of the heavenly doctrine . . . that he might allure them the more with his gentleness."[15]

The Protestants' commitment to justification by faith as the basis of the Christian life went doctrinally further than Erasmus was ever willing to go. Nevertheless, because of this very emphasis on personal faith, persuasion was just as important to Luther, if not even more so. Therefore, unsurprisingly Luther also found "allure" a useful word to describe how Christ wooed sinners back to himself:

> Thus, when the shepherd finds the lost sheep again, he has no intention of pushing it away in anger once more or throwing it to a hungry wolf. Rather, all his care and concern is directed to alluring it with every possible kindness. Treating it with the upmost tenderness, he takes the lamb upon his own back, lifting it up and carrying it, until he brings the animal all the way home again.[16]

For Luther such gentle handling was the key to people coming to personal faith: "How very kindly and lovingly does the Lord allure all hearts to himself, and in this way he stirs them to believe in him."[17]

13. Tunstall, *A Sermon Made upon Palm Sunday Last Past*, sig. B3v.

14. Erasmus, *The Manual of the Christian Knight*, sig. [A5]r.

15. Erasmus, *The First Volume of the Paraphrase of Erasmus upon the New Testament*, fols. 38r, 68v.

16. "So ist der Hirte auch nicht darumb da, wenn er widder findet, das er mit im zürnen noch von sich stossen odder dem Wolff inn rachen werffen wolle, sondern alle seine sorge und gedancken sind, das ers nur auffs aller freundlichst locke und auffs senssste mit im umbgehe, nimpt es auff seinen eigen rucken, hebt und tregt es, bis so lange ers widder heim bringet," Luther, *Weimarer Ausgabe 16. Kritische Gesammtausgabe*, vol. 18, 36, 290,38–91,17.

17. "Wie gar freundlich und lieblich lockt der herr alle hertzen zu sich und reytzt sie, ynn yhn tzu gleuben ynn disem exempel," ibid., 8, 359,5–6.

With an endorsement by both Erasmus and Luther, it was only natural that those Tudor humanists who embraced evangelical doctrine would consider "allure" an especially apt term for expressing their understanding of the process of salvation. Firstly, they were well aware that personal belief was naturally a product of individual conviction, not compulsion. Hence, conversion to the truth had to come from persuasive preaching, not just by proclamation and punishment. Richard Taverner used "allure" to stress this point in his 1540 handbook of Sunday homilies:

> The Romish bishop erreth and doth naught in that he goeth about by violence to draw men to the Christian faith. For besides the preaching of the Gospel, Christ gave nothing in commission unto his disciples. So they preached it accordingly to their commission and left it in men's free liberty to come to it or not. They said not, either believe it or I will kill thee. So ye see that infidels as Turks, Saracens, and Jews ought not violently to be drawn to our faith, but lovingly rather invited and allured.[18]

In his book against Edmond Bonner, Bishop of London, John Bale came to the same point, but rather more quickly: "The office of a Christian bishop were rather to preach than to punish, rather to feed than to famish, rather gently to allure than currishly to rebuke before the world, were he after the order of Christ and his apostles."[19]

Secondly, the connotation of "allure" as persuasion by expressing gentleness and kindness towards the hearer fit precisely with the Protestants' understanding of salvation by grace. Earlier in the same passage Bale explicitly linked gentleness on God's part with unmerited forgiveness: "The gentle spouse of Christ (which is his church without spot) is evermore ready to forgive, though the offence be done seventy-seven times."[20] In his book of sermons for Holy Days, Taverner went on to specifically define forgiveness as the means of divine allurement: "God freely pardoning all our sins doth allure us all, of whom he hath been offended, to peace and amity."[21]

For both Bilney and Katherine, it was this unexpected offer of immediate unmerited reconciliation with God that first captured their attention. For up until they encountered this good news, neither was searching for God. Bilney was allured to reading Erasmus' New Testament by its reputation for

18. Taverner, *The Epistles and Gospels with a Brief Postil upon the Same from after Easter till Advent*, sig. 42v.

19. Bale, *A Disclosing or Opening of the Man of Sin*, fol. 31v.

20. Ibid., fol. 31r.

21. Taverner, *On Saint Andrew's Day the Gospels with Brief Sermons upon Them for All the Holy Days in the Year*, fol. 49v.

eloquence. Katherine Parr was confident in her own penitential works. Yet, when they read the divine promises in 1 Timothy 1:15 and Matthew 11:28, they both realized, as Katherine wrote, that God used "such pleasant and sweet words to allure his enemies to come to him."

This gentle handling of sinners by God was the origin of Thomas Cranmer's notorious lenience towards those who had wronged him personally. As William Shakespeare had Henry VIII put it, "Do my Lord of Canterbury / A shrewd turn, and he is your friend for ever."[22] When chided about this trait, Cranmer responded:

> What will ye have a man do to him that is not yet come to the knowledge of the truth of the Gospel . . . ? Shall we perhaps, in his journey coming towards us, by severity and cruel behavior overthrow him, and as it were in his pilgrimage stop him? I take not this the way to allure men to embrace the doctrine of the Gospel. And if it be a true rule of our Savior Christ to do good for evil, than let such as are not yet come to favor our religion learn to follow the doctrine of the Gospel by our example in using them in a friendly and charitable manner.[23]

For Cranmer, the inherent drawing power of divine free forgiveness was the root of all evangelism.

Thirdly, the sense of "allure" as appealing to a hearer's own inner longings, rooted in its derivation from the whirling of bird-bait, enabled it to effectively convey the underlying existential dimension Protestants associated with coming to a saving knowledge of Christ, namely, as it were, the "feeling of their faith." Writing to Henry VIII in 1538, Cranmer described the internal effect of hearing the good news of the Gospel:

> But if the profession of our faith of the remission of our own sins enter within us into the deepness of our hearts, then it must kindle a warm fire of love in our hearts towards God, and towards all other for the love of God—a fervent mind to seek and procure God's honour, will, and pleasure in all things—a good will and mind to help every man and to do good unto them, so far as our might, wisdom, learning, counsel, health, strength, and all other gifts which we have received of God will extend—and, *in summa*, a firm intent and purpose to do all that is good, and leave all that is evil.[24]

---

22. Shakespeare, "Henry VIII," Act V, Scene III, Lines 176–77.

23. Nichols, *Narratives of the Days of the Reformation*, 246–47.

24. Cox, *Miscellaneous Writings and Letters of Thomas Cranmer*, 86.

Here is the heart of the Protestant message. Love by its very nature seeks union, for implicit within the offering of the gift of love is a calling, a wooing, an alluring of the recipient to reciprocate likewise with love. If God loved humanity so much as to endure the cross so that they might have assurance of everlasting life with him, to use Cranmer's words again, only those with "hearts harder than stones" would not be moved to love God in return.[25] Katherine was quite clear that such was her own experience:

> "Then began I to dwell in God by charity, knowing by the loving charity of God in the remission of my sins that God is charity as St. John saith. So that of my faith (whereby I came to know God and whereby it pleased God even because I trusted in him to justify me) sprang this excellent charity in my heart."[26]

Thus, for the English Reformers, to encounter unconditional divine love was to discover something deep within being touched, an unquenchable, often unexpected, longing for a relationship with one's Maker being stirred up, a transforming grateful human love for God being gently drawn out, a fervent drive to express this love in all outward actions rising up and directing the remainder of their lives. Fear of punishment could not produce such an inward, all-encompassing transformation in a sinner. Only the assurance of divine love made known in free pardon had that power. Perhaps no one expressed the results of feeling the alluring nature of the Gospel better than Thomas Becon, Cranmer's chaplain:

> As I may unfeignedly report unto you the affect of my heart, truly since you declared to us the goodness of God the Father toward us through Jesus Christ I have felt in my heart such an earnest faith and burning love toward God and his Word, that I think a thousand fires could not pluck me away from the love of him. I begin now utterly to condemn, despise, reject, cast away, and set at naught all the pleasures of this world, herein I have so greatly rejoiced in times past. All the threats of God, all the displeasures of God, all the fires and pains of hell could never before this day so allure me to the love of God, as you have now done by expressing unto me the exceeding mercy and unspeakable kindness of God toward us wretched sinners, insomuch that now from the very heart I desire to know what I may do, that by some means I may show again my heart to be full fired

---

25. Ibid., 134.
26. Parr, *The Lamentation of a Sinner*, sigs. B7v-B8r.

on the seeking of his glory. For I now desire nothing more than the advancement of his name.[27]

Fourthly, according to Cranmer, it was precisely because human beings were psychosomatic beings who "felt their faith" that God had instituted the sacraments. Since these ordinances incarnated the promises of God's words in concrete, creaturely symbols which were then able to appeal to the many varied senses of the human body, they were highly effective in alluring the hearts and minds of God's children to draw closer to him:

> And in like manner Christ ordained the sacrament of his body and blood in bread and wine, to preach unto us, that as our bodies be fed, nourished, and preserved with meat and drink, so (as touching our spiritual life towards God) we be fed, nourished and preserved by the body and blood of our savior Christ, and also that he is such a preservation unto us, that neither the devils of hell, nor eternal death, nor sin, can be able to prevail against us, so long as by true and constant faith we be fed and nourished with that meat and drink. And for this cause Christ ordained this sacrament in bread and wine (which we eat and drink, and be chief nutriments of our body), to the intent that as surely as we see the bread and wine with our eyes, smell them with our noses, touch them with our hands, and taste them with our mouths, so assuredly ought we to believe that Christ is our spiritual life and sustenance of our souls, like as the said bread and wine is the food and sustenance of our bodies. And no less ought we to doubt, that our souls be feed and live by Christ, than that our bodies be fed and live by meat and drink. Thus our savior Christ, knowing us to be in this world (as it were) but babes and weaklings in faith, hath ordained sensible signs and tokens, whereby to allure and to draw us to more strength and more constant faith in him. So that the eating and drinking of this sacramental bread and wine is, as it were, a showing of Christ before our eyes, a smelling of him with our noses, a feeling and groping of him with our hands, and an eating, chewing, digesting and feeding upon him to our spiritual strength and perfection.[28]

Only against this background of the Gospel as divine allurement can we begin to understand Cranmer's crafting of the Prayer Book's Comfortable Words.

27. Becon, *A Christmas Banquet Garnished with Many Pleasant and Dainty Dishes*, F4v–5r.

28. Cox, *Writings and Disputations of Thomas Cranmer . . . relative to the Sacrament of the Lord's Supper*, 41–42.

THE COMFORTABLE WORDS

As with most things liturgical for Cranmer, the origin of the Gospel sentences at the heart of his Communion service lies somewhere else. For Renaissance writers were encouraged to strive to be like a bee making honey "from flowers of all the sweetest and best scents and savors which are tasted and distinguishable in the honey itself."[29] Hence, literary brilliance lay not so much in originality of ideas as in the diversity of sources culled, the abundance of material artfully used, and the aptness of the adaption to circumstances of the current audience. Each of these factors will play a significant role in Cranmer's handling of the Comfortable Words.

As F. E. Brightman clearly demonstrated, Cranmer's prayer books did indeed use a wide variety of earlier material, including Scripture itself, ancient liturgies like that of St. John Chrysostom in the East and the Mozarabic Rite in the West, Sarum as the most influential Latin mass in medieval England, and various contemporary changes introduced by the Protestant Reformers.[30] In the case of the Comfortable Words, Cranmer's sources were communion services by Huldrych Zwingli in Zurich, Martin Bucer in Strassburg and, finally, Hermann von Wied in Cologne.

In 1523, Zwingli's *De canone missae epicheiresis* (Attack on the Canon of the Mass) significantly rewrote the eucharistic prayers of the traditional Latin rite so as to emphasize a spiritual feeding on the Word of God. As part of these revisions, the welcoming words of Matthew 11:28 were recited inbetween the Institution Narrative and the Words of Administration.[31] Two years later, Zwingli deleted the biblical text from the new German communion service, but retained the verse on the cover of the book.[32]

As early as 1524 Strassburg introduced a Communion service in German.[33] The order opened with a general confession and the recitation of 1 Timothy 1:15 as the absolution.[34] After several revisions guided by Martin Bucer, the city's chief Reformer, the opening section of the 1537 rite

---

29. Fox, "Statutes of Corpus Christi College, Oxford," 32.

30. Brightman, *The English Rite*

31. Egli and Finsler, eds., *Huldreich Zwinglis Sämtliche Werke*, II, 607–8.

32. Egli et al., eds., *Huldreich Zwinglis Sämtliche Werke*, IV, 9, 23.

33. The best critical edition of the liturgies used in Strasbourg during the Reformation remains the work of Hubert, *Die Straßburger liturgischen Ordnungen im Zeitalter der Reformation.* For a commentary in English on their development, see Van de Poll, *Martin Bucer's Liturgical Ideas.*

34. To make this clear, a further edition that year included a one-word introductory rubric for 1 Tim 1:15—"Absolution," Hubert, *Die Straßburger liturgischen Ordnungen*: xi–xii, 57–58.

included: (i) three possible confessions from which to choose, the last being based on the Ten Commandments; (ii) a rubric describing the verse from Timothy as "*Ein absolution oder trostspruch*" (an Absolution or Comforting Word); (ii) the text of 1 Tim 1:15; (iii) a pronouncement of forgiveness by the minister; and (iv) a list of four alternative verses which could be used instead: John 3:16, 35–36; Acts 10:43; and 1 John 2:1–2.[35]

When Bucer and Melanchthon aided Archbishop Herman von Wied in revising the liturgy for Cologne in the 1540s, the proposed Communion service began with a Strassburg-style confession and absolution which had only minor differences in the Scripture section. In the initial 1543 German version of the proposal, the previously printed rubric introducing a *Trostspruch* became a spoken injunction: "*Höret den Evangelischen trost*" (Hear the Gospel's comfort).[36] The final 1545 Latin version shortened the injunction to simply "*Audite Evangelium*" (Hear the Gospel). Both Cologne versions, however, shared the same reordering of the textual options for the single passage of Scripture to be recited: John 3:16; 1 Tim 1:15; John 3:35–36; Acts 10:43; and 1 John 2:1–2.[37]

So much for Cranmer's sources. Let's look at what he did with them. The first appearance of his version of the Comfortable Words came in the *Order of the Communion*, an English-language addendum to the medieval mass to be used from Easter 1548 onwards. Immediately after the priest's reception of the sacrament consecrated with the usual Latin prayers, he was to turn to the congregation and exhort them in their own language to receive worthily themselves. Then followed English versions of the confession, absolution, Comfortable Words (Matt 11:28; John 3:16; 1 Tim 1:15; and 1 John 2:1–2), the Prayer of Humble Access, the Words of Administration, reception by the laity in both kinds and a final blessing as dismissal.[38]

The most immediately apparent distinctive of Cranmer's use of his sources is its sheer Erasmian abundance. The "Comfortable Word" of Strassburg has become in its English version the "Comfortable Words."[39] Whereas Bucer's liturgies had recited only one biblical text during the service, Cranmer's *Order* specified four. Of course, such rhetorical multiplication is hardly surprising from a man noted for his habitual use of linguistic doublets: "erred and strayed," "devices and desires," "acknowledge and bewail," "wrath and indignation," "do earnestly repent and be heartily sorry"; not

35. Ibid., xxii–xxvii, 91–95.

36. Von Wied, *Einfältiges Bedenken,* Vol. 11.1, p. 342.

37. Von Wied, *Simplex ac pia Deliberatio,* fol. 92r.

38. Ketley, ed., *The Two Liturgies,* 1–8.

39. Ibid., 7.

to mention his love for piled-up synonyms like "succour, help and comfort all that be in danger, necessity and tribulation."[40] Yet, Rowan Williams was spot on to spot something far more at work here than merely seeking an eloquence of excess through repetition and rhythm. Rather, "a liturgical language like Cranmer's hovers over meanings like a bird that never quite nests for good—or, to sharpen the image, like a bird of prey that never stoops for a kill."[41] The Prayer Book never uses one word when more will do because no human speech, even human speech dignified by the divine's direct appropriation of it, can ever fully convey the glory of God. Cranmer's sacred diction circles that which is being described like a hawk so as to see God and us and the relationships between us from as many angles as possible.

Naturally, this spiritual hovering with intent was especially true with regards to the great mystery of God's gracious alluring of his wayward children back to himself. An injunction to "Hear the Gospel" in Cranmer's liturgy could never be followed by a mere solitary verse. Meaning through multiplication required something more. Hence, the *Order's* four scriptural texts form a *locus communis*, a commonplace, that Augustinian hermeneutical tool much encouraged by Erasmus whereby the meaning of one passage from the Bible is discerned through comparison with other passages from Scripture on the same topic. Consequently, Cranmer's Comfortable Words offer a concise, but still multi-faceted description of the Gospel itself. Here, as it were, is the Anglican equivalent of the Four Spiritual Laws embedded in its very first vernacular liturgy. To fully appreciate its insights, we need to do a bit of falcon-like circling ourselves over Cranmer's Gospel commonplace.

HEAR WHAT COMFORTABLE WORDS OUR SAVIOR CHRIST SAYETH TO ALL THAT TRULY TURN TO HIM.[42]

Note that "Hear the Gospel" has become in Cranmer's hands "Hear what comfortable words our Savior Christ sayeth." No doubt he understood the Cologne revision from "*Evangelischen trost*" to merely "*Evangelium*," since Cranmer would have agreed that the former was a tautology. The Good News of Jesus Christ literally embodied all comfort. Cranmer's revised introductory injunction highlighted the inherent interconnectedness of Gospel, comfort and Christ. It was, after all, an important polemical point.

40. For the use of these phrases in the 1552 Prayer Book, see ibid., 218–19, 234, 276.

41. Williams, "The Martyrdom of Thomas Cranmer—Sermon at Service to Commemorate the 450th Anniversary," (2006).

42. For the final version of Cranmer's Comfortable Words as found in the 1549 and 1552 *Book of Communion Prayer*, see Ketley, *Liturgies of Edward VI*, 91, 276.

Actually, it was the main point on which so much of the Reformers' thought and action turned. Here was the source of all that whitewashing of Edwardian church interiors. For what was the ubiquitous image that visually dominated most parish sanctuaries in England? Jesus as the Lord of Doom. As Eamon Duffy expressed it, "Christ would have gazed sternly down from the chancel arch" on the congregation below.[43] There on high before their eyes Jesus would have sat in judgment at the general resurrection with some people being received by the devils into Hell while others were welcomed by those golden-curled angelic choirs. Here was the apex of a "moralistic strain" in late medieval piety which Duffy himself admitted "could be oppressive":

> Churches contained not only the chancel-arch representation of the Day of Doom, with its threat of terrifying reckoning down to the last farthing, but wall-paintings and windows illustrating the deadly sins, the works of mercy, the Commandments, Christ wounded by sabbath-breaking, the figures of the three living and the three dead, or the related *danse macabre*.[44]

Indeed, the medieval church had come to rely so routinely on the terror of coming torments in the afterlife to encourage moral obedience in this one that even the very nature of purgatory changed over the centuries to reinforce it.[45] Originally, the possibility of spiritual purification after death arose as a divine concession to mercy, offering the hope of salvation even to the much less than pure who only repented at the last-minute as they lay dying. Because of the doctrine of purgatory, the medieval church could hold to its strict standards of justice while at the same time proclaiming that no earthly sinner remained beyond the hope of redemption. Hence, those undergoing punishments in Dante's *Purgatorio* were in fact joyful, cheered by their now certain knowledge of eventual salvation. However, by the Fifteenth Century this pastoral safety valve permitting death bed conversions seemed to many in the church to have become so successful as to now actually be in danger of encouraging people to put off serious repentance until that moment. In response arose Bridget of Sweden's much darker visions of extremely painful purgings which eventually dominated popular preaching and perception. Here is a brief portion of the fearful fate she saw reserved in purgatory for those guilty of lying pride:

43. Duffy, *Stripping of the Altars*, 226.

44. Ibid., 187.

45. The standard work on the history of purgatory in English remains Le Goff, *The Birth of Purgatory*.

Then I thought that there was a band bound about his head so fast and sore that the forehead and the back of the head met together. The eyes were hanging on the cheeks; the ears as they had been burned with fire; the brains burst out at the nostrils and his ears; the tongue hanging out, and the teeth were slammed together; the bones in the arms were broken and withered as a rope.[46]

Be assured, the remaining parts of the sinner's body fared no better.

With such visions of exacting retribution for each human frailty, Duffy had to admit again that the omnipresent threat of terror "must have seemed at times oppressive." Hence, the "whole machinery of late medieval piety was designed to shield the soul from Christ's doomsday anger."[47] Here was the root of Taverner and Bale's complaint against forced obedience through fear of violence, for the bishops' conduct merely modeled in the flesh how Christ himself was portrayed in art as handling wrong-doers. The medieval tonic was the kindly intercession of Mary and the saints, who naturally understood the human condition, as well as the hope of saving grace through the sacrament of penance.[48] For the Reformers, relief came through walls whitewashed of all past reminders of terror as well as all lesser saving friends whose special spiritual stature had risen at the expense of the Lord Jesus' own reputation for accessibility and mercy. In their place the Edwadians put the promises of Scripture, both painted on the walls and proclaimed through the Comfortable Words during the Sunday liturgy. The Reformers' aim was simple: to change the popular perception that Jesus was watching humanity like a hawk, ever ready to swoop down to punish their least infraction. Instead, they wanted the English people to understand that first and foremost Christ was the Good Shepherd, alluring back his lost sheep by the power of his self-sacrificing love.

The Cologne revision of 1545 had explicitly linked the good news of salvation with an outpouring of divine love. For the injunction to "Hear the Gospel" was followed by the reading of John 3:16 as the first option, not 1 Tim. 1:15 as in Strassburg. Cranmer went still further. He not only rejected the traditional emphasis on Christ as the embodiment of divine wrath, Cranmer choose not to begin with divine intent at all. Rather, his initial preaching of the Gospel began with addressing the felt needs of a hurting humanity, and he used Jesus' own words to do so. Like Zwingli before him, Cranmer turned to Matthew 11:28.

46. Duffy, *Stripping of the Altars*, 338–39.

47. Ibid., 309.

48. Ibid., 187–88, 310.

COME UNTO ME ALL THAT TRAVAIL,
AND BE HEAVY LADEN, AND I SHALL REFRESH YOU.

Human misery caused by captivity to the destructive power of sin was a favorite theme of the English Reformers. As part of the first liturgical changes Cranmer made under Edward VI, the vernacular sermons of the 1547 *Book of Homilies* were required reading in sequence on a repeating basis as part of the Sunday eucharistic service in every parish church in Edwardian England. The order was important, since the second homily preached the Law in good Lutheran fashion so that the third homily on salvation could preach the Gospel. The second homily was entitled, not surprisingly then, "The Misery of All Mankind," and concisely summed up the human condition resulting from sin: "We are sheep that run astray, but we cannot of our own power come again to the sheepfold, so great is our imperfection and weakness."[49]

Such a clear doctrinal statement of the bondage of the will could not but have had extensive existential ramifications for the feeling faith of the English Reformers. As Bilney's testimony bears ample witness, they experienced penetrating personal brokenness in the face of their deeply entrenched soul-sickness. In fact, Cranmer appears to have chosen the word "travail" instead of the more usual "labor" specifically because of its connotation of suffering and distress.[50] Hence, the promised alleviation of human misery by a sensuous Gospel was a powerful inducement for turning to God. Katherine mentioned in particular the alluring power of Jesus' offer in Matthew 11:28 to meet her at the point of her need. Cranmer gave an enduring voice to these *Anfechtungen* (spiritual anxieties) in his vernacular confession for the 1548 *Order of the Communion* which was then carried over verbatim into the 1549 *Book of Common Prayer*:

> Almighty God, Father of our Lord Jesus Christ, maker of all things, judge of all men, we acknowledge and bewail our manifold sins and wickedness . . . the remembrance of them is grievous unto us, the burden of them is intolerable.

49. Bond, ed., *Certain Sermons or Homilies (1547) AND A Homily against Disobedience and Wilful Rebellion (1570): A Critical Edition*, 74. Although John Harpesfield, a Catholic Erasmian humanist, wrote the homily, Cranmer's sandwiching it between clearly Protestant sermons made "Misery" in effect a proclamation of Lutheran doctrine. See Null, "Official Tudor Homilies," 355.

50. Whereas Tyndale's New Testament, the Henrician Primers (e.g., William Marshall, *A Primer in English*, sig. L3v.) and the Great Bible use "labor," Erasmus wrote: "Come unto me (sayeth he) as many of you as be grieved with afflictions, cares, or with conscience of your sins, and as many as be oppressed with the burden of adversity, I will refresh you, I will give you solace and comfort against all kinds of displeasures," Erasmus, *The First Volume of the New Testament*, fol. 70r.

In the face of such honesty about sinful guilt before God and humanity's powerlessness to counter its corrupting influence, the only answer lay in divine action. When the minister in the absolution which followed asked God to "pardon and deliver" the congregation, Cranmer's seemingly rhetorical copiousness was actually responding to the two separate sources of human misery—being wounded in both conscience and will.[51]

In the 1552 prayer book, Cranmer reinforced these themes by adding a new opening for the Daily Office which repristinated the image of sin-sick humanity as helpless sheep:

> Almighty and most merciful Father, we have erred and strayed from thy ways, like lost sheep. We have followed too much the devices and desires of our own hearts. We have offended against thy holy laws. We have left undone those things which we ought to have done, and we have done those things which we ought not to have done, and there is no health in us.[52]

By beginning Morning and Evening Prayer with a confession of humanity's profound spiritual neediness in the face of its ongoing struggle with self-centered waywardness, Cranmer made turning to God because of sin so as to be turned by God from it the warp and weave of Anglican worship.

SO GOD LOVED THE WORLD, THAT HE GAVE HIS ONLY BEGOTTEN SON TO THE END THAT ALL THAT BELIEVE IN HIM, SHOULD NOT PERISH, BUT HAVE LIFE EVERLASTING.

Having used Jesus' own words to acknowledge the depth of human longing for good news, Cranmer's second Comfortable Word now turns again to Jesus to establish the depth of God's own longing to respond. The divine desire and initiative to save his people is at the very heart of the English Reformers' theology. John 3:16 makes clear that God the Father, moved by the love which is his very being, sent God the Son into this world to become the visible embodiment of the divine Good Shepherd. Jesus came to seek out the lost, gently freeing lambs caught in the thicket of sin, laying down his own life so that in the end he could bear his wandering creatures safely back to the flock on his own wounded shoulders. In the face of such alluring love, the Reformers were convinced, even the sin-sodden souls of humanity could not but find themselves drawn by their own inner longings back to their Creator.

51. Ketley, *Liturgies of Edward VI*, 6–7, 90–91.
52. Ibid., 218–19.

Of course, the medieval church read John 3:16 too. In fact, the typical English depiction of Jesus as coming Judge had him display his wounds and the signs of his torture on their behalf.[53] Yet this depiction of divine love was not intended to be a means of wooing humanity back to the fold, but rather to render them without excuse if they had failed to so. In effect, the medieval church said to Christians, "Here, look at what Jesus has done for you. What have you done from him lately?" Because of that "moralistic strain" noted by Duffy, the medieval church expected Christians to prove themselves worthy of the divine love which has been so costly lavished on them.

Nothing could have been further from the reformers' understanding and, hence, the truly revolutionary nature of the Gospel they found in Scripture. The red thread that runs throughout Cranmer's writings is this simple truth: the glory of God is to love the unworthy. For the early English Protestants, nothing established that principle as clearly as God's decision not to base salvation on personal merit, not even on the kind of grace-aided merit that John Fisher had instilled into Tudor Scotistic theology in attempt to be more authentically Augustinian.[54] No, personal belief brought about salvation, as John 3:16 suggested, rather than personal accomplishment. Eternal life with God came through simply trusting his saving acts on their behalf, rather than their own. In short, by faith sinners were adopted into God's family forever, not merely made foster children having to live under the threat of being disowned as the Devil's in the face of every fresh case of disobedience.

HEAR ALSO WHAT SAINT PAUL SAYETH. THIS IS A TRUE SAYING, AND WORTHY OF ALL MEN TO BE RECEIVED, THAT JESUS CHRIST CAME INTO THE WORLD TO SAVE SINNERS.[55]

Having laid out the two sides of a falcon's gyre—the longing of humanity for relief and the longing of God to rescue—Cranmer's third Comfortable Word circles back to the human condition, but now at a higher level. On the one hand, humanity's situation is no longer described in subjective terms of felt needs but rather as the objective consequences of violating divine law. Humanity suffers from spiritual fatigue because that is merely the most readily apparent fruit of human sinfulness. As rebels against divine order,

53. Duffy, *Stripping of the Altars*, 157.

54. For Fisher's penitential theology, see Null, *Thomas Cranmer's Doctrine of Repentance*, 76–81.

55. The 1548 version of the *Order* had "worthy of all men to be embraced and received," Ketley, *Liturgies of Edward VI*, 7.

they are cut off from God's peace now and stand under the threat of the divine wrath to come. Humanity's refreshment can only come by addressing humanity's sin. On the other hand, to do so is also clearly beyond human beings. Having been so weakened by sin's power, humanity cannot co-operate with grace to achieve their salvation. According to Cranmer, that would be the "ready way unto desperation."[56] 1 Tim 1:15 makes plain that here is the reason for the Incarnation. It is Christ's mission to save sinners, not their own. As Cranmer's "Homily of Salvation" expressed it:

> Justification is not the office of man, but of God. For man cannot justify himself by his own works neither in part nor in the whole . . . But justification is the office of God only, and is not a thing which we render unto him, but which we receive of him, not which we give to him, but which we take of him, by his free mercy, and by the only merits of his most dearly beloved Son.[57]

Only upon realizing this distinction did Bilney find refreshment from his spiritual fatigue.

HEAR ALSO WHAT SAINT JOHN SAYETH. IF ANY MAN SIN, WE HAVE AN ADVOCATE WITH THE FATHER, JESUS CHRIST THE RIGHTEOUS, AND HE IS THE PROPITIATION FOR OUR SINS.

With the fourth Comfortable Word we have arrived at the top of the gyre. Now the doctrinal aspects of salvation are not seen from 1 Tim 1:15's anthropocentric view, i.e., how shall I be saved, but rather from God's prospective, i.e., how can he be true to both his own righteous nature and his enduring love for an unrighteous humanity. Firstly, 1 John 2:1–2 plainly states that the divine justice requires "propitiation." This was a sharpening of the 1548 version which had read: "he it is that obtained grace for our sins."[58] However, Cranmer's confession for Communion even in 1548 explicitly acknowledged the need for propitiation, saying that the congregation had sinned "by thought, word, and deed, against thy divine majesty, provoking most justly thy wrath and indignation against us."[59] Secondly, Christ's death is this necessary atonement for our sins, as Cranmer's 1549 eucharistic prayer clearly affirmed with typical humanist abundance—"a full, perfect

---

56. Cox, *Miscellaneous Writings and Letters of Thomas Cranmer,* 94.

57. Ibid., 131.

58. Ketley, *Liturgies of Edward VI,* 7.

59. Ibid., 6.

and sufficient sacrifice, oblation and satisfaction, for the sins of the whole world."[60] As a result, according to the "Homily on Salvation," "the justice of God and his mercy did embrace together and fulfilled the mystery of our redemption."[61] Thirdly, faith in Christ is the means by which his atonement is applied to the individual. For John's use of legal language, i.e., Christ as humanity's advocate, reinforced the Reformers' teaching that justification should be understood in its Greek, forensic sense of being declared righteous in a court of law, rather than in the Latin, factative sense of actually being made inherently just. Those who trusted in Christ's advocacy to gain their pardon from God the Father would be credited with their Savior's perfect righteousness. As Cranmer's confession for Communion expressed it: "for thy Son our Lord Jesus Christ's sake, forgive us all that is past."[62] Thus, Cranmer concluded his commonplace exposition of the Gospel as he had begun, with utter reliance on Christ's saving activity both to meet human needs and fulfill divine desires.

LIFT UP YOUR HEARTS

At last we have now come to the third criterion for humanist brilliance. Beyond diversity of sources and copious eloquence, a writer was expected to adapt his work to the needs and circumstances of his audience. Although many of his peers disagreed with him, for Erasmus that meant emulation (seeking to be better than ancient role models) rather than mere imitation (seeking to repristinate the best of the past). For example, Erasmus insisted that a Renaissance Latinist should not use the pagan religious vocabulary of Cicero to describe Christian activities. Rather, a true Ciceronian would go beyond the ancient stylist by actually acting like Cicero in treating Latin as a living language which grew and changed along with the society which used it for self-expression. It seemed obvious to Erasmus that patristic Greek and Latin diction for Christian activities were the most apt for a Christian society. To him humanist brilliance meant building on the best of the past to create a better model for the future.[63]

Such was clearly Cranmer's liturgical vision. Although deeply interested in the worship practices of the early church, he was not a patristic liturgical fundamentalist trying to recover the authentic past just so as to put new wine

60. Ibid., 88.

61. Cox, *Miscellaneous Writings and Letters of Thomas Cranmer* 129.

62. Ketley, *Liturgies of Edward VI*, 91.

63. See Pigman, "Imitation and the Renaissance Sense of the Past: The Reception of Erasmus' Ciceronianus."

in old wine skins. Cranmer was fundamentally an evangelist. Naturally, that meant first recovering an authentic understanding of the Gospel based on a *loci-communes* reading of the New Testament. However, the second task was no less important—discerning how to fit its presentation to contemporary society so as to be most effective in persuading them to embrace it. Despite his preference for the tried, his essay "On Ceremonies" for the Prayer Book made clear that for a liturgical custom to be retained it also had to be true to the Good News. Good order meant Gospel edification. The result in 1552 was, as Dom Gregory Dix commented, "the only effective attempt ever made to give liturgical expression to the doctrine of 'justification by faith alone.'"[64]

Yet, for Cranmer Gospel edification also meant local adaptation. If the saving truths of Scripture were unalterable, the church's means to commend them to a society had to evolve and change as the culture it addressed did, if it were to have any hope of continuing to reach its audience generation after generation. Hence, a national liturgy had to proclaim the good news in the light of the current needs and aspirations of that specific nation. Cranmer disagreed sharply with John Knox and the hotter sort of later Puritans on this issue, the latter believing that the Bible contained not only unchanging truths about faith and morals but also a necessary uniform pattern for church governance and worship. In the end, Cranmer's adherence to the regulative principle in doctrine but the normative principle in other areas was adopted as Article 34 of the Thirty-Nine Articles:

> It is not necessary that traditions and ceremonies be in all places one, or utterly like; for at all times they have been diverse, and may be changed according to the diversities of countries, times, and men's manners, so that nothing be ordained against God's Word . . . Every particular or national Church hath authority to ordain, change, and abolish, ceremonies or rites of the Church ordained only by man's authority, so that all things be done to edifying.[65]

Of course we have already seen this missionary strategy at work. The English reformers held head and heart together in their proclamation of the Gospel to be true to the sensibilities of their audience as much as to their own experience. Emulation through adaptation meant that the vernacular had to replace Latin as the liturgical language of the modern Church of England. If medieval English piety presented Jesus as a keen-eyed hawk scanning

---

64. Dix, *The Shape of the Liturgy*, 672.

65. Hardwick, *A History of the Articles of Religion*, 295. Note that the first section is from Cranmer's Forty-Two Articles, the second part was an Elizabethan addition which reinforced Cranmer's view.

the flock to be sure to punish the slightest indiscretion, Protestant preachers first had to seek to allure their people back to God with the good news of Jesus' obvious concern for humanity's felt needs. Only then could they begin to lead their congregations gently to greater doctrinal understanding. Clearly, all these themes came together to shape the text of Cranmer's Gospel commonplace. Yet arguably, they found their greatest expression in Cranmer's final placement of the Comfortable Words at the very center of the church's greatest form of divine allurement—Holy Communion.

Originally, in the Strassburg Communion rite 1 Timothy 1:15 had functioned as the absolution. God worked through its proclamation to move the congregation to trust Christ for the forgiveness of their sins and thus receive forgiveness. As the city's liturgy evolved, however, the Bible verse came to be followed immediately by an assurance of absolution spoken by the minister. Consequently, 1 Tim 1:15 ceased to be the primary vehicle for divine action and became simply a proof text, a logical justification for the ensuing action of the minister. The two Cologne liturgies continued this order of general confession, scriptural promise of forgiveness then an absolution by the minister. Cranmer, however, declined to do so. In the 1548 *Order*, his Comfortable Words followed rather than preceded the absolution.

This new placement had two distinct advantages for Gospel edification. On the one hand, the minister's absolution became the uncontested focal point for divine action in the face of human sinfulness. Accordingly, Cranmer rewrote the prayer to preach the good news through it and to apply its promises to the full range of human need. In the 1549 and 1552 version, the Protestant understanding of reconciliation was included as the introductory appositional description of the divine character: "Almighty God . . . who of his great mercy hath promised forgiveness of sins to all them which with hearty repentance and true faith turn unto him."[66] Even as early as the 1548 version, Cranmer had adapted the medieval Sarum rite to make the absolution's second half address the totality of divine action needed in the face of humanity's ongoing struggle with sin—compassion for its underlying spiritual weakness, forgiveness for present disobedience, further fortitude for a more faithful life in the future, and the gift of perseverance until the end: "have mercy upon you, pardon and deliver you from all sins, confirm and strengthen you in all goodness, and bring you to everlasting life."[67]

66. Ketley, *Liturgies of Edward VI*, 91, 276.

67. Ibid., 7. For Cranmer's dependence on Sarum at this point, see Brightman, *The English Rite*: II, 698. Note that in the version of this absolution used in both the 1549 and 1552 *Book of Common Prayer*, Cranmer revised the text to read: 'deliver you from all your sins'; Ketley, *Liturgies of Edward VI*, 91, 276.

On the other hand, the Scriptures in Cranmer's Gospel commonplace were now freed-up to be a vehicle for divine intervention in their own right. His 1547 "Homily on Scripture" was quite explicit that the Bible was a divine instrument for God's turning of his people to himself: "The words of Holy Scripture . . . have power to convert through God's promise, and they be effectual through God's assistance . . . they have ever a heavenly spiritual working in them."[68] In the 1548 and 1549 versions, Cranmer placed his Comfortable Words directly after the absolution but before the Prayer for Humble Access and Reception. As a result, he made the fresh proclamation of the Gospel the immediate supernatural means by which God drew his people towards a direct encounter with Him in the sacrament. Divine gracious love made known in the absolution and now reinforced through the Comfortable Words inspired grateful human love, moving the hearts and minds of the people to long for the living God, that they "may continually dwell in him and he in" them.[69] In short, Cranmer positioned his Gospel commonplace to be the divine means of alluring God's people to a sensuous embrace of the Holy Mysteries.

Despite the obvious brilliance of the Comfortable Words' new position, Cranmer's liturgical emulation through adaptation was still not yet finished. In 1552, he completely reordered the Communion service to remove any notion of our sacrifice—even one of mere praise and thanksgiving—as the grounds for the supernatural empowerment effectually conveyed during the sacrament. In the new order, nothing separated the Institution Narrative from reception. Hence, the whole Confession—Absolution—Comfortable Words—Humble Access cluster had to be moved. In the end Cranmer decided to reposition this material so as to reinforce his mature understanding of the Eucharist.

From the written description of the sacrament which he supplied during the Oxford Disputation in 1554, we know that Cranmer took the *Sursum corda* (Lift up your hearts) literally:

> We should consider, not what the bread and wine be in their own nature, but what they import to us and signify . . . that lifting up our minds, we should look up to the blood of Christ with our faith, should touch him with our mind, and receive him with our inward man; and that, being like eagles in this life, we should fly up into heaven in our hearts, where that Lamb is

---

68. Bond, *Certain Sermons*, 62.
69. Ketley, *Liturgies of Edward VI*, 7, 92.

resident at the right hand of his Father . . . by whose passion we are filled at his table."[70]

In the 1549 rite the Offertory Sentences had followed the Exhortations to Communion and directly preceded the *Sursum corda*. Cranmer must have found that awkward in 1552, for the Sentences' emphasis on Christian duty at that point in the service only reinforced the very notion he was determined to eliminate, namely, that the congregation approached God with something to offer him for which they were then rewarded with a fresh gift of grace. Consequently, Cranmer moved the Offertory to earlier in the service, between the Creed and the new position for the Prayer for Christ's Church. In considering what should take their old place before the *Sursum corda*, it must have seem patently obvious to Cranmer that here was the most natural place for the Confession—Absolution—Comfortable Words cluster. What better way to respond to the Exhortations' encouragement of a worthy reception than by confession and absolution? What better way to draw the human heart to ascend on high than by the recitation of his Gospel commonplace? In Cranmer's final setting for them, the Comfortable Words became God's divine instrument to allure believers to seek union with Christ and each other in heavenly places.

Finally, we can see the full scope of Cranmer's Gospel falconry which he tethered to the very heart of Anglican worship and, hence, its identity. In the 1552 *Book of Common Prayer*, Cranmer sent out Scripture's Comfortable Words, not so much as an eagle, but as a falcon, flying forth in a spiraling gyre, grounded in the human condition but gradually looping higher and higher towards the glory of the divine, uniting physical human senses and metaphysical sensibilities, holding humanity and the Trinity together in a dynamic mutual dialectic, funneling love from above into the hearts of the beloved below so that they at last have the power to love God and one another on earth as it is in Heaven.

On the massive dark oak organ screen which divides in two the chapel of King's College, Cambridge, amidst its numerous carved royal emblems of Henry VIII are examples of a crowned falcon sitting on a stump. The same badge can be seen embossed on the ceiling of an inner gateway of Hampton Court Palace as well as high up in its Great Hall. Few today recognize these rare heraldic references to the reign of Queen Anne Boleyn, architectural survivors from Henry's order to have all such reminders removed like his wife. Of course, with each ensuing decade of the Twenty-First Century, fewer and fewer Anglicans are familiar with Cranmer's falcon, for the continuing presence of the Comfortable Words in modern Anglican liturgies

70. Cox, *Cranmer of the Lord's Supper*, 398.

is as scant and scattered as the Boleyn badge. Yet, if Anne's falcon reminds us that Cranmer lived in turbulent times too, then the Comfortable Words give us his answer for when "things fall apart; the centre cannot hold."[71] This falcon is itself the lure, leading earthly eyes and hearts to look to and long for heavenly places. Today's falconers would do well to listen.

BIBLIOGRAPHY

Bale, John. *A Disclosing or Opening of the Man of Sin.* Antwerp, 1543.

Becon, Thomas. *A Christmas Banquet Garnished with Many Pleasant and Dainty Dishes.* London: John Mayler for John Gough, 1542.

Bond, Ronald B., editor. *Certain Sermons or Homilies (1547) and a Homily against Disobedience and Wilful Rebellion (1570): A Critical Edition.* Toronto: University of Toronto, 1987.

Brightman, F. E. *The English Rite.* 2nd ed. London: Rivingtons, 1921.

Cox, J. E. *Miscellaneous Writings and Letters of Thomas Cranmer.* Cambridge: Parker Society, 1846.

———. *Writings and Disputations of Thomas Cranmer . . . Relative to the Sacrament of the Lord's Supper.* Cambridge: Parker Socity, 1844.

Dickens, A. G. *The English Reformation.* 2nd ed. London: Batsford, 1989.

———. "The Shape of Anti-Clericalism and the English Reformation." In *Politics and Society in Reformation Europe: Essays for Sir Geoffrey Elton on His Sixty-Fifth Birthday.* edited by E. I. Kouri and Tom Scott. London: Macmillan, 1987.

Dix, Gregory. *The Shape of the Liturgy.* Westminster: Dacre, 1945.

Duffy, Eamon. *Stripping of the Altars: Traditional Religion in England C. 1400—C. 1580.* London: Yale University Press, 1992.

———. *The Voices of Morebath: Reformation and Rebellion in an English Village.* London: Yale University Press, 2001.

Egli, E., and G. Finsler, editors. *Huldreich Zwinglis Sämtliche Werke.* Leipzig: Heinsius, 1908.

Egli, E., G. Finsler, W. Köhler, and O. Farner, editors. *Huldreich Zwinglis Sämtliche Werke.* Leipzig: Heinsius, 1927.

Eliot, T. S. "The Metaphysical Poets." *Times Literary Supplement*, 20 October 1921.

Erasmus. *The First Volume of the Paraphrase of Erasmus Upon the New Testament.* London: Edward Whitchurch, 1548.

———. *The Manual of the Christian Knight.* London: Wynkyn de Worde, 1533.

Fox, Richard. "Statutes of Corpus Christi College, Oxford." In *The Thought and Culture of the English Renaissance: An Anthology of Tudor Prose 1481–1555*, edited by Elizabeth M. Nugent. Cambridge: Cambridge University Press, 1956.

Foxe, John. *Actes and Monuments.* London: John Day, 1570.

Hardwick, Charles. *A History of the Articles of Religion.* Cambridge: Deighton Bell, 1859.

Hubert, Friedrich. *Die Straßburger Liturgischen Ordnungen Im Zeitalter Der Reformation.* Göttingen: Vandenhoeck & Ruprecht, 1900.

71. Yeats, "The Second Coming," 158.

Ketley, Joseph, editor. *The Two Liturgies . . . In the Reign of King Edward the Sixth.* Cambridge: Parker Society, 1844.

Lacey, T. A. *The King's Book.* London: SPCK, 1932.

Le Goff, Jacques. *The Birth of Purgatory.* Translated by Arthur Goldhammer. Chicago: University of Chicago Press, 1984.

Luther, Martin. *Weimarer Ausgabe 16. Kritische Gesammtausgabe.* 121 vols. Vol. 18, D. Martin Luthers Werke. Weimar: Böhlaus, 1908.

Marshall, Peter. *Religious Identities in Henry VIII's England.* Aldershot, UK: Ashgate, 2006.

Marshall, William. *A Primer in English.* London: Byddell, 1534.

Nichols, John Gough, editor. *Narratives of the Days of the Reformation.* London: Camden Society, 1859.

Null, Ashley. "Official Tudor Homilies." In *Oxford Handbook of the Early Modern Sermon,* edited by Peter McCullough, Hugh Adlington and Emma Rhatigan. Oxford: Oxford University Press, 2011.

———. "Thomas Cranmer and Tudor Evangelicalism." In *The Emergence of Evangelicalism: Exploring Historical Continuities,* edited by Kenneth J. Stewart and Michael A. G. Haykin, 221–51. Nottingham: Apollos, 2008.

———. *Thomas Cranmer's Doctrine of Repentance: Renewing the Power to Love.* Oxford: Oxford University Press, 2000.

Parr, Katherine. *The Lamentation of a Sinner.* London: Edward Whitchurch, 1548.

Pigman, G. W., III. "Imitation and the Renaissance Sense of the Past: The Reception of Erasmus' Ciceronianus." *Journal of Medieval and Renaissance Studies* 9 (1979) 155–77.

Rex, Richard. "The Role of English Humanists in the Reformation up to 1559." In *The Education of a Christian Society: Humanism and Reformation in Britain and the Netherlands,* edited by N.S. Amos, A. Pettegree and H. van Nierop, 19–40. Aldershot, UK: Ashgate, 1999.

Shakespeare, William. "Henry VIII."

Taverner, Richard. *The Epistles and Gospels with a Brief Postil upon the same from after Easter till Advent.* London: Richard Bankes, 1540.

———. *On Saint Andrew's Day the Gospels with Brief Sermons Upon Them for All the Holy Days in the Year.* London: Bankes, 1542.

Tunstall, Cuthbert. *A Sermon Made upon Palm Sunday Last Past.* London: Berthelet, 1539.

Van de Poll, G. J. *Martin Bucer's Liturgical Ideas.* Assen: Van Gorcum, 1954.

Wied, Herman von. *Einfältiges Bedenken,* in *Martin Bucers Deutsche Schriften.* Edited by C. Strohm and T. Wilhelmi. Gütersloh: Gütersloher, 1999.

———. *A Simple and Religious Consultation.* London: John Day, 1547.

———. *Simplex Ac Pia Deliberatio* Bonn: Mylius, 1545.

Williams, Rowan. "The Martyrdom of Thomas Cranmer—Sermon at Service to Commemorate the 450th Anniversary." 2006. Onlin: http://rowanwilliams. archbishopofcanterbury.org/articles.php/1599/the-martyrdom-of-thomas-cranmer-sermon-at-service-to-commemorate-the-450th-anniversary.

Yeats, William Butler. "The Second Coming." In *The Collected Poems of W.B. Yeats.* Ware: Wordsworth, 1994.

19

What Should Christians Do When They Disagree?

Reflections on 1 Cor 8–10 and Rom 14:1—15:6

JAMES D. G. DUNN

PAUL HAD TO DEAL with various controversial situations in which his fellow believers found it hard to come to agreement—I refer to Paul the apostle! The churches he was most involved with had a rather mixed membership. They presumably were more or less at one on the faith in Jesus Christ which had brought them into the church (as outlined in Rom 1:3–4 and 1 Cor 15:3–6, 7). But on various matters of conduct, of the conduct appropriate for that shared faith, they were at odds. The two letters where Paul deals most fully, and carefully, with these issues are 1 Corinthians and Romans. How did Paul the pastor handle these issues, these disagreements? And does his handling of them provide an illustration of how such issues can or even should be handled today? I will focus on only the two most interesting and potentially instructive issues (1 Cor 8–10 and Rom 14:1—15:6 dealing with the conventions and proprieties of dining together.

1. HOW SERIOUS WERE THE ISSUES?

a) The Church in Corinth

The issue in 1 Cor 8–10 was whether it was acceptable for believers to eat *eidōlothyta*, "meat offered to an idol" (8.1). For many of the Corinthians the issue was one of *rights*, as signalled by Paul's repeated use of *exousia*, itself best translated here as "right" (8:9; 9:4–6, 12, 18).[1] Corinth being a Roman colony, there were probably a number of Roman citizens in the Corinthian church. For them it would be a matter of good citizenship and normal social custom to participate in civic banquets and other such celebrations; it was their "right."[2] These banquets were typically celebrated in one or other of Corinth's larger temples, or in honour of the imperial family or one of the gods worshipped in Corinth. The temples were the restaurants of the day.[3] In such circumstances it was inevitable that the surplus meat from the temple's sacrificial carcases would provide the meat dishes for the banquet.[4] On special festival days the whole population might hope to be able to participate, even if only at the fringe, in such feasts. That too would be regarded as their "right."

The problem was, and this is why the issue of "idol meat" became an issue, that for a Jew—all Jews, including Jewish believers in Messiah Jesus—to eat "idol food" was not an option, was completely out of the question. This was because idolatry was totally unacceptable to Jews. The first two of the ten commandments (Ex 20:2–5) were deeply rooted in the Jewish psyche, and were central and integral elements of Jewish self-understanding. The two commandments were interdependent: idolatry meant putting another god before YHWH. In order to remain faithful to God it was deemed necessary, therefore, to avoid not only idol worship itself, but also anything which smacked of idolatry, which might bring the influence of other gods into the community—as —the Mishnah tractate, *Abodah Zarah* ("Idolatry") goes on to spell out in detail. "Idol-meat" was precisely a case in point, a test-case

---

1. The point is missed by most modern translations which render *exousia* in 8:9 by 'freedom' (NIV, NJB) or "liberty" (NRSV, REB). The "liberty" (*eleutheria*) actually claimed (9:1, 19; 10:29) was liberty to exercise (or decline) their *exousia*.

2. See particularly Winter, *Seek the Welfare of the City*, ch. 9, "Civic Rights."'

3. The temple complexes regularly give evidence of dining rooms attached to the temple or round the temple courtyard; the give-away feature is that the entry doorway is not in the middle of one side, but has been inset lopsidedly, to allow one reclining couch to be long-ways and another with its end set against the doorway wall.

4. The temples' provision of restaurant facilities was the direct result of there being so much surplus meat after the animal sacrifices had been offered—too much for the priests and the temple functionaries themselves.

for any Jew faithful to Israel's covenant with YHWH.[5] The resistance of the attempt by Antiochus Epiphanes to force Judeans to eat pork and food sacrificed to idols was one of the make or break points in the Maccabean rebellion (4 Macc. 5–6); to eat meat offered to idols was an act of apostasy. According to *Abodah Zarah* 2:3, to eat flesh which had been sacrificed to an idol was to repeat one of Israel's most infamous acts of apostasy, when 'they attached themselves to the Baal of Peor and ate sacrifices offered to the dead' (Ps 106:28; referring to Num 25).

The issue dealt with in 1 Cor 8–10, then, could hardly have been more serious. It was not simply a matter of dining niceties and awkward social relationships. For one side, it was a matter of what they would have regarded as basic human rights—to enjoy the privilege of Roman citizenship as Roman citizens normally did. And they could justify their conduct by denying that idols amounted to anything (8:4). For the other side, however, it was a question of being faithful to the most fundamental duty laid upon Israel by Israel's God. For Jewish believers, that consideration would be far more fundamental than any civic rights of their fellow (Gentile) believers in the church of Corinth.

b) The Church in Rome

The congregatons of believers in Rome, of course, had not been established by Paul. But he evidently had a sufficient number of personal friends and colleagues in the Roman congregations (Rom 16:3–15) to be confident that the issue raised in 14:1—15:6 was not simply a generalization from his previous experience, but a real issue for the Roman assemblies. The issue in Rome was different from, though related to that dealt with in 1 Corinthians. Here it was a question particularly of believers dining together: what was acceptable in terms of what they might eat in a shared meal.

The issue was similar to that in Corinth, in that some of the Roman believers thought it quite acceptable to eat anything; the claim in this case was not put in terms of their "rights," but the attitude behind and justifying the practice would be very similar. The problem, however, was not that of "idol-meat," but that eating "unclean" food was unacceptable to others of the Roman believers. These latter were almost certainly Jewish believers,[6] who

---

5. The fact of this issue, as well as the care with which Paul deals with it, are among the clearest indications in 1 Corinthians that there were a significant number of Jews who counted themselves members of the Corinthian church.

6. The use of the terms *koinos* ('profane, unclean') and *katharos* ('clean') in 14:14 and 20 is a sure indication that the scruples addressed in Romans 14 were Jewish in

abstained from all meat.[7] If they (or most of them) had indeed been expelled from Rome by Emperor Claudius (49 CE), then we can infer that Claudius' decree had lapsed after his death (54 CE) and that Jewish believers had been returning to Rome and to the Roman assemblies.[8] This would explain Paul's repeated exhortation for the assemblies to be welcoming (14:1; 15:7)—the probability being that congregations which had been Gentile-dominated following Claudius' decree, now found that they had to welcome back more scrupulous Jewish believers.[9]

Once again the issue should not be seen as a simple matter of dietary fads, likes, and dislikes. The laws of clean and unclean were almost as central to Jewish identity as circumcision. These were two of the practices which the Syrians had made resolute attempts to root out (1 Macc. 1:60–63), precisely because they were so central to Israel's religion. The natural consequence, of course, was that in the formation of 'Judaism,' the name given to the Maccabean resistance movement,[10] these two covenant observances became central to and definitive of 'Judaism.' For Jewish believers to eat unclean food, then, was as serious as and as dangerous as eating idol-meat. This was

---

character, for *koinos* in Greek means simply 'common.' It only gains the sense 'profane, unclean' from its use to render the equivalent Hebrew terms (*kol tamē*) in the Maccabean and post-Maccabean period (1 Macc 1:47, 62; Mark 7:2, 5; Acts 10:14; 11:8). *Katharos* is clearly the opposite of *koinos* and again has the issue of clean and unclean foods in view - a regular usage for *katharos* in scripture, particularly the Torah (Gen 7:2–3, 8; 8:20; Lev. 4:12; 6:11; 7:19; etc). The maintenance of purity was a particular concern within Judaism in this period (e.g. Judith 12:7; *Jub.* 3:8–14; *Pss. Sol.* 8:12, 22; 1QS 3:5; CD 12:19–20). This does not mean that only Jewish believers were in view, since many god-fearing Gentiles had been drawn to Judaism by what they regarded as the attractiveness of the Jewish religion. See further Dunn, *Romans*, 2:818–19, 825–26.

7. The Torah food laws, of course, envisaged the eating of meat; but to avoid the possibility of breaching the law, particularly of eating food tainted by idolatry, many Jews were practising vegetarians (e.g., Dan 1:16; 2 Macc 5:27; *Jos. Asen.* 8:5; Josephus, *Life* 14); vegetarian practice was attributed to the Therapeutae (Philo, *Vit. Cont.* 37), to James the brother of Jesus (Eusebius, *HE* 2.23.5), and subsequently to the Ebionites (Origen, *In Matt.* 11:12). Similarly, in view of 14:21, we should note that while the consumption of wine was not forbidden in the Torah, many avoided it for similar reasons - in case it had been offered in libation to the gods before being sold in the market (cf. particularly Dan 1:3–16; Add. Esther 14.17; *Jos. Asen.* 8:5; *Test. Reub.* 1:10; *Test. Jud.* 15:4; *m. Abod. Zar.* 2:3; 5:2).

8. An obvious example would be Priscilla and Aquila, greeted in Rom 16:3, who, according to Acts 18:2, had been among those expelled from Rome. Romans was probably written about 56 CE, give or take a year or so either way—that is, about seven years had elapsed since the expulsion of such as Aquila and Priscilla.

9. This was the case argued particularly by Wiefel, "The Jewish Community in Ancient Rome and the Origins of Roman Christianity," which has proved persuasive for many.

10. 2 Macc 2:21; 8:1; 14:38.

not a matter of adiaphora, an issue on which they might flip-flop without damaging their integrity or their faith. It was such a fundamental factor in their identity as Jews that they could not abandon it without abandoning their Jewishness.[11] The pastoral dilemma for Paul, then, was that having succeeded in resisting Jewish believers' attempts to insist that Gentile believers should become Jews/proselytes by accepting circumcision (Galatians), he was now confronted with the de facto attempt by the Roman Gentile believers to insist that Jewish believers should cease to be Jews.

2. HOW DID PAUL HANDLE THESE ISSUES?

In both cases Paul handles the situation with pastoral sensitivity.

a) 1 Corinthians 8–10

There are fives stages in Paul's response to the issue of eating meat that has been offered to idols.

1. He acknowledges the theological logic of those not worried about eating such food. Yes, he agrees, 'An idol *is* nothing in the world'; and 'God is one' (8:4), though he immediately adds the reminder that they have "one Lord, Jesus Christ," as well as one God, the Father (8:6), with implications to be drawn out (8:11–12). Paul further acknowledges the corollary, that if idols are nothing, then it is justified to conclude that those who eat idol food are no worse off than those who do not eat such food (8:8).

2. However, Paul also recognizes the importance of the scruples of those who did not and could not eat idol meat. They identified eating the meat of sacrifices offered to other gods as a breach of the first two of the ten commandments. To accept idol meat was to dally with idols and to slide into apostasy. Their conscience, not being so robust as that of the Gentile believers, but rather having been shaped and formed by Israel's scriptures, history, and traditions, could not allow them so to eat without making them feel dirty and spiritually impure (8:7). But if they then saw a fellow believer participating in

---

11. The other issue in the Roman assemblies was whether holy days should be observed or whether all days should be regarded as alike (Rom 14:5–6). Primarily in view would be the Sabbath feast, observance of which was almost as important as the laws of clean and unclean (see Exod 31:12–17). Since the Sabbath was a sign of Israel's set-apartness, failure to keep the Sabbath law was a capital offence. For Isa 56:6, the mark of Gentile participation in the covenant would be their keeping of the Sabbath.

a banquet—that is, in a banquet held in a temple—where the meat dish would certainly be from the temple sacrifices, meat offered to idols, they might feel sufficiently embarrassed at their scruples and emboldened by their fellow believer's conduct to join in that or a similar banquet (8:10). In so doing, however, they would be acting against their conscience and so undermine or even destroy their relation with Christ (8:11).[12] Those casual about their participation in such dinners should recognize that in exercising their 'right' to participate in such civic events, even though on good theological principles, they were in danger of causing their fellow believers with more sensitive consciences to sin against their consciences and so against their Lord.[13] In so acting, they themselves were sinning against their fellow believers, and so also against their Lord (8:12). In consequence, Paul says, "If food causes my brother to stumble, I will never eat meat, lest I cause my brother to stumble" (8:13).

3. To illustrate how one might or should act in relation to claiming one's rights, Paul goes on to cite his own example of a right he was wholly justified in claiming, but which he refused to claim. This was the right of an apostle and missionary to claim support for his ministry, support particularly in terms of travel and hospitality during his mission. The other apostles exercised such rights (9:3–5). Soldiers received pay, vineyard owners ate the fruit of the vineyard, the owner of goats drank their milk (9:7). Even oxen ate the grain on which they trod; and the farmer benefited from his crop (9:8–11). The priests in the temple benefited from the surplus from sacrifices (9:13). And not least, the Lord himself had commanded "that those who proclaim the gospel should get their living by the gospel" (9:14),[14] that is, should be supported by those to whom they preached or whom they taught (cf. Gal. 6:6). So Paul's right in the matter was about as unquestioned as it could be, with natural logic, abundant precedents, and dominical authorisation. Nevertheless, Paul absolutely declined to claim that right. For him it was a higher priority to 'make the gospel free of charge' (9:15–18).

---

12. 'Conscience (*syneidēsis*)' is a critical factor in all this for Paul (1Cor. 8:7, 10, 12; 10:25, 27–29); on the concept and experience of 'conscience' and bibliography see Dunn, *The Theology of Paul the Apostle*, 54–55 n.16.

13. Paul describes them consistently as 'weak' (8:7, 9–12; 9:22). The term is expressive of a 'strong' perspective, which sees such scruples as a weakness in faith (cf. Rom 14:1–2; 15:1). But the more important point for Paul was that recognition of the reality of such scruples should condition the behavior of the "strong."

14. Paul evidently knew the tradition of Jesus' teaching recorded in Luke 10:7/Matt 10:10.

To have rights, legitimate rights, was not sufficient reason to exercise them or to claim the benefits which they enshrined and safeguarded.

4. From Israel's history of dallying with idolatry (10:1–13) Paul draws the clear and blunt conclusion: "Flee from idolatry" (10:14);[15] and avoid any suggestion that it might be acceptable for those who shared the Lord's table to participate also in meals whose host were other gods, and the demonic reality which might lie behind them (10:15–22).[16] So the strong counsel of 8:7–13, that the scruples of other believers should be a determining factor in their conduct, becomes an even stronger warning, that to participate in temple feasts was so contradictory and offensive for those who shared in the Lord's table, that it should not be contemplated.[17] By obvious implication, no believer in Corinth should even think to exercise his civic right to participate in banquets or feasts in one of Corinth's temples.

5. However, Paul envisages another situation, in which a believer was invited by an unbeliever to dine at the latter's home (10:27). In this case, Paul goes back to the theological point acknowledged in 8.8: that food in itself has no spiritual benefit or disbenefit: "the earth and its fullness are the Lord's" (10:26; quoting Ps. 24:1). The deduction he draws this time is that food bought in the meat market should be eaten without any qualms (10:25). This would be because although the temples were the principal suppliers of meat for the meat market, there were other sources—that is, other than temple sacrifices.[18] So, when invited to someone's house for a meal, the meat served could be eaten in good conscience (10:27). It would only become an issue if someone volunteered the information that the meat had come from a temple (10:28). In which case the believer guest should refuse the meat—not for his

---

15. It is important to note that Paul did not abandon Israel's traditional hostility to idolatry; see Dunn, *The Theology of Paul the Apostle*, 702–4.

16. Paul's view of other spiritual/heavenly beings at this point remains unclear: he agrees that idols are nothing (8:4) and speaks of 'so-called gods in heaven and earth' (8:5); but he goes on to add, "just as there are many gods and lords" (8:5), and in 10:20–21, for the only time in his extant letters, refers to "demons" as the spiritual reality behind idols, drawing on Deut 32:17.

17. As Gooch, *Dangerous Food*, clearly shows, it would have been impossible to treat meals in temples as purely secular and to dissociate them from the religious rites for which the temple primarily existed.

18 Meggitt, "Meat Consumption and Social Conflict in Corinth," 137–41, points out that poor quality meat would have been more widely available from cookshops (*popinae* and *ganeae*), wineshops (*tabernae* or *cauponae*) and elsewhere.

own conscience sake but because the other had raised the issue of conscience (10:29).[19]

The major principle determining conduct in this case is often called 'the principle of the weaker brother'—that the believer with less scruples should be willing to restrict the exercise of his rights or to limit the exercise of his liberty by concern for the possible impact it might have on the more scrupulous believer. There is a strong point here which Paul develops more fully in Romans 14: that liberty is most fully experienced and expressed in the willingness to limit its exercise for the sake of the other; concern for the other's spiritual well-being is more important than exercising one's own rights.

However, Paul's exposition of this principle is more nuanced than has often been recognized. He does not envisage believers restricting their rights or liberty simply because the scrupulous believers *did not approve* of their conduct. He applies the principle to the case where the more scrupulous believer is actually enticed by the other's conduct to *act* against his own conscience. That is what Paul means when he talks of some believers "wounding the conscience when it is weak" of other believers (8:12), not simply that the more scrupulous were *offended* at other believers exercising rights or liberty in conduct of which the former disapproved. That rights or liberty should be restricted simply because other believers thought the conduct wrong is not what Paul had in mind.

The point is reinforced in 10:23–30. For Paul there envisages the possibility that a believer might in fact eat idol meat without knowing it; and he shows himself to be quite relaxed about it. Only if someone else were to make, in effect, a challenge to eat idol meat—that is, a challenge to his beliefs and conduct as a member of the church in Corinth—should he decline. It has become again a matter of conscience—not the believer guest's own conscience, but that of the one who has raised the issue (presumably thinking along the same lines as in 8:10–12). For the believer himself, the fact that he could give thanks to God for what he ate (10:26, 30) was sufficient for him to eat whatever was set before him with a good conscience. Only when the issue became explicit and someone else's conscience was threatened need he act differently.

The advice to "eat whatever is set before you without raising any question on the ground of conscience" (10:27), it should not escape notice, is equivalent to the modern, "Don't ask don't tell" counsel used in some contemporary issues on which Christians disagree. Paul evidently

---

19. It is unclear whether the person who is envisaged as raising the issue is a Jew, or the unbeliever host raising an issue which he knew divided the Corinthian believers.

did not want the Corinthian believers to cut themselves off from social intercourse with their fellow citizens and fellow residents in Corinth. His counsel, however, reflects his awareness that on some occasions to maintain relations with non-believers would put the Corinthian believers in awkward and potentially embarrassing situations. If Paul's counsel be regarded as a counsel of compromise, at least the theological principles behind it are clear (8:4, 12; 10:26, 30).

b) Romans 14:1—15:6

In the situation addressed in Corinth Paul examined the issue from what might be called the more liberal perspective, of those who were aware of their rights and who thought that in principle their attitude to idols and idol-meat had good scriptural and theological grounds. His counsel was addressed throughout to those who did not share the scruples of the Jewish believers. But in Romans, while he still saw the issue from a more liberal stance,[20] Paul shows more sympathy for the more scrupulous Jewish believers (14:5–6), and addresses them directly (14:4, 10–11). By addressing both parties Paul makes clear that he wants to see a shared resolution to the issue, one which will demonstrate that the shared faith of Jew and Gentile made them one church, living in harmony, and uniting them in the shared worship of the one God (15:5–6, 7–13).

The problem was greatly exacerbated by the fact that the two parties found it hard to recognize, acknowledge, or respect the stance of the others. Those who ate without scruple "despised" the more scrupulous; those who abstained were "judgmental/condemnatory" of those who ate without scruple (14:3). The two attitudes are familiar from the history of Christian (and other) controversies: the more liberal "despise" the more scrupulous as unenlightened and "weak"; the more scrupulous "condemn" the more liberal because they regard the latters' conduct as breaching rules or conventions expected or required of the believer.

Paul first addresses the more scrupulous (Jewish) members of the Roman assemblies (14:4), those he regarded as "weak in faith" (14:1–2) and who condemned their fellow believers (14:3–4). The danger they were in, and the danger that they posed to the fellowship of shared Christian commitment, was that they regarded their stance on clean and unclean foods (and holy days) as central to the faith which they shared with the others. Consequently they regarded the more liberal attitude to food laws (and holy

20. He associates himself with "the strong" (15:1) and regards the more scrupulous as "the weak" (14:1–2).

days) as antithetical to their shared faith, and social freedom to eat anything (and to ignore sacred times) as in effect apostasy. Paul's response was to respect their more scrupulous stance, but to insist that it was valid only for themselves. Their scruples did not qualify or justify them in condemning the conduct of others.[21] The key point was that each had to decide for him/herself, before his/her Lord, what was appropriate or acceptable in his/her own case. And, evidently, the more liberal believers were acting as accountable to their Lord, just as were the more scrupulous. To judge/condemn a servant of the Lord who was acting in a way of which the Lord approved was to judge/condemn the Lord who supported that servant's stance (14:4).

There are several important features of Paul's ruling here.

- He insists that God welcomes those who differ from each other—both parties—and that the Lord Jesus approves modes of conduct which are at odds with one another. It was not necessary for one to be wrong for the other to be right. What I judge to be wrong for me need not and may well not be wrong for a fellow believer.

- The appropriate response to conduct of which one disapproved was not to condemn it, but to acknowledge that the fellow believer was fully convinced before his Lord that he was acting in a way of which his Lord approved. Rather than condemn, the more scrupulous believer should respect, truly respect the conviction and conduct of the other, even though he disapproved of it.

- The determining factor was whether each and both could give thanks to God for what they ate (14:6), always bearing in mind that it is God to whom each believer is accountable, not to his more scrupulous fellow (14:7–12).

Paul then turns his attention to the other party, "the strong (in faith)," with whom Paul himself was more in tune with (14:13).[22] The danger to them and to the community was that they "despised" the more scrupulous believers (14:3, 10).[23] Here Paul's counsel is very similar to the counsel he gave to

21. "God has welcomed him. Who are you to condemn the slave of someone else? In relation to his own master he stands or falls. And he shall stand, for the master is able to make him stand" (14:3–4).

22. "The strong" were not, then, as might be expected, those who held strongly to their traditional heritage and identity markers, or as they would no doubt have said, to fundamental elements of their traditional faith and practice. On the contrary, Paul regarded them, rather pejoratively, as "weak," that is "weak in faith." In Paul's perspective they were trusting in something other than God alone. They were trusting in God *plus* continued observance of clean and unclean and special days.

23. The verb, *exoutheneō*, has the sense of to show by one's attitude or manner of

the Corinthians, with the addition of noting that to despise another servant of his Lord is as bad as to condemn him (14:10). Paul makes it clear that he himself does not (or no longer does) regard the laws of clean and unclean as still in force (14:14).[24] But, more strongly than in 1 Cor 8:7, Paul insists that food *is* unclean for those who regard it as so (14:14). He thus shows his genuine respect for the scruples of those with whom he disagreed.

As in 1 Corinthians 8 Paul goes on to insist that love for the fellow believer should be the paramount consideration (Rom 14:15); what made for peace and mutual upbuilding was more important than eating meat or drinking wine (14:19–21). The possibility that a more liberal life-style would encourage a fellow believer to act contrary to one of his basic beliefs should be sufficient reason to restrict such a life-style (14:15–18).

Notably, Paul rounds off his advice by underlining two essential points. The first is that it is one's faith, one's trust in God, which should determine conduct: what matters is acting in accordance with one's conscious dependence and reliance on God.[25] This affirmation recognizes and accepts that the faith of different persons will express itself in different conduct, and that is OK. But it also means recognizing and accepting that "whatever does not proceed from faith is sin" (14:23), so that for the weaker brother to eat food he regarded as unclean would be sin. The second is Paul's insistence that those who claim greater insight should recognize the greater responsibility on them to "love/please their neighbour" (15:1–2),[26] always bearing in mind the model which Jesus himself had given (15:3–4), and should recognize that Christian harmony depends entirely on truly welcoming those who disagree and live differently (15:5–7).

What is particularly worth noting here is that in this passage (Rom 14:1—15:6) Paul defends attitudes and conduct with which he himself disagreed. He did *not* see the return of more conservative Jewish believers to

---

treatment that an entity has no merit or worth, "disdain"; to have no use for something as being beneath one's consideration, "reject disdainfully"; to regard another as of no significance and therefore worthy of maltreatment, "treat with contempt,'" Walter Bauer et al., *A Greek-English Lexicon*, 352; cf. 2 Kgs 19:21; 2 Chr 36:16; Ezek 22:8; Wis 4;18; Luke 23:11.

24. An echo of Jesus' teaching as recorded in Mark 7:15 is generally recognized here (Rom 14:14), and there is a probable allusion to Jesus' teaching on the kingdom of God in 14:17.

25. Interestingly, unlike 1 Corinthians 8–10, Paul gives critical weight to "faith" and not "conscience."

26. Paul's reference to the "neighbour" recalls his only other uses of the term in Rom 13:9–10 and Gal 5:14, both quoting Lev 19:18; since Jesus was the first to focus on Lev 19:18 as a summary of the second table of the Ten Commandments, here too Paul almost certainly owes the emphasis to his knowledge of Jesus' teaching.

the Roman assemblies as an excuse, or occasion, or reason to dispute their scruples, to try to re-educate them, to give them a theological lesson to the effect that Christ had banished the need for such scruples (14:1). He thought the attitudes did show a weakness in faith, the faith in and by which alone they were able to stand before God, accepted by the Lord Jesus Christ. But he fully respected that weaker faith as faith and argued on behalf of those who held it and of the conduct which their faith required. Love of neighbour in a Christian context demanded nothing less, as Jesus' own teaching and conduct so clearly illustrated.

If we regard Paul's pastoral teaching as of relevance to modern Christian disagreements, how is it best summed up?

- Christians are hardly likely to agree on many/any matters of the conduct required by or appropriate to their faith. In itself this need not be or cause a problem.

- Each is responsible for his own conduct before his Lord, who evidently could accept such differences as much less important than their shared faith and trust.

- A key test is being able genuinely to give thanks to God for what one does and how one acts.

- The fact that God approves one person's conduct provides no ground for that person to pass unfavourable judgment on a fellow believer's conduct.

- Christian harmony is impossible unless each has and shows genuine respect for the other who believes and acts differently, and is ready to speak for and defend that different pattern of living.

- The more traditional/conservative/scrupulous must not give way to the temptation to regard the more liberal as unChristian—an insult to the Lord who had accepted them. Do not make God in your own image!

- There is greater responsibility on those who claim greater insight and freedom, to exercise their liberty in a neighbourly loving concern for their fellow believers which might well require them to limit their liberty.

BIBLIOGRAPHY

Bauer, Walter, Frederick W. Danker, William Arndt, and F. W. Gingrich. *A Greek-English Lexicon of the New Testament and Other Early Christian Literature*. 3rd ed. Chicago: University of Chicago Press, 2001.

Dunn, James D. G. *Romans*. 2 vols. Word Biblical Commentary 38B. Dallas: Word, 1988.

————. *The Theology of Paul the Apostle*. Grand Rapids: Eerdmans, 1998.

Gooch, P. W. *Dangerous Food: 1 Corinthians 8–10 in Its Context*. Waterloo, ON: Wilfrid Laurier University Press, 1993.

Meggitt, J. J. "Meat Consumption and Social Conflict in Corinth." *Journal of Theological Studies* 45 (1994) 137–41.

Wiefel, W. "The Jewish Community in Ancient Rome and the Origins of Roman Christianity." *Judaica* 26 (1970) 65–88.

Winter, B. W. *Seek the Welfare of the City: Christians as Benefactors and Citizens*. Grand Rapids: Eerdmans, 1994.

20

Guard of Honor

Envoi and Epilogue

PAUL F. M. ZAHL

"I don't know what good a guard of honor does him when he's dead," General Beal said. "... How about you, Judge?"

Colonel Ross, not without grandiloquence, said: "It does us good. Ceremony is for us. The guard, or as I think we now prefer to call it, escort of honor is a suitable mark of our regret for mortality and our respect for service—we hope, good; but if bad or indifferent, at least, long. When you are as old as I am you will realize that it ought to get a man something. For our sake, not his. Not much; but something. Something people can see."

Laughing, General Beal said: "That's telling them, Judge! Only, what I meant was: how about another drink?"

— *GUARD OF HONOR*, JAMES GOULD COZZENS[1]

THE APPEARANCE OF THIS Festschrift, with its pastoral title, *Comfortable Words*, is an honor to me, personally, and a long labor of love on the part of its contributors, and especially on the part of its editors, John (Jady) Koch

---

1. Cozzens, *Guard of Honor*, 594.

and Todd Brewer. I wish to thank them all, and especially Jady and Todd, from the bottom of my heart!

Its publication also gives me a chance to write a short reflection, in late 2012 and in light of the person I am now, on three themes, underlined by the contents of the book, that have captured my mind and heart for over 40 years. These themes, summed up in the headings "Free Will—Not!," "One-Way Love," and "Strength in Weakness," have been the objects, conceptually and pastorally, of a career-long formal ministry—its preaching, its teaching, its books and articles; and also its pastoral care. Here I can look back on those emphasized "objects," and try to weigh them in present perspective. What do I retain from them, and to what, if any, aspects of them would I wish to say, "Goodbye" to all that? It is a mixture, with the emphasis being on the retention and enlargement of enduring, magnetic themes, rather than on subtraction.

Aldous Huxley wrote that it is rare for a person to actually change his or her mind in relation to long-held convictions, unless the person is "subjected to certain rather drastic treatments."[2] I feel I have learned something, or been forced to learn something, from some "rather drastic treatments." I have tried to integrate those "treatments," by which I mean experienced reversals, with the intellectual commitments of my ministry during the years prior to 2007. 2007 was the year my professional life, and my life as a human being, hit a stone wall. This epilogue offers me a chance to put what I am learning from Aldous Huxley's "drastic treatments" into writing. I also agree with Huxley's view, written down the same year, that religion is a form of "research. Research into, leading to theories about and action in the light of . . . experience."[3] From my earliest formal study of Christianity, which began in the Fifth Form at St. Alban's School in Washington, D.C., I have believed this concerning the role of experience in religion. It helps explain why I always argued that theology should be studied "from the bottom up" rather than from "the top down."

Finally, by way of short introduction to this "*envoi* and epilogue," the metaphor of a "guard of honor," borrowed from James Gould Cozzens' 1948 Pulitzer-Prize winning novel of that name, is how I would describe the labor of love that this Festschrift embodies. Whether the person to whom it is dedicated desires it, and whether it is out of proportion to what the person actually did, it's a good idea! It affirms that long service, even if indifferent, is a good thing, in itself, and something for which to give

2. Huxley, *Huxley and God: Essays on Religious Experience*, 63–64.
3. Ibid., 14.

thanks, if only for the sake of "the others" who are still pulling their oars in the hold of the galley.

There are other people, some of them parish rectors of many decades' service, who have written scarcely a line, and some of them former colleagues of mine personally, whose dedication has been dismissed, gone uncelebrated, and considered, and thus rendered, "null and void" in the world's sight, especially if they were on the "losing" side of conflicts within the church, who deserve a Festschrift like this one much more than I do. I might ask that this book be considered a "guard of honor" for some of them, too.

COMFORTABLE WORDS

Comfortable Words, which is a reference to the verses from the New Testament that accompany the minister's invitation to the congregation to receive Holy Communion according to the Book of Common Prayer, is a happy title for this book. It coheres with the view that theology should be a practical comfort to the reader or recipient of it. Such coherence should be axiomatic for a pastor, because the sum and substance of what you are doing is comforting and sustaining sufferers. Exhortation can bring about resistance, while Comfortable Words bring acceptance, and healing.

I first learned the difference between comfort and exhortation, or between "Gospel," which is "Yes!," and "Law," which is "No!," from C. FitzSimons Allison. Allison demonstrated, in several pastoral situations that we were actually there to see, the upholding power of comfort as compared with the depressing, hence also suppressing, power of admonition. These were powerful lessons and my wife and I were able to witness them early in our ministry.

Thus for me, theology was connected, from earliest days in the parish, to the possibility of an "enabling word" rather than a "lecturing," hence defeating word. There were corollaries, theologically speaking, to what we saw. But in first place was the conviction that almost all pastoral care was committed to us under the sign of comfort rather than instruction (i.e., telling people what to do). More broadly put, it was a question of placing the emphasis on God's Word of Love rather than on God's Word of Judgment. More precisely expressed, it was a question of God's Word of Love superseding His Word of Judgment. In this context, I don't think we need to shrink from the verb "supersede," because ultimately Love must supersede Judgment if we are, any of us, going to survive, either now, in the world, or in whatever form we survive after death. St. Catherine of Siena said as she was dying, that "For no reason whatever should one judge the actions of creatures or their motives. Even when we see that it is an actual sin, we ought not to pass judgment on it, but have holy and sincere compassion and offer it up to God with humble and devout prayer."[4] In my opinion, St. Catherine's words qualify as "comfortable."

Shadowing me, however, almost every day of my ministry, going back to the mid-1970s and extending right through to 2007, was the criticism, often stated and not just implied, that a purely "comfortable" Word runs the risk of being "antinomian." "Antinomianism" is the name given to the supposed Christian heresy that an overly "one-sided" affirmation of God's Grace, or unconditional love, skirts the requirement, also expressed in God's Word, that people should become holy. When the preacher of "comfortable words" is labeled an "antinomian"—and it's been a criticism I have always faced, and others with me—this means that he or she is supposedly making an end-run around the portions of Scripture that enjoin moral discipline and obedience. In traditional Lutheran terms, the charge of "antinomianism" accuses you of "privileging" God's Promise at the expense of God's Command.

The problem with this criticism that you are being "antinomian" when you preach the Grace of God—and it is a true cliché, that an almost sure sign you are preaching Grace is when you are accused of being an "antinomian"— is that it misunderstands the way Grace works in practice. Love, when it is really received by a person, and I mean, received emotionally, in the heart, so to speak, and not just as a form of words or as a concept, almost never fails to engender a response of love. When love is sincerely offered to a pretty un-loveable person, or someone who regards himself or herself as being un-loveable, the result, in practice, is that they become more loveable. A good analogy, which almost never fails to connect with listeners to sermons, is the analogy of romantic love. When an awkward and not very "good-looking" person is loved romantically by someone else, they almost always seem to "get" less awkward and become more "good-looking," almost as if on the spot. Just watch teenagers, and adolescents—and retirees! Love is reflected in love.

The fear that "love to the loveless" (Samuel Crossman) will produce the "fruit" of sin, or un-holiness, is not an observant fear. It is not true to life. People do not take advantage of love, or if they do, they begin to stop doing so if the love persists. A famous example of this is the thief Jean Valjean at the beginning of Victor Hugo's novel *Les Miserables*. Jean Valjean is the stunned recipient of "love to the loveless" on the part of a bishop in a provincial town. Rather than taking advantage of a completely undeserved reprieve on the part of the bishop, Valjean becomes a man of intense compassion and grace. He even "falls away" from grace, shortly after the bishop's reprieve,

---

4. From "The Testament of St. Catherine of Siena," written down by Tommaso di Petra and quoted in Huxley, *Huxley and God*, 283.

robbing a defenseless shepherd boy of his last sou. But he never falls again, in the sense that his response to the bishop's prior love becomes a lifetime of "grace upon grace" (John 1:16). I reject the criticism that One-Way Love leads to "antinomianism."

Now I can begin to speak about the three headings, in practical theology, under which "Jady" Koch and Todd Brewer have categorized the essays of this Festschrift. These headings are "Free Will– Not!," "One-Way Love," and "Strength in Weakness." The origin of the three phrases was a cocktail napkin that was printed up for a leave-taking party in Birmingham in the late spring of 2004. The hosts asked for a "Cliff Notes" version of what I had tried to teach for almost ten years at Cathedral Church of the Advent in that city. This is what came out:

"FREE WILL—NOT!"

All of us, and I have never met an exception, want to believe that we can control our own lives, or at least make choices that will help us accomplish our plan for happiness. This seems to come with birth. Add to this a somewhat particularized form of free-will thinking that Americans seem to grow up with. Everybody wants to think he or she can manage their lives—and maybe manage the lives of others. Personally, I think it's an illusion. (Like everyone else I know, I tried!)

What I attempted to express over the years, both in the pulpit, at the lectern, and in books and articles, was skepticism concerning choice, or the parameters of human choice. I thought that the scenario described by St. Paul in Romans, Chapter Seven, as in "the good I want to do, that I do not; and the evil I do not want to do, that I do," was closer to the way my mind worked, and my life worked out. I also observed a kind of "bondage of the will," which was Martin Luther's phrase, in the lives of others, and especially in the lives of people who would come to me in the parish to talk over their problems. They—we!—kept doing the same things, many of them self-damaging or at least not self-helping, "over and over and over again" (Dave Clark Five).

I also noticed that in several of the so-called "classical" confessions of faith adopted by the Protestant churches during the Reformation period, such as the *Thirty-Nine Articles of Religion* (1571), with which I was I familiar as an Episcopal minister, and the later *Lambeth Articles* (1595), it appeared to be an article of faith that human beings did not possess "free will."

The really convincing evidence of this, however, always remained the pastoral reality. All I needed to do was sit in on a meeting of Alcoholics Anonymous (in the church basement, usually) and it was obvious, at least to me, that sufferers are often in the grip of drives, addictions, concepts, and what the *Thirty-Nine Articles* called "concupiscence," that possess a life of their own. As Dr. Frank Lake used to say when we studied under him in Nottingham in the early 1970s, human beings are often more "lived than living." Or in another memorable phrase from that memorable man, it's your "archaeology that determines your teleology." I think, in other words, that I have free will; but other factors, some of them unconscious and buried (as far as my conscious awareness is concerned), may be the real and powerful things that actually drive me.

So I have never been able to believe in free will, first from personal observation and pastoral experience, and second from the evidence of St. Paul in his letter to the Romans.

Another, important reason to view the human will as un-free is that such a view usually heightens your compassion, both in respect to people you know who act as if they are unable to change—meaning change destructive habits or character disabilities—and in respect to yourself, who can also feel as hard as a rock in relation to compulsive traits of character. If you can see a little into human personality, and discover people in the grip of forces, many of them interior forces, that are stronger than anything they can consciously bring to their problems by way of self-help, then you begin to observe a compassion in yourself that can surprise you.

When the co-founder of Alcoholics Anonymous, 'Bill W.' (Bill Wilson), began to separate the disease of alcoholism from the human victim held in its grip, a therapeutic breakthrough took place in the understanding and treatment of addiction. The drinker was no longer regarded as an irresponsible malefactor who had "free will" over his drinking—Wilson discovered, in himself first and then in fellow alcoholics, that he didn't have "free will"—but as a poor sap who was powerless over alcohol. This one giant step, of separating yourself from your disease, became decisive. (I think Bill Wilson should have received a Nobel Prize for making this discovery. Christ had done something like it, long before, when He separated possessing demons from the people they possessed. I think Wilson learned his distinction directly from the Gospels.)

When you stop treating people as though they can implement good advice and obey solid principles of living, especially when they are instructed what to do (by you, for example), then you begin to develop an insight into how people work that can issue in compassion for them when they fail to do so. It is a priceless gift from St. Paul and the New Testament that allows us to see people as un-free rather than free. Ironically, the more compassion you develop for the un-free members of your family and your friends, the more free they begin to act. Once again, love for the loveless creates, in practical cases of unloveable people, loveable people. "Have mercy, Have mercy, baby" (Don Covay).

ONE-WAY LOVE

"People Got To Be Free," sang the Rascals.

But they're not.

They want to be free, but freedom eludes them.

Therefore they need to be freed.

My own personal experience, almost lifelong, with the bondage of anxiety—nail biting, foot wiggling, futurizing on almost every score, never feeling satisfied (for one minute) with what I have or have even earned—made me respond to the observation, both in theology and in pastoral experience, that people aren't free. Or rather, people aren't as free as they'd like to think they are.

If you're a Christian, this insight, involving both the hope of freedom and the reality of bondage, sets you on a path to the Cross. That might sound pious, but John Bunyan said it, not me. An "anthropology" of *Prometheus Bound*—the anthropology of us, in other words—makes us instant adepts of Milton's *Paradise Regained*. If you're working in Christianity, that is. I always taught that a "low" anthropology, or what I preferred to call a realistic view of human nature, led inevitably to a "high" soteriology, which is the thought-category for how a person is saved, "*sōtēr*" being the Greek word for "savior." By "saved," I mainly mean saved from your repeating faults and consequent mistakes in practice, the kinds of faults and mistakes that get you into trouble and cause you to fail. If you cannot save yourself (from a life that is failing to make you happy and at peace), yet require saving—and desire it urgently, like a man who is sinking and up to his neck in quicksand—then you'll go straight towards an agency that promises to save you.

Therefore, and to make a third step in the logic of Christian thought, you adopt a "high" Christology. In order to overcome the un-free nature of the bound human being, it takes a mighty, or simply sufficient, agency or Agent. In Christian theology, the Agent is Jesus Christ. To repeat: powerless man and powerless woman need powerful saving agent. Only God can achieve what human nature cannot achieve for itself. "Jesus Saves": Therefore, Jesus Christ is God.

The first time I ever visited the Church of the Holy Sepulchre in Jerusalem, I burst out crying almost the moment we got in the door. When you visit that church, you go up the stone steps to the "Calvary," which is an elevated stone outcropping where Christ was crucified. It is there He died.

After several visits since that visit, I still don't think I have ever been with a Christian believer who was not affected to the point of tears when they got there. It's as if something inside you recognizes that something you have come to rely on everywhere is physically focused in that particular spot.

When you stop and think about it, you are putting a very great deal, through that emotional response in the Church of the Holy Sepulchre, on a specific event of history. You are connecting the experience you have had of having been "saved" or absolved, of having received mercy on your life and on your person, with a definite place. Such a kind of visceral response to this one place, which people like me seem to have there, ought to merit a little caution. Can something or someone that specific carry the weight of the world?

While I acknowledge the almost overwhelming power of the feelings the Church of the Holy Sepulchre evokes in me—and I've had similar experiences in the Church of the Nativity at Bethlehem—I'm not completely sure I understand what connects "my" life, with all its debits, credits and conditions, with His death and life. "Sometimes it makes me tremble." I am a little more reluctant now than I used to be, to pin everything on what Lessing called "the accidental truths of history (that) can never become the proof of necessary truths of reason." When we put all of our weight, as people who believe we have to be saved in order to live and survive, on something as specific as a single three-hour event enacted on a single stone pillar that we can actually touch and see and stand on, that is a very extreme kind of bearing down. Like a circus performer diving from 100 feet in the air into a five-foot tank, it is a "death-defying" risk, a dizzying gamble.

Nevertheless, the next time I return to Jerusalem, I fully expect I shall go right to pieces when I cross the ancient threshold and ascend the stairway to the Calvary.

Strength in Weakness

Martin Luther's "Theology of the Cross," as expressed in a series of theses composed for the *Heidelberg Disputation* of 1518, embodies an understanding of life that is counter to what looks true of life on the surface. Luther argued, and St. Paul and several others before Luther, that God is actively known through His "left hand," which is to say, God's work in human experience is done through and in the midst of human suffering and human loss rather than through victory and prize-winning.

This is a "counter-intuitive" interpretation of suffering, for in the eyes of almost everyone, suffering is bad and not good. That is the way it feels, so that is the way it "is."

Constantly in life we come up against bad or obstructing experiences that become, in hindsight, occasions of grace. "The worst thing that could have happened," we hear a person say, "was the very thing on account of which something else happened that turned out to be brilliant." "If it hadn't been for that awful experience with so-and-so, I never would have met you!" "If that door hadn't been slammed in my face, I would not have discovered my life's work." "If my own child had not become ill, I would have never have been able to sympathize with that family over there." The list of "theology of the Cross" situations, once you start looking back on your life, can go on and on. "He promised to exalt us, but low is the way." (Billy Preston)

I have tried to preach and teach this message not just because it occurs in the Bible, and in some of the primary sources of the Reformation; but because I have seen it in people, and seen it in myself. A tipping point for me, or rather, an overwhelming example of the principle that there is strength in weakness and gain through loss—and life through death—came in the form of a professional reversal quite late in my ministry. My world was "She's come undone" (The Guess Who). Never had it crossed my mind that I might resign a post, for any reason whatsoever. Hadn't crossed my mind! Overnight I became Eliza Dolittle: "What a fool I was . . . What an elevated fool, What a mutton-headed dolt was I!" (*My Fair Lady*)

This is to say that I now believe in the advantageous experience of "Strength in Weakness" as much as I ever have before. It is a principle of life written in the nature of things. It's a kind of "natural law" that reaches a pitch of enactment in the way Christians use the adjective "good" to describe what took place—on the site of the Church of the Holy Sepulchre—on Good Friday.

Analogy

A few of the essays in Comfortable Words refer to my interest over the years in science fiction and Gothic horror, especially in the movies. Apparently, the more "campy," the better! What was going on with that?

There are basically three factors in a continuing and beguiled fascination with material like *The Crawling Eye* (1958) and *The Premature Burial* (1962). The number one factor is that these movies fascinated me as a child. When I watch them now, and talk about them, I am speaking from the "child" of me, 'PZ' at age 11. There is a personal authenticity to that voice, the voice of *The Space Children* (1958), which I consider precious, almost sacred. The eyes and ears, and tongue, of a child!

Second, this material, and there is almost no end to it once you start, puts you in touch with the absurd. There is a degree of entropy to human experience, culminating in physical death, that makes your self-conceived efforts to manage and control your world appear futile, at least at one point or another during the course of your life. Almost everyone asks, at some time point, "Is that all there is?" (Peggy Lee). The absurd, reflected in a movie like *Konga* (1961), in which a giant ape that is clearly a man in a gorilla suit who is wearing street shoes on his feet kicks down a tinker-toy model of London, helps me put the futility of human effort, as I see it, in the line of humor. *Konga* has always made me laugh, and it still does. What's more, it's got an excellent musical score, composed by Gerard Schurmann. (Who would have thought?) I love these movies because they make me laugh. *The Alligator People* (1959) is another one.

Thirdly, the analogy of good versus evil, altruistic sacrifice versus diabolical villainy, the child as hero—you can see this in primary colors within the 2011 movie *Super 8*: these are themes that lend themselves to religious analogy. They bear easy comparison to themes of the New Testament, such as atonement and sacrifice, "a little child shall lead them," and the ultimate hope of a New Creation.

This brings me to two further points concerning the use of art and popular culture in the practice of Christian ministry: There's a lot of material out there! Akira Kurosawa's movie *Red Beard* (1965), for example, is pure Gospel, portrayed visually to a high emotional pitch, yet without an explicit word about religion as such. Roberto Rossellini's *Open City* (1945) is a miracle of grace in practice. It depicts a Catholic priest who is grace in practice. Jacques Demy's *Lola* (1960) is pure miracle: God, I would say, speaking through a little lost ensemble of poignant characters in a "nothing" town in France. I could stand here all day and all night, listing analogies in the movies—and just the movies, not to mention the others of the seven arts. I would list analogies to the great humane themes of Christianity, analogies that fill out human experience, especially of suffering but also of credible healing. Analogy is a great tool to get across the message of Grace.

Moreover, religious people, and specifically Christian religious people, can learn about the Holy Spirit when we study the creative process of artistic people. The point of analogy is not to "co-opt" writers and film-makers and musicians for our own purposes in communicating the Word of God. If that were all it is about, then we'd be running the risk of "using" instruments that are not ours to use. Some Christian application of movie and media resources strikes me as dishonest, at worst; and at best, taking unfair advantage of somebody else's idea.

What I have learned in recent years is the potential of an artist's vision to deepen my own vision, and sometimes even to change it. I am continually edified by the novels of James Gould Cozzens (1903–1978). It started with Cozzens' 1933 novel *The Last Adam*, which gave me the first concrete insight I ever had into the flight of two generations of "upper-middle-class" Episcopalians from that church. In one devastating paragraph, Cozzens, who had grown up and been schooled in the Episcopal Church, was able to explain to me the reason I never saw one entire demographic in a church where I was rector, a church which had been erected, endowed, and supported by the grand-parents and parents of that precise demographic. *The Last Adam*, a forgotten novel, opened a door of insight to a perplexed contemporary clergyman—me!

What I am getting at is that once you open yourself to analogy, and to the immense body of human attempts to understand the world, especially in the arts, you have to be open to where it may lead you. It almost goes without saying that God is larger than the use you may want to make of Him. Analogy is therefore not just a means towards an end. It is an enlargement of the basic "research" project that religious inquiry actually is into the nature of reality.

"Some People" (Belouis Some)

Certain teachers have played a role in my theological thinking to whom I feel especially indebted, and even especially close, though some are dead.

This list, which is not exhaustive, includes two teachers in first place. John Claiborne Davis, who taught us history and also church history at St. Alban's School in Washington, D.C. Mr. Davis, whom almost all his living students would rise up and praise if he were still here, introduced me, as a 15-year-old student, to the intellectual tradition of the Christian Church. He was sharp, wry, and loyal. Then there was Zeph Stewart. Mr. Stewart was my House Master and academic advisor at Harvard College, a wise and erudite Classicist, and a person full of compassion for confused undergraduates. I loved Zeph, and wish he were here to be told this again.

Other helpers along the way, of one's "*theologischer Werdegang*," were Fitz Allison, of whom I have already spoken; Frank Lake, the same; John H. Schutz, who first taught me New Testament in an academic setting during the years 1968–1970; George H. Williams and Peter Gomes, each a mentor and later a friend at Harvard College; and James Dunn, who accepted me in 1973 as his first official graduate student. Later on, George Carey, the 103rd Archbishop of Canterbury, opened the door for me to begin doctoral studies at Tübingen; and Jürgen Moltmann took me on as a doctorand. Herr Moltmann brought a "human dimension"—the milk of human kindness— to the case of a 40-year-old man, with displaced wife and children, who was suddenly sitting on an ice-berg in the middle of an uncharted sea—the German doctoral process.

To the Tübingen years should be added Heinz-Dieter Neef, who got me "over the hump" of Ancient Hebrew; and Geiko Mueller-Fahrenholz, who rehearsed me in preparation for the famous Rigorosum, which is the final oral examination for the Doctorate in Theology. There was also the great and grave Ernst Käsemann, whose theology of justification by faith (i.e., *die Rechtfertigung der Gottlosen*) was the subject of my Tübingen dissertation, and who gave generously of his time and insight, both during and after my period of residence there. Herr Käsemann became a regular correspondent right up to his death. More recently, Dr. Thomas W. Calhoun has helped me reflect on the "upshot" of my long "*Werdegang*," deepening my understanding and also appreciation of it.

I do not include the pastoral and more personal mentors and examples who have influenced my work, especially in parish ministry. That is another list, and in some ways an equally important one. Nor do I list the students who became interested in my thinking, and have carried it on in diverse and fruitful settings. Some of them have contributed to this book.

Concluding Unscientific Postscript

After 2007, I realized that one or two things for which I had been contending, over many years of parish ministry and wider service in the church, not to mention nine years of academic research, had to have been mistaken, at least partially. Certain aspects of the form of religion to which I had committed myself in 1973 had become *The Light that Failed* (Kipling).

The so-called "culture wars" had ended in an almost complete defeat, at least as measured by worldly or political results, for the more "traditional" members of the church I had served. A pitched battle had been fought, within the church and in front of the world, during a period of roughly three years; and many bodies, mostly of clergy I had known, lay "in pieces on the ground" (James Taylor). "Someone had blundered" (Tennyson). The blunder, whatever it was or had been, needed to be explored. It needed understanding. It required research. We shouldn't just try to get "closure" and then, Poof!, "move on with our lives." I believe now that the blunder, or delusion, lay in a kind of conflict-structure—Eric Mottram's phrase—which had somehow gotten possession of the religion of Christ, at least in the expression of it to which I had been attached for over 30 years.

I now discovered myself to be part of a "lost cause." At the same time, I discovered that I had become a disillusioned person. How, I said to myself, could I have given myself so completely, as I believed I had done, to a light that had failed, and to a light that had failed within me? The practical result of this discovery was a decision to take a two-year sabbatical, a two-year period of being in "the desert." In June 2009, after completing one last church job, I "dropped my life," and moved, with Mary, to a small town in Florida, where we had a place to go. That period did in fact last almost exactly two years. Since late summer of 2011, I have been emerging a little, back into active thought and less active life. It is now mid-summer of 2012.

While I have given up pretty completely on the fever-world's conflicts, including the world's religious conflicts, I would still affirm, in basic outline, the three main headings of Christian concern that are outlined in this book. Each of them, "Free Will—Not!," "One-Way Love," and "Strength in Weakness," strikes me as sound, verified in everyday life and relationships, and set out profoundly within the Bible. But I would like to add something, by way of a postscript. It comes as a comment on a paragraph at the conclusion of William Hale White's biography of John Bunyan. This paragraph, which has intrigued me for years, used to sound threatening. It read like a counsel of despair rather than a word of hope. I see it differently now.

Here is the paragraph. I think the word "Puritanism" could just as well be "evangelicalism":

> "One last word. Puritanism has done noble service, but we have seen enough of it even in Bunyan, to show that it is not an entirely accurate version of God's message to man. It is the most distinct, energetic and salutary movement in our history, and no other religion has surpassed it in preaching the truths by which men and nations must exist. Nevertheless we need Shakespeare as well as Bunyan, and oscillate between the *Pilgrim's Progress* and *As You Like It*. We cannot bring ourselves into a unity. The time is yet to come when we shall live by a faith which is a harmony of all our faculties."[5]

My over-all reflection on theology at the age of 61 is that I can stand by the three affirmations of this book, *Comfortable Words*, supporting them from the Word of God and from life. But I have to add, with William Hale White, that they do not contain the whole truth of life. Where are the gaps? Where are the holes? Where are these affirmations silent when they should be speaking?

For one thing, they don't quite do justice to the unfailing transitoriness of all things ("All Things Must Pass," George Harrison). They don't quite cover the macrocosm, and the laws of space and time. They don't quite cover

5. White, *John Bunyan*, 249–50.

the strange sense you get sometimes, as time and your life goes on, that a number of things aren't completely or exactly real. The older you get, the more illusory and ephemeral appear some of the fixed points to which you'd thought you could cling. T.S. Eliot captured this "sneaking suspicion" concerning the unreality of certain elements in life that appear to be real, in *The Waste Land* (1922), with his repeated cry, "Unreal City."

A personal example of this sneaking suspicion—*Orpheus Rising*—concerning the unreality of certain experiences and certain phenomena follows. It really happened: One morning during my next-to-last job, I was reading something at my desk, and said to myself, "This can't be true." It can't be true that someone would actually write this and think this. It simply can't be true. But it was! I had the document before me. So now I reasoned—and it came like a flash: "If this is true, then some other things must not be true. And what have I been doing, all this time, thinking those other things were true? What was true' about me up until today, that could have believed those things to be true that are plainly controverted by what I'm looking at now?" At that moment, at that exact moment, when I realized I had been mistaken about previously cherished conceptions, the "reality" question, or rather the "unreality" question, came to the fore. This was my personal instance of Jack Kerouac's "*Satori* in Paris."

The same thing happens when a person finds out that he or she has been the victim of a long-term ongoing betrayal. They can't believe it. "This can't be happening," they reason. Here is a more everyday example of the "unreality" of which I speak. It is in a letter from a teacher of theology who lives overseas:

> This morning I went to Starbucks and saw a sign that read in large letters 'Frappuccino Journey.' It was an ad for a card where you get stamps and the 7th frappuccino is free. To connect the idea of journeying—an idea of great meaning to me, a spiritual sort of idea—to frappuccino discounts is to make a little crack in the world—the level of sheer cynicism and unconscious absurdity can only be a little unintended revelation of the world's unreality.

If you ever find yourself saying, whether in a crisis or in a Starbuck's (or both), "This can't be happening"—but it is happening!—then you're in the territory of what is real in relation to what is unreal. It is why Eliot's Waste Land cry of "Unreal City" strikes a nerve.

I wish someone had told me earlier—and these insights are all found in the Christian tradition—that life is characterized, universally, by suffering, by change, and, oddly, as I have said, by unreality. Maybe someone did try to tell me, and I couldn't hear what they were saying. It has all been true of my life, but I only understood it, or was forced to understand it, late in the day.

I was weak on metaphysics, and put a somewhat one-sided emphasis on the ethical. The ethical is pervasively present in relationships, and nothing succeeds better in helping a person who has failed ethically and morally than absolution. Mercy is the center of Christianity and is its jewel and highest, greatest good. But there is also the "space-time continuum"; and what are we doing here in light of Relativity, the Uncertainty Principle, and "Since the splitting of the atom, man . . ." (*The Phantom Planet*, 1961)?

Much of religion, or at least the form of religion to which a person tends to gravitate, is psychology in theological dress. It is possible that almost all religion could be described as psychology in theological dress. Thirty-five years of pastoral counseling showed me this. Yet there's nothing to be wary or suspicious of in that fact. In a way, not just religion, but almost all human interests and pursuits, are "forms" for psychology, pegs on which people aim to hang their psychological yearnings. A better way to say this might be that everyone wants to be happy, and is looking for some vehicle by which they can transcend their sufferings.

Christianity, with its focus on the Compassionate Christ (Thorwaldsen), the Good Shepherd, the Man of Sorrows and the Man for Others, carries a unique message of God's "One-Way Love"; a realistic perspective on who we are and what human nature consists of; and a working therapy of how to overcome our problems—by identifying with our need and weakness, and watching this work: Christ's ever-present conversion of Good Friday into Easter.

My "*envoi* and epilogue" has placed a reverent and grateful "guard of honor" around convictions that animated 35 years of formal ministry, and continue to animate me now. But I also echo William Hale White, in looking forward to a time "yet to come when we shall live by a faith which is a harmony of all our faculties." I'm looking forward to the next ten years, a decade of religion as further research into the nature of life and the revelation of God.

BIBLIOGRAPHY

Cozzens, James Gould. *Guard of Honor*. New York: Harcourt, Brace, 1948.

Huxley, Aldous. *Huxley and God: Essays on Mysticism, Religion, and Spirituality*. Edited by Jacqueline Hazard Bridgeman. San Francisco: HarperSanFrancisco, 1992.

White, William Hale. *John Bunyan*. London: Hodder & Stoughton, 1905.

Published Works of Paul F. M. Zahl

BOOKS

Zahl, Paul F. M. *Who Will Deliver Us? The Present Value of the Death of Christ*. New York: Seabury, 1983. Reprinted, Eugene, OR: Wipf & Stock, 2008.

———. *Die Rechtfertigungslehre Ernst Käsemanns*. Stuttgart: Calwer, 1996.

———. *The Protestant Face of Anglicanism*. Grand Rapids: Eerdmans, 1997.

———. *A Short Systematic Theology*. Grand Rapids: Eerdmans, 2000.

———. *Five Women of the English Reformation*. Grand Rapids: Eerdmans, 2001.

———. *The First Christian: Universal Truth in the Teachings of Jesus*. Grand Rapids: Eerdmans, 2003.

———, and Ian Douglas. *Understanding the Windsor Report: Two Leaders in the American Church Speak Across the Divide*. New York: Church Publishing, 2005.

———. *2000 Years of Amazing Grace: The Story and Meaning of Christian Faith*. Lanham: Rowman & Littlefield, 2006.

———, and C. Frederick Barbee. *The Collects of Thomas Cranmer*. Grand Rapids: Eerdmans, 2006.

———. *Grace in Practice: A Theology of Everyday Life*. Grand Rapids: Eerdmans, 2007.

CONTRIBUTIONS TO EDITED COLLECTIONS

———. "The Message of Romans." In *The Bible for Everyday Life*. Edited by George Carey. Oxford: Lion, 1996.

———. "A Retro-Future for Theology in the Episcopal Church." In *New Conversation: Essays on the Future of Theology and the Episcopal Church*, edited by Robert Boak Slocum, 177–83. New York: Church Pub., 1999.

———. "Full Circle: 'Confessing' Mainliners." In *A Confessing Theology for Postmodern Times*. edited by Michael S. Horton. Wheaton, IL: Crossway, 2000.

———. "Formal-Liturgical Worship." In *Exploring the Worship Spectrum: Six Views*. edited by Paul Basden. Grand Rapids: Zondervan, 2004.

———. "The Bishop-Led Church: The Episcopal or Anglican Polity." In *Perspectives on Church Government: Five Views*, edited by Chad Owen Brand and R. Stanton Norman. Nashville: Broadman & Holman, 2004.

ESSAYS

Zahl, Paul F. M. "The Historical Jesus and Substitutionary Atonement." *Saint Luke's Journal of Theology* 26 (1983) 313–32.

———. "E. P. Sanders's Paul vs : Luther's Paul: Justification by Faith in the Aftermath of a Scholarly Crisis." *Saint Luke's Journal of Theology* 34 (1991) 33–40.

———. Zahl, Paul F. M. "Where Did All the Galleries Go?: Pre-Tractarian Interiors in Relation to the Decade of Evangelism." *Anglican and Episcopal History* 60 (1991) 165–83.

———. "The Things that Remain." *Anglican Digest* 33/2 (1991) 35–38.

———. "Within the Inner Sanctum : Andacht in the Evangelisches Stift." *Anglican and Episcopal History* 61/4 (1992) 505–8.

———. "Holbein's Masterpiece and our Church's Message for the Nineties." *Anglican Digest* 34.1 (1992) 30–36.

———. "In the Kingdom of Dread, Justification by Faith: Reapplying an Old Doctrine." *Sewanee Theological Review* 35 (1992) 274–85.

———. "Within the Inner Sanctum: Andacht in the Evangelisches Stift." *Anglican and Episcopal History* 61 (1992) 505–8.

———. "Christmas in Zürich, 1992." *Anglican and Episcopal History* 63 (1994) 111–16.

———. The Spirit of Life: A Universal Affirmation, by Jürgen Moltmann. *Sewanee Theological Review* 36 (1993) 276–78.

———. "A New Source for Understanding German Theology: Käsemann, Bultmann, and the 'New Perspective on Paul.'" *Sewanee Theological Review* 39 (1996) 413–22.

———. "A Tribute to Ernst Käsemann and a Theological Testament." *Anglican Theological Review* 80 (1998) 382–94.

———. "Mistakes of the New Perspective on Paul." *Themelios* 27/1 (2001) 5–11.

———. "The Spirit in the Blood." *Anglican Theological Review* 83 (2001) 493–98.

———. "Lex Rex." *Anglican Theological Review* 85 (2003) 75–82.

———. "An Evangelical Episcopalian Looks at Pluralism." *Anglican Theological Review* 85/3 (2003) 527–34.

———. "The Crisis of the American Episcopal Church." *Churchman* 117 (2003) 71–76.

———. "Thoughts on the Windsor Report: What Went Wrong?" *Anglican Theological Review* 87 (2005) 575–82.

———. M. "Last Signal to the Carpathia." *Anglican Theological Review* 86 (2004) 647–52.

———. "Face behind the Mask: The 'New Perspective on Paul' as an Act of Fraud." Unpublished manuscript dated 31 May 2005.

———. "Why Pay the Cost?: Some Reasons for Defending a Traditional Position on Homosexuality." Unpublished manuscript dated 1 June 2006.

BOOK REVIEWS

———. Review of *Why I Believe in a Personal God: The Credibility of Faith in a Doubting Culture, and I Believe*, by George Carey. *Anglican and Episcopal History* 61 (1992) 109–11.

———. Review of *Jesus in the Gospels: A Biblical Christology*, by Rudolf Schnackenburg, and of *Studies in Early Christology*, by Martin Hengel. *Anglican Theological Review* 78 (1996) 504–8.

———. Review of *The Mystery of Salvation: The Story of God's Gift*, by the Doctrine Commission of the Church of England. *Anglican Theological Review* 79 (1997) 637–39.

———. Review of "Booknotes." *Anglican Theological Review* 80 (1998) 313–17.

———. Review of *Can a Bishop Be Wrong: Ten Scholars Challenge John Shelby Spong*, ed. Peter C. Moore. *Anglican Theological Review* 81 (1999) 326–28.

———. Review of *Flagships of the Spirit: Cathedrals in Society*, eds. Stephen Platten and Christopher Lewis. *Anglican Theological Review* 81 (1999) 500–501.

———. Review of *Norwich Cathedral: Church, City and Diocese, 1096–1996*, edited Ian Atherton, et al. *Anglican and Episcopal History* 68 (1999) 260–62.

———. Review of *Christology*, by Hans Schwarz. *Anglican Theological Review* 82 (2000) 219–21.

———. Review of *The New Age Movement and the Biblical Worldview: Conflict and Dialogue*, by John P. Newport, and of *The Way of the (Modern) World. Or, Why it's Tempting to Live as if God Doesn't Exist*, by Craig M. Gay. *Anglican Theological Review* 82 (2000) 229–32.

———. Review of *We Believe: A Prayer Book Based on the Augsburg Confession*, by Richard F. Bansemer. *Anglican Theological Review* 82 (2000) 613–15.

———. Review of *Jesus in the Drama of Salvation: Toward a Biblical Doctrine of Redemption*, by Raymund Schwager. *Anglican Theological Review* 82 (2000) 841–42.

———. Review of *Between Two Horizons: Spanning New Testament Studies and Systematic Theology*, eds Joel B. Green and Max Turner. *Anglican Theological Review* 83 (2001) 129–30.

———. Review of *Sin, Death, and the Devil*, edited by Carl E. Braaten and Robert W. Jenson. *Anglican Theological Review* 83 (2001) 145–47.

———. *Revisiting Paul's Doctrine of Justification: A Challenge to the New Perspective*, by Peter Stuhlmacher. *Themelios* 27/3 (2002) 94–95.

———. Review of Hawksmoor's *London Churches: Architecture and Theology*, by Pierre de la Ruffinière du Prey. *Anglican Theological Review* 84 (2002) 807–8.

———. Review of *Notes on the Holiness of God*, by E. David Willis. *Interpretation* 57 (2003) 334.

———. Review of *Prayers for the Assassin*, by Robert Ferrigno. *Touchstone: A Journal of Mere Christianity* 19/6 (2006) 55.

Review of *The Spiritual Journal of Henry David Thoreau*. *Anglican Theological Review* 93 (2011) 746–47.

SHORT ARTICLES

Zahl, Paul F. M. "Learning from the Nottingham Congress." *Kerygma* (1977) 6–7.

———. Various contributions to *The Episcopal New Yorker*, edited by J. Elliott Lindsley, 1982–88.

———. "The Church and the Zodiac." *Anglican Digest* 30/4 (1988) 11–13.

———. "Whatever Happened to Allan Bloom?" *Anglican Digest* 30/4 (1988) 39.

———. "Fall Reflections." *Anglican Digest* 30/1 (1988) 51.

———. "A Cottage Industry We Could Have Less Of." *Anglican Digest* Lent (1989) 19.

———. "Regaining Lost Ground." *Mission and Ministry* 6/3 (1989) 11–16.

———. "Undiluted Anglicanism." *Mission and Ministry* 6/3 (1989) 23–24.

———. "Tracts for These Times: Is "Choice" the Summum Bonum?" *Anglican Digest* Advent-Epiphany (1989) 46.

———. "East Europe: The Protestant Factor: Some of 1990's Dreams Date Back to Luther." *Washington Post*, 14 Jan, 1990, b.04

———. "Tracts for These Times: A More Excellent Way." *Anglican Digest* Lent (1990) 61.

———. "Tracts for These Times: Where True Simplicity Is Found." *Anglican Digest* Easter (1990) 59.

———. "Tracts for These Times: There Is a Fountain." *Anglican Digest* Pentecost (1990) 59.

———. "Welcome, Bishop Carey." *Anglican Digest* Advent-Epiphany (1990) 4–5.

———. "Tracts for These Times: On the Stunting Effect of Thin-ness." *Anglican Digest* Advent-Epiphany (1990) 59.

———. "The Things That Remain: An Episcopalian's Credo." *First Things* 10 (1991) 10–12.

———. "Tracts for These Times: Neither Do I Condemn Thee." *Anglican Digest* Lent (1991) 58.

———. "Tracts for These Times: Report from Christendom 1991." *Anglican Digest* 33/3 (1991) 59.

———. "Trojan Horse or God's Providence?" *Anglican Digest* 33/4 (1991) 10–12.

———. "Tracts for These Times: the Undefeated." *Anglican Digest* 33/5 (1991) 58.

———. "Tracts for these Times: A View From Abroad." *Anglican Digest* 34/2 (1992) 58.

———. "Preaching Hope as Retrospective: An Evangelical View." *Living Pulpit* 1/1 (1992) 10–11.

———. "Tracts for these Times: A View from Abroad." *Anglican Digest* 34.2 (1992) 58.

———. "A View from Abroad: What is it Going to Take?" *Anglican Digest* 34.3 (1992) 58.

———. "A View from Abroad: Retrieving Gold." *Anglican Digest* 34/4 (1992) 58.

———. "Love Comprehended in Faith." *Living Pulpit* 1/3 (1992) 6–7.

———. "A View from Abroad: Now is the Time." *Anglican Digest* 34/5 (1992) 59.

———. "A View from Abroad: What is Missing?" *Anglican Digest* 34/6 (1992) 59.

———. "A View from Abroad: Zugunsten." *Anglican Digest* 35/1 (1993) 60.

———. "A View from Abroad." *Anglican Digest* 35/2 (1993) 61.

———. "A View from Abroad." *Anglican Digest* 35/3 (1993) 61.

———. "A View from Abroad." *Anglican Digest* 35/4 (1993) 61.

———. "A View from Abroad." *Anglican Digest* 35/6 (1993) 61.

———. "A View from Abroad." *Anglican Digest* 36/1 (1994) 59.

———. "A View from Abroad." *Anglican Digest* 36/3 (1994) 60.

———. "A View from Abroad." *Anglican Digest* 36/4 (1994) 58.

———. "Whatever Happened To . . . ?" *Anglican Digest* 36/5 (1994) 60.

———. "A View from Abroad." *Anglican Digest* 36/6 (1994) 60.

———. "Getting the Goods to Market." *Anglican Digest* 37/1 (1995) 62.

———. "Four Helps For Sufferers." *Living Pulpit* 4/2 (1995) 10–11.

———. "Getting Serious." *Anglican Digest* 37/2 (1995) 62–63.

———. "How Good & Pleasant." *Anglican Digest* 37/3 (1995) 62–63.

———. "But Is It Preaching?" *Anglican Digest* 37/4 (1995) 61.

———. "The Holy Spirit between Scylla and Charybdis." *Living Pulpit* 5/1 (1996) 20.

———. "Protestant Joy: An Actual Possibility?" *Living Pulpit* 5/4 (1996) 40.

————. Zahl, Paul F. M. "Theses from our Cathedral Door: Makes Me Tremble." *Anglican Digest* 43/1 (2000) 13.

————. "Stephen King's Redemption." *Christianity Today* 44/3 (2000) 82.

————. "Theses from Our Cathedral Door: Easter and the Minaret." *Anglican Digest* 42/2 (2000) 39.

————. "Theses from our Cathedral Door: Ambiguity." *Anglican Digest* 42/3 (2000) 30.

————. "Theses from Our Cathedral Door: He Stoops to Conquer." *Anglican Digest* 42/4 (2000) 62.

————. "Theses from Our Cathedral Door: Is It a Mystery?" *Anglican Digest* 42/6 (2000) 29.

————. "Theses from Our Cathedral Door: Joe Canada, Wake Up!" *Anglican Digest* 43/1 (2001) 53.

————. "Theses from Our Cathedral Door: Theology Driven." *Anglican Digest* 43/2 (2001) 41.

————. "Theses from Our Cathedral Door: It's Evenly Distributed." *Anglican Digest* 43/3 (2001) 9.

————. "Theses from Our Cathedral Door: Watch." *Anglican Digest* 43/4 (2001) 16.

————. "Theses from Our Cathedral Door: the 'Jesus Boat'." *Anglican Digest* 43/5 (2001) 16.

————. "Theses from our Cathedral Door: My Sweet Lady Jane." *Anglican Digest* 43/6 (2001) 16.

————. "Theses from our Cathedral Door: A Great Unknown." *Anglican Digest* 44/1 (2002) 16.

————. "Theses from our Cathedral Door: Or Was 9.11 in Vain?" *Anglican Digest* 44/2 (2002) 16.

————. "Theses from our Cathedral Door: Avoiding Detours." *Anglican Digest* 44/3 (2002) 8.

————. "Theses from our Cathedral Door: The One Way to Pluralism." *Anglican Digest* 44/4 (2002) 32–33.

————. "Theses from Our Cathedral Door: a Christian road map to Israel/Palestine." *Anglican Digest* 44/5 (2002) 25–26.

————. "Theses from Our Cathedral Door: Slide Show with a Message." *Anglican Digest* 44.6 (2002) 19.

————. "Theses from our Cathedral Door: Cul de sac." *Anglican Digest* 45/1 (2003) 16.

————. "Theses from our Cathedral Door: a New Approach to Hispanic Ministry." *Anglican Digest* 45/2 (2003) 9.

————. Zahl, Paul F. M. "Theses from Our Cathedral Door: 'Collegiality': Is It a Good Thing?" *Anglican Digest* 45/3 (2003) 16.

————. "Theses from Our Cathedral Door: Identi-kit." *Anglican Digest* 45/4 (2003) 27.

————. "Theses from Our Cathedral Door: Are We Traveling Light (Enough)?" *Anglican Digest* 45/5 (2003) 16.

————. "Theses from Our Cathedral Door: Isaiah 40:8." *Anglican Digest* 45/6 (2003) 16.

————. "Theses from Our Cathedral Door: Top Management." *Anglican Digest* 46/1 (2004) 16.

————. "Theses from Our Cathedral Door: What Shall We Do?" *Anglican Digest* 46/2 (2004) 31–32.

————. "Theses from Our Cathedral Door: Have Mercy!" *Anglican Digest* 46/3 (2004) 19.

————. "Theses from Our Cathedral Door: If It Was Okay Then, Why Is It Verboten Now?" *Anglican Digest* 46/4 (2004) 23.

————. "Theses from Our Cathedral Door: Deployment Blues or Golden Opportunity." *Anglican Digest* 46/5 (2004) 25.

————. "Theses from the Seminary Door: Yesterday's Future." *Anglican Digest* 46/6 (2004) 19–20.

————. "Theses from a Seminary Door: Chichester Prophet." *Anglican Digest* 47/1 (2005) 16.

————. "Theses from a Seminary Door: Next Best?" *Anglican Digest* 47/2 (2005) 16.

————. "Theses from a Seminary Door: Over and Over and Over Again." *Anglican Digest* 47/3 (2005) 15–16.

————. "Theses from a Seminary Door: A Run on Puritanism." *Anglican Digest* 47/4 (2005) 19–20.

————. "Theses from a Seminary Door: Rock Lobster." *Anglican Digest* 47/5 (2005) 15–16.

————. "Theses from a Seminary Door: Liturgy for Outsiders." *Anglican Digest* 47/6 (2005) 48–49.

————. "Theses from a Seminary Door: Good-bye to All That?" *Anglican Digest* 48/1 (2006) 32–33.

————. "Prehistoric Rebels vs. Prehistoric Dinosaurs: Finding Christ in Popular Culture." *Seed and Harvest* 29/3 (2006) 4–7.

————. "Theses from a Seminary Door: Journey Home?" *Anglican Digest* 48/4 (2006) 23–24.

————. "Old Europe as a Mission Field." *Seed and Harvest* 29/6 (2006) 6–9.

————. "Theses from a Seminary Door: Anglican without the Skin On." *Anglican Digest* 48/6 (2006) 13–14.

————. "Theses from a Seminary Door: 'Bunker Hill Bunny.'" *Anglican Digest* 49/1 (2007) 23–24.

————. "Theses from a Seminary Door: A Need to Heal." *Anglican Digest* 49/2 (2007) 23–25.

————. "A Moral Wake-up Call from World War II." *Providence Journal*, 4/17/2011.

————. "Rudyard Kipling's 'Love to All Men 'Neath the Sun.'" *Providence Journal*, 7/11/2011.

————. "Death of a Great Minister: Notes on John R. W. Stott." *Providence Journal*, 7/28/2011.

———— et al. "Just War vs. Technology: Is It Wrong for the US to Use Unmanned Predator Drones to Kill People by Remote Control?" *Christianity Today* 55/8 (2011) 64–65.